# North Country Life

## IN THE EIGHTEENTH CENTURY

UNIVERSITY OF DURHAM
PUBLICATIONS

SIR WILLIAM CHAYTOR, BT.

# North Country Life

IN THE

EIGHTEENTH CENTURY

---

*The North-East,* 1700–1750

---

EDWARD HUGHES

GEOFFREY CUMBERLEGE

OXFORD UNIVERSITY PRESS

LONDON NEW YORK TORONTO

1952

*Oxford University Press, Amen House, London E.C. 4*

GLASGOW NEW YORK TORONTO MELBOURNE WELLINGTON
BOMBAY CALCUTTA MADRAS KARACHI CAPE TOWN IBADAN

*Geoffrey Cumberlege, Publisher to the University*

PRINTED IN GREAT BRITAIN

IN
HONOURED
MEMORY

# Preface

WHEN I came to Durham in 1939 I chose as the subject of my inaugural lecture 'North Country Life in the Eighteenth Century'. Little did I realize what was in store for me. In the following autumn I learnt that some five or six old chests stuffed with manuscripts had been deposited by Colonel Spain at the Blackgate, in the keep of the old castle overlooking the Tyne; and I was asked, as a local consultant of the British Records' Association, to examine them before they were consigned to the pulp-mill. It was evident at a glance—once the dust of two centuries was removed—that they were the letters, account books, and papers of the lords of the manors of Gateshead and Whickham, once the richest coal-bearing manors in this country. Many months of 'blitz' research ensued for I feared that, placed as they were, all might go up in smoke at any time. When things quietened down somewhat I arranged with the President and Secretary of the Newcastle Society of Antiquaries, in whose custody the documents were, for them to be deposited in the strong room in the Public Library at Gateshead. This was not only their natural home but, as I discovered, part of the same collection—the cleaner part—had already been presented to that library. This portion had been arranged in bundles and a hand-list prepared by the late Mr. J. Oxberry. It is known as the Ellison MSS. The contents of the chests, as yet unlisted, are to be called the Cotesworth MSS.

Work on this mass of unsorted material proceeded steadily until the slag heap of transcripts began to assume forbidding proportions and it became clear that the heap could not be disposed of without a special effort. The Council of the Durham Colleges most generously granted me leave of absence for the session 1949–50 to enable me to complete my researches. The present book is the result. I cannot sufficiently express my sense of appreciation to the Warden,

Chairman, and Council of the Durham Colleges and to my colleagues in both divisions of the university who carried on in my absence. It will always be a source of special gratification to me that this book is the first to be published under the auspices of the University of Durham: to the members of the Publications Board, and to its Chairman, Professor Butt, in particular, my best thanks are due. Others, too, have laid me under an obligation by their readiness to throw open their muniments for inspection. The Bishop of Durham most generously placed the Episcopal Registers at Auckland at my disposal; the late Lord Ravensworth allowed me to consult the papers at Eslington and Ravensworth, Sir William Chaytor, Bt., at Witton Castle, and Miss Christian Howard at Castle Howard. Lord and Lady Ridley entertained me more than once at Blagdon and Captain Carr-Ellison at Hedgeley. Sir William Chaytor also kindly allowed me to photograph and reproduce the charming miniature of the first baronet, as did Captain Carr-Ellison the portraits of William Cotesworth and General Cuthbert Ellison, and Colonel Stafford the estate maps of Ravensworth, &c. Mr. Clive Cookson not only allowed me access to his family papers but has since deposited the early records of his firm in the new muniment room at Durham—a step, one hopes, which other owners of business or family papers in the area will follow. Canon Stephenson, Rector of St. Mary's, Gateshead, readily allowed me to consult the registers and vestry books which contain a unique record of the early administration of Gateshead. To all these my best thanks are due. Nor should the wise foresight of Colonel G. R. G. Spain go unrecorded. Not least do I wish to thank Mr. Lillie, the librarian at Gateshead, and his staff and those at the Blackgate for innumerable kindnesses, Mrs. Reed for typing the manuscript chapters, and my colleague, Mr. H. S. Offler, for reading the proofs. I can never hope to repay the years of patient long-suffering endured by members of my family while this book was in the making.

A word should perhaps be said as to its scope and title.

The former has been largely determined by the character of the new manuscript material on which it is based. It is primarily a series of studies centring mainly in County Durham and the industrial north-east in the first half of the eighteenth century. A later volume dealing with west Cumberland in the second half of the century is contemplated.

18 *December* 1950

# Contents

# List of Illustrations

# Introduction

EVEN a casual visitor to the north can hardly fail to be struck by the amount of history still 'on the map', in vallum and wall, castle and cathedral, peel tower and fort. 'There is not a man amongst them of the better sort that hath not his little tower or pile' (i.e. peel), wrote Camden three centuries and a half ago.[1] And if such a visitor spent a few hours in Newcastle he may perchance have detected the agricultural shell of the northern metropolis in such place-names as Cowgate, Haymarket, Bigg Market, Groat Market—and there were formerly the Oat Market and the Flesh Market which the town's first historian, Gray, boasted was the greatest meat market in England. Indeed, as late as the first quarter of the eighteenth century, both at Newcastle and its neighbour across the Tyne, there were town 'herdsmen', 'grassmen', and communal bulls maintained at the town's expense. One, Jeremiah Anderson, deposed in 1722[2]

that his father for twenty two years before his death was one of the persons employed to take care of the cows depastured upon the Town Moore and the Castle Leeses, belonging to Newcastle. And that the Deponent knew them from his Infancy. And that no other Cattle but those belonging to freemen of the said Town have Liberty to Depasture there, Except the Bulls bought by the Town for the Service of the Cows and some few horses belonging to him and the other persons concerned in and about looking to the said Pastures; and the Town Moor and Castle Leeses neither are nor had during his Memory been used in any other mañer. And [he] believes that some other part of the said Town Moor was anciently Called the Nun Moore but the same is now in Common with the other and always taken as part of the Town Moor and Comprehended under that Name.

Yet Newcastle, despite its agricultural shell, is the centre of what is in all probability the oldest industrial region in the

---

[1] Quoted in Tough, *The Last Days of a Frontier*, 38.
[2] *Minutes of Evidence* (The Case of Newcastle), 1723. Cotesworth MSS. A threat to the Town Moor was an issue in the general election of 1774.

country.[1] Professor Nef, the historian of *The Rise of the British Coal Industry*, speaks of an industrial revolution in late Tudor and early Stuart times. Certainly the Industrial Revolution occurred here much earlier and its social consequences strike deeper than anywhere else. Perhaps for this very reason Newcastle has managed to keep its Town Moor when younger industrial growths have mostly lost their green lungs. Here, at any rate, is a standing challenge to the social historian.

What makes the story of this remarkable development on Tyneside so enthralling is that it took place on the very threshold of a region notorious for its continuing lawlessness and insecurity. Fierce, if intermittent, Border raids continued to the very end of Elizabeth's reign. Nor did the frontier disappear in 1603 or for that matter in 1707— Berwick was still an important garrison town, and a government borough to boot, in Walpole's day. In 1616 Archdeacon Morton bemoaned the fact that 'Northumberland will be Northumberland still, another Acheldama [Field of Blood] and the vallie of Hinnom'. Indeed, the reports that reached the Secretary of State's office in James I's reign of 'reputed great theeves, outputters or receitors and maintainers of theeves' bulk large in the State Papers—'for in tymes past it hath ben observed yt most gentillmen in this Co have had one maine theefe or other under their protection for private ends and great prejudice to ye publick quiett and saftie of the countrie'. The exploits of 'Capteine Tom', 'Robin of the Pike', 'Routledg the Piper', and their 'Bangester' accomplices furnish material for a veritable saga of thievery and crime.[2] Against these 'the strong lance of

---

[1] Leland mentions three families, 'merchants and men of land', who came to Newcastle to make their fortunes. Twiss, *Life of Lord Eldon*, i. 23.

[2] In 1564 the Merchant Adventurers' Company of Newcastle ordered that no person born 'in Tyndale . . . or such like place' be admitted apprentice as 'the parties there brought up are known either by education or nature not to be of honest conversation'. Brand, ii. 228. *The Household Book of Lord William Howard*, 416–69. Two acts were passed during the reign against the moss-troopers: 4 James I, § 1; 7 James I, § 1. In 1657 there was a further 'Act for the better suppressing of Theft upon the Borders'. Constables were required to prepare lists of persons 'not responsible' who were to be bound in recognisances 'to be called once a year at least', on pain of transportation. Rewards were offered for the discovery of robbers, 'Moss-Troopers or Tories'. *Acts and Ordinances of the Interregnum*, ii. 1262.

justice hurtless breaks' and the palsied arm of authority was impotent. *Sanguis Abell clamat de terra*, cried the preacher, for here crime—in the eyes of certain well-placed observers—was inextricably mixed up with religion. James I recommended the use of 'slue' [sleuth] dogs to track down the culprits and among other special remedies propounded were—that the act of 11 Henry VII which required that no person should let land to any Tindale man 'unless he have two freeholders not inhabiting in those parts, of 40ˢ/- freehold at the least, to be bound by recognisance to the King in £20', be extended to other proscribed districts; that all lords be answerable for the good behaviour of their tenants and officials; and that 'no beef be brought to be sold in any market without the hide, nor any sheep by any butcher without the skin hanging on the carcase, upon pain of forfeiture and imprisonment'. 'All which must bee reformed afore ther can bee anie hope had of planting so mutch as trew justice and so peace in these parts', wrote Morton to Secretary Winwood in 1616. Yet half a century later an act was passed against 'notorious thieves in the Counties of Cumberland and Northumberland' which made stealing of cattle and horses a felony liable to transportation, without benefit of clergy.[1] In 1670 a famous Durham citizen, a butcher by trade (later Sir John Duck, Bt.), was strongly suspected to have 'play'd booty with the thiefe' by buying cheaply seven oxen which had been stolen out of Northumberland. The attitude of Bishop Cosin when apprized of the facts is no less revealing: his chief concern was to recover £14, the price paid by the alderman for the beasts—the prince bishop having the right of forfeiture of stolen goods in the Palatinate —'without going to law'.[2]

In the sixteenth century all authorities affirm that the Border country 'lay in much poverty and penury'. If the gentry were disposed to put their trust in their peel-towers

---

[1] 18 Charles II, cap. 3. 'An act for preventing Theft & Rapine upon the Northern Borders.' 13 & 14 Charles II, cap. 22 empowered the local magistrates to raise special rates to support a police force. This act remained in force until 1751. *Infra.*
[2] Cosin, *Correspondence*, 249–50.

and in reprisals by their dependent tenantry, the poorer tenants lived in houses 'such as a man may build within three or four hours'—rude 'earth and timber' shanties that would not readily burn. 'Their castles and pallaces are sheephouses and lodges which they commonly call "pailes", of whose burning they are not sore solaced', wrote Leslie in Elizabeth's reign.[1] Moreover, 'decay', the chronic penury of many of the tenants, coupled with over-population and subdivision of holdings in some of the remote valleys, Mr. Tough contends, was itself a cause of crime and thus worked in a vicious circle. To this continuing insecurity was added in the next century military occupation by the Scots, 1639–41, and again after the siege of Newcastle in the Civil War, and the resulting heavy crop of sequestrations and confiscations of royalist estates by the victorious parliamentarians, for the feudal north, including Newcastle, was strongly royalist. What the price of all this amounted to in terms of retarded social development historians are now beginning to divine. William Marshall, Bishop Cosin's steward in Howden, wrote in 1665 that 'land is very low and tenants generally poore, as I am informed'; one Atkinson 'saith he can purchase an estate of inheritance after the rate of fourteen years' true vallew'.[2] If this was true of Yorkshire, it was still truer farther north. In 1694 when Sir Walter Calverley, Bt., of Esholt in the West Riding, an ancestor of the Trevelyans, sold his outlying estates in Cumberland and acquired others nearer home, he made the following entry in his *Note Book*: 'at the same time I brock upe house keeping there and turned away all my servants . . .'—we can hear the sturdy Yorkshireman saying it.[3] And what he did of choice, scores of others farther north did of necessity. In a word, the poverty and low-grade civilization of many of the lesser gentry, as portrayed of the Osbaldistones in *Rob Roy*, can now be tested historically.

An act of 1715 required all Roman Catholics to register

---

[1] Quoted in Tough, op. cit. 41.　　　　[2] Cosin, *Correspondence*, 155–6.
[3] *Note Book of Sir Walter Calverley*, 62.

their estates in duplicate with the local magistrates at Quarter Sessions and returns were forwarded to the government. The 'Register' of Northumberland Papists, with its detailed schedules of properties and debts, has been printed so that all who run may read.[1] There was scarcely a Roman Catholic gentleman in the county whose estates were not heavily mortgaged *before* 1715. The loans were of two kinds, either on personal 'bond' or to provide a trust for a marriage settlement and portions for younger children, the latter sort directly, the former by implication being 'secured' on the rental. In several instances the mortgage was already 'forfeited' and the creditors were reported to be 'in possession' in 1716.[2] The Carnabys of Hexham, the Claverings of Callalee, the Haggerstons of Haggerston and Ellingham, the Erringtons of Beaufront, the Lawsons of Byker, the Newtons of Stocksfield, the Ords of Sturton, the Riddells of Fenham and Swinburne, the Sandersons of Heley, the Selbys of Biddleston, the Talbots of Cartington, the Widdringtons of Cheeseburn and Horsley, the Radcliffes of Dilston and Redheugh, and many others were all, in greater or lesser degree, 'in a strait'. Indeed, one begins to suspect that the last civil war in England, the Jacobite Fifteen, was due, in no small degree, to the desperate poverty of the northern Catholic gentry. Not that bankruptcy was a monopoly of adherents of the old faith. Many others had little to lose. Moreover, as we shall see, the Papers of the Commissioners for Forfeited Estates provide, so far as those who were directly implicated in the rising were concerned, independent corroboration of the particulars in the Registers. To what extent northern Catholics 'deeded' their estates to Protestant friends and relations or were able to make leases 'by parole' will never be precisely known; but the truth of the general picture is no longer in doubt. In short, Jacobitism

---

[1] *Northumberland Documents* (Surtees Soc. cxxxi). Cf. The Charltons of Hesleyside in Charlton, *The Recollections of a Northumbrian Lady*, 123–5.

[2] Ibid. 33, 37–38, 43, 54, 57, 91. Many of the mortgagors' claims were allowed by the Commissioners of Forfeited Estates. Similarly Neville Ridley and Nathaniel Pigott were each allowed £250 'for discovering £2000 given to superstitious Uses upon the estate of Wm Shaftoe, attainted'. Add. MSS. 40843, §§ 31–32.

was the occasion rather than the cause of the final liquidation of scores of lesser gentry and freeholders in these parts. The evidence in the subsequent Northumberland registers of the almost total elimination of the ancient Catholic gentry is overwhelming. By the end of the century only a handful survived. What became of them and of their estates? Some went into trade or into such professions as were still open to them, e.g. medicine or estate management; others emigrated or conformed.[1] Their estates were bought up by new men who had made their money in trade or by merchant families, like the Liddells, who had already entered the ranks of the gentry. Thus a double revolution was in progress in the north in the first half of the eighteenth century—the disappearance of the old gentry on the one hand, and the rise of a new ruling class on the other—a change none the less revolutionary in its effects because its processes were silent as leaven. For, thanks to the profits to be made in coal-mining and satellite trades, the social process which transmuted yeomen into merchants and merchants into gentry was here greatly accelerated. Before 1745, the new men were completely in the saddle, ready enough to use their good offices with the government of the day on behalf of a Collingwood or a Bacon to get them excused from serving as sheriff on the score of their poverty and 'small estate'.

Thus, the rise of the landed gentry, the most notable social phenomenon in the making of Modern England, occurred here, thanks to the greatly retarded social and political development, a century and a half or more later than in the rest of the country. Not that the civilization in the new town houses of the rich merchants of Newcastle or in the country mansions of the new gentry was new in kind. Rather was it a belated blossoming of that which had already developed in the richer and broader acres of southern

---

[1] In 1733 George Bowes, M.P. for County Durham, instructed the constables of Gateshead, &c., to make diligent search for a person 'who calls himself by the style and name of Capt. Wheeler and who has a lodging at the sign of the Pedlar and Pack on the Fell or Moor called Gateshead Fell who has inlisted several persons to be by him conveyed beyond Seas and there to serve as Soldiers in the Irish Regiments now in the service of the King of France'. Bowes MSS. 40748, § 66.

England; but the northern gentry soon discovered that they could indulge a Gothic splendour more magnificent than any but the greatest houses south of the Trent. Witness the proportions and walk round the towers of Alnwick, Ravensworth, Lumley, Gibside, or Seaton Delaval; and mark well their bulwarks. For, paradoxical as it may seem, the great age of the gentry was made possible only by the profits derived from trade. In the north the rent-roll is not a true index of economic power. Thanks to coal, there was always a greater degree of fusion of landed and merchant interests in these parts than elsewhere. Throughout the eighteenth century the new northern gentry, the Liddells, Carrs, Ellisons, Ridleys, and Blacketts, for example, continued to reinvigorate their stock and their purses by marrying into local merchant families. The subsequent splintering of this joint interest can, for convenience, be dated from 1840 when Sir Matthew White Ridley, a typical product of the new society, resigned from the chair of the Newcastle Chamber of Commerce owing to differences with his commercial colleagues on trade policy in general and the corn laws in particular.

It may be asked if the older, displaced, gentry were ever conscious, however dimly, of the forces that had contributed to their downfall; for such an historical analogy with our own times will soon become, if it is not already, relevant. There is some slight evidence that they were. At least, some of them included in the schedules of properties and loan charges, items for 'cow sess',[1] 'rogue money', and the charge of 'setting out' half or a full 'militia light horse',[2] as capital charges on their estates, just as nowadays a pointed reference is occasionally made in wills to the crushing burden of income-tax and death-duties. Others included a full return of services due from their tenantry—heriots, 'catches', 'mow dargues and sheer dargues', spinning of 'wowl and line', and

---

[1] A special rate levied for police purposes sometimes called 'Country Keeping'. *Infra.*

[2] 'There was no lease in Northumberland but with provision to find horse and armour for each tenement held by an able man.' See 'Articles of Border Law', quoted in Tough, op. cit. 57, 154.

of 'bodwells', due to some distant lord—strange, semi-archaic, words eloquent of the conservatism and distinctive traditions of the region.[1] Thus Sir Carnaby Haggerston included in his return in 1718 'a rake or liberty for the inhabitants of Kylie to turn their cattle in the forest of Lowick'—an association of words of more than passing interest.

Strategically the Tyne region had already attained an unenviable importance in the national economy in the second half of the seventeenth century. Thanks to the necessity of securing London's coal-supply from the attentions of Dutch and Dunkirk privateers, the government saw fit to provide 'cruisers' to escort the coal fleet. And in every war of the next century the French projected 'descents' or raids on this coast, e.g. Blyth in 1744.[2] In 1759 the magistrates and townsmen of Berwick 'formed themselves into a Regiment consisting of seventeen Companys of thirty six privates, besides serjeants, corporals and drummers—in case of any attempts at a landing by ye enemy'. Three years later a Dunkirk privateer, Kerquelin de Tremaree, projected a raid on Sunderland. With six fast-moving corsairs and fifteen hundred men, he proposed to destroy 'the fire mills which pump water from the coal mines' in the neighbourhood: the work could be done in fifteen days and the resulting destruction of the coal-, salt-, and glassworks, he contended, would be quite as important as the destruction of London itself.[3] This was no isolated madcap project; in 1794 there were actually raids on the Northumberland coast by three French privateers.[4] Already, representatives of old north country families, like the Claverings and Collingwoods, now in reduced circumstances, had reminded the enemy that fighting blood still ran in their veins, as others have done in our own day.

[1] *Northumberland Documents*, 76.
[2] The report of Bishop Chandler to the Duke of Newcastle. Add. MSS. 32702, § 355; 32896, § 250.
[3] Quoted in my article on 'North Country Life in the Eighteenth Century' in *History*, 1940.
[4] *Parl. Register* (24 March 1794), 640. Sheep and cattle were carried off from two different estates 'near Newcastle'.

'We have left off beating the eighteenth century', Augustine Birrell remarked some years ago.[1] And if that be true of students of literature, it is even truer of historians. Certainly, the men who figure prominently in the following pages, William Cotesworth (1668?–1726), his friends, Sir Henry Liddell, Bt., of Ravensworth, and his manager sons, Henry and George, had their feet firmly planted in reality and were of a stature capable of measurement. There is nothing Lilliputian about them. The same is true of the second generation, Sir Henry Liddell, the fourth baronet, later Lord Ravensworth, a leading Whig in the period of Whig ascendancy, and of his friends, Henry Ellison and Henry Thomas Carr, who by marrying Cotesworth's two daughters succeeded to his fortune. And who will doubt after reading the unpublished correspondence of Sir William Chaytor, whom I have chosen as the representative of a society 'in decay' that he was typical of his kind, weak in resolution, yet lovable in adversity? He had a flavour all his own. 'Good wine—of whatever sort—needs no bush.'

[1] Quoted in *Essays in Honour of George Sherburn* (ed. Sutherland).

## CHAPTER I

# Social Conditions in the North

## 1700—50

*He that is his own pupil has a fool to his tutor.*

*(An old saying. Sir William Chaytor, 1700)*

### I

IN January 1700, Sir William Chaytor, Bt., was seized in his ancient manor house at Croft, near Darlington, by sheriff's bailiffs and carried up to the Fleet prison in London, 'for debt', so he explained, 'occasioned by the great incumbrances left upon his estate by his father who suffered for his loyalty to King Charles the First'.[1] The disaster which had overtaken him was not unexpected: twelve years earlier his principal creditor, Sir John Sudbury of Mill Green, Essex, nephew and executor of a former dean of Durham, had threatened legal action of such severity that Chaytor had complained that he would use me 'like a teague or a papist'.[2] 'I desire once more from you that you will not suffer possession to be taken by the bailiffs which will be such a slurr as cannot be imagin'd to be put upon a Gentleman at this time of day.' Part of the estate was seized in 1690 for the creditors feared that the rents would not answer the principal and arrears of interest, and after ten years more of shuffling their patience was at last exhausted. 'From Hell, Hull, Halifax and York, Good Lord deliver us', Chaytor muttered as he rode to London never to return to his ancestral home. 'I wish thou hadst seen what a day George [his servant]

[1] In the sixteenth century, Christopher Chaytor was diocesan registrar successively to Bishops Tunstall and Pilkington and jointly with his son Thomas, to Bishop Barnes. (Information kindly supplied by Dr. G. Hinde of St. Hild's College.) Chaytor MSS. (Witton Castle). 'I am here at the King's suit and the King my debtor', he wrote, 'though they all think here I am committ only upon a mean process at Thompson's suit as Administrator.'

[2] Hunter MSS. (Durham Cathedral Library) xii, § 121, *passim*. Lady Chaytor had warned her husband that Thompson 'Will have you confiend in spight of your teeth'. N.B.—Boswell used 'teague' to describe an Irishman as late as 1763. *London Journal*, 282.

and I had yesterday', he wrote to his wife as soon as he was settled in his new quarters, 'he mending my old drawers and I mending my old breetches and setting buttons on my ruff coat which was almost worn to pieces in riding up.' He was doubtless pleased with the news in Lady Chaytor's first letter that 'Lodde Hall was so vext at one Hunter of Haughton for being conserned in the takin of you as that he made the fellow strip himself and he lashed him severely'. Magnificent! but it was not war according to the new rules of the game.

Life in the Fleet for those of its 5,000 inmates who could afford luxuries was not intolerable.[1] Sir William, by reason of his quality, paid 6s. a week to the Warden for his lodging and half a crown for his bed, 10s. to the tipstaff—Mr. Madox of Exchequer fame[2]—for board, and a few shillings for coals, candles, laundry, &c., but 'there is good air in the Fleet', he wrote, 'and good walks and a booling green and many Gentlemen do remove themselves thither from the King's Bench' prison.[3] Indeed, those who could give the necessary security were free to live with their wives in lodgings 'within the Rules which is Ludgate Hill and the Old Bailey and by-alleys and many had liberty to live in the town': 'A man may live here as well as at Court.' Eventually, Lady Chaytor was persuaded, against her better judgement, to join her husband. For a time she took lodgings in Westminster until she could no longer pay the landlady or the milkman. 'I had rather you changed my peas [i.e. piece] of gold or pawned it for a ginney', she wrote pathetically, 'I have nothing now left to pawn.' She died in 1704 and was buried at Kensington. Of her surviving children, Nan, the only

---

[1] 'Tis said at least 5000 belongs to the Fleet', wrote Chaytor. 'For indeed it will not hold scarce a tenth part of those that are committt.'

[2] 'Mr Maddox is a good, hearty, blunt man and loves a bottle sometimes; he had got too much last night and he is stuff'd with a cold.' 'We eats twelve at the ordinary at Mr Maddox's ... eating but one meal a day but that very good, and bread and butter sometime in a morning or a draught of half ale with a tost butter'd with honey and a draught warmed with a bottle at night, and a penny black serves me two days.' 'Mr Maddox trusts me and has not the least jealousy upon me for making an escape.'

[3] 'Mr Woodhouse [the sheriff's bailiff] advises me to go to the Fleet where I shall be kindlier used than in the King's Bench.'

daughter, was a pillar of strength to the family until she fell a victim to consumption and followed her mother to an early grave. Henry, the eldest son, became an engineer in Marlborough's army, but he had perforce to sell some remaining ancestral properties, certain burgage tenures in Richmond, North Riding, to Lord Wharton, the Whig party manager, whose interest had secured him his commission and subsequent promotion. To the grandson of a stout-hearted cavalier this must have been as devastating as any mine he himself had sprung at Schellenberg or Ramillies. Thomas, the second son, joined Queen Anne's navy but failing to pass the examination for a commission, found consolation in the bottle. Clarvaux, the youngest, became a merchant's clerk. The tough old squire rotted in the Fleet for seventeen or more years:[1] on his death in 1721 the baronetcy became extinct.[2] It was revived a century later in the Spennithorne branch of the family.

The disaster which had overtaken the Chaytors is symptomatic of the plight of many of the lesser squires and gentry in the north at that time. Of Sir John Sudbury's other debtors, Sir Ralph Cole of Kepier, descendant of a one-time blacksmith, was reported to be 'in a strait', owing 'use upon use' before 1688; Colonel Tempest, Sudbury's brother-in-law, was 'desperately in debt', while legal proceedings were contemplated against Sir Francis Salkeld and Sir Edward Smith, only less severe than against Chaytor himself.[3] Early in the next century, the account books of William Ramsay, a Newcastle goldsmith, bear some resemblance to those of a modern building society, save that the vital social process was then often in reverse. Many ancient families, the Blenkinsops of Bellister, the Radcliffes of Redheugh, the Riddells of Shipcote, to mention only a few, mortgaged and later sold piecemeal their ancestral lands. The Register of Estates of Roman Catholics and the papers of the Commissioners

---

[1] He was buried at St. Bride's in January, 1721. Henry died at York in 1717. Surtees, *History of Durham*, iv (ii). 111, is inaccurate in some of the details concerning Chaytor's children.

[2] Debrett, *Baronetage* (1808), 1049.        [3] Hunter MSS., loc. cit.

for Forfeited Estates show that many of the lesser gentry, Richard Butler of Rawcliffe and Greenall and Hall of Otterburn, for example, who actively supported the Fifteen, had long since heavily mortgaged their properties while some of the larger estates, like the Widdringtons, it transpired, were in little better case.[1] Indeed, in one instance, the Commissioners were presented with claims for debt in respect of tradesmen's goods and tithe before the estate was actually forfeited.[2] 'It is a sensible affliction to me', wrote Colonel Cuthbert Ellison, lord of the manor of Wardley, near Hebburn, in 1739, 'to be obliged to divest myself of any part of the Patrimony of the Family', but it was a choice of evils, he explained, an amputation of a limb to save the body itself. He took comfort in the thought that 'the mortification was not due to any of my excesses but from an old gangreen'.[3] What was true of the lesser gentry was true also of great numbers of small freeholders, copyholders, and tenants. The correspondence of landlords like Sudbury and Ellison is full of complaints of the monstrous arrears of rent of their tenants. 'I believe if you informe yourself of any Country Gentlemen', wrote William Wilson, Sudbury's Durham agent, in 1689, 'they will tell you rents are pretty hard to come by and that if tenants at this time pay half a year within another it is well.' 'I have sued two of your tenants', he wrote a year later, 'and if you be willing to be served with them all, I shall readily doe it, but it will be a danger of breaking of them for there were never so many broke in this Country in the memory of man.'[4] The Audit Books of the dean and chapter of Durham for the last decade of the century lend some support to this conclusion.[5] Half a century later, Cuthbert Ellison repeatedly complained of the arrears of his Hebburn tenants. It is no part of our present purpose to analyse in detail the causes

---

[1] F.E.C. 1 (P.R.O.), C/146, 159A, W/44. e.g. The Widdrington estates were part mortgaged to Sir John Eden and Richard Townley.

[2] Ibid. The claims of Francis Brandling, merchant of Newcastle, and the dean and chapter of Carlisle against John Clavering of Berrington. *Northumberland Documents* (Surtees Soc.), 37–8, 131.        [3] Ellison MSS.        [4] Hunter MSS. xii, §§ 125, 139.

[5] 'Rents remaining in arrear', 1691–6, £1,864. 9s. 6¼d.

that had contributed to the malady which he described as 'an old gangreen'—mortgages, military occupation by the Scots, sequestrations, and confiscations resulting from the Civil War. Suffice to say that the period between the Restoration and 1750 witnessed the liquidation of scores of ancient families, both great and small, and the rise out of the ashes of new men who gradually acquired vast agglomerations of estates and whose descendants have, for the most part, remained in possession until our own day. In some cases, the Liddells of Ravensworth, for example, it is possible to watch a slow-motion picture of this process. 'I would have you to let no opportunity slip of buying any Estate that is contiguous to Streatlam, High Lands, Kirk Leavington or Gibside', wrote W. Blakiston Bowes to his mother in 1718, 'I am sure of it that you might have Red Hall, Maynards or Cowtons whenever you please and at reasonable rates.'[1]

## II

In April 1716 Sir William Chaytor had like to have been joined in the Fleet by Lady Clavering of Axwell Park as the following letter to her lawyer will show:[2]

I refer you to what I wrote last post since that suit such a concern has hapned to me as exceeds all others I met with in this troublesome affair which was yesterday afternoon vizt,—a messenger sent down with a warrant from the Lord Chancellor to arrest me and carry me up to the Fleet, he entering my house with several more to assist him with such violence and treated me with such Indignity as if I had been a publick Malefactor by pulling me out of my Chamber and pressing me against the door, he's bruised all my arm and nothing would serve him but he would force me out of my house at near 11 a clock at night, though I gave myselfe into his custody as his prisoner and offered him the keys of my house and that he might have as many people as he pleased to assist him lest he should think I should make my Escape and I offered to sitt up with him in the room all night since he would not suffer me out of his sight, soe that never Gentlewoman was soe used as

[1] Bowes MSS. 40747, § 175.

[2] Hunter MSS. xiii, § 38. Her offence was a breach of a Chancery injunction. An order of commitment was issued against four other persons, one of whom, Anthony Leaton, was arrested and carried up to London a month later. Bowes MSS. 40747, §§ 129, 135.

I have been and I was forced to give a Bond with penalty of £1,000 if I don't agree with Mr. Cotesworth by Wednesday next, the 11th inst, that then to surrender myself into his custody again and to goe along with him to London and be committed to the Fleet which is the barbarousst usage ever any one met with and especially to me that knew nothing of the concerns or what's past, saving what you informed me. . . .

Like Chaytor's arrest, this unheard-of 'barbarousst usage' of a lady caused quite a stir in the north. It arose out of a dispute concerning a colliery wagon-way over Whickham Fell in which the aforesaid Mr. Cotesworth was acting on behalf of his brother-in-law, Alderman William Ramsay, goldsmith and merchant of Newcastle, who had lately purchased the manors of Gateshead and Whickham. Cotesworth, like Wolsey two centuries earlier, was teaching people in the north the new law of Chancery. 'Tis remarkable how free you make with Dignity at a time when Dignitarys (tho' of an higher station) are so lately made Numerous by a considerable creation',[1] Sir Henry Liddell, Bt., had written to him four years earlier. He was one of the new men who had come rapidly to the fore in recent years. When Lady Clavering indited her letter, Alderman Ramsay was on his death-bed and the manors passed to her mortal enemy.

Cotesworth was a yeoman's son from Eggleston-in-Teesdale. In February 1682, a youth in his early teens, he was apprenticed to Robert Sutton, mercer and tallow-chandler of Gateshead.[2] His master died before the term was out and Cotesworth elected to complete it with the widow with whom he was something of a favourite. He was admitted a freeman of the company in the year of the Glorious Revolution and shortly afterwards, like Hogarth's Good-

[1] A reference to the creation of twelve peers in 1711. Here, as elsewhere, when no specific reference is given, the information is taken from the Cotesworth–Ellison MSS.

[2] He has been confused with his cousins of the Hermitage. Hodgson, *Northumberland*, iv. 145. *North Country Diaries*, i. 87. In May 1699 he married at St. John's, Newcastle, Hannah, sister of William Ramsay. The baptisms of their five children—the youngest Cuthbert born 1704 died in infancy—are entered in the Register of St. Mary's, Gateshead. Mrs. Cotesworth died in 1710; he subsequently paid 3s. 4d. for a 'lairstone' for her (the standard fee), but no monument to either of them appears to have survived.

child, formed a family partnership with his late master's son, on capital partly lent by the widow, and he eventually married his partner's sister-in-law. The firm of Sutton and Cotesworth, tallow-chandlers and corn merchants of Gateshead, lasted some fifteen years; it was eventually dissolved following disputes over widow Sutton's will, which was thought to be somewhat too favourable to Cotesworth, and allegations that, contrary to the deed of co-partnership, he was trading separately on his own account. In truth the partnership had become unequal—a somewhat lethargic senior partner was no match for the thrustful energetic yeoman's son who was never guilty of the sin of letting grass grow under his feet. By 1705, like the Liddells a century earlier, we find him engaged in a highly miscellaneous trade exporting grindstones, lead, glass bottles, and later salt to Holland, Hamburg, and the Baltic ports, and importing flax, hemp, madder, and whale-bone in return. At the same time he shipped vast quantities of tallow and salt to the London market, buying in return indigo and costly dyestuffs besides hops, sugar, and tobacco. When conditions permitted he imported wines direct from Bordeaux and Spain—the new northern gentry were nice connoisseurs of claret and port—and corn from the west country. In May of that year he branched out into a new line of business and obtained from the dean and chapter of Durham a lease, jointly with Dean Montague himself, of exclusive way-leave rights for a term of twenty years with leave to build a wagon-way for the carriage of coals and grindstones to Jarrow staith from half a dozen adjoining parishes.[1] He came to specialize in obtaining way-leave rights of this kind, thereby threatening to hold to ransom coal-owners of the neighbouring hinterland. The Clavering dispute is a case in point. Towards the

---

[1] Register of Leases (1700–5), § 193. In January 1706 the 'Twenty-Four' of Gateshead 'ordered their Stewards to wait on M$^r$ Lyonel Vane and M$^r$ Henry Liddell to execute a lease of Bensham way-leave formerly agreed upon and upon their refusing to sign and execute the same, it is then ordered that all the way-leaves now used be immediately let to William Cotesworth, Merchant, under the same covenants and agreements which were demised to M$^r$ Vane and M$^r$ Lidle abateing £10 per annum in the rent'. Vestry Book (St. Mary's, Gateshead).

end of Queen Anne's reign he began to acquire salt-pans at
Shields where ancient proprietors, including his kinsman,
Michael Cotesworth, were going down like ninepins, thanks
to the recent heavy duties on the commodity, vexatious
restrictions, and unequal competition.[1] By the end of the
reign he claimed to be the biggest salt proprietor in the
kingdom. Shortly afterwards he obtained the contract for
the supply of the Victualling Office. By that time his trading
turnover was in the region of £30,000 a year. Nor was that
all. Since 1710 he had been the moving spirit and paid
secretary of a powerful coal cartel or 'Regulation'. He went
to London in the spring of 1711 to oppose an important
Coal Bill which aimed at suppressing illegal combinations
in the trade and acquitted himself well.[2] Soon afterwards he
was a substantial mine-owner himself. In 1711 he negotiated
the purchase, in London, for his brother-in-law, Alderman
Ramsay, of the manors of Gateshead and Whickham, once
reputed to be the richest coal-bearing manors in the country,
and in the following year he obtained a renewal of the lease
from the Bishop of Durham. On Ramsay's death, four years
later, these manors together with the lordships of Hartleyburn and Bellister, near Haltwhistle, and freehold lands at
Newsham near Stockton, passed to the one-time tallow-
chandler. Further purchases followed of Lady Radcliffe's
lands at Redheugh and the Riddell estate at Shipcote, besides a half-share with Joseph Banks, M.P., of Winlaton and
Stella forfeited by the attainted Lord Widdrington for his
part in the Fifteen.[3] He was now 'Esquire Cotswith', of The
Park, Gateshead, which he proceeded to modernize apace.
Office as mayor and on the commission of the peace for the
two counties followed as a matter of course; he was Sheriff
of Northumberland in 1719, for, as a leading Whig, he was
the government's principal agent in the north and had close

---

[1] Register of Leases, *passim*.                              [2] Ch. V.

[3] They bought the Widdrington estates in 1719 for £7,300 but in 1727 they resold them
to the family, 'so that this £12,000 is clear again', wrote Banks. Lord Widdrington was
allowed £12,000 by George I as a special bounty, possibly to enable him to recover the
estates. B.M. Add. MSS. 40843, §31.

contacts with the ministers of the day, the Earl of Sunderland, Lord Townshend, Lord Cadogan, and others.[1] 'Black William' was a force to be reckoned with, as Lady Clavering and others discovered to their cost. He had a reputation for laying mighty adversaries 'on their backs'. 'I was resolved to make this estate as near a £1,000 per annum as the accidents of my affairs were exposed to and providing reasonably for the rest of my children', he told his eldest son. 'I never intend to cross Trent till I can sit at Gateshead Park in peace', he wrote from London in 1722. ''Tis all I desire. I think it a valuable place and I am persuaded it would be thought so by others when I have left it.'

'Gentility is but ancient riches', Lord Burghley had re-marked in Queen Bess's day. Cotesworth, it would seem, had merely deleted the adjective. In the end, fate half-cheated him of his ambition. His elder son, who had been duly apprenticed as a tallow-chandler before going up to Sedbergh and Cambridge, died while a student at the Middle Temple: Robert, the younger son, designed originally for commerce, and switched to law on his brother's death, died three years after his father. The Cotesworth fortune passed to the two daughters, Hannah and Elizabeth, who became respectively the wives of Henry Ellison and Henry Thomas Carr. In the former Cotesworth's ambition was realized. For close on half a century Henry Ellison lived at Park House as resident lord of the manor. Cuthbert Ellison, the honoured member of parliament for Newcastle until 1830, was his grandson. A new 'county' family had emerged. Yet it is entirely fitting that the name of Cotesworth is still enshrined in the place-names of Gateshead—no mean tribute to one whose own reign had lasted barely ten years.

'We have, you know, a proverb', he once wrote, 'he that is born under a threepenny planet will never be worth a groat.' Unlike Chaytor, Cotesworth put his faith in his own star not in any outworn astrology. Charles Sanderson, an eminent London lawyer who knew him well, paid him this tribute:

[1] See Appendix A. Extracts from his correspondence in 1715–16.

'Your father was the most remarkable man I ever knew, considering his education.' No doubt the margin between success and failure in this world is determined by intangible personal qualities which historians can scarcely pretend to gauge. That Cotesworth had remarkable gifts of mind and heart his closest friends, the Liddells of Ravensworth, readily recognized—a clear business head with a distinct flair for law, foresight, and astuteness, coupled with tireless energy and driving power. And withal he was a rare fighter with the spirit of a game-cock. In a sense he needed to be, for his meteoric rise to fame and fortune aroused the jealousy of powerful enemies, Sir John and Lady Clavering, Lady Bowes and her son, 'the Count', of Gibside and Streatlam, and certain members of the privileged corporation of Newcastle.[1] Fazackerley, a leading Counsel of the day, assured him 'that it was the fate of most men that had raised an estate as I had done' to be involved in costly and vexatious suits: and so it proved. One of his correspondents, Edward White, the agent at Lumley Castle, once counselled him not to be mercenary but White's master, the Earl of Scarborough instructed him to consult Cotesworth on all matters pertaining to the coal trade. To the men who knew him best and whose respect and affection he won and kept, he was always 'Honest Will' and 'Kind Friend'. In his mental outlook and speech he remained a countryman to the end. He could never bring himself to accept the permanent loss of good farm land by pit heaps: every winter gangs of men and ox teams were engaged on their removal. 'The coal fitters must not take all the cream and leave only the blue milk', he wrote in 1723. 'Thus am I kicked and cuff'd and threatened with destruction [by George Bowes], if it so fall out, I must be forced to come to the Hills and keep sheep.'

[1] Bowes alleged that Cotesworth had once been a menial servant in his family. For the Bowes's pedigree. Surtees, *History of Durham*, iv. 108. 'Your friend M$^r$ Cotesworth having obstinately persisted in his law suit against Lady Clavering and self and not hearkening to any terms of accommodation has utterly deprived himself of £3,500 per annum.' (W. Blakiston Bowes to D$^r$ Jurin, 22 April 1721.) 'I think you in the wrong for pitying M$^r$ Cotesworth for his loss was entirely occasioned by his own Covetousness and endeavouring to engross all ye Coal Trade.' Bowes MSS. 40747, § 184–6. Earlier the two families had been very friendly.

If Sir William Chaytor provides an extreme example of a society on the wane, Cotesworth is the prototype, *par excellence*, of the new men who were rising to the ascendant. Such were also his contemporaries; William Blakiston Bowes and his brother George, Alderman William Ramsay, Matthew White of Blagdon, Richard Ridley of Heaton, the Delavals of Seaton, Colonel George Liddell of Ravensworth, industrialists like Matthew Bell and John Wilkinson, and, somewhat later, John and Isaac Cookson: farther south, the Allans, Hedworths, Lambtons, Ettricks, Shipperdsons, and Whartons to mention but a few—men of enterprise, vision, and resource who were prepared to take risks and to seize opportunities with both hands. Speaking generally, the most rapid industrial and social developments of the time took place away from the islands of corporate or ecclesiastical privilege. Indeed, it was one of Cotesworth's basic contentions that the high placed officials, agents, and stewards of the great estates, both lay and ecclesiastical, had long battened upon their masters and had come to form a sort of reactionary and predatory confederacy against which he and his like had to do battle. We shall have occasion later to examine the truth of this conviction. Certain it is that the notable developments which took place in the coal industry in the first half of the eighteenth century were made not by the privileged members of the powerful Hostmen's Company of Newcastle which had monopolized the trade since Queen Elizabeth's day, but, for the most part, by new men starting more or less from scratch. Again, it is surely significant that the great ironmaster, Ambrose Crowley, set up his works at Winlaton and Swalwell and that Cotesworth himself conducted his business from Gateshead which remained outside the corporate jurisdiction of Newcastle. To some extent the same is true of Dagnias's and Cookson's glassworks at Shields and of the first blast-furnace at Gateshead.[1] True,

---

[1] Cookson and Button's 'Foundry' at Gateshead [Low Ward] was assessed for land-tax at £3 per annum in 1726. Land Tax Assessment Book. Twenty years later the Cooksons had a blast-furnace at Chester-le-Street. Cookson MSS.

the rich and privileged corporation of Newcastle—it had a revenue from tolls, &c. of nearly £7,000 a year in 1700[1]— fought a stubborn rearguard action or series of actions thanks to its chartered rights as conservator of the Tyne. As late as 1698 it had obtained a verdict confirming its monopoly control of ballast shores on both banks of the river against a powerful London financier, Shepherd, who had obtained a lease of lands on the south bank from the dean and chapter of Durham. In the next two decades it burst through its medieval bands by acquiring Wincomlee, Willington quay, and Walker estate in defiance of the statute of mortmain, and although *quo warranto* proceedings were threatened and a government inquiry was held into the 'oppressions' of the corporation in 1722–3, its privileges and possessions were eventually confirmed.

But control over the navigation of the Tyne did not extend to Wear or Blyth. The rapid rise of Sunderland as a coal-port in the first quarter of the century caused acute anxiety on Tyneside. Already by 1710 its overseas shipments of coal nearly equalled those of Newcastle and from then on the 'Regulation' or the 'Grand Allies' strove repeatedly to put a quota on the Sunderland trade. In 1712 more than a hundred of the principal inhabitants of the Wear port sub-scribed to the building of a new parish church.[2]

For that the town of Sunderland nigh the sea [so runs the preamble] is of late years very much increased to the Number of People who are now computed to amount to 4000 souls and upwards. And whereas the Church at Bishop Wearmouth (near half a mile distant) being the Pariochiall Church is not only incapable of containing one tenth part of the number together with the other inhabitants of the Parish who, being owners or farmers of lands doe in right thereof pretend to be possessed of all the Pues or seats in the said Church insomuch that other persons not soe qualified are often undecently thrust out as

[1] Cotesworth MSS. As conservators of the Tyne, the corporation had a monopoly of the ballast shores. Masters of ships which came from the south 'light', i.e. in ballast, were obliged to cast their ballast at these official ballast shores at so much per ton. Ralph Gardiner had first protested against this in 1655, in *England's Grievance Discovered*.

[2] The Rector of Sunderland now has the original document with the names of the sub-scribers.

intruders into the propertyes of other people . . . [The inhabitants of the town, therefore, desired to build a church] within their own Township whereunto they may repayr and assemble with more frequency and ease than the ways and weather in the winter season or the roome in the said parish Church will permit. And also that Masters of Ships (not free in the liberties) and other strangers resorting or trading to the said town may be thereby accommodated.

Five years later, the 'Wearmen', headed by the Earl of Scarborough, the Hedworths, Lambtons, and Allans, obtained an enabling act to make the River Wear navigable as far as Durham and to improve the harbour of Sunderland, despite powerful opposition from the county and from Newcastle.[1] This spectacular growth of Sunderland was made possible by the invention and development of colliery wagonways which enabled the mines at Washington, Lumley, Rainton, and Chester-le-Street to be exploited. Much the same thing was happening in the hinterland about Blyth. Already in 1718 John Horsley considered that 'it can scarce fail of being a town of trade', though the notable developments there and at Seaton Delaval belong rather to the second half of the century. In one respect Sunderland's increased importance in the coal trade was responsible for a curious and significant legacy: there were no hostmen at Sunderland and accordingly the Wear port's name for a coal-factor, viz. 'fitter', came to supersede the older name, hostman.

## III

History had left abundant and peculiar marks on the Border counties, not only in ancient monuments, causeways, and colliery wagon-ways, but in the underlying social conditions and habits of the people. For example, up to 1662 all the principal tenants in the village of Shincliffe still paid a uniform rent and were required to hold themselves in readiness at all times, each with a horse appropriately 'furnished,

[1] *C.J.* xviii. 516. Cotesworth played a leading part in organizing opposition to the project. The correspondence has survived in his papers. *Infra*, Ch. VI.

to attend their lord to the wars'.[1] Indeed, the peculiar northern custom known as 'tenant right', whereby the right of succession and the amount of fines were strictly regulated was being constantly appealed to in the seventeenth and early eighteenth century.[2] Spearman in his *Enquiry into the Ancient and Present State of the County Palatine*, published in 1729, states that Dr. Grey, 'a venerable Prebend, a Joseph among his brethren', often recommended his fellow prebends 'to keep to the old rule in Bishop Morton's time . . . to be easy and moderate in renewals of leases and to encourage the tenants' improvements, if they meant to avoid the evil of those unhappy civil wars he had bitterly tasted of and to which, he said, some rigid Clergymen had not a little contributed and by provoking the laity had (in great measure) occasioned'. Men in the northern counties had good reason to remember 'those unhappy civil wars', a recurrence of which they feared in 1715. It was not for nothing that every colliery lease had a clause rendering it null and void in the event of civil war. But then, some men also remembered that speculation in forfeited estates might prove a good thing and they were quick to take advantage of the misfortunes of the Jacobites.[3] Roger North tells us that at Kendal the common people walk barefoot and children leap 'as if they had hoofs, but it is almost the same all over the north' he added.[4] He noted also a certain classlessness—'I could not but wonder to see pantaloons and shoulder knots crowding among the common clowns'—a reference to gentry serving on juries with commoners. Again he remarked that the people about Hexham rode about in strange attire and 'are great antiquaries in their own bounds'—they had such abundant local material to work upon. Fifty years later Mowbray, a Durham lawyer, noted that semi-feudal conditions obtained around

---

[1] Register of Leases (1661–5), §§ 108, 126, 179. In 1666 Bishop Cosin pointed out that the Palatinate enjoyed the same laws as the rest of the kingdom and instanced the act of 1660 which abolished feudal tenures. Surtees, *History of Durham*, i, p. cxlvii.

[2] *Infra*, Appendix B.

[3] The Liddells bought Eslington, forfeited by the Collingwoods, for £21,131.

[4] *Lives of the Norths*, 173, 181.

Naworth: 'he has a sort of brutish tenants that if my Lord [Carlisle] takes their wives they dare not oppose him'.

'The country is yet very sharp upon thieves', noted North, 'and a violent suspicion, there, is next to conviction.' 'There is seldom a week but either some horses or other cattle are stoln', wrote Thomas Sisson in 1728, 'the watch is set on both in Newcastle and Gateshead.' It was not uncommon for rival gangs of roughs to accuse individuals of horse-stealing. Indeed, until the middle of the century, there was a special cess or rate in Northumberland known as 'Country Keeping' which 'the Occupiers and Farmers of land', not the owners as was the case with other cesses on land, 'had all along chearfully paid'.[1] When the magistrates at the Quarter Sessions held at Morpeth in April 1719 intimated their intention of abolishing 'Country Keeping', a petition was got up and circulated in favour of its retention 'for we apprehend that stealing of cattle will thereby be increased and that great damage will fall upon the poorer sort of Tennants who neither have money nor will be able to spare their time to go in pursuit of the thief', with the result, so it was feared, that land would fall in value. In County Durham highway robbery was so prevalent in 1670 that it provided an additional reason for giving the Palatinate parliamentary representation with a view to making a law that watch and ward should be kept in the winter as well as in summer months. Sir Gilbert Gerard, Bishop Cosin's son-in-law, stoutly resisted the demand: 'I am sure if any man should propose to bring in a bill to that purpose in parliament [it] would be thought rediculous, for if upon every aksident a law must be had to redress it, they had need to have a parlement to attend that perticuler contry.'[2] In 1692 the responsibility of the 'Hundred' for highway robbery committed within its limits was brought home to the citizens of Durham for in that year a special assessment was levied in Chester Ward

---

[1] Cotesworth MSS. 'Cunterey-keeping', or 'cow-sess', figured as a rent charge on some papist estates. *Northumberland Documents* (Surtees Soc.), 19, 40, 93.

[2] Hunter MSS. vii, § 74.

for the robbery of the king's taxes on the Durham–Chester road.[1]

Though the raids of mosstroopers had ceased and fear of the 'Bonny Blue Bonnets' had practically disappeared by the beginning of the eighteenth century, the north was still 'too prone to outrage' and violence or what Charles Sanderson, an eminent London lawyer, euphemistically called 'the Northern fashion of being perpetually conserned about other folk's business and a dear Love of Mischief'.[2] Respect for the law was scarcely skin deep, and unhappily men of standing often set an example which keelmen and pitmen were only too ready to follow. For instance, in April 1712 the board of directors of a powerful coal cartel, including gentlemen and citizens of the highest repute, openly encouraged the copyholders at Tanfield Moor to 'cut up' a rival wagon-way and further resolved that 'if they are opposed that then a joint force be raised to pull it up by force'. 'Riotts' in connexion with 'pulling the Wayes up' were endemic at Gateshead.[3] The famous keelmen's strike in the summer of 1710 led to the stationing of a regiment at Newcastle—'Kirke's Lambs' were there for a time—and although the 'soldjers' themselves were sometimes the occasion of trouble, this became the stock policy for dealing with strikes or 'mutinies', as they were called, in the eighteenth century. Commenting on 'ye days of Battle' in Newcastle, a northerner, Henry Liddell, wrote from London that he was not surprised 'at ye rude management for tho' we be at the tail of the kingdom, yet we follow the fashions of our Metropolis', an allusion to the recent Sacheverell riots. In 1712, he congratulated his friend Cotesworth 'upon his delivery out of the hands of the

---

[1] Details are given on a slip of paper in the Book of Rates.

[2] 'I hope the farmers need not be too fearful of the Scots', wrote Chaytor in 1700, 'but I wish they have good hearts to unite for the interest of England.' His daughter, however, 'did not apprehend the least danger from them'.

[3] Vestry Book (St. Mary's, Gateshead), 1681–1807, §191. In September 1713 the 'Twenty-Four' ordered their stewards 'forthwith to use the most proper methods and likelyest means to oblige the Bensham Owners to pay what money is due and in arrears for way-leave . . . and that the Grassmen be secured from all inconveniency that may attend them in Pulling the wayes up or using any other means that may be thought necessary by Councel'.

Mohocks, certainly such barbarous treatment in one's own house was never heard of. It was happy for you that you were in a condition to oppose force with force.' On the occasion referred to above, Cotesworth, the secretary of the coal cartel, powerfully aided and abetted the exploit. 'At the pressing instance' of Lady Bowes of Gibside and in her company, he assisted in pulling up a newly laid wagon-way over certain lands at Fawdonfield.[1] Hearing of the incident Sir Henry Liddell wrote:

1712. May 30. In these pacifick days we are entered upon, I find war is begun in the North and squadrons and battalions led into the Field under theyr several commanders. The cause I have heard well of; these wish it success and that you may ride tryumphant with your Female Heroine who fac't the Baronet [Sir John Clavering] with courage beyond her sex and humanity becoming it.

But the incident cost Cotesworth dearly. Legal action resulted and 'the Female Heroine' backed out and left him to bear the whole cost. Besides, a year later, he had to deal with a counter-demonstration in force.

On 15 June 1713 a gang of roughs, including some foul-mouthed women led by Sir John Clavering, Bt., Conservator of the Peace, accompanied by a constable, molested a party of Alderman Ramsay's work-people in a quarry on Whickham Fell. John Fenwick, colliery viewer, who was in charge of the workmen later deposed on oath:[2] 'That the said Sir John commanded that we should give over in the Queen's name and called us rogues with abundance of other passionate

---

1 'Mr Cotesworth has writ and sent a messenger to Mr Rood, Fawcett and Gowland [Durham lawyers] and says he should think it best to bring as many persons as you can into ye Riot betwixt this and Tuisday. And indeed I see no reason for your Ladyship paying them any compliment in forbearing to beat up theire quarters.' (Dr John Bowes to Lady Bowes, 7 March 1712.) Bowes MSS. 40747, § 116.

2 The depositions and bill of costs are in the Cotesworth Papers. There was, however, good reason for Lady Bowes's action. Her brother-in-law, Dr. John Bowes, Prebend of Durham wrote on 30 April 1712: 'Mr Gowland since writing his to you bid me lett you know that since Mr Wright is Chairman [of the Sessions at Durham] he thinks it adviseable rather to deffer prosecuting Sir John's people who were informed against by way of Indightment till next Sessions than goe on with it now and the charge will then be greater and more for them to pay.' Wright was Sir John Clavering's associate in the colliery at Tanfield. Bowes MSS. 40747, § 123.

and extravagant ill-names and words.' He told Fenwick that he was an old knave and 'wou'd make him fast'. Other witnesses testified that Sir John said, 'Ad Zounds! do not I know what Mr. Cotesworth, that curse-mother fellow is? This is Black Cotesworth's doing and many other exhorbitant and unreasonable expressions to the like purpose.' There is a distinct sixteenth-century flavour about this. Further, that one Ralph Hymers 'was also very abusive and amongst a great many malicious invectives and unjust calumnies said that Mr. Cotesworth was not an honest man, but a Rogue and a Black Devill, that had invented the work we were at when he should have slept with many other exhorbitant expressions'. All this time, the constable, John Armstrong, had 'laid or sat in our way so that we could not pursue our work'. Nor was it merely a battle of words; hacks and shovels were brought into action; one of the workmen had his arm broken and had to be treated by a doctor for several weeks. By this time, Cotesworth was an adept in getting affidavits, as Sir John discovered to his cost when the case went to the assizes at York and the tables were completely turned three years later when Lady Clavering, who kept up the dispute after Sir John's death, was arrested in her own house and required to give bond to be of good behaviour. By 1720 one of Clavering's associates, Mr. Wright, J.P., of Sedge-field, was credibly reported to have fled into Wales and another, Thomas Brumell, hostman of Newcastle, went bankrupt. It was because of the excessive litigiousness in his work-people that the ironmaster, Sir Ambrose Crowley, set up a Court of Arbitrators at the Swalwell works with quasi-magisterial powers.[1]

By the summer of 1714, 'Black William' was singled out by local Tories and Jacobites as a special object of attack. Fierce rivalries in the coal trade, notably disputes about way-leave, gave a sharp edge to political differences. 'Let me

---

[1] Add. MSS. 34555, Law No. 50, 53. 'To hear small differences . . . which cause waste of time and trouble to Magistrates.' No workman was 'to strike an officer, throw stones or snowballs, or by blowing of a horn or otherwise raise a tumult or mobb'. 'Clubbing' for drink was also finable.

entreate you to be carefull of your own safety and ride not single and unarmed (as hath bin your practise) when Revenge is threatened', wrote his friend Sir Henry Liddell from London, who sent him his own pair of neat pocket pistols with an injunction 'never to travel without ym'. 'They are clever, well made and lye in a little room.' Two years later, his son, nicknamed affectionately the 'Governor', reiterated the advice: 'Pray thee, dear Will, take a particular care of yourself. Get home betimes and never travel without a sturdy blade and an oaken towell. The party are insolent to a degree.' Indeed, the Tories and non-Jurors were so numerous about Newcastle that he really feared civil war for a time. The behaviour of some people made Cotesworth conclude that they were mad. His friend was more philosophical. 'The High party are outrageous more than ever which is not unpleasing to me', he wrote in January 1715. 'Did you never see the Gamesters when they dispair'd of success toss about their box and dice?'

Cotesworth gained great credit in ministerial circles for effectively forestalling the Fifteen in the north-east, having early impressed on the government the importance of sending a regiment of troops to Tyneside, while his friend Colonel George Liddell assembled and drilled the county militia on Gateshead Fell. He became the government's secret agent in these parts and from 1715 to 1719 enjoyed the confidence of the Whig Ministry, particularly of the Earl of Sunderland, Secretary of State, Lord Cadogan, Master of the Horse, and Colonel Williamson.[1] During these years there continued to be many alarums in the north, fears of a second Jacobite attempt, possibly associated with a Swedish descent. The intense and critical atmosphere of these years is evident in his correspondence.

His elder brother wrote from Teesdale:

1716. February 7. We have a mighty talk that ye Sueed will make a descent into Scotland. Pray think you there can be anything in that report: methink it doth not look a likely thing.

[1] Appendix A.

June 14. Fears if the King goes to Hanover the wicked party will take much liberty and be plotting to lay some scheme or other. The Duch and Swisers should not go out of the kingdom till the King return again, but rather be quartered among the roguish towns to keep down their mutiny least they take opportunity of doing wors things. . . . Pray use your Intrest to oyle some wheels of Government that they may get the rest to work that we, by what is already done, may not live in too much security. The seas should be well lined with men of war. Brother, I desire you will not let this go in at one ear and out at the other, neither let the poor man's advice be despiseable for certainly all opportunities will be made use of by that crafty Regent [of France] he hath . . . a hearty inclination to be sole monarch and certainly will let slip no opportunity.

P.S. You may think I am a lunatick but I have something for my speaking.

That year Jacobite sympathizers in the 'roguish town' of Newcastle wore 'oak branches' at the end of May. Cotesworth reported 'it is plain it has bin concerted aforehand all over the Nation more or less'. At York they were so insulting that the mayor was forced to use his authority to disperse them and four or five of the 'principals' were secured. Even Sedbergh schoolboys sent reports of armed strangers seen riding about the district.

The worst fears of a second Jacobite attempt were in the spring of 1718.[1] Cotesworth was then in London on business but Colonel George Liddell kept him fully informed:

1718. March 2.

Our Torys in this Neighbourhood are grown very insolent and in Northumberland all the Rebells meet as publicly as ever so that I see nothing but a prospect of a New Rebellion.

March 14. [Sends a report he had received.]

There were 50 or 60 armed horsemen rode thro' Winlayton: I believe the fact is true. There were 30 seen after that as you see by the

---

[1] On 20 March 1718 W. Blakiston Bowes wrote to his mother from London. 'I had partly agreed to sell what we had in the South Sea [Company] at 19¾ but upon your Orders would not stand to it: it is now fallen to 8 and will be shortly at a par and perhaps still lower: certain it is we shall have a War with Spain and Sweden, so it's your fault yᵗ we have lost above £500.' Bowes MSS. 40747, § 164.

enclosed and last week 19 Gentlemen well-mounted and well armed went over the ferry boat at Shields northward in the evening. They met a man a little way out of town; they were very inquisitive after his name, place of abode, occupation, where he had been and so forth. Several people see them but none of them knowne. Since I begun this, I had one from Winlayton on a little business who tells me that last week 6 Gentlemen well mounted and armed and with blue coates and green cockades rid thro' that town in the evening southward. The Toryes and Non-Jurors are very insolent and the Rebells meet and caball frequently and brag of their having been in the Rebellion. I am satisfied we shall have another Brush this summer if the King goes over.

April 5.

It is the opinion of all the judicious well-affected people both in this County and Northumberland that we shall have another rebellion and that very speedily unless some more than ordinary care is taken by the Government.

I formerly gave you an account of two bodys of armed men and horse, one at Winlaton and another about Sheeles and several lesser ones in Northumberland. Since that I am informed there have been several more seen in Northumberland and in Scotland near the Borders in the night time, 30 or 40 in a body. That to prevent its making a noise (in Scotland particularly) they swear all they meet not to divulge that they met any party. This I had from a good hand who tells me that both a man and boy met a party and that they made the man take the oath, but the boy hid himself and afterwards divulged it.

This day I had a letter from a friend in Northumberland who had been the day before at Wooler where he says he met with some honest men and some very great rogues. I will give it in his own words as follows: 'They are busy riding backward and forward and you may depend upon it you will have another Rebellion and worse than the first, if the Government do not take care in time to prevent it by seizing the heads of them. The Generality of the people are of opinion they will begin with a massacre. There is a fellow lives at Wooler called Carbraith or Galbraith whose house is like a Fare with disaffected persons. There will be several Scotch Lords there at a time and met by English Gentlemen. Two came there and drunk only two bottles of wine, gave the Landlord two pistoles for it and would take no Exchange but returned to Scotland again. This Carbraith or Galbraith has proclaimed a horse race upon Easter Tuesday for a cup of 20 shillings where, tho' but a mean plate, a great concourse of both Scotch and English are expected. I shall endeavour to be there to observe what bakes.'—Thus far my friend. . . . My friend is as notable a man and as brave as any in Northumberland and as well affected as any man in Brittain. The rebels swarme in Northumberland and are so uppish that they brag that they were in the Rebellion. I am told that there have been in Newcastle and in Northumberland likewise, several rebels that were transported and also several that have not plead[ed] the King's pardon. These people had appeared publickly and no notice taken by the civil magistrate.

Coll. Kirke's last battalion marcht from Newcastle last Wensday and that very night a parcel of fellows went about the streets singing songs reflecting on the Gov$^t$ and calling out James Stewart. Tom Robinson the surgeon's maid coming out of doors about nine at night, see a parcell of mobbing fellows which she endeavoured to avoid but one of them got her by the arm and ask't her where lived *James Stewart*. There was no person of that name in that neighbourhood so that it is easily understood what they meant.

There are now no souldiers in Newcastle nor I believe only Invalids at Tinmouth, but I hope neither will be long without. I hope the Gov$^t$ will order at least one Regiment of Dragoons into Northumberland to prevent mischief or I am morally sure as soon as our fleet is gone for the Mediterranean, you will see Bloody noses.

As I hear anything new it shall be communicated.

His friend and informant, it transpired, was John Horsley, the famous antiquary and author of the first history of Northumberland.

April 14. There is certainly some villany on foot; we have it from all quarters. I met a man from Bladon he was with Dr. Finney and his curate last night where he could not but observe some things remarkable. He says Dunn and Silvertop's [colliery] waggon horses are so nicely fed and kept that their workmen cannot but notice of it. One Cook, a vile Papist, at Winlaton in his liquor told his landlord that in a little town he would see brave sport, which his landlord thought was a horse race at Derwenthaugh, but the other replied it was otherwise game than that.

W$^m$ Graham, the Pedlar, had been lately in the County of Durham and in three Popish familys was told that in a little time they would see a strange turn of affaires: that they for themselves would have been quiet but others would not let them and that all the clergy would espouse the cause. . . .

James Scott came this day from Alnwick and says the people there and all up and down the country are in a strange consternation, being made believe their throats will be all cut in one night. He says abundance of transported rebels are actually returned and now in Northumberland: That partys of 40 or 50 well armed are often seen together at Bambrough and several other places where they hold Caballs.

That there are three Scots' gentlemen in Durham who have been there for some time under pretence that one of them is not well. One of their servants declared publickly in a mixt company that there would very shortly be another rebellion: that the Highlands had actually begun the work and who could blame them for the Government had banisht most of their Noblemen and now were going to sell their estates.

An honest lawyer who came lately from York says all the Romans of Lancashire and Yorkshire almost of any fashion were then in that City, among them Townly and several others that were in ye Rebellion. That a Tory lady or Roman Catholick in Yorkshire going to see her neighbour that was ill and who she knew was a well-wisher to the cause, she came in with a brisk aire and told her she must not nor should not be sick now when so Glorious times were coming, as would be seen before Mayday.

April 20.

Cosen Horsley tells me the Duke of Gordon was at Causey Park where he stayed two nights altho' he was in post haste. Went from thence to Wooler where he was met at Calbraith's (formerly mentioned) by the Earl of Hume and Ayton his brother and several other gentlemen. He says he will give me what he can from time to time but doubts he can hardly get information of anything upon oath, people being generally speaking in a pannick fear and not only so but those that did in the last Rebellion were so far from being skreen'd that they were left to the Rage of the party which many of them found to fall very heavy upon them.

I am glad to hear you are in so fair a way of getting relief for some of the officers of the militia. . . .[1]

Disaffection was a tribute to the strength of the Catholics and non-Jurors in these parts. 'Oh Will, ye Holymen have

---

[1] The government had not yet paid the officers for their services in 1715.

damnably poyson'd by much ye Greatest part of the Nation', wrote Henry Liddell to his friend in October 1715: 'Would the black coats but shew an example, doubtless ye Populace would be fond of copying after.' The government was not long in recognizing the force of this observation. Two years later Cotesworth forwarded this piece of intelligence. 'This fornoon General Wills has seized Mr. Yap [the non-Juror] and 19 of his male congregation as they were assembled at their meeting in Newcastle—they are all in the Guard House at present and tomorrow they are to be carryed before the Mayor who is a very honest man.'[1] Cotesworth saw to it that there were other 'honest' men as magistrates for he furnished the government with lists of those who should be put on, and those who should be left off, the commission of the peace in the two counties. In 1722, Mr. Flower, supervisor of the excise at North Shields, was discharged 'for turning to be a Quaker': intolerance could go no farther.

One of the most surprising things is how quickly the luxury of Jacobitism evaporated in the north-east after 1718. The subject just drops right out of the correspondence. In 1727 the Lord Lieutenant, magistrates, clergy and freeholders of Durham sent a loyal address to the king condemning the 'unexampled attempt of the Emperor to raise a rebellion among us'.[2] The Forty-Five caused more anxiety to Tynesiders domiciled in London than to people on the spot. King Coal now reigned. Besides, as Liddell had predicted in Fifteen, the populace soon became 'fond of copying after the black coats'. Witness how the news of the Jacobite retreat in 1745–6 was celebrated in Durham. 'The populace behaved on Monday at Durham pretty much the same as yours though not quite so violent', wrote Thomas Liddell to his friend at Gateshead on 31 January 1746, 'they broke

---

[1] Abraham Yapp, formerly precentor at Durham Cathedral and curate at Witton Gilbert. Overton, *The Non-Jurors*, 496. Young Bowes shared Liddell's distrust of the clergy. 'I doubt not but against I come down to prove yt he [Lodge] as well as several other Clergymen in Durham are ye meerest vile wretches alive.'

[2] Bowes MSS. 40747, § 21. 'Nourished in the love of liberty . . . we must ourselves forget, as much as our Enemies have done, the conduct of our Fathers before we can tamely resign what their arms and generous dangers have obtained for their Country.'

ye windows of one of ye Popish Chappells and plundered the house adjoining which belonged to ye Priest. They would not have finished so, but that His Royal Highness [the Duke of Cumberland] had desired the Commanding Officer of the Dutch that he would, at the request of the High Sheriff or any two Justices, assist with such a body of men as they should desire upon any disturbance. This had success in that affair and I hope will put a stop to the like hereabout.' It is known that Mr. Salvin of Croxdale and Meagher, the Durham priest, had got in touch with Bishop Chandler and sought his protection for their co-religionists.[1] In 1747 reports reached Lord Ravensworth, which he duly forwarded to the Secretary of State, of parties of armed stragglers making their way back to Scotland along 'the Papist road'.[2]

## IV

It may well be a matter for surprise that amid the apparent lack of security in the first two decades of the century men should be busily engaged in building stately mansions in these parts which are still admired for their taste and indefinable quality—Eslington, Seaton Delaval, Lumley. 'I have a house that is very near finished that will be the best in our Northern parts', wrote Blakiston Bowes of Streatlam in 1720. It is difficult to describe them, for each had its own peculiar character and lay-out. Streatlam and Gibside and most of the larger houses underwent radical reconstruction at this time. The severe, almost barrack-like appearance of

---

[1] Ellison MSS.

[2] Add. MSS. 32712, § 418. 'This road extends over the Moors from the S.S.West [at Haltwhistle] to the N.N.W. of Northumberland and may be travelled from one end of the County to the other without going through a village, or near a House unless a Herd's cottage.' The report which reached Lord Ravensworth, he assured the Duke of Newcastle, came from a reliable source. 'This town [Haltwhistle] swarms with Travellers both on horseback and on foot and by night as well as day. They are Scotch or Irish, most of them speak French, all of them have plenty of Gold. If any of them go to bed, they rest not above two or three hours. They on horseback are well-mounted and have servants, feed their horses with bread and ale and halt but a short time; and if anybody takes notice of them and asks Questions, they move off in an instant. They on foot carry a knapsack, pretend to have Stockings to sell, but sell none. One thing is remarkable that they who come after enquire after them that went before and at the very houses where they refreshed themselves. These roads were haunted after the same manner before and during the time of the late Rebellion.' (16 August 1747.)

Ravensworth Castle of Buck's print of 1728 was probably already out of date by that time and in any case was substantially modified by the alterations of the early thirties undertaken before the young heir, later the first Baron, came into residence on his marriage.[1] Seaton Delaval and Lumley were 'modernized' a little earlier by Vanbrugh. Park House, Gateshead, was 'gutted' by Ramsay in 1714–15 and extensively altered first after Cotesworth went to live there in 1716 and again fourteen years later when Henry Ellison married one of his heiresses. Cotesworth happened to be away in London on business in the spring of 1718 when the first alterations were put in hand and his good friend, the colonel, volunteered to supervise the work:

March 4.

Ventured to the Parke yesterday morning tho' the wind was so high it had almost blown off my head. See the worst plastering my eyes ever beheld and, what is worse, I doubt there can be no cure for it. I ordered Grey to be discharged and W^m Teward to go on with that work. I would advise you to latt and plaster to your boards first which will keep all dry and warm and the joints of the boards close and not only so but will take off a great deal of noise and the charge will not be above 15^s/- a room. I have ordered them to do one after this manner but to do no further without your directions.

The timber in the Rooms over the one which was the kitchen is extremely mean so that I have ordered them to put one new baulk there to support the partition which is to be betwixt Madam's room and the other. They tell me you have given orders for a sash window to be put in the North Gavell end over the brew house. We have, one and all, agreed to suspend it till further orders. The wall is very mean, being much shaken and has a great weight upon it so that it will be very hazardous. That room will not want light so that without you have any perticular reason for it, think it advisable to run no risque. Besides, if you build a kitchen where the brew house now is, as probably you will, then that window will be stopt up. I design to step over now and then tho' perhaps you will not thank me for it, but I will do my best.

---

[1] Colonel Liddell wrote from Ravensworth in April 1724, 'My papers are in confusion by pulling down the greatest part of our house'. There is an old print at Eslington of Ravensworth (by Bailey, 1782), which has no turrets.

March 18.

. . . Thence I went indoors and found W^m Tewart plastering the servants' hall which he does as well as can be expected with such lime, but he will have better for the best rooms. He has not latted to the Boards over the Hall having had no orders, tho' had I seen him 'ere he began, he should have done it for Madam's sake both for warmth and to allay the noise that such sort of cattle generally make and besides it preserves the boards. I have ordered him to do so in all the best rooms.

Had not Brown been still your Inspector,[1] I would have whipt over with my Gardner and pruned all your trees and have slasht them rarely, tho' I know you would have been provoked at me for the present, but I am sure you would have thank't me two years hence, tho' I think I can cure your wall trees when you come down.

W^m Tewart is, as well as all your friends, highly provoked at your dining room chimney, but it is too late now and therefore I only do this to teaze you.

When he was in London again in 1722–3 Cotesworth ordered the bed and hangings in the yellow room [his own] to be taken down and cleaned. 'Be sure that Jno. Hansal make all the walls right when the hangings are down in the two rooms', he continued, 'and take care that the canvas for putting up behind the hangings be bought at the best hand, which is Carlisle peices sold on the Sandhill.' 'The tops of all the three rooms must be double whiten'd with strong size wch they will make in the servants' hall that you may see the specks put in. You must bespeak boy Jack to paint what will be needful when the chimney piece in the blue room and the wainscot and chimney piece in the Blue parlour is done. I would have the pales in the Court and the gates and what-ever has been painted before painted again. . . . Consult Brown [the gardener] whether it will not be proper to buy oil and white lead here and send down and let Jack do it all by the day. . . . It will be May before things without doors can be painted, but the sooner in that month, if fair weather, the better.' 'Let the staircase out of the stone hall into my office be plain and lett the lawndry floor and the chamber floor be laid close. I wish the buffet in the new Parlour could

---

[1] Allan Brown, the gardener at Park House until 1725.

be enlarged and a new one be made in the blew parlour', he wrote later. More instructions followed: 'It was a great oversight that there was not an alcove made in the blew parlour; it might have been easily done in the north or south corner toward the mount: . . . wishes it could be done still even if some of the panelling has to be undone. Wishes to enlarge the alcove in the new parlour for they are a great ease and convenience. I have not heard whether you sash the two south windows in the blew parlour; in all cases have a care of the wall for they are rotten stuff daubed, full of only mud and not lime.' 'The doors of the alcove to do up and down like sashes will be more commodious than folding doors to open to the walls', though he had no objection to the latter 'if there be but room for them'.

A complete inventory was made of the furnishings of each room at Park House at the time of Hannah Cotesworth's marriage to Henry Ellison in 1729. The individual rooms, both upstairs and down, were usually named after the predominant colour of the wall furnishings. Thus there was the 'blew parlour' (the only room with a carpet), the 'red room' hung with 'red china', the yellow room, brown 'do', and so on. There was considerable variation in the character of the hangings; the best bedroom was hung with yellow mohair; it had a yellow mohair bed lined with thread satin, with a yellow quilt and window cushions to match; the 'withdrawing room' was hung with gilt leather, the 'brown room' with 'printed stuff', the staircase with 'Dutch pictures on lyn' and the best garrets with 'painted paper' and 'yallow china'. As in the sixteenth century, great store was set on the best bed, yellow ones were most in fashion—the one at Alderman Rudston's sale in 1733 was expected to fetch £50. In the best bedrooms mohair, in the others, cane or 'bass' chairs were usual. The dining-room chairs were of walnut; 'easies' covered with bright 'callimancoe' were replacing the 'worsted damask' or 'stuff upholdstery' which the young ladies themselves had embroidered earlier in the century. Of other new furnishings, usually obtained from London, mention might be made of 'jappaned' tea-tables and corner cupboards, round or oval mahogany dining tables, sets of blue and white china, bought at the East India Company's sales, coloured coffee-trays, a weather-glass, and a grandfather clock, though the latter was made locally. The best table linen, sheets, and huckaback were obtained from Darlington. The pictures and maps, except the family portraits which were in the 'blew parlour', together with a few 'thrumb' chairs, were in the hall.

In the subsequent reconstruction at Park House, certain things stand out—the calling in of a well-qualified London architect, Gibbs;[1] the use of brick, made locally, in place of stone—stone was sometimes 'simented' to imitate brick—and of pantiles in place of slate; the ease and convenience of alcoves in the parlours, the importance of having well-seasoned wood for the new sash-windows and panels; the use of fine-quality glass, obtained in London, for the windows in the best rooms, that made locally was good enough for the kitchen, and the great care taken in laying out the gardens, the lawn, the flower-beds, and kitchen gardens. There was clearly a tradition in the north in such matters long before the days of 'Capability Brown', and, as we have seen, one Allan Brown was the gardener at Park House in Cotesworth's day.

Like his uncle Colonel Liddell, Henry Ellison and his brother-in-law, Carr, were keen gardeners, especially fruit-growers. The yearly seed bills supplied by leading London nurserymen, Henry Woodman of Strand on the Green, Middlesex, and Stephen Switzer of Westminster, have survived and very instructive they are.[2] It is probably no mere coincidence that a famous dessert apple, Ellison pippin, bears his name. Apricots, peaches, and nectarines were

[1] James Gibbs, architect of the Radcliffe Library, Oxford, and of the great court at King's College, Cambridge. *D.N.B.* 'If I can get a clever architect I will try what he and I can make of it', wrote Colonel Liddell in 1730. In due course he received Gibbs's 'plans for your alterations . . . thinks his design is good . . . and it cannot be any great addition to your expense; it will be a great convenience as well as ornament'. Liddell counselled his nephew against being too hasty in 'making your sashes', otherwise they would sweat and stain. 'This we found both at Eslington and Ravensworth.' [2] See Ch. IX.

successfully grown on south walls though, by 1720, increased use was made of glass-houses and cloches. Colonel Liddell certainly knew what he was about:

1718. March 18.

Called at the Park where the method they proceed in does not please. . . . They are laying turfe that was cut last winter and is as yellow as saffron and I don't think will grow for 'tis in my opinion rotten. Brown was not there, nor anybody but strangers and so I could have no satisfaction. Your trees are neither pruned nor planted in my opinion for bearing fruit. But you may help the wall trees another year, as I should have done the standards this, had they been mine, by cutting off the tops of them, but you are too merciful a man to cut and slash those hopefull vigorous plants.

Incidentally, parents did not altogether approve of too much fresh fruit for children and in 1734 Mrs. Anne Liddell confessed that 'jesting apart, I am no friend to roots and puddings'.[1]

What we have in the north at this time is rather like a Caucasian spring, a sudden blossoming of civilization with the melting away of political and social disorder under the warming influence of economic prosperity. Park House and old Ravensworth have long since disappeared, but Eslington, Lumley, Seaton, and Gibside have survived as memorials of its taste and quality. Moreover, the high degree of comfort in the newly rebuilt houses was doubtless enhanced by survivals from a cruder age. At Croft, the living-rooms were fouled by dogs and many of Sir William Chaytor's important papers were kept 'in the stove'; at Park House the beds in the old servants' quarters wcre bug-infested.[2] Or there is this picture of conditions in the kitchen there in 1723 when Cotesworth ordered the dog-wheel of the spit to be moved 'on purpose to keep the dog from the fire, the wheel out of the way and the dog prevented [from] shitting upon any-

---

[1] 'The same Crato will allow no roots at all to be eaten.' Burton, *The Anatomy of Melancholy*, quoted in Drummond and Wilbraham, *The Englishman's Food*, 149–50. 'Fruit was still regarded with suspicion as a result of the survival of the medieval belief that it caused fevers.'

[2] In 1731 Francis Salkeld was paid 10s. 6d. for curing the settee bed of bugs. 'Your mother is uneasy in her [London] lodgings which swarm with Bugs', wrote Liddell.

thing it could. The dog must shit in the pot and the stoves must not be in a place where people have a constant occasion to be moveing about.' That dogs were still used as turn-spits, working a 'dog-wheel', is evident from a letter of John Aynsley, a Hexham attorney, four years later: 'My spouse desires Mary Hipson, [the cook at Park House] to remember to train her up a young dog turn-spit and she'll send for him.' And what shall we say of the social conscience which did not hesitate to send the carcase of a 'measled pig', originally intended for use by the family, to the public butcher?

Park House had a reputation for good eating, thanks to the housekeeper Peggy Gates and Mary Hipson. 'Why do you set people so agog with your raritys', chaffed the colonel, 'I wish I may be able to keep my young woman [his niece] to beef and mutton after it.' Some years later he adverted to a haunch of pork he had tasted at a dinner party at Park House. Edward Wortley, M.P., one of the guests, remarked 'it was the best meat he ever eat'; 'I think it was boiled', added Liddell and he begged the 'receipt, or I shall have no peace'. This was indeed high praise. Mrs. Gates also had a reputation for potted charrs, goose-pie, potted woodcock and grouse, and bottled mushrooms, and she made 'stoughton', a form of marmalade.[1] Her wages in 1733 were £8 per annum; the nurse got £5, the cook £4, and the best chambermaids from £3 to £3. 10s. 0d. I wonder what they had to say of Sir Harry Liddell's French chef whom he engaged in 1736 at a hundred guineas a year.[2]

In the eighteenth century domestic service was a major national industry but how to come by good servants was already a problem, especially in London. Cotesworth got some of his from his native Teesdale. 'Honest servants are so difficult to be met with in this town', wrote Fazackerley, the eminent lawyer, in a letter to Cotesworth in 1726 asking

---

[1] 'Your mistress desires you will tell Peggy Gates to preserve six oranges and make some Stoughton. She has forgot the quantity she made last year but would have double that quantity this', wrote Ellison in 1731. Boswell later praised 'that admirable viand, marmalade'. *London Journal*, 230.     [2] *H.M.C. Carlisle MSS.* 159.

for a reference concerning Isabella Pickering, formerly in his employ. Cotesworth replied that she had been a chamber-maid at Park House for two years. 'She was a very honest and orderly servant till an ungovernable underclerk made her believe he would marry her, made her grow giddy. I turn'd him away and that made her give warning. Her parents live near Teaseworth on the Yorkshire side and, I believe, are very honest people. If she be clear of the young fellow, I hope she will make you a very honest servant.' It is significant of the mobility of labour at the time that within a few months of leaving Gateshead this young woman was looking for a job in London. The 'new' housemaid at Terrie's, Boswell's landlord, came from Cumberland. Ordinarily, servants going to town travelled by sea with the luggage as neither could be readily accommodated in the coach. Continuing his letter to Fazackerley, Cotesworth observed that he had earlier contemplated a bill for the regulation of servants.

I am glad to find so great a man think the business of well-regulated servants so much for the concern of all families. . . . I was wrote to by a member [of parliament] three sessions ago for some heads for the better government of servants which would tend so much to their own benefit. I drew up what I think would be of use but the Bill did not proceed, but it seems now time for the Legislature to lend their aid. I have about 16 people of my committing in Durham and Northumberland jayles, most for capital crimes, all committed for want of a due Regulation of inferior people.

This sensible Whig J.P. did not hesitate to call for state regulation of labour as an alternative to filling the gaols and emptying them by bounties and contracts on transportation. Moreover, it is worth noting that the laws of the famous Crowley ironworks, while envisaging an abundant supply of free labour, yet felt the need of a system of regulation.[1]

---

[1] Add. MSS. 34555, Law No. 17. 'Workmen's Entrance'. Newcomers were to be interviewed by the work's surveyor who would 'recommend them to the fittest place to work, live or board in, and caution them to fix so at the first that there may not be occasion of removing'.

## V

Of the general soundness and purity of family life at this time there can be no doubt. Amid all their tribulations, Sir William and Lady Chaytor remained each other's 'dearest heart'; their letters invariably closed with a fervent prayer to 'send us a happy meeting'. 'Though you write more like a lover than a husband', wrote Lady Chaytor to the prisoner in the Fleet, 'yet I must believe you reall, having had your affection for above these twenty years and not in the least lessen'd by the charms of those who endever to captivate your sex; and though I have been in contrary circumstances these many years, you may be confedent of the like return from me which nothing but death can dissolve.' Indeed she was generous enough to hope that the children would take after their father, 'for I am sensible of my faults; but if he that you call the British lyon [? Clarvaux] have some of the Welshe blood in him, you must blame yourself for grafting on soe bad a stock'.[1] Thirty years later, Sir Henry Liddell confessed to being 'head over heels' in love with Miss Delmé, though convention dictated that he should not be with her alone until the lawyers had 'squeezed the wax' on the marriage settlement. Neither party was ever in doubt as to what constituted the groundwork of their forty odd years of happiness. Hence their profound dismay when the only child of the marriage, the Duchess of Grafton, eloped with the Earl of Upper Ossory. It was the same with Henry Ellison and Hannah Cotesworth. Before their marriage, Mr. Megault, a fashionable London jeweller, was commissioned to make four rings—a diamond hoop, the pattron, another 'with two hearts joined together which he says is very proper on this occasion', and 'the ring which will make you happy'. Ellison's sister who placed the order had a very simple prescription for married happiness—'where there is sens and good nature gos together', and she was satisfied that 'Miss Hannah

---

[1] Lady Chaytor was the daughter of Sir Joseph Craddock, attorney-general to Bishop Cosin, and M.P. for Richmond 1678–85. *Miscellanea* (Surtees Soc. xxxvii), 189. For the Craddock pedigree, see Surtees, *History of Durham*, iv. 13.

Cotesworth has a very great share of both'. And so it proved. A dozen years later Mrs. Ellison closed her letters to her husband, 'I am, my Dearest, yours entirely', and to one she added this postscript, 'I hope my dearest Jewel will remember the charge I gave him to take care of himself'. Later in the century Margaret Shafto wrote to her kinsman, William Eden, the statesman, apropos of her niece's engagement: 'I wish her to think from her heart and if she likes him not to attend to the nonsense of pedigree. Happiness is the only pursuit—the older one grows, the plainer this appears.'[1]

For courtship there was normally little opportunity in the higher social circles where so much depended on negotiating the legal settlement. Nan Chaytor had a flutter with 'her beau', Mr. Mauleverer. 'They are ancient squires', she told her father, 'he is very sober and a good scholar, loves poetry and lent me the Dispensery, an extraordinary poem done by Dr. Garth, and Dryden's Fables.' On one occasion she reported that he was 'upon much nicer airs than ordenery, he had not forgot his scarlet stockins and a tie wig which was powder'd to a nicety and he gave me a complement in verse'. The young lady was not unaffected. 'If my dear father would buy me a little book called *Reflections on Marriage* it would be very acceptable . . . it's only stitched together like a play.' Disappointment, however, and the want of fortune soured her. 'I care not how little I have to do with men either in giving them hopes or provoking their malice and so much do I think all country gentlemen slaves, I always declare against them.' Nor was she above giving her father advice on the subject of re-marriage: 'I bid my dear father will be

---

[1] *Add. MSS.* 34413, § 142, quoted in *History*, 1940, 125. Cf. W. Blakiston Bowes's negotiations for a marriage settlement in 1720 when he demanded £30,000 'on the nail' and a further £5,000 on the death of his prospective father-in-law. 'You are much in the Right', he confessed to Dr. Jurin, the intermediary, 'when you think I was not in love for my character is "Je m'attache à la sexe en generale mais jamais en particulière"; neither had I been of another temperament, had she Beauty to effect so wonderful a change as it would have been had I fallen in love. All my aim was convenience. . . . In the meantime as Philosophers of old were wont to make diligent search after the stone, so do I after the best in Christendome.' Bowes MSS. 40747, § 186.

very careful and cautious about the widdows, there is so much cheat amongst them, for nothing could be more posseatively reported than that Mrs. Godophin had £30,000 and I believe she had not five; but if you could get a great fortune it would do well and it would be best to keep it a secret after you did marry.' Sir William's own reflections on the subject are contained in a brief note he penned in the Fleet: "Twere a happiness to those that wo'd marry in their latter years to meet with a woman whose disposition is religiously good or serious inclination to be good.' And for once the pupil was as good as his tutor. Nothing could exceed the sense of shame in Miss Carr's family when she became Sir James Lowther's mistress.

Transcending the affection of husband and wife was their mutual solicitude for the 'barns' or 'the infantry' as the loveable bachelor Colonel Liddell was pleased to call them. Large families were the order of the day: the lady was often 'in the straw, as the old saying is'. Lady Cooke had ten children in twelve years, 'to all of whom, except one, she had been a nurse'. But the risks of childbed were formidable and the infant mortality rate was staggering. Seven of Lady Chaytor's eleven children died young. For one of her later confinements she took the double precaution of making her will and going to London where she was offered 'Sir Richard Temple's apartment in the house of Mrs. Brown' at 20s. a week. 'Poor Mr. Clavering is to be compassion'd', wrote Sir Henry Liddell in 1714, 'a miserable case, God knows, his whole stock of children swept away in five months and his wife like to follow speedily.'[1] Cotesworth's wife died young and his four surviving children were brought up by their aunt. In 1722 he secretly married Hannah Watson, his housekeeper, and had a daughter by her who later became governess to the elder children of George III and was said to have grown very like her father.[2] That there was little

---

[1] James Clavering of Greencroft.
[2] She had an apartment in the Queen's House (i.e. Buckingham Palace), a salary of £300, 'and a very good table kept for her the year round'. Her kinswoman, Mrs. Airey, widow of a Newcastle lawyer, frequently visited her at the palace. 'I had not the honor of seeing H. R.

prudery or mock modesty in family matters is evident from
a delightful letter written by a ten-year-old schoolgirl to her
father.

Chelsea.<br>September 9. 1742.

Dear Papa,

I am very glad to find by yours that I shall so soon have a new
brother or sister. I wish it was well over with my dear Mama and that
I may soon hear she is well recovered. We broke up yesterday and my
Grandmama was so good as to send for me.

Your dutiful daughter<br>Hannah Ellison.

When the writer of this letter was a baby, her mother sent
'an anodyne necklace' from London 'which is very much
used for making ym get their teeth easily; however, as it
cannot do any harm, your Mistress would have her wear it
constantly. It should hang loose about the neck.' Further
instructions followed for nurse—she was to lose no opportunity of carrying the child into the air in good weather—this
towards the end of February—and to see that its stays were
big enough. 'The child may be carried to Mrs. Stevenson
provided Peggy Gates [the trusted housekeeper] goes with
her and that she goes nowhere else, but she must not let her
eat anything there but what she eats at home.' Solicitude for
the children's well-being reached its apogee in the concern
for their education but this subject and that of diversions are
treated separately.

'Harry Potts has gott a son of wch hee's very fond', wrote

Highness', she wrote in 1763, 'as that is not allowed, I believe, to people who are of my Rank,
as the admitting numbers could not be done at the Queen's House, or indeed any company as
there is no convenience for it.' In the following January, on the occasion of Princess Augusta's
marriage, Mrs. Airey wrote: 'I intend to go to Mrs. Cotesworth's apartment tomorrow to
try to get a peep at their Highnesses [at the Ball].' In 1771 she reported that 'M^{rs} Cotesworth
is much affected with the Prince of Wales and Prince Frederick being taken from the Nursery,
though expected and necessary'. Dr. Markham (their preceptor) paid her this tribute—'he
was surprised to find them so well instructed, for that he had not found the *least* cause for
Reprehension in either of the Princes'. 'She certainly has great merit', added Mrs. Airey, 'as
I believe no person could be more assiduously careful or more capable of instructing them, in
every respect, thus far in their lives'.

Sisson, the steward, to his master Cotesworth in London, 'he got it in his armes the morning it was born, wch was yesterday and said "Honny, thou's my Darlin and shalt want for nothing as long as I am able to warke for thee".' Most fathers worth their salt have experienced something of this feeling but only a Geordie would put it like that. Joseph Cowen would have said that the speech of these people was 'racy of the soil'. It was extraordinarily rich in old words and phrases and in local peculiarities.[1] For instance, they used the indefinite article freely, e.g. 'he had *a* one', and the second person singular. Many words which were then in common use have since largely disappeared: 'throng' (busy), 'making rook of' (spoiling), 'hatter' (pester), 'paroll' (give my word for), 'stirridge' (things stirring), 'cant' (to check or put a value on), 'gregged' (done in), 'pin the basket' (put the lid on), 'stand buff to' (ignore). The spelling even of well-educated people was highly variable as these pages amply show, e.g. 'friend' was commonly spelt 'freind'. And for all the culture in polite circles there was an occasional streak of coarseness which would shock modern sensibility. Negotiations were said 'to hang an a—e'. Dr. Baker sent spicy medical doggerel to his friends, and T. Stockdale's letter congratulating Henry Ellison on his marriage is unprintable.

Poor Lord W^m [Poulett] sent to inquire when I had heard from his friend W^m, if dead or alive [wrote 'the Governor' in 1713] he heard not from you above a fortnight since. Besides, says my Lord, does he write you ever a smotty story? 'Yes', I reply'd. 'Oh then, he will doe well', says my Lord. 'But why does he never write me such?' I made answer that I apprehended you were in mighty favor with my Lady [Poulett] att present and had no mind to be outed by a fatt story. 'Oh' says he 'she likes itt as well as I.'

The worthy Mr. Carr in the course of house-hunting in their early married life wrote that his wife said 'she wanted a canny hole of her own to f—t in, to use a northern

[1] Archdeacon Morton wrote, 'I was not woorth the ground I went on, as wee speake in this countrie commonly'. *The Household Books of Lord William Howard*, 427, 454–6.

expression'. But of coarse and vulgar blasphemy I have found no trace. When Henry Hadley, a London musician, returned from a tour of the north in 1729, he commented on 'Old M^r Ellison's [of Hebburn] simplicity of manners', and added significantly, 'we see no such thing in these parts'.

WILLIAM COTESWORTH

## CHAPTER II

# Tyneside Merchants
## 1680–1726

> You know how natural it is to pursue privatt interest
> even against that Darling principle of a more general
> good. . . . It is the interest of the Public to be served
> by the man that can do it cheapest, though several
> private persons are injured by it.
>
> (*William Cotesworth*, 1717)

GATESHEAD or Gateside as it was more usually styled in the early years of the eighteenth century was a curious anomaly.[1] It was called a borough and its inhabitants burgesses though it had no recent charter or parliamentary representation.[2] It had gilds or fraternities, notably the composite one of mercers, tailors, hardwaremen, coopers, and tallow-chandlers, and, most important, it was completely outside the corporate jurisdiction of its powerful neighbour across the Tyne.[3] But, in fact, it was a manor belonging to the bishops of Durham, and although after the death of Robert Delaval, who was appointed bailiff in 1681, the bishop ceased to appoint a bailiff or head officer to hold the court leet and to receive the fines and profits of jurisdiction, it continued to be dominated by the bishop's lessee, the lord of the manor, who enjoyed the profits of jurisdiction, the bishop merely reserving to himself the patronage rights in the two churches.[4] It was governed by the parish vestry, the 'Twenty-Four', who levied 'sesses', and each year appointed

---

[1] Hutchinson, *History of Durham*, ii. 453. In 1685 Thomas Corbridge, the first collector of excise, entered it in his book as Goatshead. His receipts 'for rounds ended 24th June' totalled £399: Keyside, Pilgrim St., and Sandgate, Newcastle contributed £641, £532, £423 respectively. Durham Palatinate Records (P.R.O.), 196/30.

[2] Cotesworth was styled 'mayor' in 1716: he was a vestryman in 1700, auditor 1705–6 and again in 1719.

[3] *Northern Notes & Queries*, i. 15–67. Bishop Cosin's charter to them in 1661.

[4] Mackenzie and Ross, *View of the County Palatine*, i. 82–83. The Vestry Minute Books from 1626 have survived. The parish register of births, marriages, and burials from 1558, in perfect condition, has never been edited. Hutchinson, op. cit. 468, gives some population figures.

four constables and the like number of 'overseers of the highways, and of the poor', 'Grassmen', and 'Wainemen'. Such was its constitutional position throughout the eighteenth century.

Local government in the town was most vigorous and efficient in the half-century after 1676 when the Vestry was reconstituted. A public water-supply was provided and fines were imposed on vestrymen who absented themselves from public meetings. Every year a number of inhabitants found themselves presented by the borough jury and fined for a variety of nuisances or 'impeachments'.[1] Thus, in 1702, Thomas Fagon and David Brunsk were each fined 1*s*. for 'a middin'—a common offence—and several others a like amount for 'dunghills on Jackson's chaire'. In 1705 Philip Trumble and John Pattison were each fined 6*d*. for 'laying a stack of cinders [coke] in the street',[2] and every year there were a goodly number of people fined small sums ranging from 6*d*. to 1*s*. for 'sweeping dirt into the Common Vennall' or 'under the Shop stalls' and 'not carrying it away'. Mrs. Maddison was fined as much as half a crown 'for suffering her servants to team filthy water out at the back side of her hous to the damedg of her neighbour John Ratchester'. 'Frunts out of repair' were another common offence, though the fine was usually remitted if the same were subsequently reported 'repaired' or 'repairing'. In 1702 William Weightman and Anorah Hackworth were fined 2*s*. for two swine 'being unringed', William Cotesworth 1*s*. 'for a sow and five pigs', and Mark Stephenson the like sum 'for an unlawful swine'. And there were recurring items such as 'Mercell Postgait fined 1ˢ/6ᵈ for resque [rescue] of her horse when they were bringing him to the pinfold'; Henry Gray 1*s*. 'for his wife resquing their cow when they were bringing her to the pinfold'. The tallow-chandler, William Cotesworth and his partner, Robert Sutton, were frequently

---

[1] Cotesworth MSS. Some of the lists of presentments are fragmentary. One of uncertain date lists half a dozen people as liable 'for keeping a gun', including Parson Fallowfield, it being 'too martial an exercise for a Clergyman', and 'most of the millers on the Hill for keeping guns and greyhounds'.     [2] *Infra*.

indicted; in 1702 they were fined 3*s*. 4*d*. 'for setting their casks in the street to stop the passedg'; in the following year 10*s*. 'for their tallow house', and again in 1705 'for casks in Hilgate and the forestreet standing out to the disturbance of the neighbourhood—6*s*. 8*d*.; and on another occasion, the same amount 'for their workhouse in the forestreet, an annoyance to the neighbourhood'—an early instance of town regulation of noisome trades. There were regular fines of half a crown or 3*s*. 4*d*. 'for building houses on the Fell and not paying their acknowledgement' for the same, also 'for cutting sods on the common' or encroachments on it, while Ralph Farbridge was fined as much as 13*s*. 4*d*. for 'cutting Duffets[1] on the Fell'. Larger fines were imposed for more serious nuisances: in 1702, Mr. Will Ridel, the reputed owner of six pits on the Stony Flat 'lying open, very dangerous both for man and beasts', was fined 15*s*.[2] Nor did Lady Gerard, relict of the Grand Lessee, escape; she was fined a like sum for three open pits 'beside the Windmill' and other three in Barn Close field, while Ralph Farbridge was fined as much as £1. 19*s*. 0*d*. 'for two dangerous pits on the Fell'. Altogether these 'presentments' are chiefly important as revealing a strong sense of responsibility to the local community, or 'the neighbourhood' as it was called, and they are the more significant at a time when manorial economy was being overlaid by problems created by industry. Of the twelve jurymen some three or four could not write their own names but their authority was apparently never questioned.

Half a century later the same procedure still obtained but there is evidence of an increasing breakdown in administration. Whereas, at first, the great bulk of the 'Twenty-Four' regularly attended the vestry meetings, the average for the period 1714–24 was about nine. In 1745 only three, including Henry Ellison, the lord of the manor, who signed first, attended. By that time, apparently, only one meeting a year

---

[1] Duffarts = small, dull-burning coal. Wright, *English Dialect Dictionary*, *s.n.*

[2] In August 1677 the 'Twenty-Four' levied a special sess 'for and towards carrying on a Suite against William Riddell Esq'. Minute Book, § 486.

was held to authorize the levy of the rates for the ensuing year and increasing difficulty was being experienced in their collection.[1] In 1757 William Hilton, the foreman of the borough jury, took the precaution of forwarding the present-ments to Henry Ellison, 'as those which were given to the Clerk of the Court have hitherto been disregarded'. 'I find a difficulty in getting a sufficient number of Jurymen together upon any occasion', he continued, 'and should, therefore, be glad to receive instructions how to act in that circumstance and in whatsover relates to my office as Foreman.' None the less a majority of the jury, upon complaint of one Anthony Chambers, proceeded to view several heaps of rubbish laid upon the waste or lane called Wormwood Hill, alias Bailey Chare, and reported 'we do find the same to be a very great nuisance incommoding the Rights of the Lords and Ladies of this Manor and their tenants and the Neighbourhood in general', and they proceeded to indict the Rev. Charles Ward and four other persons for causing the same. In 1760 Dr. Wade was indicted and fined 6d. 'in satisfaction of a trespass for erecting a Stage in Gateshead Street', and there were two fines for 'deodands', Anthony Wilson was fined 6d. 'in satisfaction of his horse killing a boy', and Ralph Branding, whose coachman had been killed by a horse, 3s. In 1772, and again in 1791, the borough petitioned the bishop to appoint a bailiff, the beginning of a demand for incorporation, but Henry Ellison had little difficulty in persuading him of the true manorial character of the town.[2]

Alderman William Ramsay, the elder, father of the first

---

[1] Vestry Book (St. Mary's Gateshead) (1681–1807). The rates took the form of an assessment of so many weeks' sess, e.g. thirty weeks 1718–24, thirty-six in 1725. In 1745 a five months' sess was authorized. There had not been a reassessment of property since 1682. In 1742 the Vestry resolved that they would support and defend the churchwardens 'against all persons who shall commence or bring any action against them for or by reason of their levying any distress for non-payment of their assessments'.

[2] In 1772 Bishop Egerton referred the petition to his attorney-general and no more was heard of it. 'Certain persons in Gateshead have long wished to be erected into a Corporation which they say they formerly were, and are of opinion that if the Bishop of Durham should constitute, at their request, a bailiff, their long extinct corporation would revive.' (Henry Ellison to Bishop Barrington, 29 October 1791.)

lord of the manor with whom we are concerned was a leading Newcastle goldsmith. He has been called 'the best known worker of that period', 1656–98, and many beautiful examples of his art have survived.[1] From such of his business accounts as have survived we can form some idea of his other activities. In the sixteen-seventies we find him carrying on a credit and mortgage business, often for small amounts, besides supplying plate to local families. After 1680 he dealt increasingly in bills of exchange on London in conjunction with Edward Ridley, accommodating in this way Thomas, Bishop of Carlisle, and a military gentleman named Strother.[2] It was possibly this connexion with northern garrisons which accounts for a curious item in the accounts for June 1689, when over 500 muskets, some with walnut stocks, 'strapped', 240 'Dutch-made' pikes, besides 'halberts, drums, cartouch boxes', 6½ barrels of fine 'cornpowder', 6¼ cwt. of musket-shot, and 6 cwt. of match were consigned to him 'for the service of Colonel Beaumond's regiment at Carlisle'. By that time, he could possibly have supplied plenty of shot himself for since 1687 he had been the leading partner and virtually sole proprietor of lead-mines at Haydon-field and Setlington Groves, leased from the Earl of Somerset. Two former partners, John Blakiston and George Morton, formally assigned the management of the concern to him in 1690, while two others, Mr. Bacon and Mr. Ridley, appear to have been sleeping partners. Work began in earnest under the management of John Thompson in November 1687: two old shafts which had fallen in were repaired, a dam was built across the Terret burn, and in

---

[1] Jackson, *English Goldsmiths and their Marks*, 341. *Arch. Ael.* xxi. 1–34. The earliest-known example is a flagon from Sawley, near Ripon, dated 1670. This and three cups and patens were in the 1897 exhibition of silverware made in Newcastle. Boyle, *The Goldsmiths of Newcastle. Arch. Ael.* (N.S.), xvi. 397. As late as 1717 the Newcastle goldsmiths ante-dated their quarter-day in order to accommodate customers at the Cowhill Fair. Richardson, *Rare Tracts*, iii. 87. Brand, *History of Newcastle*, ii. 352. The plumbers separated from them in 1717.

[2] In a letter to Ramsay, dated 27 June 1684, Ridley noted the apprehensions of the Newcastle magistrates 'of the King taking away your charter', adding, 'their civility to Mr L'Estrange would have saved them the trouble'.

course of time new shafts and 'stoups' were driven. 'You shall not nead to feare', wrote Thompson at the end of December, 'but we will get all things well a neugh ordered for your advantag, but would have you come and see us as shortly as you can and if aney of your partners thinke the charge great, let them goe of[f]. I do not feare to make hir doe well aneugh, so restes your servant.'[1]

For the next four years he lived up to his promise. By June 1688, nearly sixty workmen were engaged at day-wages but Thompson soon became convinced 'that it will tend to beter advantage' if the ore-getters and sinkers were put on piece-rates, the former at 15s. or 16s. a bing, and the latter at 11s. a fathom, which was accordingly done.[2] Thereafter, Jeremy Roberts, Wm. Ree (Rey), Andrew Little, and half a dozen other working partnerships drew varying amounts each quarter, sometimes as much as £40 per gang, less sums paid for candles. At the same time nearly a score of ordinary labourers continued to be engaged at day-wages, repairing the dam, pulling and leading 'threaves' of ling, or carting coal, timber, and other materials from Hexham, at rates varying from 8d. a day to 1s. or more, according to whether they supplied a horse and cart or not. Eighteenpence a shift was paid for drawing water with teams of horses. The man who 'kept the gin' got half a crown a week and manager Thompson a 'covenanted salary' of £25 per annum. One interesting feature of the work was the employment of women as washers. Thompson had complained in July 1688 that men would not wash the ore under 6s. a bing. Thereafter, half a dozen women, some the wives or daughters of the miners, were paid day-wages rising, according to age, from 4d. to 10d.; but soon, they, too, were put on piece-rates at 3s. 6d. per bing, though Anne Roberts was paid double that rate for washing 'waiste' ore. The local terms used for fractions of a bing—'poakes', 'horses and foales'—led to some confusion and Thompson asked for instructions how to

---

[1] Cotesworth MSS.
[2] In 1690 the rates for 'getting' were increased to 18 or 20 shillings.

enter them in the accounts. By December 1690 some of the workings were so deep that wooden pipes were built to convey air to the miners.

Unfortunately, it is not possible to give comparative figures of output, partly because the mining partnerships themselves changed in personnel, but also because the quarterly payments were not only irregular in point of time but overlapped from year to year. Some indication, however, may be gained from the following: the gross salary bill rose from £17. 19s. 0d. for the period November 1687 to the following January, to £197. 18s. 11d. from November 1688 to April 1689, and £213. 18s. 4d. from December 1689 to 1 May 1690. At the same time Jeremy Roberts's output went up from 33 bing in 1689 to 73 in 1691 and Andrew Little's from 56 to 102. Unhappily, the accounts end in the latter year and we do not know what happened subsequently. A shrinkage in the number of working partnerships in 1691 perhaps indicates that the veins were failing.[1] We know that two years later Ramsay leased a third part of Sir William Blackett's mines, on a front of 600 yards by 40, in Bollihopeburn and Rookhope near Stanhope in Weardale, and that the Ramsays continued to export lead for another twenty years. In Queen Anne's reign the price got up to nearly £9 a fother. Consignments were stamped with special marks like silver or gold. It is perhaps not altogether fanciful to suppose that the brand most in demand in Amsterdam and Hamburg, marked WB,[2] was in fact the product of this family of Newcastle goldsmiths and that the despised metal had laid the foundation of the fortunes of a Tyneside merchant, and not for the last time.

Even before he speculated in lead-mining, the elder Ramsay had entered another field. As early as 1675 he

---

[1] The London Lead Company for smelting lead with pit coal was founded by royal charter in 1692. *V.C.H. Durham*, ii. 352. In 1717 Lady Mary Radcliffe stated that 'those rakes or mines of lead ore in East Coneywood Forest and Hargell-rigg . . . in possession of Matthew Bell, John Routledge, Hugh Ridley, Thomas and John Ornsby . . . hath never been wrought'. *Northumberland Documents* (Surtees Soc.), 71.

[2] This should be compared with the mark on Ramsay's silverware, Jackson. loc. cit. Another brand was stamped G. M. (? George Morton).

purchased for £50 from John Garrick of Fouletown two 'messuages or farmholds' in Plenmeller, near Haltwhistle, and eleven years later the lands of William Pattison 'yeoman' in the same manor, a district with which the Ramsays seem to have been earlier associated. Further purchases were made as opportunity offered until, in 1697, he bought the two manors of Bellister and Hartleyburn from young Robert Blenkinsop for £734. The goldsmith was undergoing a significant alchemy, from plate to land. His son left 'the shop in the Side' and went to live at the foot of West-gate.[1]

In 1686 Alderman Ramsay paid the churchwardens of All Saints, Newcastle, 13s. 4d. 'for a burial place adjoining unto ye vestry wall on the south side and Mr. John Otway's stone on ye North side, lately Mr. Wm. Robinson's'. This Robinson was apparently a less fortunate fellow goldsmith, for Ramsay also acquired his tools and working kit. If Ramsay intended the burial place for himself, the purchase was distinctly premature for he lived for another dozen years. He was mayor of Newcastle in 1691 and his son later held the office of 'Troner and Peisor' in the port.[2] That he was a person of very considerable fortune and importance is clear from the elaborate and expensive arrangements at his funeral—Ralph Mitford's bill for mourning gloves, hat-bands, and narrow 'allemode' came to more than £16; Dorothy Ornsby supplied 10½ yards of fine black cloth at 19s. a yard for Mrs. Ramsay; Mrs. Trumble great quantities of muslin at 6s. 8d. a yard—the 'fine black serdge' provided for the men cost less than half that rate. William Gibson, shoemaker, made 'shamah' shoes for all the near members of the family at 5s. a pair for men and 3s. 6d. for women; Richard Crawforth's bill for black hose and lute string came to nearly £7; Thomas French provided the 'cosing, hatch-ment and hearse' and Dorothy Hankin loaned 'ye velvet

---

[1] Sir John Allaburton became the tenant of Westgate House after Ramsay moved to Park House, Gateshead. The original home, 'Whitehall in the Side', was let to Andrew Halliday at £20; Dr. Kipling had his 'shop' under it for which he paid £5. 10s. per annum.

[2] *Calendar of Treasury Books*, xiii. 353.

paill', besides supplying eighteen mourning cloaks and twenty-four hatbands.

Although William Ramsay, junior, was frequently styled 'goldsmith', he had, in 1686, been admitted to the Merchant Adventurers' company of Newcastle and was more properly addressed 'merchant'.[1] As such we find him, a decade later, trading to the Baltic, importing flax and madder through his factors, John Tyreman at Narva, and Bothomley and Mallabar at Danzig, and we know that for over twenty years he traded largely with the house of Pickfatt and Forster of Rotterdam, the former a cousin of the Durham Hedworths. His outgoing shipments to Holland included lead, grindstones, coal, and consignments of glass bottles (for Holland gin) in return for madder, flax, whale-fins, and occasionally hops. There is some evidence, too, that he was interested in the Newfoundland trade. From 1703 to 1709 we have fuller information relating to his loan and mortgage business. In 1703 his kinsman, Rev. Benjamin Bewicke of Soar in Leicestershire, heir and executor of Robert Bewicke of Close House, Northumberland, deposited with Ramsay 'for custody and safe keeping' some twenty-five 'Bonds, Writings, Mortgages and Securities'.[2] The goldsmith gave a formal receipt for them and continued, for the rest of his life, to collect the interest on the securities and to pay out annuities to various Bewicke nephews and nieces. The list includes loans on bond of £50 to £100, mortgages on house property in Sandgate, Newcastle, £250 to Mr. Mehittabell Partis on salt-pans at Shields, £300 to Mr. Edward Fawcett on lands at Richmond, £400 to Mr. Ralph Ogle, mortgage on lands in Kirkly, £500 to Mr. Lyonel Vane, mortgage on Stella colliery, £800 to Mr. Roger Fenwick on lands in Stanton, and £1,000 to Mr. Edward Delaval on lands at Aydon Castle. Ramsay must have scanned the list often and pondered it carefully for on the reverse side, entered in a beautifully

---

[1] Surtees Soc. ci. 303. He continued to lend money on bond.
[2] Some of the correspondence of Ramsay's brother-in-law, Calverley Bewicke, a London grocer, and of two of his sons is in the Cotesworth Papers.

neat clerk's hand, is another list headed 'Lent by W.R.'.
I give it as it stands:

*'Lent by W.R.'*

| | |
|---|---|
| Mr. Geo. Sanderson of Herly upon his Estate | £500 |
| Rec[d] interest due 10th October 1704 | £15 |
| Mr. Milburne of Chirton upon bond | £100 |
| Febry. 14, 1704. Mr. Robt. Sutton, Mr. Wm. Coatsworth, and Mr. Peter Bernardeau bond | £500 |
| June 11, 1705. Mr. Hall's[1] securitys of lands at Otterburn | £1300 |
| Mr. George Whinfield of Bavington upon bond | £300 |
| January 1st 1705. Mr. Robert Lawson upon bond | £150 |
| Febry. 13th 1705. Abigall Carr and others upon their bond | £100 |
| May 18th 1705. Geo. Ledgard and Wm. Johnson upon bond | £100 |
| March 1st 1705. Edward Harle and his brother upon bond | £200 |
| Robt. Cay and others upon bond | £100 |
| May 10th 1707. Alice Mallabar pd. halfe a year's Interest | |
| 18th March for Lawrence Heslain and others upon bond | £100 |
| August 1707. Mr. Francis Baker | £300 |
| August 1707. Mr. Ralph Wallis | £1300 |
| March 25 1708. Sir Edward Bl[ackett] | £500 |
| December 1709. Mr. Charles and James Mont[ague] | £2000 |

The names and date of the last entry are significant. We
know that the Montagues, kinsmen of the Dean of Durham
and of Bishop Crewe, were then owing over half that amount
for 'dead rents' on certain collieries in Gateshead and Whickham. Two years later Ramsay had to find £6,880, being the
purchase money of the two manors and the moiety of
Newsham, and in the following year a further £1,364. 6s. 0d.
for the renewal of the bishop's lease of the manors. His
surplus capital was temporarily exhausted; in fact he himself had to borrow £1,000 from 'Cousin' Ord.

In the remaining four years of his life he nursed assiduously his new treasure, Park House, Gateshead, whither
he removed from the house in Westgate. Elaborate altera-

---

[1] ? John Hall, the Jacobite. Patten, the historian of the Fifteen, records an alleged conversation in Newgate gaol between William Shaftoe of Bavington and Hall. 'Your grandfather
and my grandfather got most of their estates as sequestrators and now we must lose them
again for being rebels.' Quoted in Dixon, *Notes on Jacobite Movement in Upper Coquetdale.*

tions were put in hand—Nicholas Cockerill supplied no
fewer than 100,000 bricks at 4*s.* a 1,000 for a garden wall
and a new 'duff coatt'. John Oliver, the gardener's bill for
£23. 2*s.* 0*d.* included 1,000 tulip roots, 600 'narcisis', 400
'hya-sints', besides 618 yards of 'Dutch box', yews and
hollies, and 18 lime-trees. A new coach was bought and the
monthly smith's bills began to mount up. Indoors, William
Henderson supplied a dozen walnut-tree chairs at 8*s.* 3*d.*
apiece and two 'elbows' at 11*s.* 9*d.*, besides 66½ yards of
'blew print' and 1,000 gullets with nails and thread. His
bill 'for hanging the room' was 5*s.*, and 9 more were paid
'for making three pair of window vallance and curtains'.
John Dagnia, a local glass-maker, supplied a dozen 'egg and
goblet' wineglasses for 4*s.* and another dozen of 'six square'
for 3*s.* 6*d.*[1] 'Brother' Calverlcy Bewicke sent occasional
presents of cherry brandy from London and consignments
of *materia medica* for Mrs. Ramsay who consumed increasing quantities of medicines including 'a Bottle of Bitter
Infusion', besides ointments, glysters, and plasters. And
she had the kindly attentions of Dr. Richard Kipling of
Newcastle—'dressing a sore on Back, what you please'.
That the alchemy of the former goldsmith was now complete
is attested by two facts: in 1715 the Ramsays bought a new
silver teapot, weighing 15½ ounces, and a solid silver pint
tankard from John Younghusband—a leading local goldsmith:[2] and in the last months of his life he commissioned
the purchase in London of two marble statues, of a shepherd
and a shepherdess, 5 feet 6 inches high on pedestals of
Portland stone, the work of Mr. Vannost, costing £26.
*O fortunata . . .*

It is surely significant that prior to 1711, and thereafter
only as landlord, Ramsay was never a coal-owner or concerned
in the salt industry at Shields, both notoriously precarious

---

[1] His glassworks were then situated in Newcastle: he moved to South Shields later.
*Arch. Ael.* vi. 163; xxiv. 147. Joseph Tissick's (Tyzack) glassworks at St. Lawrence were
rented from the corporation of Newcastle at £10; Mr. Davison's at 'Easter and Middle
glasshouse' at £50 and Jacob Henzell at 'Wester glasshouse' at £60. Corporation Accounts
(1701–2) in Cotesworth MSS.     [2] For samples of his work, see *Arch. Ael.*, loc. cit.

trades. One could wish that more of his correspondence had survived but the following letter to his brother-in-law Cotesworth, who had lately negotiated both the purchase of the two manors and the subsequent renewal of the bishop's lease, gives a glimpse of this upright man of business.

Dear Brother,

    I hope I have no cause to blame your management in that business of the way-leave but I have great reason to complain of its not being finished as it ought to have been near 20 month since. The Gentlemen for whom you are concerned cannot say but I have been very true to them, and my affaires, you know as well as I, requires an end to be put to that matter. And, therefore, without more words, as you brought me into the bargaine, bring me out and that I may see what it is I have been doeing and take measures accordingly.

It should perhaps be explained that as a result of collusion between Henry Jackson, late steward of the manors, and Sir John Clavering, the latter fraudulently claimed an ante-dated and most valuable lease of way-leave rights over Whickham Fell which became the subject of protracted and expensive lawsuits.

Ramsay's large, open handwriting reveals a firm but kindly man. His friends spoke of him as the 'honest Alderman'. He could detect a knave, albeit a near relative, as surely as he could alloy in gold. A few weeks before he died he gave his two nephews, the Cotesworth boys, who were just going up to school at Sedbergh, a Jacobus each—a gold coin not readily come by—and this advice at parting: 'Fear God, Honour your Father, Love your Relations, and be Gracious.' Pure Gold!

Many people had wondered how this childless man would bestow his fortune. His brother-in-law, Calverley Bewicke, a London grocer, had astutely placed his daughter 'Dolle', as companion to Mrs. Ramsay at Park House. But the young lady ('housey', her father called her) proved ungovernable and was sent packing. In the end, the great bulk of the fortune went to William Cotesworth—a signal compliment, for the one-time goldsmith had had ample opportunity of assaying the yeoman's son and goldsmiths do not wittingly squander their treasure.

We have seen that Cotesworth was originally a tallow-chandler and he was careful to apprentice both his sons to the trade while they were mere boys before they went to school at Sedbergh.[1] For more than twenty years the tallow and candle business constituted his main trading interest. He collected raw tallow all over the four northern counties, melted some of it at his 'shop' in Gateside into 'fine', and sold both 'rough' and 'fine melted' in bulk in the London market. It was shipped in casks or hogsheads weighing several hundredweight each. In addition he made candles—the wick was obtained from Holland—for which there was a steady and surprisingly large demand in the coal- and lead-mines and in private houses. Some idea of the value of the candle trade alone may be gained from Cotesworth's accounts with Sir Henry Liddell for a single year, 1716—£237. 17s. 1½d. for the collieries, £6. 10s. 7d. 'for the house'. A certain Margaret Laing might be seen almost every day of the year taking consignments of 'twenty dozen' on horseback to the various collieries in County Durham and on occasion she attended her master farther afield to Richmond and elsewhere. But it was on the London wholesale market that he concentrated. In Queen Anne's day and until the extended use of oil-lamps and of spermaceti oil to make wax candles some twenty or thirty years later, tallow candles were still the main luminant for rich and poor alike, and provided employment for over 400 master chandlers in the city of London alone.[2] *Ex luce lucellum* had already occurred to needy financiers like William Lowndes, Secretary of the

---

[1] *Northern Notes & Queries*, i. 67–69. One of the indentures has survived.

[2] *Treasury Papers*, cxvii, § 22; clxxxvi, § 41; cccxviii, § 26. In 1739 the Commissioners of Excise represented to the Treasury that there have been of late great quantities of candles made of spermaceti oil and other ingredients in imitation of wax candles, which being sold at a lower price and though little inferior to wax candles, greatly prejudice the sale thereof. Moreover, the revenue from candles 'already considerably lessened, . . . must suffer much more should the said candles come into more frequent use'. Under 8 Anne, c. 9, tallow candles paid a duty of one penny per lb. and wax candles one of eightpence. Dowell, *History of Taxation*, ii. 76.

Treasury under Godolphin, and bright spirits had not been wanting to suggest a tax on raw tallow.[1] But in the interval between suggestion and official adoption a significant metamorphosis occurred: in 1711 the tax was imposed not on the raw material, as had been first suggested, but on the manufactured product, doubtless with a view of placating the powerful weaving interests since rough tallow was also a principal ingredient in soap making. This had the inevitable, if unforeseen, result of encouraging numbers of poor people living in cellars or garrets to make their own candles and so evade the duty, much to the concern of the master tallowchandlers.[2]

Competition in the wholesale market for tallow was keen, for large supplies came not only from the Smithfield butchers and from northern collecting centres like Newcastle and York, but also because of the considerable, if irregular, importations from Ireland and Russia.[3] Weekly spot quotations for both 'rough' and 'melted' were eagerly followed on Tyneside. Cotesworth traded through a number of London agents in turn, Dan Collyer, James Dixon, Robert Hodshon, all of whom sold on a commission basis. Some scores of their business letters and invoices have survived. In the early years of the century the ruling prices ranged from 1s. 8d. per stone for 'rough', to 27s. 6d. per cwt. for 'melted', but by 1711 the latter had jumped to 39s., and before the end of the reign, topped 40s. Here are a few excerpts from Dixon's letters and advice notes.

1710. April 15.
We have had cold weather for 3 days past wch made the markets for

---

[1] The principal advocates of the tax were Edward Stracey and J. Denham. The former contended that a duty of a half-penny per lb. on candles would produce £200,000 and that without the addition of officers, 'the burthen of all excises'.

[2] They pointed out later that 'such who are allowed to burn oyl (fish oyl only) in lamps in their shops, instead of fish oyl use other and very many poor people make use of any nautious oyle to burn in lamps even to work by in close rooms with a family, which must be of ill consequence to their healths as well as to the tallow-chandlers' trade'. T.B.P. (1729–30), p. 23, clxxxvi, § 41. The original act had imposed a small duty on linseed, neat's foot, and other oils.

[3] Some 17,797 cwt. were imported from Russia in the years 1753–63, despite the interruption of trade during the Seven Years War. Add. MSS. 38337, § 71.

ruff ye same as last week and ye buyers a little brisker or else could not have sold it at this price, for last week and beginning of this, people would not bye expecting it still cheaper and I find ye butchers are of opinion it will be lower, being little demand.

August 19.

. . . Your tallow proves soe soft and bad that I cannot yet dispose of it, ye Sope boylers prefer Stuff before it, wch they bye at 32/- [per cwt.] or under. I hope with laying cool in ye warehouse, it will harden soe that I may sell it.

September 26.

Trade was never known worse nor ye demand for Tallow less than at this time. Shall not sell any under 33/- till I have your order.

October 5.

. . . I cannot tell what to say to Tallow; tho' we had wett weather last week, yet the markit fell. I am of opinion with both Butchers and Chandlers till trade mend and money Curranter yt commodity will not advance. Ye quantity made in Town is very large wch near supplies ye whole demand; ye Chandlers are so full yt they are indifferent whether they bye fat or not. At the price they sell I think I had better sit still.

Cotesworth, expecting prices to rise with the approach of winter, instructed Dixon not to sell, though he had over £600 stock on hand in London and needed the money. 'This is such a time as we have never had before', wrote Dixon early in November, 'I cannot see but other people are as hard sett to get money for their Masters' notes as I am . . . I cannot take money from people whether they have it or noe; shall endeavour as much as I can to obleidge you but will not pretend to impossibilities.' The economic and financial crisis of the autumn of 1710 was upon them. In the event Dixon made a bad deal. He sold all the remaining hogsheads of tallow, worth £589, to a government contractor, one William Parker, hitherto a trader of repute. Unhappily, the Navy Bills which Parker held were then at an unusually heavy discount, and a disappointed rival promptly took out a commission of bankruptcy against him. His creditors were eventually paid 10s. 3d. in the £1 and Cotesworth lost £300 on the deal. Sharp recrimination followed and the Dixon agency was terminated. His successor, Robert Hodshon, acted for the rest of Cotesworth's life. 'Chandlers uses a pritty deal against the King's coming', he reported a month after Queen Anne died—it was a custom in the eighteenth century to put a candle in every window, indeed in every pane, at coronations and such occasions. Complaints of the poor quality of Cotesworth's tallow continued to be made. 'Your tallow is worse this year both for culler and smell', wrote Hodshon in 1715, 'and if you please to take a drawing iron and run it a pretty way in, you'll find what I say to be true, for it smells worse than any necessary house.' He suspected that some of the country tallow was tainted before Cotesworth got it. Smell or no smell, Cotesworth's account with him for that year totalled £4,423. 'If one cou'd forsee what wou'd happen, it wou'd be an easy matter to get an estate', wrote Hodson four years before the South Sea Bubble. His client had already shown the way.

All these tallow agents and fully a dozen others at one time or other, supplied the Tynesider with quantities of indigo, argoll, cochineal, copperas, galls, logwood and sanderswood, fustick and woad, and other curious and expensive dyestuffs imported from both the East and West Indies and the Levant, besides various kinds of ashes (potash), soap, and oil. Thomas Bard of Thames Street, 'understanding that you deale considerably in those commoditys', sent Cotesworth a price list in 1702. This reverse trade from London is a reminder that there was a very important textile industry in the north-east. The best huckabacks, damask, and sheetings were obtained from Darlington, as Lady Gerard and Lady Sudbury knew well.[1] More than half a century later Ralph Ward of Gisborough sold his annual clip of wool, over 90 stone, to 'Cosen' Pease of Darlington. That there were dyers in Gateshead is clear from the fact that one John Harrison, dyer, witnessed

---

[1] Sir John Sudbury to Wilson, his Durham agent: 'my Wife desires me to put you in mind of her huggaback'. Hunter MSS. xii, § 132.

Cotesworth's apprentice indenture in 1682, and twenty years later his son commissioned Cotesworth to collect the rents on certain house property while he was absent in London 'improving his trade'.[1] It was this north-country linen industry which accounts for the regular purchases, by Ramsay and Cotesworth, of flax, tow, madder, and whale fins from Rotterdam and occasionally of alum from Hamburg.[2] In 1713 Hodshon, the London factor, was supplying small quantities of 'Siprous cotten' at 22*d*. per lb. There seems little reason to doubt that Cotesworth supplied the weaving centres of Morpeth, Kendal, and Carlisle with dyestuffs.

Nor does this, by any means, exhaust the range of his activities. He supplied sugar, tea, and chocolate to Sedbergh landladies and ill-paid clergy in Cumberland, as well as tobacco, all obtained as yet from London. The latter was usually made up in 14-lb. packets, at prices ranging from 15*d*. to 18*d*. a pound. Alderman Ramsay bought his in bulk, 'provided it be good leaf'. After 1730 Whitehaven cut out London from this important trade. We know, too, that Cotesworth imported wines, cherry brandy, and prunes from Peter and Jacob Albert of Bordeaux whenever the intermittent wars with France permitted. (We shall presently have occasion to notice his pertinent queries regarding the commercial clauses of the Treaty of Utrecht.) Nor is that all. In 1698–9 we find Peter Albert, his London wine agent, sending him current prices of wheat, rye, barley, and beans at Exeter, at the other corner of a famous trade triangle represented by London–Amsterdam, the west country, and Spain. 'Cotesworth and Sutton' were also 'Corn merchants'. Already the industrial north-east, where farming was mainly pastoral,[3] could not grow enough grain for its own requirements; some of the barley and rye for the famous 'geordie' loaf had to be imported. Cotesworth also

---

[1] In 1726 the Dyers' Meeting-house in Gateshead was assessed for land-tax at £1. 10s. 0d.
[2] The great development of the alum works about Staithes came later in the century. Baker–Baker MSS.          [3] *Infra*, Ch. IV.

regularly imported from Thomas Shepton of London, considerable quantities of hops. The coal-miners, keelmen, and
wagon-men were notoriously heavy drinkers. We know that
the brewers of Newcastle were powerfully organized and
determined to maintain a local monopoly. The local brands
of beer and ale were already famous, though gentlemen still
brewed their own.[1] At one time, Cotesworth's son-in-law,
Ellison, seriously considered embarking in the brewery
business himself, but was dissuaded by his uncle, Liddell,
who anticipated difficulties and bad debts from gate-keepers
and wagon-men. Whenever a northerner found himself
domiciled in London for any length of time he took care to
have regular consignments of home-brewed ale and beer
sent to him.[2] It was found not infrequently that barrels were
tampered with on shipboard and recourse was had to bottles
which, when packed, could be more conveniently disguised.
Cotesworth's account with Shepton for hops from December
1709 to September 1711 amounted to £237. 11s. 6d.

Five points of general interest to the economic historian
emerge from this highly miscellaneous trade between London
and the north-east. (i) The growing tendency of London
merchants to specialize in one branch of trade. Thus,
Thomas Bard of the Black Lyon, Thames Street, advised
Cotesworth in 1702 that his former partner, Mr. Shepton,
and himself had parted company 'he dealing in the Hopp
trade, myself only in Dyeing goods', and thereafter each of
them dealt only in his special line. (ii) The general effect of
this expanding entrepôt trade on the industrial development
around London is also worth noting. In 1716 Mr. Sam
Buck added this advice note to an invoice for three hogsheads
of best ground sanderswood: 'Hopes to send 3 hogsheads of
Fustick with the next ship, but we have had so great a
demand for ground wood for ye Town consumption and
water has fallen short at all our mills that I could not possibly
get it ground sooner.' It is known, for example, that the

---

[1] Inquiry into the 'oppressions' of Newcastle, 1722–3. *The Note Book of Sir Walter Calverley* (Surtees Soc. lxxvii), 127 n. [2] Chaytor in the Fleet wanted 'an anchor of ale'.

calico-printing trade was centred in the environs of London for the greater part of the eighteenth century.[1] (iii) A similar tendency towards increasing specialization was noted in shipping: the big colliers could not afford to wait to carry general cargo, they wanted a quick turn-round. 'There is few or no colliers takes in goods for Newcastle', wrote Bard in 1705, 'most people shipping in the smaller vessels it has not been worth the colliers' while to lye for loading.' (iv) Both the East and West India interests competed to some extent in the supply of these costly dyestuffs. 'Indico seems to decline, tho' these East India company ships have bought none and yesterday we had an account *via* Flanders from France that several Spanish West India ships are come into Rochell and have brought near 400 chests of indico, so suppose we shall not have further demands from Holland and Flanders, wch places the French will now supply. At present I see no reason why indico should bear this price, it's now 9s. 2d. to 9s. 8d. per lb.', wrote Bard in 1705. Five years later, Dixon advised Cotesworth: 'Have bought you one barrel of Indicoe. . . . I cannot find ye people are very willing to sell, tho' this quantity be com'd from the East Indies, that being generally bought for ye Holland's markit. . . . What comes now from Jamaica not soe good as formerly.' (v) The problem of balancing payments was not so great as might be supposed. Already in Cotesworth's day, London was a great clearing centre for bills of exchange. The trade in dyestuffs and other luxury goods went some way towards balancing the payments for coal, tallow, salt, and lead. True, each merchant encountered credit difficulties from time to time—Cotesworth was notorious in claiming long credit for himself and in pressing for prompt payment from his customers—and on occasion it proved difficult to get bills on London in Newcastle. But local merchants were generally able to get notes or bills by arrangement with the local collectors of Customs or Excise.[2] For normal purposes the passage of specie was a thing of the past if indeed it had ever obtained.

---

[1] Excise Board (Correspondence with the Treasury), *passim.*  [2] Ward, *Journal.*

Three other branches of Cotesworth's trading interests have yet to be mentioned. First the trade in grindstones and whetstones of varying shapes and sizes. There was a proverb in the seventeenth century 'that three things were to be found the world over—a Scot, a rat, and a Newcastle grindstone'.[1] The axes which rang in the forests of the Baltic countries and in the American plantations were sharpened on 'grindlestones' obtained from the Tyne; the scythes and sickles which were put into meadows and golden cornfields were whetted by handstones obtained from the same area. And, as yet, the log cabins in the colonies were lit by the glimmer of tallow candles made in the homeland.[2] The grindstone quarries were situated along the low fells south of the Tyne stretching from Whickham to Hebburn, the most famous being those on Gateshead Fell. At Wracken Dyke (Wrekenton) there were eleven working quarries in Cotesworth's day some with strange-sounding names—'ye World's Wonder', 'Luke's Hole', 'Vinegar Chapple'[3]—and the men who worked them, the Todds, Rogersons, Dawsons, and Stoddarts mostly from 'Great Uzworth' and High and Low 'Iton', were equally awesome or so the sub-agent, John Lowes, believed. He reported in 1714 that some of them were 'sectaries that comes not to be subject to civil order except forst [forced] by compulltion, nor is anything likeing to them but what's forg'd on theire own anvil'. 'If you doe not make a publicke example of some of these insolent fellowes', he told his master, Alderman Ramsay, 'they'll ride on your shoulders as long as you live.' They were notorious offenders in ignoring or removing 'bounder' stones and in dumping waste rock just where it suited them. The quarries were ordinarily held on short-term leases or yearly licences which often contained a stipulation that not more than four men were to work them at a time. The lessees tended to be

---

[1] Quoted by Gray in *Chorographia*, and by the Earl of Oxford. *H.M.C. Portland MSS.* vi. 104.

[2] In 1711 the London tallow-chandlers pointed out that the duty on candles 'must be like to keep the price so high . . . our usual supplying the Plantations must be lost which is a large article to us'. T.B.P. cxvii, § 22.   [3] The remains of some can still be seen.

hereditary family partnerships, for quarrying was a difficult and dangerous art. There was first the problem of deciding on the right 'throat' in the line of the natural dip; the surface layers where the rock had become too soft or brittle to be serviceable had then to be pared off. The stones themselves, from the great circular 'eight foots' to the small 'knife' stones were cut and shaped 'in the hole' by skilled crafts-men and sold at so much per chaldron according to size. Unfortunately, the advantage accruing from the universal distribution of grindstones was largely offset by their long-wearing qualities with the result that the trade in them was dull and was probably already on the decline in the early eighteenth century. Besides the grindlestone quarries, there was one stone quarry in Quarry Close, Gateshead, leased at the time to two Newcastle masons and a few slate quarries, though locally made bricks and pantiles, and some 'Dutch-made', were tending to replace stone for building and slate for roofing.[1]

Doubtless it was the presence of millstone grit and local iron-stone which accounted for the location of a colony of German sword makers at Shotley Bridge as also for the Crowley ironworks at Winlaton and Blaydon.[2] The English Sword Blade Company was perhaps the strangest under-taking with which Cotesworth was ever associated. In April 1703 Henry and John Wopper, Adam Olligh (Oley), William Schafe, and Pieter Tiergarden, sword-blade makers residing at Shotley Bridge, signed articles of agreement bind-ing themselves to make exclusively for the company some thirty-seven different varieties of swords (as per an attached schedule) at stated prices for a term of six years.[3] The list ranges from 'Large Latsons' hollow ground, 32–36 inches long, at £1. 4s. 6d. a dozen, to 'byenetts', plain, 12–13 inches long, at 7s. per dozen. The average price for double hollow-ground rapiers, scimitars, and 30-inch swords ranged from

[1] Thomas Wright, the Durham scientist, used the more expensive Dutch pantiles for his house at Byers Green.     [2] *V.C.H. Durham*, ii. 288.

[3] The agreement was signed by 'Jno. Blunt, secretary' to the company and the schedule of prices by Thomas Lake and J. Bellamy.

11*s*. to 14*s*. per dozen, delivered in Newcastle.[1] It is clear
that the Germans had settled at Shotley Bridge before 1703
for two years later Cotesworth wrote to John Beardmore,
that 'Clem Schaff is very old; let us know if he be able to do
our work; if not, we will endeavour to get one from abroad
but it will be a great trouble and charge for they are very
stiff and proud when they know they are wanted'. Indeed,
at the time when the Sword Blade Company was formed,
Herman Mohll had gone to Solingen in Germany to recruit
more labour.[2] By 1709 the colony had been joined by others
besides Mohll—John Hartcop, William Palds, and John
Voes. In 1703, the Germans agreed to take over the existing shops and mills, tools and equipment, and to hand over
the same in good repair at the end of the contract. The list
included a dozen anvils, 11 pairs of bellows, 2 tempering
troughs, 2 water hammers and 30 double-headed hammers,
4 earthen engraving pots, 6 grindstones besides rules and
compasses and a quantity of miscellaneous tackle. The steel
was bought by each German on his own account from Dan
Hayford's 'forge' at Roamley, near Pontefract ('Direct to
me *per* Bawtry post') in bars at 5*d*. a lb. This is interesting
because although the famous Crowley works at Winlaton
clearly made steel from imported Swedish iron for their own
use, they manufactured mainly ironware, nails, fire-irons,
shovels, &c.[3] Moreover, in 1715, Hayford seriously proposed to take over the Shotley mill himself.

'Sir, all the cutlers complain of the blades being soft and
ill-tempered', wrote Henry Benson, an official of the company, to Cotesworth in 1705, 'there is very few of them,
especially ye tukes but what stand like lead: it would give
great satisfaction if they were made of such steel as was used
formerly, for our workmen by reason of their softness can-

---

[1] The highest price in the list was for 'India Backs', 1–3 hollows, 35–38 inches long,
£1. 8*s*. 0*d*. per dozen.

[2] On his return to this country he was imprisoned for a time at Morpeth as a suspected
Jacobite.

[3] Add. MSS. 34555. In 1714 John Lovett imported a cargo of Swedish iron into Newcastle but it was seized on the ground that he was not a member of the Merchants' Company.
Minutes of Evidence, § 35–36.

not bring them to coller like the German blades.' Clearly,
Cotesworth was also selling swords made elsewhere. Again,
a year later, acknowledging the receipt of four chests of
swords, Benson wrote, 'they are prety siseable, but a little
of ye weakest. Pray tell them to make them very stiff and
well glased and especially well tempered. I have a great
many blades by me wch stand like lead.' 'Your workmen
need not grave any more of the blaides seeing they will not
yield twopence per dozen more than the plain ones, being
not deep enough done', wrote Benjamin Sleigh in 1714.
The swords were mostly consigned in chests to London,
though some were sent to a cutler in Glasgow possibly to
return later with the Jacobites.

In 1710 after the original contract expired, the Germans
at Shotley Bridge, now joined by Mohll and others, signed
a three-year agreement with Cotesworth to make swords for
him 6*d*. a dozen cheaper than the present rate. Two months
earlier he had made another contract with John Saunthop
and partners to make swords 1*s*. a dozen cheaper than the
Germans. By that time the English Sword Blade Company
had been virtually taken over by Cotesworth. For the next
three years, so long as the war lasted, he took off the bulk,
if not the whole, of the output of the Shotley Bridge works—
his account from 30 November 1710 to 21 August 1712
amounted to £935. 13*s*. 3½*d*., representing some 1,600
dozen blades. Thus with the naval ordnance and stores supplied by the Crowley firm, the north-east was already an
important munitions centre: half a century later, in the war
with the American colonies, Tyne shipyards began building
frigates for the Admiralty.[1]

The fate of the German colony at Shotley Bridge can only
be surmised. They were palpably hard hit once the war was
over; so much is clear from their dunning letters to Cotesworth and from the Sheffield steel-maker's concern about
their debts. As early as September 1713 the aged Adam

---

[1] At Howden Pans. North MSS. b. 56 (Bodleian). At the beginning of the eighteenth
century shipbuilding at Newcastle had declined. Minutes of Evidence, §§ 49–50.

Olligh (Oley) 'yeoman' signed a covenant with Cotesworth by which, in consideration of a loan of £5. 1 5s. 4d. he agreed to assign over to him his two cows 'one all black and the other a hank one withal', to be returned if the money was ever repaid. There is nothing to indicate that it was. Olligh's signature on this document suggests a Rembrandtesque hand that could scarcely push pen along. In 1715, Hermann Mohll wrote asking Cotesworth's permission for 'we grinders to ground Mr. Hayford's blades made by our smith here, that is when we have not full imploy', making Cotesworth an allowance for the use of the mill. This confirms the view that not all the Germans at Shotley Bridge actually made swords; some were grinders or engravers. A fortnight later he wrote again:

Mr. Hayford is for the Company works here: his ingineers viewed and measured all housing, shops and mills and taking the level of the water and everything where he cut gite [could get]. Some tells he is for buying it: howsoever he is for taking it and I hear the Company will bestow no more money here and hath offered to let it at a reasonable price. Sir, I thought it convenient to let you understand, if ever you have a kindness for the works or me to hold the old husie back if possible, and if you have no mind for yourself to do, then help us for it as [we] will make sword blaides for rent and we will pay rent every month.

He was very pressing to prevent Hayford's design, 'the sliye youth', and threatened not to buy 'one steel or iron of him'. What happened subsequently is not clear as Mohll died in the following year. (There are still families of Mohll in County Durham, though the word is now spelt like 'the little gentleman in velvet'.) The relation of Cotesworth to the titular company in London at this time is uncertain. One may doubt, however, if either was prepared to take 'blades for rent'. 'Your blaides are at last sold for 14s/- per dozen', wrote Sleigh to Cotesworth in the autumn of 1715, adding that the buyer would claim an allowance 'for the rusty ones and such as they call children's blades for some such there are amongst 'em'. The war was over, and impending social changes were destined to depress still farther the sword-making business. With greater security and greatly increased travel facilities, men no longer carried swords. Undergraduates and M.P.s tended to beat them into walking canes and later to emulate Jonas Hanway's innovation.[1] Almost the last thing we hear of the Shotley works is contained in a letter dated 1724 in which Cotesworth reported that the mill had changed hands.[2] 'Those of the Sword Blaide Company that were there concerned are all in adversity and misfortunes by haistening to be rich.' A Jarrow in miniature two centuries ago!

This will be a convenient place for saying something of the London firm of Ambrose Crowley which set up works first at Sunderland and later moved to Winlaton and Blaydon on Tyne.[3] The date of the transfer can be ascribed with some certainty to the year 1702 from the correspondence which passed between Crowley and Sir William Bowes of Gibside.[4] Crowley promised to take effectual care to prevent the destruction of fish whether by his works or his workmen and inquired if Bowes could supply him with cordwood for

[1] On the occasion of Henry Ellison's marriage, his friend Joshua Geekie wrote from London: 'Can't get a handsome sword for £5 to £6, so have ventured to £8/10/-'; 'It is certainly proper on this occasion you should have a handsome gold-headed cane'; accordingly he purchased one which cost £10.

[2] See the rejected petition of the Sword Blade Company in 1724. *C.J.* xxi. 246. The signatories of the petition, S. Swinsen, H. Trollope, T. Beech, L. Brightwell, H. Symmonds, who styled themselves 'Proprietors Governors and Co. etc.' prove that the business had changed hands. 'Cutlers Hall', 1787, the home of the Ollighs still stands—the mill is derelict —and I am informed that there are still Ollighs at Shotley Bridge.

[3] Crowley was satirized in the *Spectator*. *V.C.H. Durham*, loc. cit.

[4] Add. MSS. 34555. I have found surprisingly few references to iron-making in the region at this time. In August 1728 George Bowes, a London merchant, wrote to his namesake: 'I took leave to hint Mr Wood's scheme for your Iron Works for pig iron and Malleable iron, etc. The Queen wore a rose in her Breast made of this Iron: they say there is none in the world comes up to it. He has raised twenty two thousand pounds to begin his fund upon. His Cumberland works goes on prosperously & so does those upon ye Severn near Bristol for the Jemaica Trade & your Countrey for the Conveniency of Carriage to London, York etc. and all ye adjacent countrey, Crowley works. Mr Wood sets out on Monday for Cumberland will call as he comes through your Countrey. Cou'd you agree to build him Furnaces to smelt his Iron, I cannot think but it would be an improvement to Mr Bowes's Estate without Hazard. I hope you have got him some of the Iron mine about Gibside you have great plenty all around you of the hardest sort as appears by the Iron Backs and Barr in Gibside Hall which was made by the Forges in Sir Ralph Blakiston's time and that family raised themselves by those works in the Infancy of the Coale.' Bowes MSS. 40748, § 53.

making charcoal. He also desired to enter into treaty with Bowes for some land near the mill 'to keep a draft and cowes for my workmen' and before leaving the north he desired to choose six trees from Bowes's woods, part of a quantity which he proposed to buy. These presumably were intended for the great timbers of the mill itself. At the same time he expressed great regret 'that I am not in London to show how sensible I am of the great favors I have had from you even to the enabling of me to establish the Iron Manufactory in this Cuntry which will be to your immortal glory'. For over twenty years Cotesworth had regular dealings with the Crowley firm supplying it with cordwood, coal, and grindstones, and buying picks and shovels and miscellaneous hardware in return. In 1712 a small dispute arose because Cotesworth's agent refused to allow Crowley's people to cut and lead away turf from Thornley wood along with the cordwood for which he had contracted, Crowley pointing out that 'it was a favour he enjoyed from all those who sold cordwood to him'. (The turf was probably used to 'bank' the fires in the process of making charcoal.) After 1719, when Joseph Banks, M.P., and Cotesworth jointly purchased the forfeited estates of Lord Widdrington in Winlaton and Stella, J. B. Crowley, M.P., became their tenant. Four years later there was an incident which may throw some light on the origin of one of the social regulations in the famous code governing the ironworks. William Hancock, one of Crowley's workmen, was arrested for debt at the suit of one Robert Atkinson, brewer, of Newcastle. Whereupon Mr. Crowley wrote to his 'good friends', Mr. Cotesworth and Colonel Liddell, that he was far from screening any of his servants from paying their just debts and he had often requested Atkinson not to give his work-people credit 'they standing in need of none, having their wages paid them every week'. He declared that Atkinson had been 'vexatious . . . arresting and ruining 'em by troublesome prosecutions for ale-wife's scores of many years standing'. He was prepared, however, to close the incident on condition that the brewer, through Cotesworth's good offices, made apology and gave an assurance that he would not arrest his work-people in future; otherwise he was 'determined to move the House'—i.e. to assert his parliamentary privilege—no small threat in those days—'and summon the offenders to answer their offence here'. Law No. 85 required the works' treasurer 'to make it his business to Pry and Enquire' into the actions of the work-people 'and when any clerk or servant shall make a Frequent Practice in going much abroad, particularly to Newcastle, which hath been the ruine of several, to inform me'. It continued,

> Whereas Mr. Crowley hath made it his observation that Morning Drinking hath been of fatal consequence to all that have made a practice of it (1) It is of all things the most destructive to business (2) it destroyeth health, memory and understanding (3) produceth nothing but folly and madness (4) it wastes the only time to do business in . . . all which Mr. Crowley hath taken into consideration in a most serious manner and hath totally broke it at London[1] and hath found the same to be obligeing and not offensive to the best of his customers . . . and will for the future take effectual care to discharge any of his work people who drink strong liquor before they go to dinner.

This regulation belongs to the age of Hogarth's *Gin Lane* not to some nineteenth-century temperance enthusiast.

We have seen that Cotesworth claimed to be the biggest salt proprietor in the country, paying over £1,000 a year in duties. In April 1715 he obtained the contract for the supply of the Victualling Office.[2] His interest in the ancient industry at Shields came relatively late in his career and then

---

[1] i.e. at the firm's London office.

[2] The negotiations were conducted by Benjamin Sleigh. Cotesworth had a good friend in 'Honest Denzill on whose friendship you may depend', wrote Henry Liddell, 'as far as in him lyes wch is thus far only that in case another should bid as low as you, he may perhaps contrive that your proposal shall be preferred'. Actually, Cotesworth's was the lowest tender 'but a very hard bargain as most people call it'. 'By what I can discover', wrote Liddell, 'ye old Contractors offer'd at £8/10/-, others at about £9/6/- and some at £9 [per weigh] thinking that none would bid again ym. But when Sligh's proposal appeared they were struck, saying you could not gett a farthing by itt: they blame you for lowering ye market.' Cotesworth had submitted a tender to the Victualling Board in 1711 which was rejected as he would not lower his price. Victualling Board Minutes, 8 October 1711, quoted in Miss Marjorie McHattie's unpublished thesis (Manchester University) 'Mercantile Interests in the House of Commons, 1710–1713'.

largely as a result of two considerations: (i) the fact that, as a coal-owner, he had abundant 'pan-coal'—small coals or slack which could not be sold on the London market, (ii) the parlous condition of many of the Shields' proprietors confronted for the first time by heavy taxation and regulation of their trade. Cotesworth's kinsman and namesake had gone bankrupt at the beginning of the century and his pans had been sold. Clearly the position of the pan-owner *vis-à-vis* the coal-owner had recently undergone important change for, as late as 1691, some twenty-three colliery proprietors on Tyne headed by Sir Samuel Gerard, lord of the manors of Gateshead and Whickham, Matthew White, and Nicholas Fenwick 'being concerned in the working and selling of pan coals and having considered and sufficiently experienced of the largeness of the messur to which the owners of the panns have brought their boates to our great loss and disadvantage',[1] made an agreement not to sell coals to the pan-owners except at stipulated rates, ranging from 8*s*. to 10*s*. 6*d*. a chaldron. They further covenanted to insist on prompt payment, 'either redy money or upon demand', and severally not to load at their staiths any pan-owner who owed money to any in the combine. The three named gentlemen were to constitute a committee with power 'to advance the Rates at any time'; the association agreed to meet together once every week, or oftener if the committee thought fit, absentees to be fined 6*d*. A supplementary article provided for a weekly levy of 2*d*. per boat towards providing a common fund and any member who broke the contract was liable to a fine of £50. The agreement, in the first instance, was to last for twelve months. This seventeenth-century combine, the child of acute depression in the coal trade, is an interesting anticipation of the famous 'Regulation' of 1710, the first of the so-called 'Grand Alliances'.[2] By that time the position had completely changed. Cotesworth contended that he could furnish pan-coals at 5*s*. a chaldron, a rate much

---

[1] The pan-owners clearly owned or hired boats independently of the Newcastle fitters and keelmen.  [2] *Infra*, Ch. V.

cheaper than any other proprietor in the kingdom could afford. This figure gives the measure of the screw which coal-owners applied to Mr. Mehittabell Partis and his fellow salters at the river's mouth. Small wonder that they went under one by one: the independent salter, like Mr. Partis's Christian name, soon became extinct. They were bought out by bigger industrialists like Cotesworth, Wortley, and the Liddells, and in the thirties by John Cookson and the Dagnias's who erected glassworks on the pan sites.[1] The plaintive letters of Margaret Liddell, widow of a former pan-boat owner and herself the erstwhile manager of Cotesworth's warehouses at Shields, are the swan song of an ancient industry.[2] Apart from the new glass-houses, the Shields were a depressed area before the middle of the century.

It was for the reason that Cotesworth could afford pan-coals so much cheaper than any one else that he was not attracted to Thomas Slyford's plan in 1717 to form an incorporated society of all the salt proprietors in the kingdom under government charter. Superficially, this was a throw-back to the projects of Caroline patentees but with important differences. The governors of the company were to be styled 'Directors' (an early use of the term in its modern connotation) and it was to provide a sort of central advisory service on overseas markets to encourage the manufacture of improved qualities. Actually, Slyford's project savoured of the later 'Bubble' schemes, since the government was to be induced to grant a charter in consideration of the salt proprietors accepting the repeal of the allowances for waste and prompt payment of duty which were making such large inroads on the revenue.[3] Cotesworth would have none

---

[1] In 1724 Mrs. Margaret Cole, Mrs. Cowland, and Mrs. Browne assigned their saltworks at South Shields to Robert Blunt. These later passed to Thomas Jeffreys of Snow Hill, London, and Francis Hawkes, glass-maker, of Vauxhall. In 1737 Jeffreys formed a partnership with Thomas Cookson, merchant of Newcastle, for the manufacture of crown and plate glass 'at their glass house shortly thereafter intended to be built at South Shields'. (Articles of Partnership in Cookson MSS.) Dean & Chapter Register of Leases (1727–31), § 202; (1737–9), § 100; (1739–42), § 153–6.

[2] See my *Studies*, 407.            [3] Ibid. 243.

of it. His economic philosophy, a virile and sensible *laissez-faire*, is summed up in the passage which appears at the head of the present chapter.

Dr. Slyford was on intimate terms with the Bishop of London, one of the commissioners who had negotiated the commercial clauses of the Treaty of Utrecht. On learning of this, Cotesworth wrote

> I wish I had freedom of conversation with that Rev^d Prelate. There are two circumstances in the articles of trade and commerce, signed by his Lordship and the French agents, which I very much covet to have explained by his Lordship who certainly can best do it. The one is how, being restrained to five ports in France for importation of fish into that Kingdom, and that in barrells only, could facilitate the fish trade from England to France: the other is the concession that was made the French for catching and cureing fish at Newfoundland by the people of that nation in which I think it is stipulated that France shall have liberty for building sheds or stages for cureing their fish and that only during the summer season, for as I understand the trade, fish can only be cured there in the summer season. My head was from the beginning much set on the Newfoundland trade.

On these two points he felt the treaty to be delusive. The day had gone when bishops could safely be entrusted with the negotiation of vital commercial treaties. 'Trade is the game of the Politick Public', wrote a merchant, George Bowes in 1728, 'who screen its industrious arts from the idle Nobility and Gentry by glaring, dazzling notions and starve 'em even in Lace and Grandeur, and make them administer to their Riches and plenty and are only guilded Blocks to mount them and their Families upon.'

This then makes up Cotesworth's claim that he traded 'for upwards of £30,000 a year in anything he could gain by'. By 1710 he held shares in various collieries and as paid secretary of the 'Regulation' became the brain and spokesman of the coal trade. After 1716, as lord of the manors of Gateshead and Whickham and joint lessee of Heaton colliery across the Tyne, he became a principal proprietor. In 1721 W. Blakiston Bowes accused him of 'endeavouring

to engross all the Coal Trade to himself'. His clear-sighted-
ness and driving-power alarmed competitors, notably
Richard Ridley of Heaton,[1] who staged a rearguard action
in the Newcastle Corporation to defeat Cotesworth's move
to get way-leave from Heaton through lands owned by the
town. This in turn led Cotesworth to petition the government to refuse His Majesty's assent to the acquisition, by
the corporation, of Walker estate obtained some years earlier
in defiance of the statute of mortmain. For a whole year,
1722–3, he battled almost single-handed in London in 'the
town affair'. He was, in fact, a second Ralph Gardiner
fulminating against the 'oppressions' of the corporation in
their capacity as conservators of the Tyne in such matters as
ballast shores,[2] jurisdiction over wrecks, and 'restraint of
trade'. Indeed, he seriously contemplated publishing a
revised and up-to-date edition of Gardiner and did in fact go
into print with his 'case' of grievances.[3] Although in the
end he was beaten on the particular issue of a threatened
*quo warranto* in respect of the Walker estate, he firmly
believed that he had not fought in vain. He lived just long

---

[1] *Arch Ael.* (4th series), xxiii. 151. Ridley and Matthew White of Blagdon bought Heaton
estate in 1719. Ridley MSS.

[2] Coal ships returning from London and the south came up in ballast. As they approached
the Tyne they proceeded to dump some of it overboard in favourable weather; the rest could
only be unloaded at official ballast shores on the Tyne. Some of these, e.g. Willington quay,
were directly owned by the corporation of Newcastle but a few, St. Anthony's and Jarrow,
were privately owned but licensed by the corporation. The charges for casting ballast varied:
to induce ships' masters to come higher up the river, rather lower rates were charged on
ballast shores nearer the Tyne bridge. No loaded ship could 'clear' the river until its master
had paid his ballast charges at the Ballast 'office' in Newcastle. In 1722 many people testified
that the corporation showed partiality in this matter: it was feared that the town might compel ships' masters to load coals at their staiths and not with gentlemen proprietors higher up
the river. Moreover, it was contended that owing to the faulty siting or building of new
ballast shores, the course of the current had changed making navigation unsafe, also that the
corporation had failed to remove wrecks, sandbanks, &c., that were a danger to shipping.
Edward Ord, manager of Joseph Bonner's ballast quay at St. Anthony's, stated 'that tho'
the Quantity of coals exported be much encreased, the quantity of ballast in general was not
so great as formerly, occasioned as he had heard, by Masters stationalling their ballast from
voyage to voyage and great quantities (as he believed) thrown at sea, besides the ships new
built are contrived more commodiously for the Trade & carry less ballast than formerly'.
Minutes of Evidence., loc. cit.

[3] Cotesworth is known to have borrowed a copy of Gardiner's tract from Mr. Fawcett, a
Durham lawyer. There are several printed copies of his own *Case* and his original draft and
corrections in the Cotesworth Papers. Brand, op. cit. ii. 414.

enough to witness the formation and to be one of the signatories of the 'Grand Alliance' in 1726 which dominated the coal trade for the rest of the century. At first, neither Alderman Ridley nor the Newcastle Hostmen were members of it. The gentlemen coal proprietors who lived south of the Tyne now gave the law to the men of Newcastle. 'The power of the Coal Trade being thus vested in the Town of Newcastle', he had written in 1722, 'they will have an entire dominion over the Country for whoever are the chiefe Proprietors in the Coal Trade of Tine will have the influence over the people as appeared on the Late Rebellion when Colonel Liddell mustered on 12 hours' notice 1200 horse and foot on Gateshead Fell in the neighbourhood of Newcastle in defence of His Majesty's person and Government.' A shift of economic power in the region was already in progress.

CHAPTER III

# The Professions

The Setting a young Fellow out into the World well
at first, all his future happyness depends on it and 'tis
an affair that ought to be well considered.

*(John Baker, 1754)*[1]

I entirely agree with you in your resolution of breeding up all your sons to some profession . . . but I would
suggest certain general rules by which I would point
out to them the professions which I should severally
wish them to apply to. I would recommend the Army
or the Navy to a boy of warm constitution, strong
animal spirits and a cold genius; to one of quick,
lively and distinguishing parts—the Law; to a good,
dull, and decent boy—the Church; and Trade to
an acute, thinking and laborious one.

*(Lord Chesterfield, 1756)*

## I

OF the several occupations pride of place should clearly
be given to what Colonel Liddell called 'A Country
Life in Business'. A country gentleman, if he was on the
Commission of the Peace, or served as Commissioner for
Highways or the Land-tax or as an officer of the militia, was
very fully employed, if we include the oversight of his estate
and business concerns. And if to these be added, as in George
Liddell's case, a term as Governor of the Hostmen's Company and a dozen years' service as a local M.P., it was more
than most tough eighteenth-century constitutions could
stand. What most impresses one about these people is their
fine sense of service, mostly unpaid, to the local community
in which they lived. They knew well enough that their
official duties soon brought much non-official and personal
service involving large inroads on their time in trying to

[1] Ellison MSS. It is not possible to distinguish sharply between a 'trade' and a 'profession'
in the eighteenth century. Entry to both was still by the time-honoured system of apprenticeship. After 1710 the premiums paid by apprentices were subject to a stamp duty and the
returns in the Stamp Office, P.R.O. Inl. 1/41 seq. form a kind of Domesday Book of the
professions for the whole of the century.

smooth out the difficulties of individuals who were in trouble
or help in placing children in jobs. The correspondence of a
conscientious gentleman is eloquent of the many claims that
were made upon him. Witness, for example, the efforts of
Cotesworth and the Liddells to save young Jack Pearson
who had rashly joined the Jacobites in 1715 from execution
or transportation. One may smile at Ralph Ward of Gisborough who some time after receiving an express telling of
the outbreak of war with France in 1756 and of the need to
maintain a constant watch on the coast, records in his journal
that he 'got new strings for my four crossbows', but one can
have nothing but admiration for the conscientious discharge
of his multifarious official and non-official duties.[1] For
example, after meetings with his fellow Enclosure Commissioners for the division of the common fields of Marske
and Redcar over a period of several months, they eventually
made an award that satisfied all parties. Or consider the
number of times as Highway Commissioner that he rode
out on to the Whitby moors to supervise the work of road-
and bridge-building, often meeting his fellow commissioners
at nine in the morning and not getting home until four or
even later.

> Went to the Highways [runs a characteristic entry in his journal]
> where we had 8 or 10 carts leading stones and gravel where we put in
> a Gantree or Bridge against Cook's ground in Yarm Lane. Where I
> attended the whole day till near 6 without meat or drink, save a little
> water. Ye work was done to my satisfaction.

And again, six weeks later,

> Went with Mr. Hide, Mr. Jackson, Docter Wain and Mr. Proddy
> to view the place where ye Bridge is about building betwixt Tockets
> and Skelton Ellers, Jno Bennison (of Kirkletham) ye mason, being ye
> Undertaker: we all stayed about an hour and Bennison was there
> when was fixed upon ye place for building it, but ye foundations was
> partly begun with 'ere we got there.

On one occasion he was called upon to settle a nine-year-old

---

[1] MSS. Journal, loc. cit. Ward was descended from the preacher at the alum works near
Whitby.

dispute between two neighbouring farmers which was 'done and a final end made' to their mutual satisfaction. On another he was asked to use his good offices on behalf of a local lad who had signed an indenture, without his parents' consent, with a Whitby shipmaster and who 'now wanted to be off'. Even matrimonial squabbles and moral delinquencies came before this bachelor for settlement:

Richard Stevenson of Brotton came to me concerning a child he had fathered upon him, ye woman of Marske parish. . . .

Kit Johnson's wife came here to inform me her husband had been very good last week and not in the least in liquor, [I] having promist them before his Master, O. Pressick, that if he and Johnson's wife gave him a good report weekly for ten week, that I would give ym 12$^d$ a week for that time, so she came today to give me an account of his behaviour ye last week, which being good, I gave her 1$s$. for the first time.

But alas, as no more payments are recorded, there would appear to have been an early relapse. Punctilious in church attendance, Ward got 'a faculty' for building a gallery in Lofthouse Church and later supervised the pew arrangements. All this and much more interspersed with journeys over the moors to his farms at Boulby to arrange about the selling of fat sheep and oxen and of his 90 stone clip of wool to 'Cousin' Pease of Darlington, and on to Staithes to inspect the extensive alum works. So his days were spent. No less honourable, if less popular, was the service of those gentlemen who each year signed the land-tax assessments and the local men who were responsible for its collection.[1]

Life for a country gentleman with a large estate would have been impossible but for the untiring devotion and efficiency of the 'agent' or steward.[2] Such was Thomas

[1] *The Note Book of Sir Walter Calverley, Bart.* (Surtees Soc. lxxvii), 51, 57, 68, 88, *passim*. Many assessments for County Durham have survived. At Gateshead there were usually four 'assessors' and four 'collectors' each year. A reassessment for the purposes of the poor-rate was carried out in 1682 to be 'confirmed' by the J.P.s at their general sessions. Vestry Book (St. Mary's Gateshead), loc. cit.

[2] See my article, 'The Eighteenth Century Estate Agent' in *Essays in British and Irish History* (ed. Cronne and Moody). Calverley, op. cit. 57–58, 104.

Sisson at Gateshead from 1716 to 1736, and his successor, Thomas Sill, whose reign lasted nearly half a century; such were also Dr. Hall and William Robson at Ravensworth, Edward White at Lumley, Mr. Burton at Streatlam, the Stonehewers at Durham, William Emm, the bishop's secretary at Auckland, and Charles Udall at Workington, to name but a few. The agent was responsible for setting farms, arranging leases, holding courts, collecting rents, keeping accounts, supervising the collieries, keeping an eye on poachers, and if the master and mistress happened to be away in town or recuperating at Scarborough or Bath, he took over control at the hall, reported regularly on 'the infantry', engaged and paid the indoor and outdoor staff, and generally assumed responsibility. Serving at a salary of £50 or £60 a year—at Ravensworth Henry Ellison got £400 but he was an exception—the estate agent provided an important element of continuity in estate management, which was highly desirable at all times but quite essential during a minority or when, as sometimes happened, overstrain and financial anxiety brought on a mental breakdown in the lord himself. They were 'the men of business', and I have likened them to the 'efficient' secretaries of the Treasury who made it possible for a duke of Newcastle or a Younger Pitt to preside over the nation's finances without disaster. As early as 1736 Major Ellison remarked that capable 'agents' were to be had more readily in the north than in the rest of the kingdom.[1] Be that as it may, recruitment was not easy for there is no sure highway to posts requiring tact, acceptance, and reliability.

Below the agent or steward, but still strictly subordinate to him, were the skilled 'viewers' of the collieries—men who knew where to sink a shaft, what seams to expect at a certain depth, the direction of the dip, the state of the roof and thill, and the probable weight of water. 'The Viewer', writes Dr. Raistrick, 'was the equivalent of, but something more than

---

[1] In 1759 the Duke of Portland appointed as his steward John Brown, formerly surveyor of the Newcastle–Carlisle road.

our present Mining Engineer.'[1] The history of coal-mining
in these parts will not be complete until account is taken of
the technical advances made in the century that separated
such famous viewers as John Barnes and John Bullock at
the beginning of the eighteenth century and Buddle a
century later. At first these men were without any kind of
professional training; they had to pit their native wit and
slowly accumulated experience against novel and difficult
problems, knowing well that on the correctness of their
decisions the lives and livelihood of scores of their fellows
depended. They deserve to rank among the real makers of
England and some of them carried to their graves the royal
blue of miners' scars. Safety in mines has always depended
more on the skilled man at the job than on safety regulations
and mines' inspectors—there were none in the eighteenth
century. Nearly all mining leases contained a clause allowing
the lessors' viewers and agents access at all times 'to ride or
descend . . . any pit', &c.

These are to satisfy my Lady Gerard or whom itt may conserne
that we John Fenwick and John Dennoldson, Viewers, viewed Rob[t]
Lawes' workeings in Mr. Lewen's Corn moore pitt and find them all
brought togeather sence oure former veiw, occationed by Irreguler
workeings of the said Lawes and his workmen, on purpose, as we
aprehend, for drowneinge my Lady's other adioyning Colliery by
stopping the Watter Course and causing the thill and Roof to come
togeather and if ever [to] be retreved will be att greate charge and cost,
and is not possable to be maid good or won but by the helpe of the
Easter and Wester Corne moore pitts wch Robert Lawes and his men
will not permit nor suffer. The present Damaege cannot be well
Computed and if a speady remedy be not found may be £500 damage,
nay perhaps may be the Totall ruine of all my Lady's other collieryes.

Early mining was not without an element of 'tooth and claw'
and only skilled and acceptable men could settle such disputes. Four years later, in 1701, this same Fenwick reported

[1] *Newcomen Soc. Trans.* xvii. 162. Cotesworth MSS. 'If you want a writer for writing
alone without viewing', wrote W. B. Bowes in 1718, 'I think ye more ignorant ye person
you pitch upon is of the people and manners thereabouts, so he writes but a good hand, he
will hold less Correspondency with Mountague's Agents.' Bowes MSS. 40747, § 162.

'that a man may walk upright along the Watter course from Messrs. Richardson and Usher's Corne moor pit' but there 'they were forced to have a pump seated for throwing their watter into the main gutter'. In 1722 Barnes, Bullock, and Weatherby stated in evidence that they had viewed Walker estate and certain adjoining lands recently acquired by the corporation of Newcastle and 'taking the main Coal Seam to be but one yard and a quarter in thickness'—in some places it was half a yard more—'and allowing half to be left for Staiths and Pillars', they computed that in one acre of ground there would be 1,743 London chaldrons of mineable coal and in the whole estate nearly two and a half million London chaldrons. This is the first quantitative estimate of probable production that I have found.

In 1747 William Newton and William Dryden made a view of three pits on Gateshead Fell: their report is valuable for the light it throws on the 'board and pillar' method of working.

We could only view and line the North and West [they reported] there the coals are regularly wrought at nine yards to the winning and no shake or thrust made thereon. Ye Boards are from 4 to 5 yards broad, headways some 2½ and some 3 yards wide; the Pillars' length from 20 to 30 yards and about four and a half yards in thickness. Ye height of ye coal beginning at the thill is, first coal 36 inches, Black band 1½ (feet), coal 14″ Band, two foul coals mixt with Brassten and coal 24″, in all 87½ inches or 7 feet 3½ inches, exclusive of eight inches or thereabouts of coarse Bandy coal left for a binding. We have examined every particular board and headway adjoining the whole mine and not drown'd, but find no outstroke nor communication between. . . .

In short, they were satisfied that no damage could be done to the above pits by Messrs. Carr and Ellison opening up 'the old water course drift in Saltwellside'. At Matthew Ridley's Tanfield colliery in 1748 the Hutton seam was being worked 'which is 29 fathom below the Brass Thill and the Brass Thill is 9 or 10 fathom below lower Busblades'. Before the close of the century every substantial colliery-owner had his own salaried 'viewer'.

## II

Next to the country gentlemen in brilliance was the legal constellation—the Ords, Aireys, Cuthberts, and Greys of Newcastle; the Spearmans, Mowbrays, Rudds, Gowlands, and Fawcetts of Durham, and 'Lawyer' Gilpin of Carlisle, to mention only the chief.[1] In the first quarter of the century these all pointed, as to a polar star, to Charles Sanderson, attorney, of the Inner Temple. Sanderson was himself a north countryman by origin and seemed to be 'cousin' to almost everybody. He had a vast practice and there were in his chambers, at one time or another, both Cotesworth's sons in turn, their elder cousin, Edward Heslop Cotesworth of the Hermitage, their future brother-in-law, Henry Ellison, besides Sir Henry Liddell and Bob Ord.[2] Sanderson transacted much business for Cotesworth and became his close friend. Indeed, during the ten years that the latter was lord of Gateshead, he was involved in no fewer than twenty-one suits; at one time he had no less than six pending in Chancery alone. Sanderson's account with him for these years amounted to nearly £2,000 and the appropriate papers, so Sanderson's clerk reported later, would fill several cartloads. Besides the legal business proper, there was his attendance at a House of Commons' Committee on the Coal Bill in 1711, on the Wear navigation in 1717, and the protracted inquiry into the 'oppressions' of the Newcastle Corporation in 1722–3.[3]

It was a great age of litigation in the north, thanks to the fundamental social changes that were taking place and the problems that accompanied the rise of modern

---

[1] 'I observe Clapham is counsel for all Papists', wrote Sir William Chaytor in 1701. In another letter he stated that 'Ned Burdett's two clerks work on Sundays, I presume making leases for Papists to secure their estates from the Crown'. Chaytor MSS.

[2] 'He grasps after more business than he can goe thro' with', wrote Henry Liddell in 1711, and again two years later, 'you know C. S. is a man so full of business that we can never see him but of a Sunday & but then for half an hour'. Rev. Leonard Shafto, Rector of Gateshead, records in his book (17 November 1705): 'Mr Ralph Sanderson in the Middle Temple did compound my First Fruits to ye Crown. . . . Gave him for his trouble £1/1/6.'

[3] Minutes of Evidence in Cotesworth MSS.

industry. Surprising as it may seem, it was not until 1693 that a firm legal ruling was given as to what constituted a colliery, and Comberbach, when he edited the *Reports* thirty years later, noted that this ruling still applied mainly to County Durham.[1] Much business came to the local attorneys in connexion with the registration of papists' estates and they were consulted on a host of points, large and small. Could a wagon-way be laid along or across the king's highway or over common land without the consent of the lord and copyholders without risk of forfeiture? Did every copyholder, as George Bowes contended, have a sort of *liberum veto* in such matters? Was a lord of the manor free to enclose common land provided he left enough for the requirements of the copyholders? All these were burning questions in the north at the time. Questions like these were invariably referred, through Sanderson, to the leading counsel of the day—Sir Joseph Jekyll, Sir John Cheshire, Fazackerley, Lutwyche, or Talbot—and even they were not always able to give an opinion offhand. If an action was feared, Sanderson was promptly instructed to retain eminent counsel, including the Attorney or Solicitor General if they were available, in major actions such as that between the Liddells and Bishop Crewe over Blackburn Fell in 1716. Altogether, thanks to the disputes about mines and way-leaves, copyholds, and enclosures, and the problems arising under the act of 1715 which required Roman Catholics to register their estates, it would be difficult to find a keener or more lucrative practical law school than that at Newcastle and Durham in the first half of the eighteenth century—a fact which is sufficiently reflected in the surprising appointment in 1756 of Robert Ord of Newcastle as Chief Baron of the Scottish Exchequer and possibly in the legal eminence of Eldon and Stowell half a century later. Ord had the experience of at least two generations of practising lawyers,

---

[1] Comberbach, *Report of Several Cases argued in the King's Bench* (1724), 201–2 (*Ambrose v. Whittingham*). 'As to Mineris, one mine may go through a whole Manor, but when there are several shafts, they are called several mines.' 'Such ejectments [pro Mineris Carbonorum] have been usually brought in Durham.'

his father and grandfather, to draw upon.[1] Lord Chancellor
Hardwicke told his son that 'the law was the most independent and advantageous profession a man could enter'. 'I
wish that my godson may take a liking to the law for that is
the truly independent profession', wrote Lord Chesterfield:
'People will only trust their property to the care of the
ablest lawyer, be he Whig or Tory, well or ill at Court.'
This was the great age of conveyancing.[2] With the steady
agglomeration of new landed estates and the piecemeal buying out of yeomen and copyholders, lawyers were kept busy
searching for titles, preparing marriage settlements, arranging transfers of tenancy or enforcing semi-moribund claims
to ancient fines and heriots. Above all, they kept a keen look-
out for worth-while investments in real estate for their
clients, the new gentry, and this often meant dangling an
anonymous bait before small freeholders whom they knew
to be in financial difficulties. Mr. Lowes, a Hexham attorney,
anxious to accommodate Mr. Ellison of Gateshead, tried for
years to induce William Arthur of West Harle, and later his
widow, to sell his freehold which Lowes knew to be heavily
mortgaged. Indeed, he was expressly commissioned from
time to time to look out for small estates. In 1752 Ellison's
lifelong friend, Dr. Baker, now domiciled in London wrote:

This day I dined with Mr. Burroughs, the Master in Chancery,
who I believe you have heard me speak of. Having not seen him
before since his return from his Estate at Gunnerton [Northumber-
land], I mentioned some circumstances of it, particularly with regard to
the draining some parts where there were springs. He told me tho' he

---

[1] John Ord prepared 'the writings' for the Calverley–Blackett marriage in 1706. Calverley, *Note Book*, 113, 133. There is a portrait of the Chief Baron at Eslington. Eldon first won his spurs in a coal case at Durham; 'perhaps they thought I had an advantage over them in having been born and bred in a coal country'. His income from fees alone in 1810 amounted to £22,730. Twiss, *Life of Eldon*, i. 127.

[2] For the attempts to prevent schoolmasters and other non-qualified 'solicitors' from draw-ng conveyances and to regulate the numbers of attorneys, see *C.J.* xxi. 266, 274, 891; xxix. 445. The move against non-qualified attorneys was started by the Yorkshire magistrates in 1728 and resulted in the important act of 1729. Ten years later 'the Society of Gentlemen Practisers in the Courts of Law and Equity', the precursor of the Law Society, was formed. Carr-Saunders and Wilson, *The Professions*, 44–45. For fuller information see my article on 'The Professions in the Eighteenth Century', *Durham University Journal* (N.S.), xiv. 46–55.

was in no hast, he had resolved to *sell it* and to buy nearer London and in Yorkshire. He has a House, at present (how good I know not) at Dewsberry near Wakefield. Inclosed is a Copy of a Paper that he left with Mr. Horsely who takes care of his Estate, tho' he is steward to Mr. Widdrington and lives at the Grange. . . .

Mr. Burroughs told me he apprehended there were betwixt 11 and 12 hundred acres, though in Mr. Horsely's paper, only 1000 sett down.

That Mr. Reed of Chipchase had formerly told him he did not doubt when the Leases were out (which was last May d[ay]) to lett the Estate for £300 p.ann. nearly.

In answer to me why he then let it for £200 only, he said he did not care to rack Tennants and to have his Rents ill paid: besides that in that case he must probably be obliged to lay out more money in building wch he did not care to do, having had thoughts for a considerable time of selling it, in which case he would expect his Advantage in the Price. For this reason he did not lett it for longer than *six years*.

I know he left the letting it intirely to Mr. Horseley, who probably might have had more offer'd but he soon agreed with a substantial man.

This man, Mr. Burroughs tells me, has since taken a partner. If there should be fewer acres than 1000 or any other outgoings of Quit Rent etc., they ought to be deducted.

I observe the Paper left with Mr. Horsely was dated 6th August. How has it happen'd it is not sold? or have there been yet any bidders? *N.B.* Mr. Horsely is not a very active man, and Mr. Burroughs having told him he was not in hast, probably it has not yet been inserted in the Newcastle papers.

Probably the Title is very good and there will be very little trouble in the purchase, Mr. Burroughs being a man of Business and I believe a fair man. I apprehend (but am not sure) there is very little part of it but with a little good management wd bear corn provided ditches were made in the higher parts of the out grounds wch wld serve to fence the ground and drain the Land.

It appears to me *at 1st view*, exceedingly worth buying. I would have the price kept private, except for your own use or a particular Friend. He was somewhat unwilling to name his price viz, £6,200. I believe there will be no haggling.

My Bro[ther][1] tells me no one knows at present how to make 3 per Cent of mony, the Stocks are so much above Par.

£6200 at 3 per cent is, I think, only £186 per ann. Mr. Burroughs,

[1] John Baker, a director of the Royal Exchange Assurance Company, *infra*.

I think, mentioned the Purchaser would make above 3 p. cent at the present rent.

I belicve Mr. Burroughs has some fancy to buy in Yorkshire and seems a man of a disposition that loves not trouble. 1000 acres (only) at 5ˢ/- is £250 p. an. I think, if the estate was mine, I should expect a far dearer summ.

When Launcelot Carr bought Mr. Wren's estate at Helmington Row for Mrs. Carr of Durham in 1733 he declared that it would yield 4½ per cent. on the capital outlay and considerably more when the common was enclosed.[1]

When land was sold not by private treaty but by order of Chancery the services of a well-placed London lawyer were quite indispensable. Cotesworth acquired the manors of Gateshead and Whickham for 'Brother Ramsay' in this way in 1711, although at the time he was careful to mask his identity behind legal anonymity. Mr. Craddock got Hartford estate in this way in 1718 and the estates of Lord Grey of Wark were sold by order of Chancery in 1732. A letter from Joshua Geekie, one-time clerk and later the successor, though hardly the equal, of Charles Sanderson, admirably illustrates the cumbersome procedure in such cases.

Inner Temple,
1 March 1753.

This day Mr. Craister shew'd for cause that I was ready to bid £300 more for Carham Estate, and to deposit £500 on which I made the Bidding and offered to make the Deposit. Mr. Ord opposed it very strenuously, and pray'd Costs in case it went back. He said opening Biddings discouraged so much all Purchasers, that there was not a single Bidder last night for the great Hilton Estate, which was then to be sold before a Master. Lord Chancellor said as to Costs, it was agreable to the Rule of the Court to give any on the day for shewing

---

[1] 'Tho' this is a time for extraordinary advantage for money. . . . I doubt not of your quick return', wrote Sanderson to Cotesworth when negotiating the purchase of Gateshead and Whickham in 1711. 'I wonder you should talk so strangely as to say there is no buying of land under 30 years' purchase when I know no body has ye face in the North to ask above 22', wrote W. B. Bowes to his mother in 1718. 'Money lowers every day so I advise you to let no purchase slip, though you pay 22 [years'] purchase for it.' Bowes MSS. 40747, § 151–8. Bowes bought two estates adjoining Kirk Lympton at this time. For the sale of Lord Grey of Wark's estate, see *Proc. Soc. of Antiquaries of Newcastle* (5th series), i, No. 1, 21–23.

Cause, but he thought as £14,200 had been already bid, that £300 only was too small a sum on which to send it back, so I bid £500 and it is referred back to the Master to approve of a better Bidder and whoever is so reported is to deposit £500 before he takes the Report from the Master.

The possibility of an astute and well-placed lawyer pulling off a really great bargain is obvious. When negotiating land purchases, lawyers kept an especial eye on burgage tenures in the small parliamentary boroughs for by judicious purchases over a number of years they might one day find themselves in a position to offer a block of such to a powerful patron and with it a controlling influence in elections. It was in this way that Lord Wharton built up his interest in Richmond (Yorks.) and the Earl of Lonsdale came to control Haslemere in Surrey.

Some idea of the cost of a legal education is afforded by Charles Sanderson's reply to an inquiry from Cotesworth in 1720 as to the probable expense of maintaining a student at the Middle Temple. He gave a figure of £178. 17s. 0d. a year, made up as follows: to eating £45. 7s. 0d., to chamber rent £22. 10s. 0d., clothes, including wigs and laundry bills, £37, books £5. Included in the estimate were 17 guineas to a music master, 9 to a dancing master, and 13 to a French master. The gross figure was nearly four times the contemporary cost of maintaining a boy at Eton and fully three times an undergraduate's college bills at Cambridge.[1] But even at that rate there appears to have been no shortage of readers. Such was the importance which the landed gentry attached to a legal training or career which, said Burke, 'has this peculiar advantage—that even a failure in it stands almost as a sort of qualification for other things'.[2] Before the middle of the century, the lawyers had organized themselves in 'the Society of Gentlemen Practisers in the Courts

---

[1] Winstanley, *Unreformed Cambridge*, says that in the eighteenth century 'law was the refuge of the indolent undergraduate' at Cambridge. It was very different in Charles Sanderson's chambers.

[2] Burke, *Correspondence* (1852 ed.), 395. He speaks of the legal profession 'which is so leading in this country'.

of Law and Equity', the first profession to organize itself as such.

## III

The martial qualities of the men of Northumberland and Durham were already well known; in these parts fighting is bred in the bone. Undoubtedly the most distinguished northern representative of the military profession in the first half of the century was General Cuthbert Ellison, lord of Hebburn from 1730 until his death at ninety-one in 1785.[1] Though the eldest son, he chose the army as a career in the early seventeen-twenties, possibly because his family was in somewhat straitened circumstances. He obtained a commission in the Dragoons, thanks to the good offices of his uncle Liddell, and was for twelve years, 1728–40, on the Irish Establishment. A connoisseur of horses—he prided himself on being the 'best mounted' in his regiment—he had frequent commissions for his younger brother at Gateshead, 'this country [Ireland] seldom or never producing horses for our purpose', he wrote. In 1728 he told his brother that he had sold his chestnut gelding for £25 'as I was apprehensive his wind was in danger from constant coughs': he had his eye on 'a Dane' which Brigadier Churchill wished to dispose of though 'he asks too much'. A year later he wrote that he had had 'very ill luck in horse flesh lately. . . . I have scarce a horse that I can ride with safety between bad eyes and bad feet.' 'At Hexham I made a swap with Geo. Delaval. I gave him a bill upon you for 15 guineas which was the difference between his mare and my gelding.' Nearly ten years later he asked his brother to look out for 'a good, genteel gelding that moves well and would become furniture, from fourteen hands and a half to fifteen'. For a cavalry officer, smartness in equine turn-out was evidently a help to rapid promotion. By 1733 Ellison was 'Captain-Major' in Sir Adolphus Oughton's regiment, getting

[1] His father, Robert Ellison, had acquired the estate in 1680. Horace Walpole's *Letters* (ed. Toynbee), vi. 153; xiii. 340.

12*s.* 1*d.* [English] a day subsistence; later in the year he was appointed, thanks to Liddell's influence, aide-de-camp to the Lord Lieutenant of Ireland. There was a saying in that country 'that a man may live here for nothing', but Ellison did not find it so. 'What I can expect from my Troop being next to nothing, the arrears being so exceedingly ill-paid and the deductions from officers that are absent so exceedingly high.' Moreover, he found it almost as expensive to live in Dublin as it was in London and so he retired 'into Country Quarters' as much as possible. At various times he was quartered at Longford, Sligo, Lough Neagh, and once in 'the mountains of Moran where I was drinking goats' whey for a month'. From time to time he came over to England 'to recruit horses for the troop', 'to pay my Court to His Majesty as I have never been presented to him since he was pleased to make me a Field Officer', to visit his colonel at Tachbrook in Warwickshire, or to recuperate at Bath. When the War of Jenkins' Ear broke out, he got his desired promotion to lieutenant-colonel, though transference to a 'line regiment' involved a loss of 5*s.* 6*d.* a day in his pay. 'As my lot has fallen in the Foot', he wrote, 'I am very glad it has happened in the Welsh Fusiliers as it has the reputation of a good Regiment and a favourite Corps of the King's'—it was George II's own regiment—and, as we shall see, the parent of the Durham Light Infantry. Lamenting the drop in his pay he added philosophically, 'people in our Trade should always look forwards and it may be an advantage to me hereafter'.

On the outbreak of war in 1739 he was drafted to England and spent the following year in various camps, first in Windsor Forest, then at Newbury—'ground bad and no good water within a mile and a half', he reported—and in winter quarters at Marlborough. He wrote in 1740,

I am so young a Lieut.-Colonel that I have neither hopes or pretensions to have a higher rank. If I was in charge of a Regiment I would make my kinsman, J. Ellison, chaplain. On the raising new Corps the Colonel seldom or never has the appointing of the chaplain, the Govt. generally nominating to that as well as the other employments.

In 1741 he expected to be drafted to Flanders, and moved into camp at Colchester where in September they were 'reviewed by General Wade, H.R.H. the Duke of Cumberland, the Duke of Marlborough, Lord Albemarle and the Secretary at War and many other people of distinction complimented us on our appearance and performance. The whole line was reviewed together in the front of the camp, the sight was as well worth seeing as anything of that kind that has been in England for a good many years, and accordingly there was 40 to 50,000 spectators.' Later in the year he was in Bruges, expecting to be sent to the *Pais des Juliers*, but after many orders and counter-orders, while the allied chiefs deliberated in Brussels, he was sent to take possession of Ostend and Nieuport, pending the arrival of more reinforcements from England. He dreaded 'being cooped up in two of the most unwholesome, nasty, places in Europe'. After a short visit to England, he went into winter quarters at Ghent, 'our numbers much reduced by a tedious campaign' and long marches to and from Germany, 'men and horses very sickly . . . and not enough room in the Hospitals here'.

All the Regiments are so weak that some extraordinary method must be taken to fill them up . . . for the ordinary method of recruiting with volunteers will not bring us the tenth of what we want. . . .

'The campaign at St. Steven's Chapple, I imagine, will be a more active one than ours was on the Rhine', he added sardonically, 'the good people of England will want to know what we are doing with their money in Germany.'

In the spring of 1743 there was an invasion scare. 'For some days past the town [London] was made to believe that part of the Brest squadron has got to Dunkirk in order to carry transports from thence . . . to make a descent on the Eastern coast.' The government accordingly concentrated ten regiments near London and demanded the 6,000 Dutch troops to which we were entitled under treaty obligations.

Before the real crisis materialized, however, Ellison had fought his most strenuous campaigns on the Rhine at Dettingen and above Mayence in an effort to relieve French pressure on the army under Prince Charles of Bavaria. Writing from near Spires in October 1743 he explained that the British troops were 'much weakened by fluxes and feavers, 'tis impossible to restrain the men from making too free with the grapes'; 'they would prefer to go into winter quarters in Flanders if they had their choice', he added, 'preferring Flanders and a Flemish reckoning to this Country and Free Quarters'. 'Though the days are warm, the nights are very cold', he continued, 'this trys a crazy constitution on the Grand Guards which are out and have no cover for twenty four hours together: mine holds out fairly well', he added, 'though there is only one Capt and 5 subalterns and myself that are now well enough to keep the field.' In the following summer he got leave to go to Bath having been more or less out of order for several months from 'numbness and weakness in his limbs which frequently swell but with little or no pain; also violent cramps, with exquisite pain, followed by stiffness or rather lameness', all which he attributed to a weak constitution, 'much application to business and little exercise'.

By the spring of 1745 he wanted to retire from the army, and 'had lately asked for his *Quietus*, but I doubt I shall not find favour enough to obtain it, His Majesty (I am told) thinks so much better of me than I deserve that he seems unwilling to let me out of his service. The door that has been open to numbers now seems to be shut in my Face. Tis neither for want of zeal nor inclination to the service that makes me desirous of leaving it, but merely for want of a better constitution than what I have. A good one is necessary to every military man that expects either to serve with convenience or reputation. At present, I am too sensible it is by no means fit to take the field with and therefore I am anxious to quit. My Lord Stair has not only given his leave but has promist to interest himself in procuring me the

King's.' Actually, though Ellison would probably not readily have admitted it, there was another reason for his anxiety to leave the army in the middle of a war. Colonel Peers of the Welsh Fusiliers had died of wounds received at Dettingen: normally the lieutenant-colonel might expect to succeed to the command, but unfortunately Ellison had lately been seconded as adjutant-general to the commander-in-chief, Lord Stair. As such, he was 'constantly employed in providing horses and other necessary supplies for the Regiment before we take the Field'. This honourable transference robbed him of promotion. By the beginning of May, however, he 'at length obtained leave to retire from the service and my commission of Lt.-Colonel is filled up by Sir John Whitefoord', a name destined to become famous in military annals. Ellison had sold out when prices were high. 'I could have wished to have made this one campaign more for my own satisfaction and pleasure', he confessed, 'but without any views of further advancement, having been long convinced that a constant and even a long application to the Service will never intitle an officer to the rank of Coll'l and command of a Regiment, unless powerfully assisted by a Parliamentary Interest.'[1] He had long been 'ashamed' of soliciting his friends, notably Sir Henry Liddell, 'ever my constant protector'. 'My present scheme is to purchase an annuity for my life with the £3,500 I am to receive for my Commission.'

Curiously enough, after he had sold his commission he remained for a time adjutant-general to Lord Stair, though this did not entitle him to any rank and 'is not attended with either pay or profit'. In this capacity he was yet to experience what was perhaps his most exciting military venture. On the 7th of December 1745, two days after the Council of War at Derby, he wrote to his brother:

I write this from Coventry where I was sent yesterday before our Army then encampt between Coleshil and this place to make out another camp in this neighbourhood, it being then supposed from the

[1] See my article, 'The Professions in the Eighteenth Century', loc. cit.

motions of the Rebels and the long marches they made that their intention was to slip between us and London, but the long and forced marches we made from Stafford to this town with our Cavalry and followed close by our Infantry rendered that design of theirs abortive. But I question much wether that ever was their real intention and am of opinion that their principal attention is to avoid coming to any action either with this or Marshal Wade's army. And I am afraid from ye badnes of the roads and weather and the shortness of the days etc. that they may avoide both armys and reach Scotland before we can possibly get up to them, tho' there is not a single man under His Royal Highness' command but what longs to engage them were it only to put an end to the fatigues we must undergo till that happens when we make not the lest doubt of giving a thorough good Account of them if they will allow us to get up to them. But their heels are good and they have early intelligence of every motion we make towards them. By the last Intelligence we had of them they were return'd towards Ashburn in Derbyshire and we are now following them that way with all the expedition possible, tho' perhaps before night we may hear that they have taken some rout which will oblige us to alter ours, as our motions must depend upon theirs. This is the only moment I have had to myself for 8 days past. . . . Though our troops are a good deal fatigued with constant marching, yet they are in good spirits.

So much for the myth of Derby!

Despite his crazy constitution, the colonel lived for another forty years. In 1747 he was returned, along with Pitt, as member of parliament for Shaftesbury in Lord Ilchester's interest.[1] In 1759 George II, remembering his old colleague in the Welsh Fusiliers, promoted him lieutenant-general. He wrote 'the Rank is of consequence to an able and healthful man but 'tis none to me who have long been fitter for an Hospital than the Field', adding that the promotion was 'a mark of approbation for past service'. The general became an expert prognosticator of the gout and an *habitué* of Bath, but this did not prevent him going with his friends on shooting parties to Norfolk and elsewhere or relaying to his northern friends, though scarcely himself enjoying, the social scandal of town.

[1] *Infra*, Ch. VI.

GENERAL CUTHBERT ELLISON

Ellison's younger brother, Robert, was also in the army, holding a commission in the marines. He was sent to Boston early in 1746 and saw service at Louisburg: he died in America in 1755. Some of his letters and papers are now in Columbia University Library in New York. He seems to have acted as regimental quartermaster; his brother wrote in March 1746,

Bob is at Boston . . . has to see to clothing being made up and raising men for the Regiment wch I am afraid will not easily or soon be done there as the price of Labour is very high in that part of the Continent and consequently a bad country to recruite in. However, the situation at Boston is infinitely more agreeable than at Louisberg.

In the following year he wrote again,

Had a letter from Bob at Louisberg. His situation is extreamly disagreable not to say a melancholly one . . . has endeavoured to get a Lieut.-Colonel to exchange with him but Louisberg is now known to be so terrible a place that no one can be prevailed on to go thither. I have also applied to the Secretary at War to put him into any Regiment in Europe in case of a vacancy.

The disagreeableness of our overseas garrisons at this time and the influence necessary to obtain a commission are both admirably reflected in the correspondence concerning Robert Carr, Henry Ellison's nephew. This young man, whose father was a friend of Lord Holdernesse, Secretary of State, was sent in 1749 to the Royal Military Academy at Caen.

My son [the father wrote from Cocken, Co. Durham] was fifteen days in reaching Caen where there are at present at the Academy 8 English Gentlemen, 3 Russians, and 2 Swiss barons. The French are now all in the country but about the beginning of next month [October] they expect 49. They all wear an uniform dress, no coat either summer or winter except when they go into town, but only a scarlet waistcoat and breetches, a large hat with a narrow Gold lace and Black Feather, and a pair of boots, by which, I suppose, the Riding Exercize is most esteemed and I find that Master is reckon'd to excell the best there is at Paris. And at any time of the day, after the Riding hours are over the Foreigners are farther allowed any of the horses to ride about the menage and the under-Riding Master attends them. Since the war each Gentleman pays 200 livres a year more and some other articles are advanced.

'May order Bob home from Caen this summer as he is big enough for the Army', he wrote in the following spring, 'for though he is not 17 till next month, his size may make him pass for a year or two older at least.'

I have consulted some military men and am advised by all means to get my son into the Guards,[1] upon account of Rank, and to avoid his being sent either to Gibraltar, Port Mahon or the West Indies and they tell me the sooner I can get him in the better and I have a friend in London now making an inquiry.

Hearing of a possible vacancy in the regiment that was stationed at Newcastle, Mr. Carr wrote to Mr. Hutton 'to use his influence with Sir Conyers D'Arcy who may probably prevail on the Earl of Ancram for a promise of the refusal of the first Ensigns'. Later the father saw Sir Conyers in London,

who told me Lord Ancram saw but one chance of a vacancy in his Regiment, except the common one of Mortality, which it could not be worth a young man's while to wait for, *viz*, a Capt acquiring a Coy of Invalids, wch he said would require a great interest. My friends advise getting my son into the Guards upon account of obtaining Rank soon and losing no time and it affords a great opportunity of cultivating an acquaintance wch may be of use to him. The next choice is the Horse or Dragoons as being generally more genteely officer'd than the Marching Regiments and as from a Cornetcy a Coy of Foot may at once be had. A gentleman whose son is now in the Army told me the most likely way to succeed was to employ a Commission Broker, his son had lost a great deal of time by applying to Colonels of Regiments and the other procured him a good Commission in a month, as he had since done for two or three of his acquaintance. The strong objections to me against a marching Regiment is the officer's being sent with a small party to some distant Quarters where

---

[1] The military aspirations of this young man merit comparison with Boswell's in 1762–3. *London Journal*, 132–4, *passim*. In each case there was no question of buying a commission. Boswell tells us that colonels of regiments got the 'profits' of the purchase price when a commission was sold.

they have nobody better to converse with than their Serjeant and the chance they stand of being sent to the West Indies or to Gibraltar or Port Mahon where they may probably stand some years, notwithstanding the late intended Regulation, for with the expence of transport, ships etc, I am told the last change cost the Government about £80,000.[1]

(Boswell was clearly on the right tack in 1762.) 'If my son's commission is arranged', wrote Carr a fortnight later, 'I will write to order him home by the first ship from Caen to Newcastle or to Hull, in case the coal trade is again stopped by a new rising of the keelmen.'

By August, however, Mr. Carr was thinking in terms of finding 'the advance money' for another quarter at Caen and it was eventually arranged for the son to stay there until the following February.

Capt East of Bland's [Regiment] dined with me yesterday and mentioned a vacancy in Hawley's (to be filled up on the King's return). As to the Foot, besides the danger of being sent abroad they are sure, if at home, to be quartered in Scotland 7 years out of 11, and a Cornet may at a step get a company of Foot. . . . Could have got a Cornetcy in either Ligonier's or the Dragoon Guards and in Hawley's Dragoons, both very old Regiments, [he wrote later] . . . if fail here I will get him into the Foot Guards.

In the end, however, 'thanks to Lord Ravensworth's friends', the young man was fixed up in Lord Ancram's regiment, then stationed at Canterbury. Powerful and persistent political influence was indispensable in such matters. 'I have not restricted him to a certain allowance at Caen', wrote the father, 'so that he might keep the best company in the place, but now it may be right to teach him decent frugality at least.' He desired Colonel Robert Ellison 'to inform me as to a proper allowance over and above his pay'. Unfortunately, any reply which the colonel may have sent from America is not forthcoming.

[1] Sir John Fortescue's statement that 'the War Office had as yet no idea of an organised system of reliefs for overseas garrisons', needs some qualification. *Johnson's England*, i. 71. It is very probable that agents of regiments acted as commission brokers. Mr. Calcraft was agent for no fewer than thirty-six regiments in 1759, practically half the army. *Army List* (1759).

After fifteen months' service the young man was drafted to Minorca. 'Colonel Rusane who used to be sea sick the whole voyage has obtained leave to go through France', wrote Mr. Carr, 'only the Major who was the commanding officer was to dine with Commodore Rogers (of the Le Mars) and all the Captains and sub-alterns mess with the Sea Lieutenants.' Mr. Carr, senior, had ideas on army reform far in advance of his time.

I had recommended to my son the Study of Fortification and Spanish during his stay at Port Mahon; the latter he had got a Master for but there was nobody to instruct him in the former. As our Marching Regiments are at home moved so frequently from one town to another, there is little time or opportunity for the officers to learn anything. During their four years' continuance at Gibraltar and Port Mahon there would be time and opportunity both of learning a great deal if there were proper masters to instruct them and some kind of establishment for that service would be so useful in the Military way that a hint of that sort convey'd properly to His Royal Highness the Duke [of Cumberland] might perhaps give occasion for one. A small established salary for a Mathematical or a drawing Master and an Engineer fixed there who should be obliged to instruct the young officers might answer the purpose at a very easy expence to the Govt, for to prevent the idle from disturbing the studious, every officer who learn'd might be required to allow the Master something each Quarter. That allowance would deter those from coming who had no inclination to learn and an officer who was really desirous of learning would not grudge to be at a little expence about it.[1]

After a year in Minorca the young subaltern had orders to hold himself in readiness to return to England 'to recruit when the next relief arrives, and as he won't beat up till October, if they have anything of a quick passage, I shall hope to have him here for a few weeks, tho' he apprehends he shall be to recruit in Devonshire or Somerset'. Mr. Carr, who had now moved to Mobberley in Cheshire, was full of praise for the subaltern's 'ideal disposition', gaiety and good spirits.

My son is gone to see the old City of Chester and to take a view of

[1] The navy had schoolmasters afloat.

a well-sized recruit wch his Serjeant has pick'd up for him to his great satisfaction.

In October, he reported that his son 'is gone to his recruiting Quarters at Shipston-upon-Stour on the edge of Gloucestershire', but he met with no success in beating up volunteers, 'the Regiment being at Minorca is, I suppose, the occasion of it, the country fellows being unwilling to go abroad'. Unfortunately, owing to Mr. Carr's serious illness, the correspondence closes soon afterwards. The young officer was apparently not at Port Mahon when the French seized it in 1756. He later saw service in Germany and came home wounded in 1760.[1]

Any list of north-country military men at this time would include the names of Generals Lambton and Clavering. The former was appointed Colonel of the 68th Foot (now the 1st Durham Light Infantry) in 1758: it had been raised two years previously as the second battalion 23rd Royal Welsh Fusiliers 'but had been chiefly recruited in Durham'. Lambton commanded it at the attack on St. Malo and when county titles were bestowed on line regiments in 1782, it was styled the 'Durham' regiment.[2] Clavering, 'the real hero' in the capture of Guadeloupe in 1759, was later the commander-in-chief in India, a member of the Council set up under North's Regulating Act and a violent critic of Warren Hastings. Nor was the senior service unrepresented, witness the names of Admirals Delaval and Collingwood, though it seems likely that the 'protections' issued in every war to seamen, keelmen, and coblemen engaged in the coal trade, kept the number of Tynesiders serving in the royal navy to small proportions.[3] In 1781 young Midshipman Richard Bates, Henry Ellison's first grandchild, was killed on the *Argus*, a forty-four gun man-of-war built on the Tyne, in an engagement with the French in the West Indies.

[1] His letters from Germany are among the Ellison Papers.

[2] *D.N.B.* (General Lambton).

[3] 'Lives are frequently lost in that disagreable and cruel service of pressing', wrote General Ellison in 1759, 'the practice however long customary is still arbitrary. 'Tis greatly to be wish't some other way cou'd be taken for speedily manning the ships of war on an Emergency.'

Nor had the navy reason to be proud of the contemporary exploits of the Cumbrian, Fletcher 'Christian of the Bounty'.[1]

## IV

As early as 1746, a clause in the Militia Bill proposed to exempt physicians, surgeons, and apothecaries from compulsory military service; the latter had been exempted from jury service and from serving as parish officers since 1717. These were already highly organized professions. 'Whereas in 1724, taking into consideration the deplorable state of my honest and laborious workmen and their families when visited with sickness or other bodily infirmities, who for want of a proper and speedy relief have languished for a longer time under their maladies than otherwise they would', so runs the preamble to Law No. 113 of the Crowley iron-works. The proprietor accordingly appointed, at his own proper charge, a surgeon skilled in physic as a works' doctor. He was to be a person of sober life and conversation 'not addicted so much to pleasure as to be withdrawn from a due attendance on his business'; he was to give daily attendance in the factory, though he was allowed to have a private practice within 10 miles of it. All workmen who had been in the firm's employ for twelve months and their families were to be attended gratis.

Yet such hath been the unparallel'd ingratitude of some persons and the villany of others that they deserve punishment more than the benefit thus intended them, first in obtaining medicines on every light occasion and, on the disorder naturally abating, not only kept them till spoilt but have also destroyed them; others have unreasonably demanded medicines for their children when they have returned indisposed from foreign service and also I have been credibly informed that such hath been the villany of some others that they have feigned themselves sick or disabled by bodily infirmities and have thereupon obtained medicines which they have afterwards disposed of to Countrey people.

Persons abusing the scheme in future were to be de-

[1] See my article in *History*, 1940.

prived of its benefits.[1] All this has a distinctly modern ring about it.

Actually, one gets the impression that all classes were over-addicted to medicines; certainly people did not hesitate to call in the doctor and they bought considerable quantities of drugs from the apothecaries. In 1714 Sir Henry Liddell, though he protested that he was 'no friend to the apothecary's shop', was full of praise for the virtues of Barbados tar as a cure for colds: 'It has recovered Mr. Freeke to a miracle in less than a fortnight.'[2] He insisted on sending his friend Cotesworth 'a small gally pot' of it; 'it is extraordinary good and the fame of it spreads apace. The Ladys make no difficulty to make use of it with success.' At the same time Calverley Bewicke sent regular consignments of medicines from London for his sister Mrs. Ramsay at Park House. Patent cures and quack remedies were regularly advertised in the newspapers though a few people were getting wise: Robert Hodson sent Cotesworth a bottle of tincture, as desired, 'but in my opinion it's no safe for anybody to take ym for you may fully perswade yourself that ye person who put in the advertisement is a man of no character'. Occasionally, a patient ventured a pointed comment on the limitations of the medical profession. 'My Complaints', wrote Colonel Ellison in 1744, 'are what the Modern Physicians term nervous, a cant word the Gentlemen of the Faculty are pleased to make use of when a distemper proves obstinate and does not yield to their medicines.' Henry Liddell was perhaps nearer the truth when he remarked, 'I am now sensible that a constitution when once broke thoroughly as mine has bin, can never be united again. The learn'd with all their skill can but make hatch'd work on't.' Miss Elizabeth Ellison, whose sister Dr. Small had been treating for four years for

[1] For the decision of certain London physicians in 1696 to set up a free dispensary for the poor, see Samuel Garth's *The Dispensary*.

[2] Rev. Thomas Freke, pastor of the Dissenting chapel in Smithfield. *Diary of Dudley Ryder* (ed. Matthews.), 164, 227–8, 276. In 1744 Bishop Berkeley wrote a treatise, *Concerning the Virtues of Tar Water*. Mullett, *Public Baths and Health in England, 16–18th Century*, 28–29.

'straitness in the gullet' wrote, 'I must own, I think, he has troubled himself just to put his fees in his pockett; he only ordered her stweed pruens which I should wonder if that could carry off her disorder'. Mr. Henry Liddell suffered much at the doctors' hands: he now lived in London and sent a unique series of confidential reports to his friend in the north.[1]

1713. May 8.

My legs are more inflammed of late and the same humour has struck into my body, stomack and head. The Doctor has tried several new experiments by altering of his prescriptions but without ye least success, all which have weaken'd me extremely, besides want of appetite and rest have perfectly confounded me. My wife would have the D[r] sent for last night after 11 to take a perfect view of my legs, who gave me a dose of opium immediately, but alas, I waked at one and never slept till 7 this morning, after which I slumbered till 9. Am in a bad condition but conceal it as much as I can from my friends to avoid trouble.

That year he went to Bath and was somewhat better.

1714. February 16.

A cold rhume wch fell upon my gums gave a sharp tast of an infirmity to wch I was all along a stranger and that was the tooth wark. . . . Took two doses of opium to sleep and at last ventured to pull a tooth. My tongue fail'd me, I had no strength in my limbs, and my eyes were contorted I could scarce see anybody; in short, it was a palsy or apoplectick fit tho' not to the degree that I had last spring. The Surgeon took 18 to 20 ounces of blood. The swelling in the mouth disorders the whole fabric.

1716. May 11.

I have had but another scurvy night. Ye feaver lies in my head and stomack and a load on my spirits. The D[r] talks of sending me to Hampstead for the air. I have bought a horse at Smithfield at the Doctor's pressing instance wch cost me £25: I dont approve of him, he trots hard and a very plain nagg.

---

[1] Ellison MSS. Dudley Ryder records in his diary the opinion 'that the business of a physician required the least time to be perfect in of any profession'. When Colonel Liddell went to Bath in 1740 he took Mr. Burgess, his apothecary, with him.

1716. May 24.

... Tis impossible I should touch answering letters this morning or indeed till 4 oc before my German Spaw be wrought quite off during wch time am neither to read nor write. They dont pass as formerly neither do I reap the like benefit. Every other afternoon at 4 my horse is at the door and I ride out till near 8; the other days I must return a visit with the old gentleman [i.e. Sir Henry Liddell]. If I did not trespass sometimes on my Doctor's Rules I should never have an opportunity of the least correspondence with any friend and when I am drove to that extremity, farewell to one of ye comforts of life. I can barely keep on foot tho' have followed pretty strictly my Doctor's prescriptions. He ordered me to take a new house wch is just on the back of where we are, called East Street. We have a little more room, a better neighbourhood but I carn't say so much of the air.

For a time, he moved to Hampstead, but was back at East Street 'in the fall'.

Early in December he wrote, 'the excessive cold has made me very uneasy in my body corporate. My blood does not circulate especially towards the extreme parts which obliges me to nibb my legs with camphyrated spirit of wine to bring me to a sense of feeling.'

1716. December 20

Alas Will, I am pester'd with an old humor wch haunts a great toe. I have been in Small's hands almost every day this fortnight. Imagine the pain I undergo by having the nail even to the very root forced out and the Surgeon's design seems to be to leave me none. Besides his cutting and slashing he never leaves me without an application of Precipitate corrosive powders which keep me warm day and night. Last night I did not sleep an hour.

On Christmas day he wrote,

The humour that is fallen on my great toe gives him [Dr. Small] many opportunitys of distressing me with his crook'd shank'd sheers and eating powders. I am not entirely confined to the house though 'tis with great pain that I can suffer an old shoe or slipper to go next door. Am obliged to take a quieting pill after two sleepless nights. This added to my old complaints makes the burthen almost insupportable.

Before the end of the year he was 'now laid up in earnest'.

1717. 1 January

. . . My bodily infirmitys flow so fast upon me that I can't expect any of ym to [abate]. Life itself under my circumstances is a daily trouble; I had like to have said a burthen. I am now confined to the house and have daily three dismal visitors—the Doctor, the Apothecary and the Surgeon.[1] The first prescribes, the second prepares and administers for my complaints of head and stomach in order to prevent that flying goutish humor settling in those parts; the third has bin near a month in hand with a hot fiery toe where there was a swelling. He has raised the nail and cut half away, root and all, . . . thought he has pursued with his corrosives so sharply that he would needs persuade me a fortnight ago that there was no further occasion wch I could not readily come into, finding still a sharp pain, but he persisting, I paid him off. In three days' time the pains increased and I sent for him again. When he opened it out, he found my suspicions too well founded and renewed his sharp applications with vigor and has every day since ply'd me oft with his crook-shanked sheers, lancet and incision knives, besides his fiery oyles and burning powders and is raising the remainder of the nail to clear it out root and branch. I can't propose getting out of his hands this month at soonest. I have gone thro' one fiery trial yet a sharper is to follow. You will excuse this ungrateful detail; it is some allay to ye affliction when one has told the story to a friend.

[1] The eighteenth century was the great age of the apothecaries. In an appeal to the House of Lords in 1703 (*Royal College of Physicians* v. *Rose*) they won a decisive victory. The Lords ruled that the function of an apothecary consisted not only in compounding and dispensing, but also in directing and ordering the remedies to be employed in the treatment of disease. 'Thenceforward the apothecaries came to form an inferior order of medical practitioners.' Carr-Saunders and Wilson, *The Professions*, 78. The controversy had occasioned Garth's *Dispensary* (1699). The acts 10 Anne, § 14, and 10 George I, § 20, gave the company of the Apothecaries the right to examine and search all drugs and compositions used in medicines and a further act of 1748 empowered it to appoint a board of examiners without whose licence no one was allowed to dispense medicines in London and within a 7-mile radius. Meanwhile in 1745 the surgeons had successfully petitioned to be constituted a separate corporation distinct from the Barber-Chirugions and thereafter their importance and status advanced rapidly. *C.J.* xxiv. 729, 738, 773. By Dr. Johnson's time the term *doctor* was practically synonymous with *physician*. See, however, Dr. Memis's of Aberdeen action for alleged defamation. Boswell, *Johnson* (ed. Croker), 428 *passim*. Also Smollett, *Humphry Clinker*, and Austen, *Emma* (Mr. Perry, the apothecary) and *Johnson's England*, ii. 273. Of eighteenth-century medical studies at Cambridge, Winstanley, *Unreformed Cambridge*, says 'the Medical School was held indeed in justified contempt'.

This, as it proved, was his last letter: before the month was out his father, the baronet, wrote despairingly:

his leg is in a worse condition than ever I knew it. .... My fears are great: I wish they be ill grounded. His Doctor and Surgeon had the same apprehensions yesterday, tho' the former seems to have better hopes tonight. Sorry to have to write so unwelcome a letter.

A month later he was dead.

Cotesworth himself went through excruciating pains from a strangury and was confined to his room for the last two years or so of his life, though he had the advice of the leading physician of the day, his cousin, Dr. Jurin. His son-in-law, Henry Ellison, was dyspeptic and was frequently in the hands of doctors in his early married life. In 1743, his friend Charles Elphinstone, who had lately consulted a leading Paris physician, Attenosia, forwarded his advice: 'Drink nothing spirituous, good wine but little, but drink cold water. Let your meat be plainly dressed, take exercise on horseback and use no drugs': to which Elphinstone added 'what he himself had found to answer better than anything else, namely cold baths'. Ellison had already adopted that regimen, which was just then becoming fashionable, when he was at Bath in 1741. The cult of sea bathing came later. In 1742 Ellison visited Spa in the Netherlands where he was attended by Dr. Alexander Hay who for over twenty years sent regular consignments of Spa water, in flasks, to Gateshead Park together with powdered magnesia—'only good against heart burning and people that is troubled with too much sowerness in their stomacks'. In course of time Dr. Hay came to supply the Greys of Howick and other northern families with Spa water. The consignments sent to Ellison cost over £20 a time. In return Dr. Hay desired the favour of some 'Scotch' snuff and bottles of 'Durham mustard', a commodity for which Durham was famed on the Continent.

Happily, it was the medical care of children rather than of adults on which attention was focused. Infant mortality and the ravages of smallpox were all too familiar. 'Sorry to hear smallpox reigns so much with you', wrote Bowes in

1718, 'but ye more you fly from them ye sooner my sisters will catch ym.' Inoculation was far more common in the second quarter of the century than is generally supposed, the governing factors being the question of expense and the courage of parents. Prince Frederick and the royal children were inoculated as early as 1723, Charles Maitland, the surgeon in attendance, receiving a special allowance of £1,000 out of Privy Purse monies.[1] The only child of Sir Henry Liddell, the future Duchess of Grafton, was done in 1742 when she was about five and the youngest of the Ellison girls five years later, though this involved a special journey to London. On these occasions, bachelor uncles and spinster aunts were profuse in attention and advice. 'Miss Liddell, poor little soul, is to be inoculated', wrote Miss Jenny Ellison; 'there was nothing appear'd in the skin last night but she complained of a pain under her arms which the learned say is a sure Simtom that the small pox had took place.' Her brother, the colonel, learning that Henry's children had had the smallpox wrote, 'if they are not disfigured with it 'tis a happiness to you and them that they have had the distemper'; indeed, there were some kinds of smallpox that were called 'good'. In 1746 'Ralphy', the youngest of the Carr children at Cocken, had it so badly that Mr. Reede, who was called in, 'wanted further advice and got Dr. Bedford over in an hour who gave him a warm and bracing powder and laid a blister on his leg wch though he got very little rest in the night has had a good effect. The Dr. now thinks him much better.' At Gisborough in 1754, when Jenner was a mere boy, Ralph Ward gave Dr. Charles Bisket 15s. 'for inoculating a poor child'.[2] Practice in the matter seems to have varied with families and districts. In

[1] Add. MSS. 40843. Dr. Thomas Rentone received £5,000 from this fund 'for making known his art, skill and mistery in cutting ruptures' and Dr. James Douglas £500 'for his performance and publishing his anatomical observations'. Douglas became the Queen's Physician and is mentioned in Pope's *Dunciad*

> There all the learned shall at the labour stand
> And Douglas lend his soft obstetric hand.

It was another Douglas who treated Boswell for gonorrhoea in 1762. *London Journal*, passim.

[2] Journal, op. cit.

1781 Henry Ellison II wrote from Gateshead, 'You will hardly credit that in this populous country Ingham has in vain for almost an entire month, searched for a patient in the small pox from whom he might procure matter to inoculate his own, our little boy and theirs.' Nine years later, when his two sons were at a fashionable 'prep' school near High Wycombe, the headmaster, Mr. Lloyd, was surprised that he should want to have them inoculated so young. At Eton there was a recognized school doctor, Dr. Hayes of Windsor, before the middle of the century. We know this because he attended young 'Bob' Ellison in a critical illness in 1750. Here is the report he sent to the boy's uncle, the colonel, in London, which was duly forwarded to Gateshead Park.

ETON
Monday Morning.
past 10 o'Clock.

Sir,

Yesterday between twelve and one I gave the first dose of Dr. James's Powder,[1] which in some time after, put Him into a gentle Sweat, which held but a little while; about six o'clock it vomited Him once. In the afternoon he slept a good deal. Finding no other operation, I gave the other half between seven and eight in the Evening, that sweated Him more than the first. He was sick once or twice but did not vomit, since which it has purged Him three times which is the effect I desired. He complains but little of his side this morning, His Spirits are better, and he is visibly stronger, being able to turn Himself in His bed which he could not do all day yesterday or the evening before. He has little or no Heat, and though the Urine continues almost the same, yet I think Him in the main better. I shall repeat the Powder occasionally as the present appearances encourage me to do it. Mrs. Young [the dame] will write by the Post and I hope every account will be more and more agreeable.

I am, Sir, Yr most obliged
Humble Servᵗ.
C. Hayes.

[1] Dr. James's celebrated fever powder was a specific for both man and beast in the eighteenth century. Dr. Johnson had collaborated with him in writing his medical dictionary. 'I knew a Physician', wrote Johnson, 'who for twenty years was not sober', though he was careful to conceal the fact from his patients. He got Johnson and Garrick to vindicate him from a charge of drunkenness, *Johnson's England* (ed. A. S. Turberville), ii. 276.

Later on the same day, Dr. Hayes reported again, this time to the boy's aunt:

Monday Night
past 8 o'clock.

Madam,

I can with Pleasure acquaint you that the third dose of the Powder, which was given this day at half an hour after 12 has done as I expected viz, laid him into a sweet Sleep attended with a kind, universal sweat, which lasted between four and five hours. He has taken proper nourishment and is now asleep. I hope it will act by Stool before morning and that our next account will be still more satisfactory.

When the colonel consulted his medical friends in town about getting further advice, he was assured that Dr. Hayes was as good as any of the London doctors and had a great practice in Windsor.

The social status of doctors, though not of surgeons, was probably higher than it is today.[1] They were frequently friends of the gentry and guests in their homes. Cotesworth ordered that Dr. Brady should have the 'sparrow grass' (asparagus) and first strawberries if he were still at Park House. Mr. Carr reported that Lady Stanley of Alderley 'has a very careful Physician who constantly lodges in the House and sees her four or five times a day'. Dr. Hollins was a friend of the Ellison family at Rathbone Place: Drs. Baker, Cooper, and Lowther were close personal friends of Henry Ellison, occasionally borrowing his coach to visit their country patients, and advising him on visits to Bath and Scarborough. In 1741 Dr. Lowther advised him to consult with London doctors 'whether the waters at Aix or Spa or Pyrmont would be of any use to you or any of those in France'.

Recruitment to the profession was still by the time-

---

1 The basic pay of army surgeons at garrisons in this country was £45. 12s. 6d. a year. *Army Lists, passim.* Naval surgeons were warrant, not commissioned, officers at £5 per month, and they had to supply their own instruments and dressings. During the Austrian Succession War those who were captured by the enemy were treated as ratings. Sir D'Arcy Power in *Johnson's England,* ii. 267. The social status of surgeons rose rapidly after their separation from the Barbers' Company in 1745.

honoured practice of apprenticeship, as is clear from the following letter from William Keenlyside, Jun^r, to Henry Ellison.

12th January 1760.

There being a Vacancy for a Surgeon in the Infirmary at Newcastle by the resignation of my late master Mr. Hallowell, I'm advised by my friends to offer myself to you, Sir, and the rest of the Governors, for his successor and to lay before you, Gentlemen, the whole of my Education in business as follows: In the last seven months of my apprenticeship by the leave and indulgence of my Master, I went through a course of Anatomy and Surgery with Dr. Monro at Edinburgh and at my return hither (when the Infirmary was just opened) at the desire of my Master and for farther improvement, I returned to his Shop and continued with him and Mr. Lambert as their principal Dresser in the Infirmary for about sixteen months and immediately afterwards went to London for farther instruction and attended three courses of Anatomy and Surgery with Dr. Hunter and continued there a year and a half, during all which time, I also attended St. Thomas' Hospital and afterwards in January 1754, I returned hither and was immediately upon the recommendation of the Physicians and Surgeons chosen Apothecary to the Infirmary in which capacity I constantly attended the Surgeons in all their operations etc. and am not a little happy in the lately public approbation my services therein met with and hope from what is said above, I may venture to add that no one can offer to succeed Mr. Hallowell with more knowledge of his approved method and Practice in business than myself and shall only beg leave farther to add that if I am thought worthy by you, Sir, and your friends to succeed him as I am by Mr. Hollowell himself (as will appear by his voting for me and more his want of health and Delicacy to the Public will not allow him to do) the Honour of your Vote and Interest will lay the greatest obligation on Sir,

Your most obedient humble servant,
(Signed).

P.S. I am afraid time will not allow me to wait on you personally, therefore beg leave to refer you to the public Papers for the Day of Election.[1]

He was not the only applicant in the field; four days

[1] Ellison MSS. Bishop Butler laid the foundation stone of the infirmary in September 1751.

earlier Henry Gibson also addressed a letter to Mr. Ellison, 'Mr. Hollowell, one of the surgeons in the Infirmary being so ill that his life is despaired of and Mr. Keenlyside, having already begun to push his interest to succeed him in that appointment, I think it not, therefore, improper, Sir, to acquaint you with my Intention to offer myself as a candidate'. We may be sure that Ellison, who was one of the governors, would appoint the best man available. The north could already boast some famous surgeons, Richard Lambert and Philip Jefferson, both of Hexham, and more were to follow: the midwives and male *accoucheurs* have mostly perished in anonymity.[1]

## V

By the middle of the century it was becoming difficult to find careers for the younger sons of gentle families. In the summer of 1754, while his second son Robert 'now turned of sixteen' was still at Eton, Ellison consulted various business friends about the prospects of placing him as apprentice to a merchant or banker. 'We were advised that London was the best scene for business.' Lord Ravensworth sounded Mr. Mellish, a prominent civil servant in the revenue branch[2] and Ellison wrote to his friend Dr. James Baker who passed on the inquiry to his brother, Mr. John Baker, a director of the Royal Exchange Assurance Company, who replied as follows:

Sir,

I am favoured with yours of the 11th inst. and since my last have made all the inquiry I could amongst the Merchants to know if any are willing to take an apprentice and have desired them to inquire of their Acquaintance. The most eligible are determined never to take any. There is a gentleman, Mr. John Peter Blaquire, of French extraction, who trades to Holland and Italy and has good Commission; he keeps a very regular, sober, family and will take great care of your son; but he asks much more money than I think any Merchant

---

[1] *Northumberland Documents*, 21–22, 49. *Calverley Note Book*, 118, 134.

[2] William Mellish, Receiver General of Customs, 'a good employment', remarked Henry Fox. The salary was £1,000. Add. MSS. 40758, § 276.

deserves which is Seven Hundred Guineas and will not abate of that. I take him to be a very Secure man and is director with me at the Royall Exchange Assurance Office. I have already given you my Sentiments of Merchants and need say no more. The difficulty lies when they are out of their times, how they are to begin in the world: however, this would not be an impracticable thing, if they are sober and dilligent, tho' will be attended with some difficulty. I will still make further inquiry, but as I am so much out of town, cannot do it so well as in Winter, when I am constantly here. You will be pleased to consider of it and use your own Discretion in this affair. It would give me great pleasure to help your son well out into the world and no endeavour shall be wanting in . . .

In an earlier letter, originally intended for his brother, Mr. Baker explained 'that the best of them [the merchants] are resolved against taking any [apprentices], they have proved so bad of late and instead of minding their business have nothing but pleasure in their heads and being fine Gentlemen and I think a merchant is the last thing I would propose to Mr. Ellison. Trade to all parts of ye world is at so low an ebb, they ask £500 and £1,000 [premium] and when a young fellow is out of his time, he is as much to seek what to do or how to begin busyness as when he first came. He may learn Book keeping etc. but what is that to help bring him into the world.'

The letter continued,

*The Country Gentlemen have a much better opinion of Merchants than we have of ourselves* and half of them that take apprentices do it for the sake of the money and care not what becomes of them when they have served out their time and give them such liberty as if they designed they should not come to anything. If a young man were to go to Lisbon tho', by the by, the trade there is so bad, that I have intirely quitted it, yet I believe in a little time it will be better: there a young man may begin busyness without any assistance from his master and there are but few Merchants there of any note that will have apprentices, Auriol, Bristow and others have all refused.—Had I a son of my own, I should be very much puzled how to dispose of him. I should first think of sending him abroad, where he would be more out of harm's way than here; this place is grown so very bad and vitious, that it would be very difficult for a young man to steer clear. However I will do all I can to find out a proper person, but first I sh^d know what money Mr. Ellison would be willing to give, as any merchant of credit demands a large sum [—]¹ has taken several apprentices only for the view of the money, for which he ought to be ashamed for none that have ever been with him have ever engaged in busyness for themselves not knowing how, his master correspondents w^d not leave him to serve them and they have no knowledge of any one abroad, how or what are they then to do.

I should think if he were to go a factor in the East India Company Service there is the most probability of success, but then there is one very disagreable thing attends it which is he being absent from his friends for 20 years or more which few parents care to come into.

A very good wholesale busyness in town I should think is much better than to put a son to a merchant. When he comes out of his time, he is personally acquainted with all his Master's customers and must have a share of them, if he takes care to make himself well acquainted with them. The Setting a young fellow out into the World well at first, all his future happyness depends on it and 'tis an affair that ought to be well considered. I cannot express myself so much by writing as I could were I to converse with Mr. Ellison. You may make my compliments to him and assure him that no time shall be lost in making inquiry and will write to him as soon as I can find anything out that I think will be proper. . . . I find Mr. Ellison's son is now at Eton. He cannot come from thence into a Merchants' Compting house without being some months at School in London to learn to write and also Accounts.

P.S. You may assure yourself I will do what I can in this affair to serve you but I cannot answer for success.

That London merchants were asking premiums of £500 and upwards for apprentices is clear from the records of the Stamp Office. For exactly a century such premiums were subject to a special stamp duty and the returns giving the names and trade of the master and apprentice and the amount of premium paid have survived. W. B. Bowes told his mother in 1718 that his younger brother 'cant be put out to a merchant under a £1,000':² this presumably had reference to

---

¹ Manuscript mutilated.     ² Bowes MSS. 40747, § 153.

London, for the highest premiums recorded for the pro-
vinces at that date were £130 paid to Liverpool and Yorkshire merchants. By the end of the century, however,
premiums of £1,000 and upwards were being asked by
London merchants—I have found one instance of £1,260—
and amounts of £700–800 were commonly demanded by
lawyers and surgeons, which effectively restricted entry to
the sons of the gentry, clergy, and rich merchants.

Meanwhile, Mr. Ellison had consulted Mr. Peareth of
Usworth, who three years earlier had apprenticed his son to
a London banker, Mr. Godhard Hagen of Fenchurch
Street.[1]

Everybody finds it a difficult matter to get a young man put out well
[Peareth replied]; my son is bound for six years and I gave £600 and
paid the duty which made it guineas . . . as I remember, £200 to be
returned in case of my son's death within 2 years. He is now in his
third year and the youngest apprentice; there's an elder apprentice and
book-keeper in the Counting House and the father and son both do a
great deal of business.

P.S. The son is a batchelor and lives in Fenchurch St. where the
business is done, is much at hours and very regular.

In due course Peareth mentioned the matter of taking
another apprentice to Mr. Hagen, and the question of
premium was discussed:

They [the Hagens] said several merchants had considerable greater
sums than they had with my son but as they expected a diligent
attendance on business, if other things were agreable, would take your
son on the same terms as mine. . . . They suppose as your son is bred
at Eton and may not have learned accounts and book-keeping, that
may require a few months to give him knowledge that way. My son
found it necessary to learn the German language but that he got after
he was with his master.

In September 1755 an agreement was reached; the term
was to be for five or six years at Mr. Ellison's discretion;
he was to pay a premium of £600 plus the stamp duty, to
give bond in £1,000 for his son's good behaviour, i.e. to

[1] For the Peareth pedigree, see Surtees, *History of Durham*, ii. 44–45.

make satisfaction for embezzling or other misdemeanours, to find his son in clothing, washing, and other necessaries, and to pay any physician's bills; 'we to find him convenient lodging and diet at our own table and to inform him of the occurrences in our trade with such other good advices for his further improvement'. Since the boy was still at Eton it would be necessary to discover, at an interview, 'what advancement he has made in writing and arithmetic' and further instruction in these subjects may be necessary 'as such are not much regarded at Eton'. 'Being placed at one of the Academys here for about three months may be of service', Hagen added. At the end of the year he wrote that 'Robert's time in the morning is employed at Mr. Futter's academy and afterwards in our Counting House'. 'He seems very willing to be instructed in which suitable directions shall not be wanting; in a few days he will make a beginning with a German master and afterwards he may continue to learn the French language: his inclinations seem sober and of an obliging temper, hoping the continuance thereof for his own benefit and the satisfaction of his parents.' We know that the apprentice started to learn Italian for he wrote that 'the time and money [4 guineas] were very ill spent; he [the master] was a person very incapable of what he promised of teaching a language though recommended by the French master'. Accordingly, another tutor was engaged, recommended by Mr. Hagen, 'his common fee is 2 guineas entrance and 2 guineas for 12 sessions; he comes thrice a week and stays a full hour'. The apprentice's washing and barber's bills were not inconsiderable—'a year's shaving 30s/-'; 'I only wear my Bag Wig on particular occasions', he wrote. The young banker was now launched on a career.[1]

A year before the term was due to expire, the father wrote to inquire about the possibility of the Hagens admitting the son into the partnership. At first the elder Hagen refused point blank, alleging that the articles of partnership with

---

[1] For the rapid growth in the number of banks in the second half of the eighteenth century, see Clapham, *History of the Bank of England*, ii. 1–2.

his own son 'did not admit of a third partner during their joint lives', though he offered to assist in placing the young man with another firm. When the apprentice came out of his time he began to trade on the stock market on his own account, making some shrewd purchases on a tricky market;[1] but, in August 1763, 'a thing of infinitely better prospect just then offered'—Hagen offered him a quarter share in his business, Ellison to pay £5,000 into the partnership. Terms were quickly arranged which included a clause to allow of admitting a certain Mr. Horne, 'now in the Counting House', into the partnership on a like basis in the future. 'The truth is', wrote young Ellison, 'his business is grown too great for him.' 'The annual profits of the House may very fairly be calculated at £4,000; last year they amounted to £12,000 but that was a matter of chance proceeding from a well-timed speculation', he wrote. Surprisingly enough, young Ellison was to have 'the chief direction of the business' and the firm was to be styled Ellison, Wolpman & Coy. The reason for this was not at first apparent.

There have been many terrible bankruptcies in Amsterdam and Hamburg which have threatened little less than Ruin to some of the best houses here [wrote Ellison to his father] and I had many apprehensions for Mr. Hagen who might have been a great sufferer, but things have happily turned out much better than was at first expected and he will escape free from us.

Affairs at Hamburg and Amsterdam [he wrote a month later] begin to put on a better appearance but the mischief, I fear, is not yet ended, at least we shall always have something to dread as long as credit continues in its present stagnation.

We can perhaps begin to suspect the elder Hagen's motives. Later, however, the name of the firm was changed to Hagen, Ellison & Co, 'as some customers construed his intention to take out all his money'.

The partnership lasted for rather less than three years: it was terminated by Ellison himself in April 1766. In a

[1] Government 3 per cent. stock fluctuated violently at the close of the Seven Years War. In 1760 it stood at 80, fell to 64 in 1762, and jumped to 90 in the following year. Add. MSS. 34417, § 18.

long and illuminating letter to his father the young man gave the reasons for his decision. He explained the nature of the Hagen business, a kind of credit shuttlecock between Exeter, London, and Amsterdam, which, in Ellison's considered judgement, was too tenuous and risky but which Mr. Hagen was unwilling to restrict or abandon.

(1) The merchants of Exeter, in general, not having money enough of their own to carry on their trade borrow of those in London . . . we have at present five of these correspondents.[1]

(2) The nature of our transactions by which we have the use of this sum is as follows; we draw every Post day upon Holland at two months' date; at the expiration of that time we make a remittance for the discharge of the first Draft, the next Post day another for that of the second etc. . . . but drawing always at the same time as much as we remit, we constantly have the use of the money drawn in the course of the first two months.

(3) The yearly interest of money raised by these means is commonly 10 per cent. to 12 per cent. as appears by accounts . . . but cannot be particularly ascertained on account of the fluctuation of Exchange.

(4) The sum paid was £7000 to £8000, that accepted £10,000 to £12,000.

(5) We may at any time be called upon to pay off that debt in the course of 2 months by being obliged to remit for the payment of Bills falling due, without being permitted to pass other drafts in the manner explained above.

'We had no means of making the advances required by the Exeter people', he continued, 'in which four fifths of our capital is constantly engaged.' He put 'the present yearly circulation passing through our hands at about £40,000'. If either end of the Exeter–Amsterdam business failed— and he already had misgivings—the firm would be 'engulphed'. 'I objected to it on point of security, but Mr. Hagen looked upon it as some of the best business that we had and intended to carry it on.' In brief, Ellison complained

[1] The names of two are known, Colombies and Passarant.

of his senior partner's 'fondness for transactions of Exchange which were constantly undermining our credit and our fortune'. And Hagen had already failed once. In view of the serious collapse of Amsterdam banking houses five years later, the young man's misgivings were probably justified.[1]

In any case, his action earned the approval of his uncle, the general, 'as right and prudent and a proof of his good understanding and attention to business'. He was immediately taken as a partner by another banker, Mr. Walpole. 'That gentleman's connections are great and the fortune he has acquired by commerce is supposed to be very considerable', wrote the general; 'his offering to engage with Bob convinces me of the correctness of the latter's transactions with Hagen and that the men of business at the other end of the town think as well of your son as his friends here do of him'. The new partnership lasted until the disasters of the American War when the French captured Tobago and other islands in the West Indies where Mr. Walpole's interests were heavily engaged. In 1781, while important law cases were pending in Paris in which his chief was involved, Ellison retired to Switzerland—a courageous decision which earned the admiration of his friends who discovered that he was no mean poet.[2] He died in 1783.

The flimsy basis of Hagen's banking business should be compared with the modest and unpretentious beginnings of the first Newcastle bank in 1756, a year after Ellison had begun his apprenticeship. Robert Bell, John Cookson, Ralph Carr, and Joseph Airey subscribed equally to a joint stock of £2,000 'to be jointly concerned in the business or employment of Bankers and Dealers in Exchange at the house in Pilgrim Street where Joseph Airey now lives commonly called the Bank'.[3] The partnership in the first instance was to last for ten years. Mr. Maberly Philips considered that this, 'The Old Bank', was the first successful

[1] e.g. the House of Clifford. Wilson, *Anglo-Dutch Commerce and Finance in the Eighteenth Century*, 97 seq. Fortescue, *Correspondence of George III*, ii. 362, 436.

[2] His Swiss Journal and some of his letters are in Columbia University Library, New York. [3] Original deed of partnership in Cookson MSS.

provincial bank in England.[1] The beginnings of another Newcastle bank, Burdon & Surtees, were even less auspicious for in its first year, 1772, it had to weather one of the most serious financial crises of the century. But the country gentlemen and local merchants rallied nobly to its support and both banks survived.[2] Thus, banking, like law, medicine, and the fighting services came to offer an outlet for the younger sons of northern gentry. Undoubtedly, the high traditions in these professions derive from eighteenth-century standards of gentility: the welfare state is at present living on this accumulated capital.

Nothing has been said about the two largest professions—the civil service and the church. Admittance to both of these was governed by patronage, a subject that will be discussed in later chapters; but it may be remarked here, as an interesting comment on the social scene, that the pressure on 'places' was greater in the north than in other parts of the country.

[1] *Arch. Ael.* (N.s.), xvi. 452.
[2] A few letters in the Baker–Baker MSS (Durham) throw light on the banking activities of the Quaker family of Backhouse. Wm. Surtees was receiver of land-tax for Durham and Northumberland. T.B.P. (1731), 62.

# CHAPTER IV

# Farming

And shall perform all such orders as the said Dean
and Chapter . . . shall set down concerning and
touching good neighbourhood.

*(A clause in all dean and chapter of Durham farming
leases)*

THE great Puritan lawyer, Serjeant Maynard, counsel for
the defence in an important case *Sir Arthur Haselrigg,
Bt.* v. *Robert Staplyton* (1658) concerning a forfeited estate,
formerly Collingwood's, in dispute in Whittingham, Northumberland, made these notes on his brief:[1] 'That it is an
ancient fine and of lands in a County farre remote where
persons in those days (*temp.* Henry VIII) were not well
skilled to give instructions to draw up Fines and being then
of small value because of the spoyles and wasts made by the
incursions of the Scots, lying within 8 or 9 miles of Scotland
. . . and much barren land there was which in those tymes
might not be thought valuable to be putt in with other
Lands. . . .' The plea that lands in that remote region might
not have been always carefully surveyed or particularly
described in sixteenth-century deeds was successful.[2] In
1693 a not dissimilar ruling was given in respect of a colliery in County Durham and according to Mr. Carr, a
gentleman lawyer, Lord Chief Justice Holt noted that it
was the practice in that county 'to make their declaration in
that general way, as in mountain land in Ireland'.[3] In fine,
the law relating to land tenure might be interpreted less

---

[1] Ravensworth MSS. There had been frequent disputes about this property to which the
Haselriggs laid claim in the sixteenth and early seventeenth centuries. In 1637–8 an information was laid in Star Chamber but the case was never heard. An historical résumé is set out
in Maynard's brief. A list of Sir Arthur Haselrigg's and the Vanes's extensive speculations in
fee-farms in County Durham during the Civil War has survived in a land-tax assessment
book.

[2] The Collingwoods recovered the estate at the Restoration, only to forfeit it again in the
Fifteen. The Liddells bought it for £21,131 in 1718 and it has remained in their hands ever
since.          [3] Comberbach, *Reports*, 201–2.

rigidly in the north than elsewhere and for good reason. In the middle of the eighteenth century it was confidently asserted that there were lands in upper Tynedale that had never been 'acred', and as late as 1786 odd parcels of land in the East Riding of Yorkshire, about Staithes, were still reckoned in ox-gangs.[1] Here, then, at the outset of any study of agrarian conditions we have the possibility of important local variants in the conditions attaching to land tenure.

Nor was the lack of precise and adequate surveys the only difficulty. In 1704 William Ramsay exhibited a bill in chancery against one John Hornsby touching encroachments on certain lands in the manor of Plenmeller in which he pointed out that his father, the Newcastle goldsmith, being seized of the said manor 'did, in or about 1670, convey part of the waste called Ramsay Rigg' to the said Hornsby with leave to enclose the same with a wall or other fence but to be 'noe way severed from the said manor'; that Hornsby had subsequently 'encroached on the said waste . . . and enclosed some considerable part thereof', over and above the purchased land, with a wall which he had contrived to build 'when your orator's said father was at a great distance, thirty or more miles from Ramsay Rigg, minding his trade of goldsmith in the town of Newcastle and your orator was then in remote parts beyond the seas'.[2] On being challenged in 1673, Hornsby protested that he had enclosed no more than he had actually purchased 'containing by estimation fourteen acres' and an accommodation was then reached. 'But the said Hornsby still takeing advantage of the distance your said orator lived from Ramsay Rigg . . . did continue making further encroachments and plowed up several parcels thereof' and joined them to his own freehold. At last in 1689 the elder Ramsay, finding how he was dealt with, took legal action and obtained a verdict requiring the defendant to pull down all hedges, walls, &c., and to throw open all such intacks as he had made before 1687. Baffled but not dismayed, the defendant Hornsby, 'by combining

[1] Baker–Baker MSS. (Durham).    [2] Cotesworth MSS.

and confederating' with one Thomas Bindloe of York and other persons, known and unknown, had proceeded, it was alleged, to overstock the common, 'to deny suit and service to the manor court', and by collusive concealment of cattle and stock had so far prevented the plaintiff from obtaining redress. Disputes of this sort, including boundary disputes between great lords, were frequent in the north throughout the century.[1] 'The manors of Bellister and Hartleyburn have suffered greatly', wrote the steward in 1753, 'from the encroachments made from the Commons especially from Hartleyburn Common, where not only several tenants have inclosed . . . but the tenants of neighbouring Lords, viz. Lord Carlisle and Mr. Algood, are claiming parts of this common and indeavouring to establish a right thereto by turning cattle thereon and enjoying the same.'[2]

Surreptitious encroachment and 'concealment' of lands on a grand scale, it transpired, had taken place at Shipcote, adjoining Gateshead, in the course of the seventeenth century, as Cotesworth discovered when he acquired these lands and certain of the deeds in 1718. Starting from a nucleus of freehold land, known as St. Edmund's—'the mansion house [there] being always made use of for a mass house and for a Preist to reside in'—a certain William Riddell, kinsman of a former bailiff of Gateshead, had proceeded surreptitiously to appropriate some of the adjoining copyhold lands. 'And the better to conceal the same from appearing to be copyhold', wrote Cotesworth, 'altered some of the names thereof particularly that of Whitehill Close to Whitefield and two other closes called Swangpool and Punderhill and that of Shipcoate close to North Awards, though the house called Shipcote house in the surrenders, and which is called by the same name at this day stands in the corner of the field called Shipcoat Close, but changed by Riddell to North Awards.' Moreover, the said Riddell had

---

[1] e.g. lands in the manor of Glasonby in dispute between the Musgraves and the Duke of Somerset. The former claimed it 'by several good and perfect boundaries, one rode in 1506'. Carlisle MSS. (Castle Howard) xiii.  [2] Ellison MSS.

'changed the names of some of the freehold closes from their real names to others, but in the doing thereof hath left one . . . without a name'. Eventually, he had sold all the lands, both copyhold and freehold, to Sir Mark Milbank, reserving to himself the mining rights and had proceeded to work the coals under the copyhold lands and to lay pit heaps on them without paying any rent or compensation either to the bishop or his lessee. He had been able to get away with this deceit, Cotesworth alleged, because the lord of the manor, Sir Gilbert Gerard, 'lived mostly in the south part of England and at a great distance'.[1] If these things were done in the open what might not be done in the dark places below ground?

The solution to difficulties of this kind lay in more scientific surveying and 'viewing' and, as we have seen, there were noted northern practitioners of these arts before the close of the seventeenth century. The outlines and acreage of the several fields at Gateshead may still be dimly discerned in T. Winship's 'survey and map' of 1689.[2] Joseph Dickenson's survey and map of Ravensworth (1712) and William Cuthbertson's of Farnacres and Whickham (1715) are works of art and there is a later one of Kibblesworth.[3] John Warner of Team's Bridge who was 'brought up to the Mathematics', made an exact survey of three farms at Byker in 1720. It so happens that all these concern farm lands in close proximity to mining and intensive urbanization and where, in consequence, farming was likely to be most progressive. Such surveys form an indispensable basis for any detailed study of farming and until more of them are found and analysed, any treatment of the subject must, of necessity, be summary and partial. But before turning to examine the evidence in these north Durham surveys, we must consider another matter of more general moment.

Throughout the northern counties there was an ancient,

[1] Cotesworth pointed out that he had been denied a perusal of certain of the deeds by the Riddells.

[2] Cotesworth MSS.

[3] Ravensworth MSS. The maps are in the Estate Office in Newcastle.

though variable, custom known as 'tenant right'.[1] In origin this derived from the eminent desirability of giving effective security to tenants who might at any time be called upon to defend the Border against the Scots. In the case of the tenants of the dean and chapter of Durham it had come to mean, by the middle of Elizabeth's reign, the payment of no more than the ancient rents and fines with an undoubted right of succession first of the widow and then of the eldest son and as such it was confirmed by order of the Council at York in 1577.[2] In 1639, two tenants, George Grey and Anthony Smith on behalf of themselves and others petitioned the king and council against alleged violations of the custom by the dean and chapter but they received short shrift from the hands of the Court of Star Chamber dominated by Archbishop Laud and were only released from custody when parliament met in 1640.[3] After the Restoration there were more complaints of infringement of the custom and although the dean and chapter obtained a verdict in their favour yet, according to Spearman, both the king and an old prebend, Dr. Grey, enjoined them not to oppress their tenants.[4] It can be proved beyond all doubt that the dean and chapter rents remained absolutely stationary for more than a century after the Restoration.[5] The question of 'fines' taken on renewal of leases, however, is a very different story, as we shall see. It is clear, moreover, that tenant right meant

---

[1] See Appendix B.

[2] Hunter MSS. xxii, § 5. Tough, *The Last Years of a Frontier*, 57–58 states: 'there was no lease in Northumberland but with provision to find horse & armour for each tenement, to be held by an able man.' 'Some tenants, for example those in Tynedale, claimed to hold their lands " by title of tenant right".' 'They were bound to serve . . . but might sell all or part of their holdings & could not be evicted if unfurnished.'

[3] Allan MSS. vii. 231, 234. The 1577 Council Order applied only to 'tenants at will or who claim to be holden or occupied by Tenant Right' and not to leaseholders for terms of years. *V.C.H. Durham*, ii. 230–1.

[4] *Enquiry*, 115–18. Spearman adds that 'during the Civil War and Interregnum many of the tenants were forced to purchase the inheritance of their estates from that arbitrary government'. On the other hand, Bishop Cosin stated in 1665 that 'the present tenant [of the manor of Sadberge] taking advantage of the late Rebellion, pretended to possess it as a copyhold', whereupon the bishop made a new lease 'for the trial whereof and for reducing it to a leasehold'. The chapter, however, refused to confirm it. *Infra*. Ch. VII.

[5] Register of Leases, *passim*.

different things in different manors and on different sides of the Pennines. John Lowes, a sub-agent of Alderman Ramsay, quoting from a deed of enfranchisement of two copyholders in 1656 spoke of it thus: 'at the death of every Lord a fine; at the death of every tenant a fine and a harriote [heriot] which is to be the best beast such tennant dyes possest of. At the death of the latter, the Lord calls his court and requires a tenant to appear and take his or her admittance and pay a fine and enter her or himself to pay suite or services therein mentioned. Note that the custom of every such manor is, failing maile heirs, the eldest sister inherits, all other sisters excluded.' Now in the manors of Bellister and Hartleyburn, beyond Haltwhistle, the essential features of such customs obtained throughout the eighteenth century.

Thomas Sisson, the steward, writing about 1720, was more specific as to what these fines and services were.[1]

The Custom of the Bellister Manor is that the tenant on the death of the Lord pays a 20d fine, and the same fine on the death of the tenant and also a herriott. Also a 20d fine on alienation and a 10d one on mortgage of the premises. This manor also performs the following services vizt, Each tenant performs one day's mowing and two day's shearing and also at Christmas they bring each two load of coals but does not pay for them at the pit; the tenant has meat and hay for his horses the time he is at dinner. They also spin, each, one hank of yarn and when they bring it home [i.e. to the mansion-house within the manor where they live] they have their dinner. They also each of them carry a load of anything to Newcastle for which they are paid 1s 2d or otherwise they pay 1s 10d. There are no sesses, taxes or repairs allowed [by the lord] in this lordship but there is a mill dam which is to be repaired by the tenants, according to custom, which repairs are uncertain, but one year with another will not exceed £1. The mines and wood growing within the premises belong to the Lord in both manors.

Query. Whether the load be a horse load or cart load; also the meat and hay be ancient custom or a matter of civility from the tenant of

---

[1] Cotesworth MSS. Almost identical fines and services were levied on Thirlwall manor in 1724 where the mowing and shearing days were still called 'dargues'. *Northumbrian Documents* (Surtees Soc.), 82.

Broomhouses to whom the service is paid by agreement from the Lord of the Manor?

It should be noted that the spinning and carrying services or 'catches', as they were called, presumed a resident lord of the manor, not one living at distant Gateshead or Newcastle.

The names of the tenants on these manors in 1726 with their rents, fines, and services were set out as follows:

| BELLISTER | Rent | Fines | Heriots | Mowing days | Shearing days | Catches |
|---|---|---|---|---|---|---|
| John Coulson | 11ˢ 4ᵈ | £11. 6. 8. | 3 | 3 | 6 | 'As you please' |
| John Bell | 11ˢ | £11. | 1 | 2 | 4 | 'do' |
| John Armstrong | 5ˢ 4ᵈ | £ 5. 6. 8. | 1 | 1 | 2 | 'do' |
| Edward Hutcheson | 5ˢ 4ᵈ | £ 5. 6. 8. | 1 | 1 | 2 | 'do' |
| Thomas Snowball | 5ˢ 4ᵈ | £ 5. 6. 8. | 1 | 1 | 2 | 'do' |
| George Cowens | 2ˢ | £ 2. | 1 | 0 | 2 | 'do' |
| Mr. Thomas Carr of Haltwhistle | 1ˢ 8ᵈ | £ 1. 13. 4. | 1 | 0 | 2 | 'do' |
| Totals | £2. 2. 0. | £42. | 9 | 8 | 20 | |

| HARTLEYBURN | | | | |
|---|---|---|---|---|
| George Jackson for Escleugh | 6ˢ 8ᵈ | £ 6. 13. 4. | 1 | The 'service money' for each of these had been commuted to 2ˢ/6ᵈ |
| 'Do' for Ulwham [Ulgham] | 4ˢ 8ᵈ | £ 4. 13. 4. | 1 | |

These tenants owe to the Lord annually 1 Mowing Day, 2 Shearing days, 1 Catch and to lead 2 fothers of coales.

| | | | | |
|---|---|---|---|---|
| Thomas Hewetson (Double Dykes) | 8ˢ 2ᵈ | £ 8. 3. 4. | 1 | 'Do' 3/- |
| (Ditto) Mill | 5ˢ | | | |
| Totals | £1. 4. 6. | £19. 10. 0. | 3 | |

It will be seen that the annual rents were little more than nominal, but the 'twenty penny' fines—i.e. twenty times the yearly rent—and heriots, when they occurred, were substantial. On the death of William Cotesworth, Sisson, the steward, held the first court for Robert, the new lord, in 1727 and reported,

All I received of fines and outrents was but £15 out of about £110 but the tenants made an objection I never heard of before *viz*, 'That the Manors of Bellister and Hartleyburn belonged to Mr. Blenconsop of whom Mr. Ramsay purchased and by whom the tenants are admitted, so they say Mr. Blenconsop is still alive and therefore they are not liable to fines at the death of either Mr. Ramsay or Mr. Cotesworth. They allow to pay you a fine at the death of any of the tenants or any change by sale and also at the death of Mr. Blenconsop. This argument has some weight in it [continued Sisson], but the case will pretty much differ from their state[ment] as above, because none of the tenants who were admitted by Blenconsop are alive save one, from which many querys will arise: Counsellor Grey's opinion to be taken.

Unfortunately we do not know what Counsellor Grey's opinion was but we know that Lawyer Gilpin of Carlisle supported the tenants' claim while Lawyer Rudd of Durham upheld the landlord's. Moreover, Sir R. Shafto had evidently been consulted on this point some years earlier for a note by him reads:[1]

I think admitting the fyne due by custom, an action of debt lyes by the Lord, but if there be a custom (as was in the Countess of Pembroke's case) that if such customary tenant does not pay his fyne that the Lord may enter and retain the land till he be satisfied, that the Lord's lessee upon such entry may maintain an *ejectione firme*. I think the fine due to Mr. Ramsay, ye admitting lord, unless the custom hath been that ye fyne hath not been paid until the death of the selling lord.

On making further inquiries, Sisson discovered that the purchase deed of the manors was dated 3 June 1697 and that 'old Mr. Ramsay' died in October 1698, so that, on a strict interpretation a fine was due when Ramsay succeeded his father but whether it was paid or not 'does not appear from Mr. Ramsay's book', and, added Sisson, 'I am afraid it will be too long now to enquire into that affair'. William Cotesworth certainly claimed a fine when he succeeded to the estate in 1716—he was not the kind of man to let such things go by default—and his son Robert did in 1727 and Carr and Ellison again two years later. Tenants had then good cause to pray for their lord's health. In 1716 Bishop Nicolson of Carlisle noted the restlessness and dissatisfaction

[1] Shafto was Recorder of Newcastle from 1685 to 1705. Brand, ii. 216.

of the Earl of Derwentwater's tenants who had only lately paid one fine and were now faced with a demand for another.[1]

Forty years earlier Roger North noted that 'in Cumberland the people had joined a sort of confederacy to undermine the estates of the gentry by pretending a tenant right which, there, is a customary estate not unlike our copyholds': he added that in cases of dispute a local jury was sure to give a tenant a favourable verdict 'in all cases'.[2] In Cumberland and Westmorland tenant right, it would seem, was already established on the principle now being claimed by the tenants at Bellister 'by which the last general admitting Lord, notwithstanding his selling or aliening the manor, does continue reputed lord, till the time of his death with regard to the payment of a General Fine, and upon his death only, it becomes due and not upon the death of any non-admitting lord, or of any minor lord or of any lord who had only admitted upon the death, alienation, or surrender of the tenants'. Sir James Lowther successfully challenged this view in a Chancery suit in the early seventeen-thirties, but the verdict was reversed on appeal to the House of Lords in 1734.[3] Lord Harborough, writing to his friend Henry Thomas Carr, Cotesworth's son-in-law, who was himself well versed in the law relating to tenures, explained 'that what the Lords went upon was this . . . that it was not reasonable that it should be in the power of a Lord to alien to persons who are lying a-dying and by that means load the tenant with a General Fine', an opinion that was based on a ruling by Littleton 'that change of the Lord ought to be by act of God alone'.[4] However, on scrutinizing the Bellister customs, Carr

---

[1] *Ellis Letters*, iii. 364.    [2] North, *Life of Lord Guilford*, 180.

[3] *Lowther* v. *Raw et al.* Early in the seventeenth century the tenants in the barony of Gilsland, Cumberland 'claimed a customary estate of Tenant right for doing service upon the Borders of Scotland which pleaded custom being by decrees & orders in Chancery adjudged to be void in law, most of the Tenants did therefore submit themselves'. In 1611, however, Thomas Salkeld and John Dacre, together with Christopher Bell and John Hodgson organized a meeting of protest at 'Gelt Brigg', at which 200 persons were present. This resulted in a Star Chamber action in 1617 and Bell and Hodgson were heavily fined and committed to the Fleet prison. *The Household Book of Lord William Howard*, 425–7.

[4] Ellison MSS.

was able to assure his brother-in-law, 'I find the customs there run very much in favour of the Lord and the tenants can't boast the privileges which are usual in some other parts of England'. The Lawyer Rudd was of the same opinion, and the great Coke had ruled in a Northumberland case 'that a fine was due upon every change of the lord by whatever manner it happens'. The tenants at Bellister might justly complain that they lived on the wrong side of the Pennines. Clearly everything depended on what the custom was in any particular manor, but nowhere did custom envisage frequent changes of ownership.

In 1738, on the death of one of the tenants, Carr wrote 'I directed Thomas Tinlin to take the best beast by way of keeping up the custom, for as I recollect they [the tenants] were aiming to have it the best beast or 40/-ˢ *at their own election*'. Again in the following year, Henry Ellison informed his steward,

> I charge the Heriott at two guineas because the Tenants, as we have sometimes taken £2 for one, wou'd, without any other pretence, have that sum established to be paid in lieu of a Heriott, so have charged it £2. 2. 0 to vary it, but we have a right to the best beast if we please.

As late as 1773 he wrote, 'it is quite right to vary the sum taken in lieu of the heriot and very kind to take what you do in lieu thereof, as the value of the best beast is generally more'.[1]

Fortunately, fairly full records of these remote lordships have survived for the greater part of the century. For a time after the death of Sisson in 1736 and until the appointment as steward of Robert Lowes, attorney of Hexham, in 1752, manorial custom had tended to fall into disuse greatly to the prejudice of the lord's rights. 'I find upon enquiring of some old people in Haltwhistle parish', wrote Lowes a year after his appointment, 'that a Court was held at Byershall for Hartleyburne by old Mr. Aynsley about sixteen years' agoe and yet no papers relating thereto are to be found in his

---

[1] On the estate of William Hodshon of Tone 'the last heriot paid was ten guineas' (1784). *Northumberland Documents* (Surtees Soc.), 121.

office'.[1] It subsequently transpired that the last manorial court had been held in 1739. Lowes set about putting matters right. He found, for example, that Hartleyburn 'being both a Court Leet and a Court Baron', required a general court to be held each year within a month after Easter or Michaelmas, whereas Bellister being only a court baron, courts could be held at any time by arrangement. At his first Bellister court held in May 1753 he found plenty of irregularities. For instance, both John and James Carr, sons of one Thomas Carr, the tenant in 1726, had enjoyed the tenement in turn though neither had been formally admitted: both had since died. George Cuthbertson of Newcastle is 'now in possession but how he claims 1 know not, nor do I see how he can have a right to it as he is not heir at law and John Carr and James Carr . . . never admitted tenants, they could not [legally] convey the same to him'. 'I take for granted these Customary Estates cannot be conveyed by will.' Lowes's own opinion was that as neither John nor James Carr had ever been duly admitted, the landlord was not entitled to a heriot on their deaths and he was in some doubt whether he could claim a fine either. 'This I know to be the case in other manors', he wrote. There was a similar difficulty in respect of Mr. Algood, 'our Member', who, it transpired, was not the heir at law of the last tenant, Mr. Robert Algood, but had only assumed the name of Algood on his marriage. Lowes found the court rolls 'very deficient in respect to the Lord's dues upon an absolute surrender, some of them say that a 20d fine is only due and others that a 20d fine and a Harriot is due thereon'; he desired instructions as to what the custom had been on this point. This was a matter of considerable importance for there were many cases of copyholders selling or alienating their birthright. For example, Henry Wallis desired to surrender his tenement to John Snowden 'by way of mortgage', and accordingly Snowden was admitted on condition that the arrears of

---

[1] Aynsley, another Hexham attorney, had acted as steward in these remote lordships in Cotesworth's day.

fines and rents were paid. Edward Robson was allowed to convey his holding to Hugh Dryden in the same way. Again, John Coulson had formerly mortgaged his tenement to William Watson but Coulson's son, having paid off the mortgage, now desired to be re-admitted, but was unwilling to pay the appropriate fines and the heriot. He was told that he must be prepared to attend at the next court and pay his fines 'or that methods would be taken to seize the tenement into the Lord's hands'.

'At Hartleyburn Court', wrote Lowes, 'I found that the Number of free Tenants have been increased since the last Court by parting Estates amongst Children by wills and several changes in respect to them; that the Earl of Carlisle has purchased the free tenement which belonged to Thomas Dobson, in all probability to acquire Common right upon Hartley Burn Common near to which he has several other Estates'; that of the three other tenements on this manor two, Escleugh and Ulwham,[1] were in the hands of one person, George Jackson. On Jackson's death in 1757 it was found that he owed 'monstrous arrears', viz. three fines since Alderman Ramsay's death in 1716, forty-two years' arrears of customary rent, thirty-five years' arrears of 'service money', two fines for mortgages, besides another fine and a heriot. Evidently it was all too easy for manorial custom to lapse if lords and their stewards were not ceaselessly vigilant. Nearly twenty years later Lowes thought he knew of a specific for dealing with the continuing evil of tenants' encroachments on the common. 'Something appears to me to be absolutely necessary to be done to prevent their claiming these enclosures as part of their freehold Estates from a long enjoyment thereof as some of them already pretend to say they have acquired a legal right by an Enjoyment for above Twenty years.' He proposed to put the offenders, 'the very people', on the manorial jury and to require them at the next court to state, on oath, what encroachments there had been and when: 'then that will

---

[1] Alias Ulgham = owl valley or nook. Ekwall, *Place-Names*, p. 463.

fix the parts so taken from the Common . . . and prevent the length of Enjoyment from prejudicing the Lords either as to the Royaltys or upon a Division of the Commons.' He desired directions also in another matter. 'If I should not have the company of Mr. Sill',[1] he wrote in 1757, 'be pleased to acquaint me whether a Dinner must be given as I perceive is usual sometimes to the Jury or only to some particular persons attending at either and which Court?' In many places the traditional 'tenants' dinner' on rent days continued into the present century but it has now almost entirely disappeared, I understand, or been commuted on some estates into a half a crown rebate.[2]

That surreptitious encroachment was practised at different times by all the Hartleyburn tenants is clear from the following letter of Thomas Smith, a comparatively new tenant of Ulwham, in 1766.

Some time ago I took an enclosure from Hartleyburn Fell and had it two years when I received a letter from Mr. Sill that it should be forthwith laid open to the common and so I laid it open. Likewise a neighbour of mine made an enclosure from the same fell, one John Robinson, and he laid it open at the same time, whereas John Bell, John Whitefield, John Jackson and Joseph Whitefield each have an enclosure from Hartleyburn Common. . . .

He desired the lord that these, too, be required to lay them open 'otherwise you will be very partial'. 'As for holding a Court, I would not have you to be at any more expense in regard to our agreeing for that will never be.' It is significant that all four alleged offenders were old tenants. Agreement was none the less occasionally possible. In 1723, half a dozen of the tenants 'interested in the Eatage of Bellister Common and knowing the Bounder hedge . . . to stand crooked and on bad ground for making a new wall . . . do, therefore, for us and our heirs and assignes for the sake of good neighbourhood, consent and agree that Mr. Cotesworth . . . shall be at liberty to set a new stone wall on the

---

[1] The estate agent.
[2] We know that boon days and other services continued at Bellister at least until 1791.

said common . . . according to the Dowells set out by his customary and other tenants for that purpose'.[1] Half the signatories could not sign their own names, but for them 'good neighbourhood' was no empty phrase.

There can be little doubt that the plight of many of the Bellister tenants was unenviable. Taking the list of tenants as it stood at the time of Cotesworth's death, it is possible to trace the fate of many of them. In 1727 John Coulson owed in all £48. 14s. 8d., including six years' arrears of rent; he then proposed to mortgage his tenement to one Nicholas Waugh of Morrilee but the lord insisted that the arrears of rent and fines be paid off first. When Coulson died in 1738, the sub-agent reported that 'the widow had but two mean cows . . . she hath a great mind to keep the herriet'. The lord subsequently abated the heriot to 35s. but the holding was alienated to one Thomas Wallis. Fifteen years later, as we have seen, Coulson's son had paid off the mortgage and was anxious to resume possession but he scrupled to pay the fines which had accrued and there is some doubt whether he was in fact ever admitted. The case of John Bell was even worse. In 1719 he owed a fine and nine years' arrears of rent besides the greater part of a loan of £50 made to him by Cotesworth in 1714, a total of £84. 19s. 0d.; one is scarcely surprised to find that his name dropped out of the list of tenants after 1727. The farm was acquired by Wallis, but thirty years later Wallis's heir sold it. Thomas Snowball's son sold his holding to Richard Watson, but Watson's son in turn, did not take up farming—in 1762 it was reported that he 'lives and trades in London'—and, in that year, he sold the copyhold to his kinsman, Tinlin's brother, the vigorous leaseholder of the adjoining farm of Broomhouses. By that date the families of Armstrong and Hutchinson were the only clear cases of direct continuity since Cotesworth's time. When Matthew Hutchinson of Linshields,[2] 'one of your very old tenants', died in 1769, he was succeeded by

---

[1] Cotesworth MSS.

[2] In 1950 this farm comprised 170 acres including about 30 acres of fell.

his nephew, Cuthbert Wigham. At Hartleyburn, after 1757, the heirs of George Jackson farmed Escleugh, but not Ulwham; Thomas Hewetson, surgeon, had alienated Double Dykes to Mr. Algood as early as 1725. Sir Launcelot Allgood was in possession in 1773, though he had never been formally admitted. 'He has been wrote to and spoken to about it', wrote the steward, 'still no admittance has been taken up, nor does there seem a disposition in him to do it. He should be spoke to seriously and that which is right done.' At that time the steward was experiencing some difficulty in getting a manorial jury together, but there was never any difficulty in selling a copyhold and would-be purchasers were prepared to pay the expenses of holding a special court to register changes of tenancy.

Whatever the causes of the liquidation of the copyholders on these remote manors, it can certainly not be attributed to the high rents or even to the severity of the fines. Unlike his immediate predecessors, Henry Ellison, the new lord, had a particularly good life, from 1730 to 1776. Moreover, he was genuinely paternal where the well-being of his tenants was concerned. A good example of this was afforded in 1769. Learning that John Snowdon, the tenant at Park[1]—his name is carved over the lintel—'gives offence locally by wanting to transfer it to his young son by his second wife, passing over two by his first wife', Ellison caused inquiries to be made as to what provision Snowdon had made for his sons by the first marriage. He found that the eldest 'enjoys something in the manor of Cornwood under his father, but he has no settlement in it . . . but is merely tenant at will there'. 'If so, this cannot be called any provision for him', Ellison commented. 'If Snowdon has bore too hard upon the elder part of his family', the steward was to lay the matter before a manorial jury and 'to recommend to him such measures as are just and equitable'. Nor were these copyhold tenants tied down to a strict course of husbandry as was their

[1] Snowdon acquired the holding from Henry Wallis 'by way of mortgage' and was duly admitted in 1753.

thrustful neighbour, Thomas Tinlin, who held Broomhouses on a lease paying a rent of £55 per annum: yet the latter and his son clearly thrived. We have seen that enclosure must be ruled out as a cause of their plight; indeed it is arguable that if they could only have made more 'intacks' from the fells, more of them might have survived. Nor can it be held that the liquidation of the copyholders was hastened, as it undoubtedly was elsewhere, by spreading industrialism for these manors have remained purely agricultural in character. It looks as if their disappearance must be attributed to more subtle and intangible personal factors. Intermarriage was common and marriage of young women to old men was not infrequent. Robert Lowes, the steward, knew only too well what a harvest of troubles resulted—family quarrels, litigation, and worse. Perhaps, after all, new seed is as necessary for men as for wheat or other grain.[1]

The liquidation of the great bulk of the copyholders in the manor of Whickham had already taken place before it was purchased from Cotesworth's heir by Sir Henry Liddell in 1728. Here the total rents of some twenty-five nominal copyholders amounted to £33. 17s. 8½d.—Liddell paid £22,000 for the purchase of the lease! Considerably more than half the rents were already being paid by the neighbouring gentry, representing in each case the buying out of copyholders who had originally paid only a few shillings. Thus, prior to 1728, the Liddells were paying £8. 12s. 7½d., Sir Francis Clavering £8. 7s. 3d., Lady Clavering £3. 0s. 6d., the latter 'for what she had purchased of Hindmarsh' and four others, while George Bowes, a late-comer, paid 11s. 5d. 'for what he purchased of Matsin'. A good illustration of

---

[1] There had been various proposals to abolish copyhold in the seventeenth century. In June 1642 Thomas Brewster, Esq. petitioned the king to disfranchise the copyholders on all the royal manors and to permit others to do the like 'which will bring not only a great benefit of estate to your Majesty but also a general good and contentment to the commonwealth'. The proposal was vitiated by the rider that Brewster should manage the same and be allowed a sixth of the profits. Egerton MSS. 2651, § 117. Roger North later commented on the distress of the copyholders 'devoured by fees, so that if it were only to relieve the poorest of the landowners of the nation from such extortions and oppressions . . . there is reason enough to abolish the tenure'. 'That, perhaps', he concluded, 'may tend to some repopulation which is more needed than any means of extortion.' North, op. cit. 31.

how the gentry acquired these copyholds, snowball fashion, is afforded by the case of Michael Crawford or Crawforth. In 1723 Colonel Liddell got wind that Crawford, who 'lives somewhere about the Mint in Southwark and (I think) keeps a tavern', contemplated selling his copyhold. He knew, too, that Lady Clavering and Alderman Ridley were only too ready to buy him out. Accordingly, he asked his friend Cotesworth, who happened to be in town, to hunt Crawford out and 'stop his proceedings'. Cotesworth faithfully discharged the trust. Sure enough, four years later, we find the Liddells were paying Crawford's rent. He had sold his birthright. By 1727 the number of genuine copyholders in this manor could be numbered on the fingers of one, certainly of two, hands. Indeed, in 1727 when the grieves, Carr and Barras, attempted to collect the fines and arrears of rent for Robert Cotesworth, only three or four copyholders put in an appearance although due notice of the meeting had been given in the parish church.[1] Some scrupled to pay the fine 'pretending it was customary to have a year to pay it in'. Yet the steward of the manor was not unduly perturbed; he knew well enough that in due course the neighbouring gentry would fully honour their obligations. Fortunately we have a list of the copyholders at Whickham half a century later.[2] The total number and the amount of the rent remained substantially what they had been in Cotesworth's day but here, unlike Bellister and Hartleyburn, continuity of ownership was very conspicuous. In 1774 the Liddells and Claverings still accounted for slightly more than half the total rent; next on the list came Bowes, now the powerful Earl of Strathmore, followed by a few titled newcomers like Lady Windsor and Lady Kerry. William Pitt paid 5s. 3d., precisely what George Pitt had paid at the beginning of the century. In short, copyhold here had nothing to do with farming: it had come to signify no more than the proverbial egg-cup holding up the crust in the pie of colliery wayleaves and staith rooms.

[1] Cotesworth MSS.    [2] Ravensworth MSS.

A very different economy obtained on the estates of the dean and chapter of Durham farther south. The great unbroken series of Registers of Leases which have survived at Durham are an unrivalled source of information regarding farming leases. For the present purpose I have chosen those relating to the village of Shincliffe, some 2 miles east of the city. For the first two years after the Restoration every tenant here was required 'to be ready at all times when occasion of service shall be made to find and set forth one able man with horse and furniture to serve the King's Highness, his heirs etc. . . . in their wars when and as he [the tenant][1] . . . shall be thereunto commanded by the said Dean and Chapter . . . and shall lead with his cattle or draught to the said Dean and Chapter such timber, fuel and cole as they shall have for their use, as other tenants of the same town do, taking no more than . . . as before the Dissolution of the late monastery of Durham'. After 1662, these feudal obligations disappear and the form of the lease was standardized.[2] The term was invariably for twenty-one years; each tenant was required to plant yearly during the term six oaks, six ash, and six alders 'for the better maintaining of the house, hedges, fences etc. in sufficient and tenantable repair'. Then followed the curious obligation that the tenant was 'to do, undergo and perform all such orders as the said Dean and Chapter . . . or their officers shall set down concerning and touching good neighbourhood'. There were the usual clauses against sub-letting without the landlord's consent and the exception of woods and mines. The rents, which were still mostly uniform and in no case exceeded £4. 6s. 8d. per annum, were to be paid in two instalments into 'the new Exchequer over the East Gate' and by way of extra security each tenant was required to find two sureties in sums varying from £40 to £100—no empty formality for the names of the bondees were entered when the lease was registered.

[1] The uniform rents which still obtained reflect the common obligation of military service. Similar conditions had existed in Northumberland earlier, Earl Percy, 'Dargs and Dayworkers' in *Arch. Ael.* xix. See Appendix B and *supra*, 13.

[2] Their disappearance lagged somewhat behind the statute which abolished feudal tenures.

Failure to pay the rent when it was due rendered the lease null and void. Finally, there was a clause relating to the tithe charge which in most cases was almost as much as the rent itself. After 1669, this read 'provided always that whereas upon the late enclosure of the fields of Shincliffe there may be a decrease of the former tillage there to the prejudice of the said Dean and Chapter within the rectory of St. Oswald's in the city of Durham . . .': failure to pay the tithe rendered the lease itself void.

Now the surprising thing is not that a twenty-one-year lease at a very modest rent came to be standard but that the rents never varied for the next century and a half. The result, so far as the tenantry was concerned, is a foregone conclusion—an extraordinarily high degree of stability and continuity. In short, they enjoyed the security of tenure which all agrarian reformers laid down as a prerequisite of good farming. I have found a few cases over the period of an apparent 'foreigner' coming in where the line of succession had failed, but no case of a tenant failing to pay his way. Another consequence may also be noted—the increased dividends of the Durham prebends in the eighteenth century came not from increased farming rentals but from fines on mining and similar leases.

In 1698 the chapter inserted a novel clause in their leases at Westhoe, Harton, and South Shields requiring the tenants 'to grind their corn at the ancient corn milns of the said Dean and Chapter . . . now in occupation of Nicholas Burdon', but it was promptly pointed out that 'there is no such custom as is mentioned above' and that the said Burdon would have 'more grist than he could grind'.[1] At that time Burdon was a salt merchant at Shields—the evolution from miller to banker, colliery proprietor, country gentleman, and M.P., came later.[2] About the same time Bishop Crewe inserted two new covenants into his farming leases 'that were never in his or his predecessors' leases before since St.

---

[1] Quoted in my article in *History*, loc. cit.
[2] Tristram, *The Burdons of Castle Eden* [privately printed].

Cuthbert's dayes, viz, that he, the said Bishop may cut down and carry away the wood on all his farms without making any satisfaction for any manner of waste and that he may also make ways through any of his tenants' grounds even without exception to houses and gardens and without a penny damages'. Our authority for this is William Cotesworth who volunteered the further information 'that there is a currant report that one of his Whimsical Tenants has in his own time planted ten thousand trees which are all lyable to this covenant'. 'There is an end of Planting and of all improvements', concluded Cotesworth, 'for who will have his corn, meadow, nay even Gardens made wayes of without the least recompense and yet must pay a fine for full improvements and which may afterwards be thus laid waste.' Wood was a controversial question on many estates. The tenants at Bellister were still allowed 'hedgebote' and 'ploughbote' but they were strictly forbidden to cut or lop growing timber without the lord's consent: a clause to this effect was usually inserted in tenancy agreements.

We turn now to the evidence in the extant surveys of Ravensworth, Farnacres, Kibblesworth, and Byker. In the first place these surveys should correct a statement or inference that County Durham was 'inclosed in great part before the eighteenth century'.[1] Not only were large tracts enclosed by act of parliament in the course of the century— Bailey gives a list in his *View*,[2] e.g. Willington and Helm Row Commons (1755), Brancepeth (1758), Wolsingham (1765), Lanchester (1773), Hebburn (1779), and Framwellgate (1801)—but even in those 'townships' where there were already enclosed farms in the seventeenth century, the 'town fields' remained common though grazing rights on them were restricted to those who had 'gates' or 'stints', a circumstance which profoundly influenced the whole farming

---

[1] Orwin, C. S., *The Open Fields*, 62. Thomas Wright stated that he could see from his house at Byers Green 'upwards of 500 beautiful inclosures in a most picturesque situation truly pastoral'. *Gentleman's Magazine*, lxiii. 214.

[2] Bailey, J., *General View of the Agriculture of the County of Durham* (1810), 86–99.

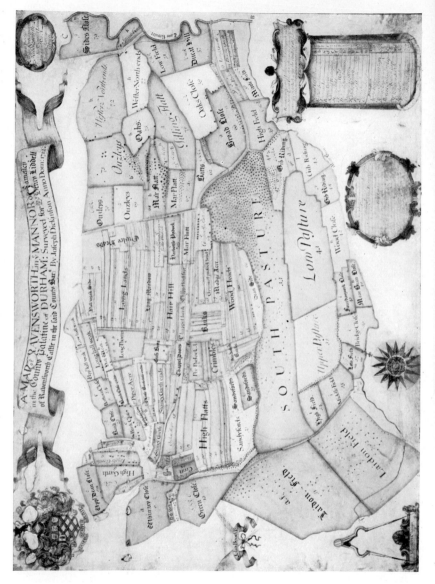

FIELD MAP OF RAVENSWORTH, 1713

economy. Indeed, at Gateshead, Wolsingham, Ryton, and
Crawcrook, the 'Townfields' were enclosed by separate acts
passed subsequent to the main enclosures.¹ On the Liddell
estate at Ravensworth in 1712, the enclosed lands comprised
some 233 acres, the open or 'field land' some 82.² At
Kibblesworth, towards the middle of the century, there were
some 1,015 acres of enclosed land and 380 common. And
even in such quasi-urbanized townships as Gateshead,
Whickham, Framwellgate, and Gilesgate the commons
remained 'open' throughout the century. J. Atkinson's
beautiful survey of Ravensworth sets out the variegated,
quilt-like pattern of 'riggs' and 'butts', with the number of
'gates' held by each freeholder or tenant. In one instance,
Langthorn, comprising 'about nine days' mowing', it shows
that land which had formerly been enclosed had become
open again. Not that landlords, old and new, and perhaps
we should add 'concealers' with doubtful titles, were not
fully alive to the obvious advantages accruing from enclosure.
When Launcelot Carr bought 'Helmington Row' estate for
Mrs. Jane Ellison in 1733, he wrote, 'I hope if you can get
a good tenant and can get a Division of the Common, as I
shall use my best endeavours to effect for you, I doubt not
(God willing) but you will make £5/10/- per centum of
your money and I hope, before a Division, you may make
£4/10/- very easily'.³ Just over twenty years later this was
the first of a series of estates in the county to be enclosed by
private act. Where there were potential mineral deposits,
the temptation to purchase and enclose was so much the
stronger especially if, as George Bowes claimed, a single

¹ Ibid. At Gateshead in the seventeenth century 'new incumars at the first entry' paid
4s. 8d. per cow if freemen, and double that sum if they were resident non-freemen and thereafter both paid 2s. per beast per annum—raised to half a crown in 1665 and to 3s. in 1677.
These sums were collected by the four 'grassmen', who were appointed each year by the
vestry, and paid over to the town. In 1660 there were eighty-three cows in the town fields
but the figure tended to rise quickly, for example, 116 in 1666; the increased charges were
intended to check the numbers. Vestry Minute Books. At Newcastle freemen were restricted
to two cows each, but I have found no such restriction at Gateshead.
² Ravensworth MSS. J. Atkinson's survey.
³ Ellison MSS. At first Mrs. Ellison hesitated to complete the purchase following a report
that the Bishop of Durham claimed the estate.

copyholder had a *liberum veto* on all 'improvements'. There was a proposal to enclose Gateshead Fell, hardly rich farming land, by Chancery decree in 1691.[1] The procedure suggested was that a proper survey be first made and 'after the number of acres is known . . . that every person be considered that hath any intrest therein and the most contiguous and convenient allotment be settled where and in what places to lye'. In this case 'a proportion of land convenient to Park House' was to be set aside as the share of the lord of the manor. Given the assistance of a skilled surveyor, a body of enclosure commissioners who commanded respect, and a measure of 'good neighbourhood' among the interested parties, a quick and amicable 'division' might be effected as at Marske and Redcar in 1755–6.[2] 'I knew a great part of these commons in their native state', wrote Bailey later, 'and think that, upon an average, the lands are at least ten times more valuable by enclosure than they were in a state of common.'[3]

The next outstanding feature which emerges from these north Durham surveys is the smallness of the farms and the fact that they were almost entirely given over to pasture. The Liddell estate at Ravensworth, comprising some 316 acres, was farmed by thirteen tenants in 1712—the demesne in this lordship consisted of only 5 acres but there were other 42 acres in the adjoining manors of Farnacres and Whickham. The biggest farm was Edward Liddell's, just over 74 acres, at a rent of £31, the whole listed as pasture save 14 acres described as 'meadow and arable'. Next in order of size came Thomas Lee's, 43 acres, rented at £31. 16s. 8d. and Ralph Surtie's 39 acres, at £34, neither of which had any arable land at all. In no case did the proportion of 'arable and meadow' to pasture rise above a third. At Farnacres and Whickham, twenty-four tenants farmed a total of 668 acres. Of the two biggest, William Hutchinson farmed 79 acres only 13 of which were arable, and George Gibson, 64 acres only 5 of which were arable. Here only two other farms exceeded 50 acres and in every case the amount

[1] Cotesworth MSS.     [2] Ward, *Journal.*     [3] *View*, 99.

of arable was fractional or non-existent. And when one remembers that every tenant, in addition to his enclosed lands, had a specified number of riggs on the 'townfield', e.g.

Edward Liddell 48 containing in all 14 acres 3 roods 36 perches.
Thomas Lee 64 „ „ 16 „ 3 „ 28 „
Ralph Surties 51 „ „ 18 „ 0 „ 12 „

the preponderantly pastoral economy is self-evident.[1] Of the three farms at Byker surveyed by John Warner in 1720, the proportion of arable to pasture was somewhat greater. At Byker Farm itself there were 25 acres under the plough out of a total of 69; at West House Farm 28 out of a total of 66, and at St. Anthony's 36 out of a total of 140 acres. The respective rents of these were 17s. 1¼d., 16s. 6d., and 11s. 5d. per acre; the surveyor considered they were all worth 25s. per acre.[2] By contrast, the farms in the rich flat lands of Northumberland were very much bigger: rents of £140 to £200 were not uncommon.[3]

Later in the century—the precise date is uncertain—all the Ravensworth tenants had a common, printed, form of lease or tenancy agreement, a draft of which was submitted to Henry Ellison, a former steward. It contained many covenants identical with those of Ellison's own leasehold tenants at Broomhouses and Brancepeth. In the seventeen-thirties the half-dozen tenants at West Park, Brancepeth, who were all on nine-year leases, were required to fallow a third of their tillage ground every year, and to take but two crops, one of which was to be oats, between each fallowing; 'not to tear out, pare, or burn any fresh ground without consent'; to lay on a stipulated quantity of clod lime each year besides all manure 'bred' on the premises (additional lime was to be used if any hay or straw were sold during the year). Then, a

---

[1] Besides the tenants proper, certain freeholders had a specified number of riggs, e.g. 'Esq. Clavering' and Rogers, 104 comprising 23 acres; Lady Bowes 82 (= 20 acres); Elizabeth Cuthbert 30 (= 5 acres).

[2] Sir John Lawson let the manor of Byker to Richard Ridley shortly afterwards. The rents of the several farms in 1726 are given in *Northumberland Documents*, 94–96, 118–19.

[3] Ibid. 95–125. In 1760, Hallington Farm, Beaufront, was let at £240. For the farm rentals of Lord Grey of Wark, see *Proc. Soc. of Antiquaries of Newcastle* (5th ser.), i, No. 1, 18–23.

point on which great stress was laid, a rood of hedge was to be scoured each year for every £1 of the rent and if the tenant failed to do this the landlord was at liberty to have the work done and charge the cost to the tenant. The Ravensworth agreement, however, was only for a yearly tenancy. Otherwise it did little more than elaborate the above conditions. For example, a penalty of £5 per acre was incurred for any grass land 'pared, burnt or converted to tillage'. Most of the farms at West Park, Brancepeth, were much larger than those at Ravensworth, with rents up to £100. Anthony Scorer paid £50 for a farm of 140 acres, and all of them clearly depended on corn-growing. In the first week of September 1737, although he had not 'inned' all his corn, Thomas Wardell was reported as having 'sixteen stacks in the yard, nine of which I take to be hard corn, the rest oats'. The tenants here had a dispute at the time with the rector concerning the payment of Easter offerings.

Easily the most detailed and elaborate covenants were contained in Thomas Tinlin's lease of Broomhouses in 1741. It was for twenty-one years at a rental of £50 per annum. He was required to fallow a quarter of his tillage ground each year 'so as not to take two crops of the same kind between one fallowing and another . . . and so as he have not in tillage, in any one year, above forty acres of ground'.[1] A suggested cropping-plan for each field over the entire term was included, based on a simple sequence—oats, haugh,[2] wheat or other 'hard corn' or peas, then grass with the declared object of having the best fields laid down to grass again at least four years before the lease expired. But this was exceptional. The joint landlords had had experience of Tinlin, 'so sharp a

---

[1] Bradley in his *Survey of Husbandry and Gardening* (1726) writes concerning 'Ploughing of Fallows which is a very great Benefit to land as appears by the common Practice of it and in the great care that Landlords everywhere take to oblige their tenants to a strict observance of it once in three years, few lands as they imagine, being able to bear more than two crops without it; and I don't know but that a year's fallowing will be beneficial to them let their land be what it will, nor yet can be persuaded that the true ploughing of it though it is chargeable will not pay for their labour'.

[2] Strictly speaking 'haugh' is low-lying pasture ground by the banks of a river (Wright, *Dialect Dictionary*), but in the eighteenth century the word appears to have had a wider application in Northumberland and Durham, and to have been virtually synonymous with fallow.

fellow'. 'He lays it down as a maxim that he can do no harm as long as he pays his rent', wrote Carr, 'I see plainly according to his notions he looks upon it that it is a great hardship to restrain a tenant from ruining the land at the latter end of the term that he has bestowed any pains upon before.' 'Loving corn land' Thomas did not scruple to rive up grass land and grow catch crops or even to take the same crop two years running 'which I look upon as the worst husbandry that can be practised', wrote Carr. 'Unless he is tied up strictly to covenants in a short lease no farm in his hands can possibly improve and in all probability will abate in value.' Yet Tinlin 'thinks himself the best husbandman in that Country and says 'tis unusual to restrain tenants thus in that country where they seem to claim a sort of priviledge of doing what they will with their lands'. Despite the irritating restrictions imposed upon them, Tinlin and his son prospered greatly.[1] Between them they farmed Broomhouses for the greater part of the century. But they discovered that, placed as they were, salvation lay in grass not in the plough. Before 1740 Carr was instructing them as to how the farmers in the southern counties of England sow trefoil and the landlords were prepared to build hembles in which cattle could winter instead of sheltering in the woods thus losing the manure so necessary for improvement. No such compelling restraints operated with the neighbouring customary tenants at Bellister: they were free to take 'white' crops until the soil was bled white. Indeed, it is probable that the policy of subsidizing corn-growing by granting bounties on export which obtained from 1689 to 1766 gave an entirely wrong twist to farming in many English counties and that the subsequent changes in crop husbandry were a matter not of choice but of necessity.[2]

We have very detailed information of the 'improved

---

[1] The elder Tinlin was drowned in crossing a swollen river in 1749. Broomhouses is now some 336 acres (158 of which are moorland), but it now incorporates Throstle Hall, formerly a separate farm. [Information supplied by Mr. Lawes, the present owner-occupier.]

[2] The sudden abandonment of the policy of export bounties has not received the attention it deserves. It marked the first defeat of the landed interest.

husbandry' practised by Cotesworth on the enclosed lands at Gateshead and Shipcote from 1718 to 1726 where, for a time, he farmed some 500 acres. In the first place, each field was fenced with quicks—he planted scores of thousands each year, and began to raise them on a considerable scale in his own 'nursery' or 'plantations'.[1] Each field was heavily limed and manured with street sweepings laid on in slack periods. Barley, bigg, oats, wheat, or vetches 'for the pigeons', were grown on a simple rotation with a fallow year or 'haugh' intervening when the field was ploughed and cross-ploughed four or five times in preparation for wheat, but the main emphasis throughout was on clover and grass. 'You know corn is no further our interest than to improve the ground', he told the steward in 1722. All the ploughing and 'leading' was done by oxen—he had twenty-four, or six working 'draughts' in all, at the time of his death, besides fourteen draught horses, though the latter were used mainly on the colliery wagon-ways. He insisted on doing the bulk of the ploughing in summer and early autumn when the oxen, at grass, were in good fettle. His will, curiously enough, makes no mention of cows or other livestock (asses excepted)[2] and we know from other sources that he obtained butter from his kinsman in Teesdale. The crops of hay and clover were mostly sold to local chapmen doubtless as winter fodder for the cows which grazed on the town fields during the summer months.[3] In any case he had no intention of farming so large an area indefinitely; once the land was 'improved', he intended to let it off in separate farms. By 1735, tenants had been found for about half of it but over 240 acres remained 'on our hands', and was farmed directly.

A farm of 500 acres required a considerable labour force for men with mattocks did the work now done by cultivators

[1] The names and acreage of the fields at Gateshead are given in Winship's survey, 1689.

[2] Asses' milk was greatly valued for medicinal uses especially for nursing mothers. Drummond and Wilbraham, *The Englishman's Food*, 148, 231.

[3] In addition 'Esq. Coatsworth' contributed 88 'coks' of hay, 50 'thrave' of bigg, 49 'do' of oats, 24 'do' of wheat, and 17 'do' of rye to the rector (Leonard Shafto) as tithe. The Rector's Book (1705–26). These quantities represented about a third of the tithes of the parish.

and disk harrows. The standard rates of pay were 8*d*. a day
for men and 4*d*. for women, with an additional 2*d*. to 4*d*. a
day at harvest time.

We have had a sore struggle among our workmen upon our keeping
off a week's wages as we have usually done in former years to oblige
them to stay with us in hay and corn harvest [wrote the steward in
1722]: they protested none of them would work unless they had their
money, but upon my arguing with them of the justness of my keeping
it off they all set to work except Harry Lacock who had the least
reason to leave us of any we employ, for he had had employment in bad
weather when we have turned those off that have deserved it better. . . .
Thos Leighton and Wm Dockwray [?] left without reason but that they
had hired themselves by the year wch is very false for now in mowing
time they are seeking mowing in their neighbourhood and Thomas
Armstrong and partners agreed with a Scotsman to mow their fields
beside ours and he took Harry Lacock and Thomas Leighton to be his
partners, but when I saw them begin in the morning I discharged
Harry Lacock and Thomas Leighton from coming either in that close
or any other that belonged to you. If anything they will be for coming
again but they will be more sensible of their fault before we admit them,
for the more kind you are to them the worse they'll be to you, but they
shall have no work hereabouts that I can prevent them off.

This was pretty drastic. In any case employment of agricultural labour was definitely seasonal. 'You have done well
in discharging useless hands and reducing wages at the
proper time', wrote Cotesworth in the following October.
Although work was found for a number during the winter or
dead months in threshing corn, leading manure, or breaking
limestone, other hands were discharged 'in the fall'.[1]

A list of the tenants and rentals at Gateshead in 1735 with
Sisson, the steward's, comments has survived. The rents
would have caused the customary tenants in other parts of
the estate to rub their eyes. A few samples are appended:

|  | acres | roods | perches |  |
|---|---|---|---|---|
| Thomas Armstrong and partners held | 93 | 1 | 1 | on a four year lease at £100 per ann. |

This farm is let at a price I think it will continue.

[1] Cotesworth MSS. ('Farm Accounts').

|  | acres | roods | perches |  |
|---|---|---|---|---|
| Edward Amory | 30 | 1 | 10 | at £47. lease expires 1735 but has taken a new one for seven years at the same rent. |

This farm is let so as if the times are tolerable it will continue, but it depends upon the milk trade which is now much worse than formerly by means of so maney following that way of liveing that the demand is less and larger pennyworths given than were formerly.

| Thomas Thompson and partners | 113 | 2 | 35 | at £140. Their lease expired Ladyday 1734 and from that time they took it for three years at £140 which was £20 abated of what they paid before, viz. £160. |

This farm depends the same way as Amory's.

| Matthew Clover [a nurseryman] | 3 | 2 | 16 | at £9. No lease, only from year to year. |

This is dear and by means of his ill-payment of rent have taken it from him this Candlemas 1735, and fancy a good tenant would not give above £7 per ann. for it.

| Henry Potts | 18 | 1 | 0 | at £38/10/-. lease expires Ladyday 1737 |

This is the dearest ground we let and is used with cows on which there is the same remark as Edward Amory above. He designs to leave at Ladyday 1737, when I doubt we shall not get above £30 per ann.

| William Robinson | 8 | 3 | 25 | at £16. lease expires 1742. |

The tenant manures well and I hope it may continue at this rent.

|  | acres | roods | perches |  |
|---|---|---|---|---|
| George Jameson | 12 | 2 | 8 | at £20. a nine year lease from 1735. |

He's a new tenant and I believe will be a good one. He uses it with cows and, if that answers, fancy he may continue at that rent.

Rents for dairy farms of £2 or more an acre and in the case of Clover, a market gardener, of £3 an acre reveal a state of affairs which economic historians have not as yet considered. By 1742 the milk sales of these Gateshead farmers were being taken into account for purposes of land-tax assessments. Of the remaining 'lands in our own hands', one group of 44 acres odd and another of 96 should deserve 'one parcel with another' 20s. and 30s. per acre respectively; the latter figure was given also for some 74 acres at Shipcote 'being all is improved or in our own hands improving'. But there were some 26 acres at Shipcote 'almost covered with pit heaps, whins and other rubbish that I cannot call it above 7s. 6d. per acre'. The total rental for lands, let and unlet, amounted to £1,075. Many tenants were able to pay these high rents because of the earnings in what was termed the 'land carriage'.[1] Indeed it was frequently a condition of a farming lease that the tenant should maintain a horse team to haul coal along the wagon-ways 'at the usual rates'.

Dr. T. S. Willan has noted that from about 1730 considerable shipments of butter begin to figure regularly in the Port Books of Newcastle.[2] The northern counties already imported corn, barley, rye, and seed oats from Scotland and elsewhere, but thanks to the character of its farming, the north had a surplus of butter.[3] Soon after their marriage, the Carrs settled for a time at Grendon in Northamptonshire whence H. T. Carr wrote,[4]

The greatest difficulty we find is the inconvenience of getting good

[1] *Infra*, 254.
[2] *The English Coasting Trade*, 84, 116. There was a considerable export also from Stockton.
[3] 'There is abundance of Rye comes in by Shipping which is sold for 3ˢ/8ᵈ–3ˢ/9ᵈ [per bushel] which keeps down the market', wrote Sisson in 1723. Both rye and barley were used in the 'geordie' loaf. [4] Ellison MSS.

butter, for this being a very great cheese country,[1] the farmers don't care to break into their cheese making. We are obliged to send all round the country for butter that you would not eat in the North . . . and we (lately) condemned ten pounds to be used for greasing chair wheels.

It will have become obvious that what was called 'improved husbandry' in the north left no place for green crops, turnips, or potatoes. (Defoe in his *Tour* makes no mention of the latter.) Indeed, Cotesworth was very angry with Peter Bamlett, his Newsham tenant, when he grew 7 acres of potatoes *c.* 1720. Twenty years later Carr, after informing his partner that a prospective new tenant at Newsham 'seems a substantial man and of very good character . . . and to have very good notions of husbandry', added, 'I hope he won't boggle at an article I propose inserting to restrain from growing rape or potatoes, as they rob the ground and leave no manure for it that answers, rape none at all'.

Bailey, in his *View of Agriculture in County Durham*, published in 1810, states that potatoes, if not first grown, have been 'longest known' at Hamsterley, in the parish of Witton-le-Wear 'where it has been the principal employment of several families for upwards of eighty years'.[2] That would roughly coincide with Cotesworth's denunciation of his tenant Peter Bamlett. Now Hamsterley is situated in a somewhat isolated and remote part of the county, possibly out of sight of officious 'improving landlords'. Bailey went on to explain that the people there 'are very particular in having their sets as perfect as possible; and in cutting them

---

[1] Near Stilton.

[2] Bailey, 165–8. Drummond and Wilbraham, *The Englishman's Food*, 215–16. Salaman, *History and Social Influence of the Potato*, 464, 478. R. Bradley, in his *Survey of Husbandry & Gardening* (1726), 207, says of the potato that it is 'a root of extraordinary use to mankind, both for Food & the making of Starch; but however it happens I know not, we do not find it cultivated in any great Quantities in England, except near London'. 'The Duke of Buckingham's steward considered that tenants should be forbidden to grow potatoes, except in small quantities for their own use' on pain of £10 per acre. As late as 1795 Rev. M. Forster, *Annals of Agriculture*, xxiv. 89, noted that most of the gentry insist on the inclusion of a like clause 'in their leases, notwithstanding that experience had shown that to ban the potato from the field was as detrimental to good husbandry as it was inimical to the poor', quoted by Salaman.

throw aside all deformed potatoes and all such as they suspect have a tendency to run wild'. The favourite varieties, he added, 'are the red nebs, the red streak or pink eyes, the one a kidney, the other a round variety'. By 1760 a few discerning men knew that 'the profit from a small piece of potatoe ground could not have been made in any other way'. The basis of the new husbandry in the north was clover, ryegrass, trefoil, and other 'foreign' grasses, the seeds of which were obtained from Holland, via London, in Cotesworth's day. Then, as later, some farmers were conservative.

The objections to sowing clover which I've heard both from Yorkshire and Northumberland [wrote Robert Swinburne of Hebburn in 1748] prove nothing but ye great want of experience in ye objectors. I don't wonder to meet with objections of this kind in Northumberland . . . but was much surprised that Yorkshire, a county famed for acuteness in other respects should advance so great an absurdity as that clover impoverishes land, though to do the County justice, I met with one Yorkshire Gentleman from Leeds who had long experienced it and acknowledged it to be the greatest improver he knew. I can guess what led so many inexperienced farmers into this mistake. . . . I can show you the famous Dr. Hales' opinion on this subject which weighs more with me than all Northumberland and Yorkshire put together. Nothing but the study of Nature can qualify a man to be either an accurate farmer or Physician.[1]

Owing to an over-liberal dressing of lime and street sweepings, the clover in a barley field at Shipcote in 1718 grew so high up in the sheaves that, when harvested, they got 'hot' in the stack and the barley could not be malted in consequence.

Thanks to the predominant type of farming practised in Durham and Northumberland, great importance attached to the cattle fairs and markets at Newcastle,[2] Morpeth, Penrith, Durham, Darlington, Barnard Castle, Gisborough, and Yarm, where young cattle, sheep, and oxen might he had for summer grazing. For besides dairy-farming, the

[1] Ellison MSS. Bradley commended 'Milk Trefoil' (cytisus), 286.
[2] 'Haymarket', 'Bigg Market', 'Groat Market' are reminders of the town's agricultural shell.

beef potential of the 'Durham Ox' was already famous. Ralph Ward of Gisborough killed a black fat ox, 'Rook', in 1756, 'the admiration of all for size and fatness'; its carcase (dead weight) was 120 stone besides 21½ stones of tallow, and the hide weighed 9 stones 1 pound, so that its live weight must have been over a ton. It and two others were sold to Mr. Mewburn, a Sunderland butcher, for 30 guineas apiece and went for ships' provisions.[1] Clearly the brothers Colling had their predecessors in this branch of farming.[2] Gimmers or store sheep were bought at Hamilton in Scotland; one wether which Ward killed in 1756 weighed 'near eight stones in the quarters'.

Oxen [writes Bailey in his *View of Durham*][3] were within my remembrance, much used in this district, but were then beginning to give way to horses: the late Earl of Darlington, about thirty years since was their last great advocate: he kept 10 or 12 ox-draughts for several years; had them yoked in collars one before another, three to a plough and driven by the ploughman, his Lordship not allowing a driver. Each ploughman had six oxen, three working four hours in the forenoon, and the other three, four hours in the afternoon. I lived in the neighbourhood at the time and recollect that they were the standing jest of the adjoining farmers, for the small quantity of work they performed and the expense it was done at. At present, I have not heard of a single ox-draught in the county.

The agrarian revolution of the eighteenth, as of the twentieth century, was partly a question of logistics.

It was at the cattle marts that one could have met those, now mostly anonymous, masters of their craft—the men who 'knew a beast' and could correctly appraise it and pronounce it free from 'cliers', 'red water', or other diseases, and who knew the specific for an ox that was 'bound in the guts'. In 1748–9 these men and the cattle-dealers and drovers watched anxiously the northward spread of the cattle plague through Yorkshire. As early as 1714, when the distemper was confined to the London area, the government had introduced a

[1] *Journal*, loc. cit.   [2] Bailey, *View*, 'The Durham Ox', 230–4.
[3] Ibid. 246. Oxen were still used in west Cumberland in Napoleonic times. *History* (1940).

policy of compulsory slaughter of infected animals with
compensation 'bounties' to farmers of £2 per cow and 10*s*.
for a calf, together with restrictions on the movement of
cattle within the infected area.[1] Official 'surveyors' and a
slaughterman were appointed to carry out the order. This
policy had proved effective at the time and it was revived by
an Order in Council of 22 March 1747 to cope with a much
more serious outbreak.[2] Opinion was most sharply divided
on the question of compulsory slaughter. In March 1749,
Mr. Carr of Whitworth wrote to his brother Ellison:

I have this last week been endeavouring to prevent the ill effects of
a very idle, silly paper entitled *Remarks on the Distemper among Cattle
in Essex*, which some of our Justices, (Dr. Johnson, Mr. Wilkinson
and Alderman Wharton) have been so inconsiderate as to order to be
dispersed round the county without knowing that it contains any truth
and though it seems to encourage people to disobey the Order in
Council which as Justices they ought to enforce. I have remonstrated
strongly against it, telling them that dispersing a paper to induce people
to believe the Distemper was not contagious is striking at the founda-
tions of every order hitherto made by the Justices of this and the
neighbouring Counties, and was with them on Thursday last at the
private Sessions, when an order was made to enforce obedience to all
former orders, but nothing more could be obtained. However, this is by
no means an Antidote against the poison of the former which the
Countrey by the order for dispersing it, supposes to be a paper of great
authority, though it was only picked up accidentally in Yorkshire and
brought by a clerk of a turnpike bill to Dr. Johnson, for they know
nothing of the author or whence it really came. This has occasioned
my writing some letters into Essex and other counties where the

---

[1] Add. MSS. 32704, § 153, 'An Account of what was done in 1714 on the Breaking out
of the Distemper among the Cowes'.

[2] The alarm in the southern counties is reflected in the following letter from an anonymous
clergyman 'situated in ... ye Province of Canterbury; [it] gives him ye pain of seeing the Country brought into very great distress by the Distemper that rages among the Cattle. Perhaps
His Grace [the Archbishop of Canterbury] will be pleased with hearing that there is so much of
a Sense of Religion still among us as makes every one express his wishes that Orders were
given for a particular mention to be made of this Calamity in our Publick Prayers. We hop'd
it would have been taken notice of in ye Office for ye Fast and were not a little disappointed
when we found 'twas not.' The writer assured the archbishop's chaplain 'that he had heard
these things not only from many of the best affected to our Church Establishment, but from
some, too, who dissent from it, who with a kind of Triumph acquaint me that it has not been
overlooked by their Ministers'. Ibid. 32710, § 110.

Infection has raged and to people of sense as well as fortune from whom I expect some accounts which may be useful to my countrey.[1]

A few days later he added 'I have not heard what the new Act is to be and some people in Yorkshire, I find, think the Government may as well save the reward', i.e. the compensation payments. From 1746 to 1750 the Treasury paid no less than £162,919. 18*s*. 0*d*. in 'issues for infected cattle': the peak year (1747) accounted for £70,000.[2]

I applaud your Resolution in executing the Order in Council [wrote Carr in February 1750]. Dr. Cooper (who I saw yesterday at St. Helen's) tells me they will certainly do it in Northumberland, which I'm extremely glad of. The Gentlemen of the Southern Counties must, I think, soon be sensible of their own indiscretion in not doing it, for within this last month great numbers of cattle have been bought in this County at infected places and even out of infected herds which have been drove southward and I wish I could not say that Certificates [authorizing the movement of cattle] have been granted for most of them. I refused Certificates to people I knew were not intitled to them, but they got them elsewhere without any difficulty.

Meanwhile, General Ellison in London sent to his brother at Gateshead 'Dr. Wintringham's receipt for treating diseased cattle'; it was the method used abroad, he said, though 'hitherto all remedies have proved ineffectual in this part of the world'. For himself he was convinced that slaughtering was the best policy 'but as 'tis impossible to persuade or even force the Country people to do so, I send you the receipt'.

In April 1750 Carr wrote that he had not heard 'how they go on in Northumberland with regard to the Distemper. If they don't shoot about Stannerton, it might be worth while to let Dr. Baker know that at Sir Rowland Wynne's they at last thought of trying mashes made of a large quantity of onion and did not lose one they were given to; they also gave onion broth.' Carr was evidently greatly concerned and discussed the subject at length with his friends when the original act was about to expire.

[1] Ellison MSS.     [2] Add. MSS. 30203, § 18.

I am sorry to hear the Distemper among the Cattle rages now at Witton on the Were [he wrote from Cheshire in January 1753], I hope Gateshead may still escape it. The newspapers lately gave an account of several being cured by Dr. James' fever powder being kept in the house and having warm water to drink.

In the autumn of that year the outbreak reached its climax in the north. In October the Newcastle justices at their General Quarter Sessions, in conjunction with the county magistrates at Alnwick, issued an order forbidding any cattle to be driven across the Tyne bridge or Derwent 'or to pass from any part of Co. Durham' to the great Old Martinmas Fair in Newcastle on 22 November. This order was quickly followed by another from the authorities at Gateshead refusing to allow cattle to be assembled on Gateshead Fell or at the public markets on that date. They declared that they were determined to use all legal means to prevent cattle being brought into Gateshead and 'to proceed with the utmost rigour against offenders and all jobbers who shall offend against the Order in Council'. We can well imagine that the dairy-farmers at Gateshead were as much concerned as anybody. The distemper never raged in the north with the same fury it had in the southern counties. It may well be that the widespread popularity of the Durham shorthorn later in the century arose from dairymen in the south replenishing their herds from the north at this time. Mr. Carr's letter of 1750 refers to 'great numbers of cattle' being driven south. English dairy-farming and stock-raising took a long time to recover from the visitation. Two important consequences deserve mention. The outbreak gave the first impetus to the upward trend in prices which was manifest in the first decade of George III's reign.[1] In 1766 high

[1] 'A Letter to Lord North attempting to shew the Causes and the Remedies of the High Prices of Provisions', by Amicus Patriae, 1772. 'I date from that period—twenty five years ago, when the great mortality befel our cattle—an extraordinary revolution in the price of provisions.' 'The Dairy business has scarcely been remarked upon by writers', he added, 'yet it is an object which claims a principal attention as it already occupies a great proportion of our lands.' He noted that dairy-farmers in the south did not rear calves but 'are supplied with fresh stock as it is wanted from distant counties'. For the rest it was his opinion that the improvements in husbandry 'consist more in theory than in general use'. As to remedies for

prices and social discontent among the masses forced the government to abandon willy-nilly the time-honoured policy of subsidizing the export of corn. Shortly afterwards a group of doctors and scientists, English and European, were engaged in trying to find a specific for 'the distemper among horned cattle'.[1] In 1769 the Court physicians, Sir John Pringle and Dr. Layard, corresponded with one Dr. Petrus Camper, Professor of Anatomy in the University of Groningen, 'who makes the distemper among horned cattle his particular study'. 'The French are still ignorant of the advantages of inoculation', wrote Layard later, 'in Denmark it is now authorized and its utility acknowledged, as well as in Holland.' Experience in England, however, continued to favour the policy of compulsory slaughter.[2] Memories of the 'plague' years burnt, as with quicklime, a lasting impression on our forefathers.

*(Postscript)*

*An Account of what was done in 1714 on the Breaking out of the Distemper among the Cowes*

The distemper first appeared in August 1714 at Islington and as soon as the Lords Justices had notice of it, the Lord Chancellor by their directions ordered four Justices to take an account of the stocks of all the Cowkeepers in or near the place who had any infected cows or calves and also to agree with them for all their cows and calves which were or should be taken ill.

This was done at 40s/- a cow and 10s/- a calf. On receiving information that the Distemper was chiefly propagated by the selling of infected calves, the Justices bought and killed all the calves, sick and well; they

---

the prevailing high prices he was convinced 'that no times would ever submit to the rule of Legal Commissaries to apportion our farmers, to settle our Rents, to prescribe the course of our husbandry or stamp a price upon our property'.

[1] Calendar Home Office Papers (1770–2), § 95, *passim*; (1773–5), §§ 469, 1222.

[2] There continued to be some opposition to slaughtering infected animals for one 'inspector' in Suffolk complained in 1774 'of the absurd spirit of liberty and folly prevalent among the common people'. Ibid., §§ 606, 745. Even haystacks were burnt as a precautionary measure. Dr. Layard disapproved the original order which required hides to be 'slashed' and cut, believing that the resulting effusion of blood caused the disease to spread. The purpose of the original order was to prevent any surreptitious salvaging and sale of infected hides.

also appointed a slaughterman at 5ˢ/- a day and proper surveyors who
every day visited each cowherd, killing every cow as soon as it was
taken ill, burying them ten foot deep with unslaked lime and covering
them well with earth to prevent infectious steames. They also every
week checked the accounts of the cowkeepers' stocks to prevent their
buying in new cattle or old cows of small value which practices tended
to increase the Distemper.

By this management and other proper directions for separating the
sound [animals] from the sick and even the sound from each other as
soon as was possible, keeping them all in the fields and open air and
drying up their milk as soon as could be, many were preserved and
their Distemper confined to Islington and Hogsden, where it first
began, for more than a month. But then, the power of the Justices
being suspended by an accident or mistake for about five weeks, and
afterwards while the Dutch medicine was trying, the Cowkeepers
were at liberty to doe as they pleased and their cattle were suffered to
live till they dyed of the distemper in a natural way, whereby it spread
all round London, till on renewing the former powers, the former
measures were renewed which kept the distemper from spreading
further into the country and at last put a stop to it intirely.

All sorts of medicines were tried but without any success (the Dutch
medicine only excepted of which I have the receipt by me) that cured
8 out of 50, but did much more harm than good by suspending the
other method of killing as soon as they were taken ill and thereby, as
there is a very good reason to believe being the occasion for the loss of
several hundred cows that might otherwise have been saved, the
Distemper being always observed to rage with the greatest violence
and most fatal effects whenever the cows were suffered to live any time
after the Distemper first seized them. The prodigious quantity of
putrid effluvia emitted by them every time they breathed infected the
aire more strongly and carrying it further to other cows and herds.
9th April 1745.                                            John Milner.


*(Enclosure)*

### *Copy of the Order to the Justices of the Peace*

(i) That the Justices of the Peace do buy the infected cows at a
    price not exceeding ½ the value of them and those also that
    were dead.

(ii) That they give public notice near the place . . . that they will buy any infected cow at the same rate to be killed and burnt. And such sums as the said Justices shall expend in this service shall be forthwith reimbursed by the Solicitor of the Treasury.

(iii) That the Justices report the number of uninfected cattle in the possession of those who are the owners of cattle that are infected.

*Note.* Burning was found inconvenient and therefore changed into Burying with lyme.

## CHAPTER V

# The Coal Trade

But what signifies all your Balls, Ridottos etc. unless
Navigation and the Coal Trade flourish.

*(Sir Henry Liddell, Bt.,* 1729)[1]

## I

At the beginning of the eighteenth century the coal
industry on the Tyne had reached a critical stage in its
development. The relatively shallow seams on the rising
ground south of the river in the manors of Gateshead and
Whickham, the scene of the great expansion of the industry
since Queen Elizabeth's reign, were practically worked out.
Skilled viewers, Fenwick and Dennoldson, surveyed and
reported on the state of the several pits there in 1697–8 and
the yearly output figures for the period 1693–1710 leave
the matter in no doubt. Whereas in 1696 the pits at Gateshead and Whickham had produced 886 and 1,147 tens
respectively, the corresponding figures in 1710 were 728
and 673. At the same time, the number of proprietors had
shrunk from twelve and fourteen to four and nine respectively.[2] True, three or more 'brogling' partnerships continued for another generation or more to work the remaining
seams of low-quality coals that found a market at the salt-
pans at Shields or were converted into 'cinders', i.e. coke,
used in malting and other concerns in the neighbourhood.[3]
It is true also that deeper mines were eventually 'won' at
Bensham, Felling, and the Park and that Gateshead Fell
colliery, on lease to Sir William Blackett, continued to be of
some importance. But of the general position there can be no

[1] N.B.—The material for this chapter has been drawn almost entirely from the uncalendared
Cotesworth and Ellison MSS. For the earlier history of coal-mining see Nef., *Rise of the British
Coal Industry in the Sixteenth and Seventeenth Centuries*; also for measures, e.g. ten, chaldron,
used in the trade, and technical terms.

[2] Allowing for newcomers who took over from other lessees.

[3] *Infra.* 'Brogling' from 'broggle' = to poke.

doubt. In 1735 the manorial steward, Thomas Sisson, added this note to the town rental of Gateshead, 'the same—a total of £22/6/- —is very ill paid by reason the coal trade is almost quite gone from Gateshead; although the houses we have are generally tenanted, they are by such as are not able to pay their rents'. Unlet and partly derelict staiths on the river front told the same tale. In a sense Gateshead was already a depressed area in the days of Walpole's *quieta non movere*. The centre of mining activity had shifted farther afield.

There were two alternatives before the industry—to go deeper or to fan out laterally: neither was easy and both were attempted. It was known that thicker and more valuable seams lay at a greater depth near the river—reliable borings had already been made to a depth of over 70 fathoms[1] and the technical difficulties encountered in sinking shafts to this depth were soon to be surmounted by a north Staffordshire mining engineer, Stonier Parrott.[2] But so far persistent and costly attempts to win them had failed. Stephen Owen at the Park, Mark Riddell and others at Bensham, Ralph Brandling at Felling, and on the other side of the river, Hugh Bethell at Walker, Alderman Matthew White and Robert Fenwick at Willington and the Bentons, William Bowman at Fenham, and others at Elswick, Kenton, Heaton, and Byker had a dismal tale to tell. Cotesworth stated in evidence before a government commission in 1723 that

[1] In 1722 Joseph Gill, 'Manager of Collieries' (the earliest use I have found of this title) stated in evidence: 'the Main Cole Seam being about 40 or 50 fathom lower than the Levell of the River Tyne and that it generally lyes 50 fathom lower than the Top Cole and that the Top Cole in the present Working Pitt in the Town Moore [i.e. Bland's & Rutter's] is about 30 fathom from the surface & to the Main Cole nigh 80 fathom deep.' Minutes of Evidence, §§ 75–76.

[2] In 1716 this ingenious gentleman proposed to drain Park colliery, Gateshead, from a shaft on the other side of the river. 'I have been ruminating whether it may not be Practicable or possible to drive two parallel drifts from the bottom of the pits . . . under the River till those drifts reach so far into Park colliery . . . and by that means drain both at one recovery', i.e. the first proposal for a Tyne tunnel. Parrott was a Staffordshire man, cf. Rhys Jenkins, *Collected Papers*, 95. 'In sinking Pitts it has been a difficulty till very lately and now we do it with ye Greatest ease by setting ye foot of ye Engine pump in a small cistern which goes down as ye pit sinks & keep two men to Jack or pump ye water from ye way of ye Sinkers into that cistern about a yard high and by a small ware chain from a Buoy in that cistern to a small Cock in ye Engine house, ye Engine will stand still when the cistern wants water and goes again on its own accord as ye water raises up the Buoy again in ye Cistern.'

'Elswick Colliery lying near the Town Moor and Nun Moor was attempted to be won about 40 years agoe to the best of deponent's remembrance and saith that he had been credibly informed that the undertakers failed in endeavouring to win the said colliery and that the fortunes of several considerable familys were greatly impaired thereby'. It was first effectively won by Mr. Ledgard and partners in 1712. In 1722 Michael Bland surrendered the lease of the collieries under the Town Moor for 'want of mine' five years before it was due to expire. All the above were known to be 'water collieries', where the 'weight' of water proved too much for horse ginns, windmills, pumps, water-courses, and other approved devices. Only a 'fire-engine' operated by 'water-catchers', that is, one of the improved Newcomen steam-engines, could answer. But owing partly to a vicious corner in the patent rights, partly to technical difficulties in casting and boring the 'cylinders' or boilers, the new steam-engine only became generally available in the late seventeen-twenties.[1] One was successfully installed at Heaton in 1729 and another about the same time at Byker and the installation of others at Jesmond, Plessey, and Longbenton in or around 1742 revolutionized output there.[2]

The other way—fanning out laterally—presented equal difficulties, owing partly to the highly controversial question of way-leaves and the great cost of building and maintaining timbered wagon-ways. 'Last Monday', wrote Bowes from Gibside on 22 April 1721, 'we begun to lead down ye new Waggon-way which is ye beginning of my profitt: it is a

[1] See my article 'The First Steam Engines in the Durham Coalfield' in *Arch. Ael.* (4th ser.), xxvii; Raistrick, *Newcomen Soc. Trans.* xvii. 131–63. Cf. Rhys Jenkins, loc. cit. The cylinders and pumps were made by Harrison and Waylett, ironmasters, at a foundry near London. 'Old Mr Newcommen' was reported to be present in January 1729, the year of his death. 'We were very unlucky in our Heaton affair', wrote Colonel Liddell in February, '. . . had a messenger from the Founder [Waylett] that by driving the horses too fast they had cracked the Cylinder' [at boring] 'and that they cannot undertake to make a new one under six months.' Stonier Parrott was the first to suggest a 'cylinder' made of iron plates.

[2] Raistrick, loc. cit. At Jesmond colliery in 1742 Samuel Calley was allowed £5 a month 'for keeping the engine'. In the following year the output was 7,425 chaldrons, worth £4,455. Ridley MSS. Long Benton began production in 1744. Ashton and Sykes, *The Coal Industry of the Eighteenth Century*, 241.

work of such great importance and crosses so many Mountains and Vales which are all levelled that I can compare it to nothing more properly than to ye Via Appia.'

Wayleaves [Joseph Banks, M.P., explained to the Commissioners for Forfeited Estates in 1719] are wayes from such mines to the said staithes (or wharves) laid with good Frames of Timber to fitt the waggon wheels, which being laid levell and descending, one horse will draw 3 or 4 chaldrons of coal several miles from the mines to the staithes. These wayes or wayleaves are so valluable that they are often farmed on the River Tyne at ye Rents of £100, £500 or £1000 per annum and without such wayleaves, staithes are of no manner of use, nor will yield any profit.

He was not exaggerating. In 1722 William Dent, a lease-holder at Swallwell paying £40 a year rent was offered £500 a year for way-leave over his ground. Cotesworth stated in evidence before a House of Commons Committee on the coal trade in 1711, that the overland haul in some instances was as much as 6 miles. In fact, Mr. Hedworth's wagon-way which Defoe saw in 1710 and the Earl of Oxford fifteen years later, actually crossed the main Durham–Newcastle road from his colliery on 'Chester Waists' to Biddick and thence to Sunderland.[1] And besides the oldest known wagon-way, the Ravensworth–Main Team, so graphically depicted on Cuthbertson's survey map of Farnacres in 1715, there was already a 'trunk' to Chopwell. By that time others were feverishly contemplated and as fiercely contested to the 'Western collieries', Burnopfield, Byermoor, Bucksnooke, and Tanfield Moor. Indeed, in that very year, the Liddells, Cotesworth, and Hedworth were competing for the lease of Urpeth colliery, some 2 miles north-west of Chester-le-Street, the coals from which it was proposed to lead to either Tyne or Wear. And not only were quite fantastic rents demanded for way-leaves by landowners, great and small, as Banks indicated, but the cost of laying and maintaining a wagon-way was very considerable. The materials alone for one at Ravensworth in 1726, some 10,000 yards in length,

[1] *H.M.C. Portland*, vi. 103–4.

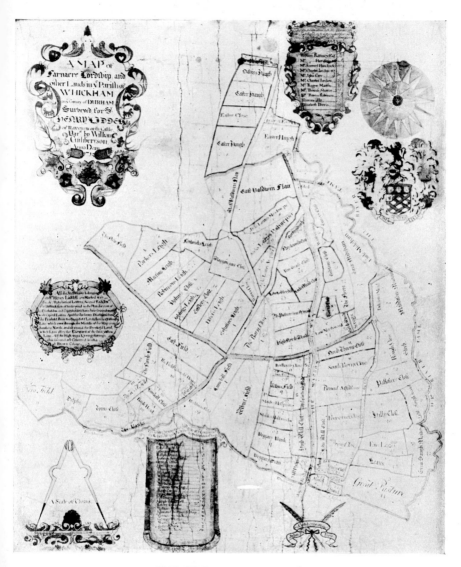

MAP OF FARNACRES, 1715

*N.B. The wagon-way runs due north*

Plan
of the
COLLIERIES
on the RIVERS
Tyne and Wear
also
Blyth, Bedlington and Hartley,
with the Country 11 Miles round
Newcastle
Taken from actual Surveys by
JOHN GIBSON.
1788.

J. GIBSON: MAP OF THE COLLIERIES (*Inset*)

cost little short of £500, while the charge for laying one some 5 miles long came to £2,677. There was little to choose between the high rents demanded for the use of the improved steam-engine and the landlord monopoly in the matter of way-leaves.

A notable pioneer in wagon-ways was Thomas Brumell, an elder hostman of Newcastle. In 1710 he obtained a lease from Sir John Clavering of Axwell Park to build a wagon-way, 10 yards wide, from Byermoor to the Tyne. This is of special interest because the use of iron rails was apparently contemplated, some sixty years before the first iron railway at Coalbrookdale. Expensive and protracted lawsuits prevented the realization of the dreams of this 'bold undertaker', but he deserves a special niche in history as the maker of the first model railway. Let an opponent, Henry Liddell, relate the story:

Last night [wrote Liddell from London on 20 November 1713] Brumell entertained the Dealers with the sight of a waggon way in frame, three yards in length and a little waggon carrying a bushel of coals.[1] *N.B.* This minature of a waggon and the way was brought up by sea in order to have shewn to the C$^{tee}$ (if oppertunity offer'd) thereby demonstrating at once the excessive charge that attends coal owners and therefore an inducement to them [i.e. the House of Commons] to grant readily a Bill for settling of wayleavs at a reasonable rate. This notable machine has laid concealed in a box at the Salutation [Inn] ever since, which is about a 12 month ago, as I take it. However, I shall leave that Gentleman where I found him viz, at the Gate. [Billingsgate.]

Unhappily, Brumell's 'notable machine' has probably perished long since but the purpose for which it was made,

---

[1] William Row, aged about seventy-nine, stated in evidence in 1736 that the wagons used at Gateshead Fell colliery were built by himself and his brother in 1694: 'The dimensions given for making them were taken from the wagons used at Fellon Colliery as follows, Height 3′ 6″ from the sole to the top of the overing, Breadth 4′ 5″ insides at the top and 2′ 2½″ at the bottom of the deales, Length 6′ 11″ top insides, and 4′ 3½″ at the bottom.' A wagon of these dimensions was reckoned to carry 15 bowles. He added that Sir William Blackett had ordered him to keep the wagons to the same gauge ever since 1694; that 'loose ledges' were put up only *after* the wagons were loaded 'to prevent runs' (i.e. overspill), and that the overman 'pulled them down' if they were put up beforehand. Nef has a print of a colliery wagon. See inset in Gibson's map of 1788.

'to demonstrate at once the excessive charge that attends coal owners', is even better served by a document written for the same occasion.

### Reflections on the Coal Trade from its first rise.

The Countrey adjacent to Newcastle affords variety of seames or veines of coal some of which are to be found and wrought from 10 to 73 fathom from the surface of the earth, and generally speaking, the Deeper the veine lyes, the better and stronger is the coal. The thickness of the vein is in some places a yard, in others ½ yd, it is in some few nere two yards.

Where the seam lyes deep you are allways attended with vast quantityes of Watter which must be drawn by horses and att a prodigious Expense from £500 to £1500 yearly. To add to this infirmity you generally are disturbed with sulphurious Damps which for want of Circulation of Air to purge them are verry apt to take fire and frequently (though the nicest care to prevent be used) does blow up numbers of workmen and consequently where this Hazard is run men will have a proportionate addition of price for the working. These collierys generally lye nere the River and by that means the shortness of land carriage does in some measure putt them upon a ballance with other collierys that lyes at a distance from the River.

The charges of winning a colliery thus attended and situated is knowen to be selldome less than 4 sometimes £7000. Nay frequent instances within this 20 years make it appear that sometimes the undertaker looses his venture and never able to compass the working of the seame. But suppose he shuld, your sume is actually sunk; then to manage the work of such a concern, a less sum than that cannot be supposed to be advanced and lyes dead. *Quaere.* What interest one might reasonably expect for hazard of monies? At least 20 per cent; so that if £10,000 should be required to manage such a concern the profit should be £2000 yearly profit. The charges of work, the sinking the pit and drawing the coals above the ground at 70 fathom may be computed, [for] 17 chaldrons Newcastle measure (as follows). [*See table opposite.*]

Where the Pitts are so deep you may be supposed to raise from 500 to 800 of these tenns, the profit of which is little more than £600 for the interest of your monies, supposing noe loss in the way of Dealing by the [Ship] Masters' notes and failing of your fitters. Nay, if you

do not sell that quantity and at the price neer, you are actually runing
out your principall stock.

As the seames are of several dipths and sortes so are the veines of each
coal, some proper for smiths where only ye strongest caker is sought for,
and others of a lesser strength are fittest for Brewers, Glass, Sugar
Baker(s), Lime, and those that are still more open are the most coveted
by the housekeepers.

| | | | |
|---|---|---|---|
| 17 cha. Work[ing] | £4 | 17 cha. [selling] price at | |
| Drawing water | 10s/- | 10s/6d | £8/18/6 |
| Rent | 15s/- | Fittage and owner's | |
| Leading | 15s/- | wages to be deducted | |
| Repair of ways | 7s/6d | at least 1s/6d per cha. | £1/5/6 |
| Wayleaves, servants' | | | |
| wages, charges at the | | | £7/13/- |
| Pitt | 10s/- | [Deduct Cost] | 6/17/6 |
| | | | |
| | £6/17/6 | [Leaves] | 15s/6d |

Till of late years fitters, that is people employed per the owners to
sell the master coall, had so much per chaldron and one owner would
give leave to 10 or 12 fitters to use his steath and these fitters perhaps
had the liberty of vending from as many different steaths: by this means
there was a generall mixture, insomuch that noe consumer could rely
upon any commodity that was brought up to market as intierly fitt for
his purpose upon which continued complaints were made, to prevent
which the sume . . . . chief the cole owners[1] came to an agreement to
work the best of their severall seames and send them unmixed with an
account of each vessel's loads and employ siveral lightermen to Encourage and recommend these best sorte of coles to their customers and
for their pains are content to allow them a small Recompense of the
nature of factoridge. These Dealers are actually loosers by the bargain
for having formerly used to buy ordinary coals at an easy Rate and
mixing them with the best, sold at the Topp of the Markett and this
was put in their pockets, but the consumer being disappointed was the
sole sufferer.

It is matter of fact that at some concernes that are led by wain or
cart carriage, the price of each ch[aldron] led is advanced $\frac{1}{3}$, others $\frac{1}{4}$,

---

[1] A copying error(?) it should read 'the chief cole owners. . . '.

not any less than ⅙ and this is not solely owing to the Dearth of provisions, but allso to the great demand of carriage of Pan coal.

The prices of working and drawing are considerably advanced on account of the price of corn which is double the price at least of former years and it cannot be supposed that a man's family can be mentained with less than formerly, the Price being double, he accordingly sets a vallue upon his Laboure and all this goes out of the Coalowner's Pocket. Nay, I am certain that one with another all charges to the staith, the owner is [the] sufferer by [the] additional charge at least 14 or 15$^d$ per cha [ldron] Newcastle measure, the Master has his 53 [cwt.] with only [an] advance of sixpence in price while at Sunderland they have raised theres at least 12$^d$ per cha within this two years.

On the question of finance two things may be said here. The landed gentlemen who engaged in mining ventures were often 'hard run' for cash and borrowed heavily from lawyers and goldsmiths, but it is not until the middle decades of the century that one hears complaints of the 'shortage' of money because of the greater attractiveness and security of government funds—and even then, curiously enough, the complaint came from one who was over-stretched and whose landed estates were put at only £600 a year.[1] 'As this is a time when so much money is turning on Government Securities', wrote Matthew Ridley in January 1747, 'it is not easie to raise any immediately on Land.' 'No one knows at present how to make 3 per cent. of money, the Stocks are so much above Par', wrote Dr. James Baker in 1752. More will be said on the subject of capital for mining ventures presently. Such was the importance of way-leaves that Alderman Matthew White, owner of the colliery at Jesmond, seriously proposed in 1711 a clause to enable mine-owners to impress carts and wains for the carriage of coal to the Tyne, and shortly afterwards powerful interests in Newcastle promoted bills, on at least three occasions, to 'lay open' way-leaves.

Nor were these the only problems facing the industry at

---

[1] Letter Book (Ridley MSS.). Sir John Sudbury wrote in December 1689, 'Money is hazarded with lying in Goldsmith's hands'; but in 1711 Henry Liddell remarked 'Now on the best land security no money can be had; credit is so sunk'. *Infra*, 247.

the beginning of the century. True, old proprietors, like the Liddells, were convinced that some restraint must be put on 'the Western Collieries' up the Derwent valley. By the middle of the century 'Tanfield Moor' headed the price-list of coals on the London market, followed by Byker and Pontops and as early as 1712 Bucksnooke was a name to conjure with as 'the darling at the Gate'.[1] But the great concern of the coal interests on the Tyne, as the Earl of Oxford discovered when he visited Newcastle in 1725,[2] was the competition of Sunderland. 'They seem at present a little jealous of Sunderland', he wrote, 'which has of late shared with it pretty considerably in this trade and as I am told is likely to gain more and more upon it every day.' The Wear port had certain advantages—virgin seams in its immediate hinterland, no chartered hostmen or powerful corporation to 'oppress' traders, and it was some hours' sailing time nearer the London market. How serious was Sunderland's challenge is evident from the following figures for 1710 found among the papers of a Newcastle cartel.

|  | Coastwise | Overseas | Total |
|---|---|---|---|
|  | (chaldrons) |  |  |
| Newcastle    .    . | 157,719 | 10,375 | 168,094 |
| Sunderland    .    . | 67,151 | 10,182 | 77,333 |
| Cullercoats    .    . | 6,051 | 138 | 6,189 |
| Blyth & Seaton Sluce | 4,230 | 95 | 4,325 |
|  | 235,151 | 20,790 | 255,941 |

From then onwards repeated attempts were made to 'regulate' the proportions of the rival ports and from time to time a measure of agreement was reached.[3] At a conference of the principal owners in London in February 1731 'My Lord [Scarborough] would be content with 125,000 [chaldrons] to our 300,000', wrote Colonel George Liddell, 'but Mr. Hedworth says they cannot start under 130,000 to our 315,000'.[4]

This I take to be the same as we offered them last year [he

---

[1] Add. MSS. 38331, § 121.   [2] *H.M.C. Portland*, vi. 105–6.
[3] *Infra*. 241.   [4] Note the increase since 1710.

continued] but would be more agreeable to them I find. I told them if we were to increase in proportion and abate in proportion, for my own part I should come into it. This must not be said [save] among friends, because they have put Harry Lambton at their head and he will be drawn but not ledd. We parted very friendly and promised each other to use our Interest on each river.

That was easier said than done. Until an agreement could be reached among the principal proprietors on both Tyne and Wear, a larger 'Regulation' was impossible. Among Newcastle men the large measure given at Sunderland continued to be a matter of the gravest concern. Friends joked with each other if one sent an unusually long letter, remarking that they were giving 'Sunderland measure', but the competition from 'the Wear men' was no matter for joking.

That Sunderland owners were prepared from time to time to discuss accommodation is symptomatic of a more general malady from which both were liable to suffer. They had common marketing problems: both had to contend with the demands of ships' masters and London middlemen which, if submitted to, they were convinced would 'enslave' them both. For truth to tell, the trade as a whole, and shipping in particular, were overdone. The alternative to a 'Regulation' as James Clavering saw it in 1711, was 'a fighting trade run in a tempestuous shallow stream'. Official statistics of the total yearly shipments from Newcastle from 1660 to 1710 show plainly enough that the volume of trade in the two decades since the Revolution was no greater—indeed it was less—than for the period 1678–88.[1] Coal-owners were not likely to forget the disastrous year 1690, when the total shipped was the lowest since the Plague year and when they had been obliged to give 'gift coal' up to five and six in the score in order to get rid of their stocks. The next two years were little better. At no time since the Glorious Revolution had the figure reached that of the peak year, 1688, when 23,126 tens were shipped: in only two years, 1699 and 1701,

---

[1] Cotesworth MSS. Yearly shipments to London are given in Lansdowne MSS. 846, § 282. Cf. Nef, ii. 95; Ashton, 249–51. Willan, *The English Coasting Trade*, 210–20.

had the figure since topped 20,000. 'A true description of the lamentable state of the Newcastle trade would appear almost past all belief', wrote Charles Povey in 1700.

Now my good friend [wrote Henry Liddell to Cotesworth in July 1711] give me leave to tell you that you will find the Coal Trade draw near a period for this year. Scarce a master that comes over the Barr that can clear £10 a voyage, even supposing he come and goe well: very few that save themselves and most have made a great hole in their stocks so that necessity rather than inclination obliges them to lye by. Nay, the common saylors are reduced to such a low ebb that they cannot so much as feed their familys with Bread and water.

A year earlier, as we shall see, there had been 'combinations' among both the ships' masters and the keelmen and the government had seen fit to send a regiment to Newcastle to suppress the 'mutiny'. 'They that work in the Coal Trade', wrote Cotesworth in 1717, 'do not eat Roast beef and it is well they can keep anything in the meal poke and all that want employment and have a mind to work Coal worke may now be as fully imployed as if the coals were exported from forty ports.'[1] We can begin to appreciate why thoughtful men were already thinking in terms of 'Regulation' and a quota system.

But the coal trade had a dangerously seductive quality about it. 'The Colliery never made less than £1,500 per annum these last thirty years past', wrote W. B. Bowes in 1720, 'and made me last year £2,500.'[2]

There will always be something or other to fight about in the coal trade [wrote Thomas Sisson in 1728] though, for all that, there's few that gets into the trade that is willing for to out, the profit is so great.

Certainly, men outside the industry imagined that handsome profits were to be made in it. Were not the mines about

[1] In answer to an allegation of a Tyne monopoly.
[2] Bowes MSS. 40747, § 176. He admitted, however, that his estate 'is prodigiously encreased by a Wayleave I have procured by which I shall improve my Colliery above £3000 per annum'. Until 1720 his colliery had been let to the Wortleys on a twenty-one-year lease at a tentale rent of 17s. per ten. They offered to increase the rent to 30s per. ten if the lease was renewed. Ibid., § 160.

Newcastle 'England's Peru'? Accordingly, plenty of adventurers embarked, 'blinded by yellow dust' to use Clavering's phrase. Henry Liddell, a sober realist, had a different tale to tell. 'Methinks the gain of about £2,000 in twelve years' service is no very extravagant allowance for one's service and pains, not to mention the entire ruin of a man's health which at this time is a sawcy rent charge', he wrote in 1711: six years later his brother confessed that the family had lost £3,000 in shipping.

Gray, the author of *Chorographia*, the first history of Newcastle, had noted earlier,

I can remember one of many that raysed his estate by coale-trade: many I remember that had wasted great estates. . . . They labour and are at a great charge to maintain men to work their collieries, they wast their own bodies with care and their collieries with working. The kernel being eaten out of the nut, there remaineth nothing but the shell; their collieries is wasted and their monies is consumed. This is the uncertainty of mines, a great charge, the profit uncertain.

He instanced some 'south gentlemen', in particular 'one Master Beaumont, who within a few years consumed all his money and rode home upon his light horse', and 'some Londoners of late who had, upon great hope of benefit, come into this country to hazard their monies in coale-pits'. 'When they come to crack their nuts', he repeated, 'they find nothing but the shells: nuts will not keep thirty years [the term of a colliery lease] there is a swarme of wormes underground that will eat up all before their time. They may find some meteors, *ignis fatuus*, instead of a mine.' In the last years of the century, Stephen Owen of Gray's Inn, Gent, the lessee of Park colliery, Gateshead, Sir Charles and Captain Philip Bickerstaffe at Whickham, Mark Riddell and partners at Bensham, Mr. Rogers, once reputed to be one of the biggest proprietors on the river, and more than one merchant of Newcastle discovered to their cost the truth of Gray's observation.[1] The Gateshead and Whickham colliery

---

[1] Evidence of Henry Atkinson in 1736 who stated that he had been 'bound' to Mr. Rogers in 1685.

rentals for the period 1693–1710 reveal a steady process of attrition and elimination: only those with long purses survived.[1] But the supply of 'south gentlemen' and others continued. In 1686 George Pitt of Strathfieldsay, Dorset, progenitor of a noted family, took a lease of a colliery at Tanfield Moor. A decade later Charles Montague, nephew of Bishop Crewe and kinsman of the Dean of Durham, took a lease on the usual 'tentale' basis of certain pits in the manor of Whickham. By 1709 when he borrowed £2,000 from Alderman Ramsay, the Newcastle goldsmith, he owed over £1,000 in 'dead rents'. The Montague-Wortleys had long purses and their persistence was rewarded. When Edward Wortley died in 1761 the size of his fortune surprised contemporaries—he was reputed to be worth nearly three-quarters of a million, exclusive of his landed properties. He was one of the meteors. His partner, George Bowes, was another; yet in 1730 Bowes confessed 'that he had long weaned himself from expectations of profit'. Against the few overgrown fortunes that sprang up there were many that fell by the wayside. Brumell, the most controversial figure in the industry in the early years of the century, went bankrupt and his partner Wright, a Sedgefield justice, fled into Wales.[2] How far the big London dealers financed industrial ventures will never be known. That they did so is indisputable. In 1715 two of them, Coltman and Blunkett, were credibly reported to be 'deeply soused' by Brumell and Wright's undertakings and the Oldners were also involved though they had pulled out, on advice from Liddell, before the crash came. Richard Ridley was certainly looking for

---

[1] The Bickerstaffes, for instance, were under contract to lead 250 tens per ann. at a rent of £100. They did moderately well for the first three years (1693–5), but in 1696 they led none and less than 20 tens in each of the next two years. At the end of 1701 there were 1,549 tens 'unled' on their lease, representing a rent deficiency of £619. 12s. 4d. They threw in their hand. Similarly, Charles Montague, who had taken over Thomas Owen's lease in 1697 and those of A. Barnes and G. Airey a few years later, had 2,553 tens 'unled' in 1709, a rent deficiency of £1,021. 10s. 9d.

[2] William Scott, the father of Lord Eldon, was apprenticed to Brumell in September 1716, but was assigned to Joseph Colpitts, another hostman, in the following year. Twiss, *Eldon*, i. 23–24.

help from this same quarter to make his Byker and Dipton pits going concerns in 1729, and he was known to be on terms of close friendship with Maltis Ryall, another of the big London dealers. It is clear, too, that a leading City financier, Tom Gibson of Lothbury Street, was heavily engaged in financing colliery undertakings at the close of Queen Anne's reign. In short, until more men had burnt their fingers in the industry, the situation was highly fluid.

The position at the turn of the century was made even more confused by another set of not unrelated circumstances. Since the middle of Queen Elizabeth's reign certain freemen of Newcastle had enjoyed the 'Grand Lease' of the manors of Gateshead and Whickham on a ninety-nine-year lease. Before the term had quite run out Bishop Cosin of Durham granted a new lease to his son-in-law, Sir Gilbert Gerard, whose family remained in possession until 1711, when the manors were bought by Cotesworth for Alderman Ramsay.[1] The question arises, How had the powerful Newcastle Hostmen reacted to the changed position? Cotesworth contended that under the 'Grand Lease' the Hostmen had been the real proprietors and that of necessity the coal-owners must continue to dominate the trade. It must not be supposed that the powerful freemen of Newcastle, doubly entrenched behind chartered privilege, surrendered to the new *entrepreneurs* and landed gentlemen without a struggle. Time and again the cry went up from the coal-owners in the early years of the eighteenth century that they should avoid 'falling again into the servitude of the fitters', i.e. the hostmen. Now we know that individual hostmen like Alderman Matthew White had a half share of the colliery at Blaydon as well as at Jesmond, Sir Ralph Carr was the proprietor of Field-house, Alderman Robert Fenwick had pits at Whickham, while the very name 'Grand Lease' was perpetuated in Stella colliery farther to the west. Another influential alder-

---

[1] Cosin granted the lease in March 1665 but it was not confirmed by the dean and chapter until 1667. Register of Leases, § 581. *V.C.H. Durham*, ii. 326, is in error in supposing that the Grand Lease was granted to Col. Liddell after 1681.

man, Francis Rudston, a merchant-shipper, had a lease of
the colliery at Heworth and in 1712 John Wilkinson, Sir
William Blackett's agent, of the colliery at Jarrow.[1] The
successful exploitation of Scotswood, Elswick, Kenton,
Jesmond, Gosforth, and Byker was due to individual hostmen like Robert Fenwick, George Ledgard, Matthew White,
Philip Hodgson, and Richard Ridley. Conversely, William
Bowman failed at Fenham and Brumell at Bucksnooke. The
result is easy to see. The Hostmen's Company experienced
the same oligarchical tendency that was the fate of most
gilds and companies. In course of time, all semblance of
equality among its members was lost and the relative status
of the rank and file deteriorated. In short, the position of the
hostman-fitter *vis-à-vis* the colliery proprietor was already
undergoing a revolutionary change when the century opened.
The author of the *Reflections on the Coal Trade* suggests that
important changes had lately taken place in marketing, e.g.
the arrangement with the London lightermen which profoundly affected the fitters, while in 1712 Henry Liddell
frankly confessed that he preferred to give the London
dealers a premium rather than let the trade fall again into
the hands of the fitters. So it came about that each coal-
owner contracted with individual fitters—George Liddell
later explained that he employed nine of them—on a yearly
basis and normally a fitter could serve only one owner, the
very reverse of the former position. In other words, Cotesworth's basic contention that the coal-owners must continue
to dominate the trade was fully vindicated, only they were
no longer principally the Newcastle Hostmen. In course of
time the fitters, like the pitmen, wagon-men, and keelmen,
became 'tied' by a yearly bond to the coal-owner, but with
this important difference: they themselves retained more
than a semblance of independence since they both owned the
keels and engaged, took bond of, and paid the keelmen.
Some indeed, like Lord Eldon's father, were able to make

---

[1] Rudston went bankrupt in 1733. *Infra.* The yearly output figures of Jarrow colliery are
given in the Durham dean and chapter Audit Books; e.g. 142 tens in 1700, 329 in 1740.

considerable fortunes and to buy lands in County Durham.[1] The coal-owners eventually discovered that tamed fitters, who were servants and not masters, were a very useful buffer or smoke-screen between themselves and the consumer on the one hand, and some hundreds of sturdy keelmen on the other. It was an accidental arrangement, the product of a curious evolution, that could scarcely be bettered from the coal-owners' point of view. Labour troubles with the keelmen were obviously acute from 1707 onwards before they reached a climax in the famous 'mutiny' of the summer of 1710.[2] To what extent were they the result of the screw which the owners were applying to the fitters? By the latter date matters were clearly moving to a crisis, and the interest is enhanced by the fact that since 1709 there had been a powerful combination of owners, known as the 'Regulation' or 'Contract', the most advanced experiment in industrial organization that England had yet seen. To that we must now turn.

## II

### THE FIRST 'REGULATION'

'It was two years gone Michaelmas since the agreement was first spoke of', Cotesworth stated in evidence before a House of Commons Committee in April 1711, 'and about two years this month since the paper book was brought to me to see if it was according to the discourse they had at several times.' Three months earlier his friend, 'the Governor', had written to him, 'with most people, you know, 'tis customary to Christen their own child first, and as the world goes, I don't see why you should not practice that Rule'. Cotesworth was in truth the father of the 'Regulation': in 1710 he became its chief executive officer and paid secretary.

---

[1] Twiss, op. cit. i. 102. As freemen of Newcastle, hostmen could engage in foreign trade. *Infra*, 249.
[2] Dendy, *The Newcastle Hostmen's Company*, 172–7. The keelmen formed a combination in 1707. Brand, ii. 508–9; Ashton and Sykes, 195–7. 'The rise of the independent fitter', writes Nef, 'appears to have taken place during the second & third quarters of the seventeenth century', ii. 86. He agrees (p. 133) that the success of any vendors' ring depended on a monopoly of keels.

The minutes of the meetings of its five 'Directors' with other important documents are preserved among his papers. The earliest of these is a draft of 'Articles of Agreement Tripartite', dated 1708, between the following ten proprietors— Henry Liddell, Sir John Clavering, James Clavering, John Wilkinson, Sir Ralph Carr, George Pitt, Matthew White, Philip Hodgson, Robert Fenwick, and James Montague on the first part, some twenty-three Newcastle hostmen or 'fitters' on the second part, and a certain Daniel Poyen 'ye principal agent' on the third part. There followed the suggested 'Proportions' as under:—

| | | |
|---|---|---|
| Gibside and Benwell | James Montagu | 4000 tens |
| $\frac{15}{24}$ of Stella Grand Lease | | 1050 ,, |
| Ravensworth: Mr. Liddell's pitt Coachy field, Chauden & $\frac{3}{8}$ of Blackburn (Sir Henry Liddell) | | 2400 ,, |
| Bensham colliery (Sir Henry Liddell) $\frac{6}{8}$ | | 900 ,, |
| Chopwell ,, | | 1400 ,, |
| All Stella Grand Lease | | 1400 ,, |
| Kenton | Mr. Wilkinson | 1300 ,, |
| Gateside & Heworth | | 1400 ,, |
| Darwent, Byer Moor, Fawdon field, Rideingfield and all other Sir John Clavering's collierys | | 550 ,, |
| Field House | Sir Ra(lph) Carr | 800 ,, |
| Tanfield Moor | Mr. Pitts | 550 ,, |
| Jesmond Colliery | Mr. White & Mr. Hodgson's | 1000 ,, |
| Lord Widderington's Stella & Ryton: Parson's Collierys | | 300 ,, |
| Two several fourth parts of Blaydon colliery | White and Wilkinson | 400 ,, |
| | | 16400 tens[1] |

Then came this cryptic statement: 'Sir Henry Liddell Bart. £200 per an and he or Henry Liddell Esq. to have the nomination of ye principal agent.' In other words, the 'Regulation' was to be launched like a ship, not as a joint stock, but as a regulated undertaking with a levy according to the estimated output of the several concerns; and, as in shipbuilding, the chief promoter and subscriber was to have

[1] The discrepancy in the total would appear to be due to the fact that the entry for Stella Grand Lease was duplicated in part.

the right of nominating the master or principal agent. Unfortunately, the role of this official and his relations with the twenty-three fitters is nowhere precisely stated and can only be inferred from later developments.

That a 'Regulation' on these lines was in fact launched in the spring of 1709 is certain, though we have no clear idea of how it worked until the summer of 1710. From June of that year there was an executive committee of five, 'commonly called the 5 Directors', said Brumell, viz. Mr. Liddell, Mr. Clavering, Alderman White, Mr. John Ord, and Mr. Wilkinson, with a paid secretary in attendance. At first the 'Five' met at least once a month or oftener at a local coffee-house or inn in Gateshead (Hull's, Shepherd's, Percival's, or Hutchinson's) and very occasionally at Ravensworth Castle or at Cotesworth's own house on 'Battel bank'. By that time 'the proportions of the several collieries' and their respective contributions to a common fund had been tabulated. It will be noted that the names of certain proprietors or concerns which had appeared in the original articles had dropped out.

| Tens | No. | | [Levy] |
|---|---|---|---|
| 4000 | 1 | Hutton and Benwell [Mr. Montague] | £266/ 6/8 |
| 2400 | 2 | Main Team [Sir Henry Liddell] | £159/16/2½ |
| 1300 | 3 | Scotswood [Mr. Wilkinson] | £ 86/11/2½ |
| 1400 | 4 | Fellon [Sir William Blackett] | £ 93/ 4/2½ |
| 1200 | 5 | Bencholme [Sir H. Liddell and partners] | £ 79/18/- |
| 1400 | 6 | Stella Grand Lease [In partnership] (for ye whole) | £ 93/ 4/2½ |
| 1400 | 7 | Clavering's Stella [Sir John Clavering and others] | ,, |
| 1000 | 8 | Jesmond [Alderman White and P. Hodgson] | £ 66/12/-½ |
| 200 | 9 | Bladon [Sir W. Blackett's ¼] | £ 13/ 6/5 |
| 200 | 10 | New Stella | ,, |
| 460 | 11 | Smith's Team | £ 30/12/5¼ |
| 59 | 12 | H'y Water's Darwen | £ 3/18/-¼ |
| 15019 | | | £1000 [approx.] |

It is obvious that there was to be an output quota for each colliery with a proportionate levy towards a 'common fund' which at the start was to be £1,000.

The minutes of the meetings of the 'Five', numbered seriatim by the secretary, have survived. Those of the first meeting are here given in full.

No. I. *Orders agreed upon 19th June 1710 by the Five.*

1st. It is agreed that all the coal owners use their authority with their several fitters to oblige the skippers and boundmen [i.e. keelmen] in their several works to load their coals without loss of time from their respective staiths and Ly them in the Host to be ready against the ships come in to give them a better dispatch.

2nd. It is agreed that no coals be led to any steath in the Regulation from this day till there be another meeting of the Five and that there be a meeting called as soon as ever there is any account of any ships coming to the barr.

3rd. Bucksnooke wayleave. The colliery to be laid in till further orders.

4th. That the offenders against W^m Cotesworth and his informer be prosecuted at the publique charge.

5th. That Mr. Alderman Fenwick be acquainted from the Five that seeing the Regulation has been very offensive to him and that he has expressed himself dissatisfied with it, and it being like to prove some expence to the Gentlemen concerned in it, though it be now laid aside, they desire to know whether he agrees to contribute his proportion of such charge as shall so happen and if he answer he will contribute nothing to the charge that he be then told that he must not expect then the coals promised him by the several owners, nor to be paid any salary for his fitters, their promises or obligations for both depending solely on the continuance of the said Regulation of trade.

The first of these orders has reference to the existing strike of shippers and of keelmen who had refused to load the summer fleet of colliers. The last proves that the 'Regulation' had in fact been in existence in the previous year though 'the charge', i.e. the levy, for that year had not yet been collected. It also shows the kind of screw which it was proposed to apply to recalcitrants. For the rest, it is clear that the 'Committee' was already proceeding upon certain recognized principles, viz., a stint, involving, if need be, the closing down of certain pits, and a common fighting fund.

In the next nine months, until the middle of March 1711, when Cotesworth was 'desired by the Five to go forthwith to London to negotiate and solicit the coal trade depending before the Parliament', these principles were elaborated. Thus, at the July meeting, steps were taken to secure uniform measure of the keels, ostensibly on the pretext that some had been 'so long lying up', with a view 'to make out 15 chaldron to a keel'. Two officers, Edward Grey, a former hostman, and John Bowes, were accordingly appointed to inspect and mark 'with a scrieving iron' all keels employed by the 'Regulation'.[1] Three other officials were appointed to accompany the keels 'in going down the river and casting on board of the ships at Shields and elsewhere', since it was generally held that grave abuses were practised, prejudicial both to coal-owners and ships' masters alike, by keelmen throwing coals into the river when going down. (It was easier to unload them thus than into the ships' holds.) A special allowance was to be paid to one of these officers in view of the fact that he would be stationed at Shields to supervise the loading of ships. At the same time, further measures were taken to apply the stint. In August Mr. Ord, Mr. Wortley's agent, was ordered to 'take up his Dunston way and not finish it till the defficient steaths are made up to his proportion, or until further order', and a month later it was 'resolved that Hutton and Benwell lead only two Gates a day for this week and the leading to be regulated at the meeting next munday'. It was then agreed 'that Northbanks shall lead only six gates in a week, that is, either two gates a day for three days a week, or three gates a day for two days in a week ... with 85 waggons, and Benwell five gates a day with 28 waggons three days a week or any other way they please themselves, not exceeding that quantity'. In other words,

---

[1] Grey had previously acted as treasurer of the keelmen's 'Charity'. Dendy, 166–7. *Infra.*

Mr. Montague's 'Hutton and Benwell' pits were exceeding their quota while other owners had 'short coals', i.e. they were not able to dispose of the stocks at the staiths up to their quota. Henry Liddell stated in 1712 that 'Mr. Montague was the greatest owner in our day, would scarce pretend to exceed 1400 tens a year such tens from his Hutton [colliery] which was ever allowed to be ye chiefest colliery in either river'. Early in August Mr. Wilkinson was instructed to write to the London dealers asking them to give equal dispatch to the fleet 'now going up' and 'proportionable price' and on their return 'to recommend some ships to Jesmond colliery and such others as are in defficiency by their [previous] discouraging the sale of such coals at the market'. In September it was decided that 'no promise be made to any [ship's] master from this time nor in this fleet to make good any deficiency in price'. In other words, the prices of the different grades of coal (if we may use such a term for convenience) were fixed and no reductions were to be allowed. This decision produced an immediate reaction from the London middlemen. Mr. Poyen was instructed to write to the three 'agents at the Gate, that he takes their silence to his letters to be a breaking off all correspondence and their own and the dealers quitting all claim to any sallery or gratuity from the coal owners'. A curious proviso was attached to this resolution of the 'Five', to the effect that 'if Sir H. Liddell do not approve this order it is to be void'. The baronet and his son, 'the Governor', lived in town and, as we shall see, were in close touch with the London dealers. At the end of September, Mr. Wilkinson was instructed 'to acquaint his Fitters that he will allow them 12ᵈ a cha. out of 11ˢ/- for his coals at Bladon, to encourage the sale of them' and to enable him to dispose of his quota. The 'Regulation' was obviously getting into deep water.

In view of the recent trouble with the keelmen, the orders of the 'Five' relating to the number of keels that their fitters were to engage are of especial interest. In the middle of November it was agreed 'that the several owners give notice to their fitters not to hire any keles till further orders to be given them'. This was followed a week later with an instruction 'that the whole owners of collierys in the Regulation do abate 8 per cent. in the number of keles for all the keles they have imployed this year and that for every 100 keles they have imployed for the year 1710, they do but imploy for the year, 1711, 92 keles, always remembering', as a later minute put it, 'that a superfluous number of keles starves their men and forces the skippers to get fit tides of such people as hires none which enables those people to injure the trade of the Gentlemen concerned in the Regulation'. Early in December it was resolved 'that 260 keles be imployed for the year 1711 for vending the coals within the Regulation according to a list produced this day by Mr. Cotesworth'.[1] A month later this was implemented by two further orders 'that if any fitter shall entertain in his service any keles more than is allowed him by his owner, that such fitter shall not be allowed any rent for such kele or keles' and, secondly, 'if any keles in the Regulation be taken shipping any coals [of proprietors] out of the Regulation, the fitter to whom such kele or keles do belong shall forfeite the rent for the same'. Henry Liddell made this comment on the decision to reduce the number of keels.

The number of keels you propose will be sufficient, but how to menage the men is a difficulty. Is it that the generality of them have combined not to enter into bond and what pretence have they for so doing?

The yearly 'binding time' for keelmen, Christmas, was drawing near but, as has been pointed out, the keelmen bound themselves to their respective fitters, not to the coal-owners.[2] Liddell continued:

Can't the Hoastman's Company frame a severe law that no fitter shall employ his neighbour's keels on any other pretence than by leave of the Chief Owner? I think ther is such an order, but I mean whether can't it be made more Effectual?

---

[1] This list has not been found.          [2] *Infra*, 251.

On 4 December he wrote again:

If the Partys could be brought to lessen their numbers of waggons, as also their winter works, it would effectually remedy the complaints under which the Trade groan'd this last year, and this may be don without Exception. The abatement of Keels will likewise contribute to make matters go more glibly in several Respects. 'Tis to be hoped that by your prudent menagement below, the Keelmen will be brought to Reason and see what is their true interest, which I take to be, the joining in with their owners and endeavouring to serve their interests with Zeal. . . .

'Had you any discourse with Dan D[ef]oe when in the Countrey?' he continued. 'What sort of Spiritt possesses that man, who seems by the print, of which he is suspected to be ye Author, to encourage modestly speaking a Refractoriness among that sort of people?' Defoe, Robert Harley's agent, had lately visited Newcastle—a Tory stronghold—and in an article in the *Review* had championed the oppressed keelmen.[1] Their grievances were many and various but it is only fair to point out that their famous strike in the summer of 1710 was not caused by the recent combination among the coal-owners. Both keelmen and coal-owners— and we may add ships' masters—were suffering from conditions in the trade, a glutted market, intense competition, and redundant numbers. But Londoners who were required to pay increased prices for coal in the winter of 1710, reading Defoe's article, began to smell the noisome, sulphureous odour of 'monopoly' and 'combination in restraint of trade'. 'For what age ever did or can out-do this in Subtil Devices, Perfidiousness and all manner of sinister Practices?' wrote Povey in his *Discovery of Indirect Practices in the Coal Trade*.

Before turning to the sequel we may briefly summarize other developments in the policy of the 'Regulation' during the autumn and winter of 1710–11. The September meeting approved the levy of 4*d*. per chaldron on its members to defray the expenses for 1709 and the same for 1710, and when it was found that a 'groat' would be insufficient for the

---

[1] *H.M.C. Portland*, v. 14, 143.

current year, an additional penny was authorized. These monies were to be collected by Poyen and Grey, who were to submit a statement of accounts at the end of the year, and Mr. Wilkinson acted as treasurer. As we have seen, the levy was based on output: Mr. Montague's proportion was originally assessed at £266. 6s. 8d. and Sir Henry Liddell's at £159. 16s. 2½d., but, in fact, for 1710–11 they paid very much more, the former £1,647 odd, and Sir Henry Liddell £950. Clavering Stella at £315. 7s. 10¾d. and Mr. Wilkinson at £295. 12s. 3d. came next in order. Meanwhile, difficulties were encountered with recalcitrants, notably Brumell, whose pit at Bucksnooke, it will be recalled, had been ordered to close in the previous summer, both in respect of arrears of groats for the year 1709 when he was in the 'Regulation', as also of his stocks of coal on Derwent staithe. The cartel also threatened legal action against Brumell's partner, Sir John Clavering, in the matter of a disputed way-leave, the cost to be met out of the common fund. By contrast, gentle persuasion was to be used with Clavering's kinsman, Mr. Rogers, who was 'to be waited on to know if he will please to let his coals at Stella come into the agreement'—with what result is not known. In the middle of February it was agreed that Mr. Ord attend the mayor and aldermen of Newcastle 'to solicit them to apply by proper hands to the Queen and Council that the convoys and six cruisers appointed for the coal trade may be made more useful by such ways as shall seem most meet'. A fortnight later a representation to this effect was sent to the Admiralty, a copy of which was shrewdly forwarded to the lord mayor and aldermen of London and their assistance requested. On 29 November it was agreed 'that an account be taken of all ships that cleared for overseas for this year 1710, how many of them loaded coals in the Regulation and by whom vended?' In January it was agreed 'that each owner give notice to their respective fitters that they load no coals for oversea but at New Stella, Bladon and the Burn and that they have leave to sell the coals for foreign vend from the two former at ten shillings

per chaldron and from the Burn at ten shillings and sixpence',
i.e. below the stipulated price, the intention being to dispose of 'inferior' coals, which the owners had not been able
to sell in the home market, abroad—the reverse of the policy
of the National Coal Board. At the same meeting, it was
decided that the secretary 'discourse Mr. Starkin about
making an interest at Zur¹ [*sic*] and with the correspondents
at London in order to sell coals for forreign vend and also
that Mr. Poyen write to the Agent for the garrisons in
Flanders to see if an agreement can be made with him for a
quantity against winter'. Finally, members of the 'Regulation' were concerned about the larger measure being given
at Sunderland and decided that 'some instances of the difference of measure between Tyne and Wear be procured
and given to the Collector of this port to be laid before the
Commissioners of the Customs and that a new commission
for the admeasurement of keles be solicited'.

In mid-November 1710 Mr. Wilkinson, one of the
'Five', was instructed to write to his chief, Sir William
Blackett, M.P. for Newcastle, 'whether he will be pleased
to attend the meeting to be held by Sir H. Liddell and Mr.
Ord [Wortley's agent] in relation to the coal affair', or
alternatively, 'whether he be pleased to submit his intrest
to the manadgment of these two gentlemen'. Sir William's
reply was read at the meeting a fortnight later; he 'desires
to be excused meeting them on account of the coal trade but
he gives Mr. Wilkinson assurance that he is a well wisher
to the agreement and will do all in his power to the continuance of it'. At the same time Cotesworth was instructed
to write to Mr. Wortley and Sir Henry Liddell 'and request
of them to name such agents, solicitors and councell as they
think proper to manadge the intrest of the coal trade *in case
any complaint should be made in Parliament against the Coal
owners of this River*'. The 'Five' had got wind from their
London agents that a movement against them was afoot in
the City.

¹ ? Zoom = Bergen-op-Zoom in the Netherlands.

The proprietors in London unanimously agreed that Cotesworth himself be earnestly requested by the 'Five' to proceed forthwith to London. At the meeting on 1 March 1711 it was agreed that Mr. Wilkinson write to Mr. Wrightson, the other member for Newcastle, 'for a copy of the clause in the Lottery Bill relating to contracts in the coal trade and which is mentioned in the Newcastle Gazette of Wednesday last'. Further, that Alderman White 'give Mr. Liddell an answer to his letter wherein he is to represent to him the hazard of setting on foot any treaty with the Dealers, till the contents of the clause mentioned in the Newcastle Gazette be known and that then the Gentlemen here are willing to concur in such measures as shall be thought for the good of the trade and that that part of his letter which relates to the bargains made by any, on account and with a design to save the public shall be duely considered'. On the 12th it was agreed 'that Mr. Poyen wait on Sir John Clavering and let him know that there being complaints made to Parliament of the coal owners in this River meeting together for the better manadgment of the Coal Trade and more complaints being threatened to be made against them for such their meeting, they will be obliged to forbear the same for the future and therefore cannot undertake to be any way concerned in the selling or providing means for selling his coals for this year and were willing he should know it as soon as possible'. Thus was a potential critic to be disarmed. Three other decisions were made and duly minuted:

> That Mr. Cotesworth propose to Mr. Hedworth [M.P. for County Durham] a meeting of the coal owners of both rivers in order to consider of what may be proper at this juncture to be done for the common good of the Coal Trade. That he write to Mr. Liddell that money will be raised without loss of time for defraying the charge that shall acrew in soliciting the coal trade now depending in Parliament:—1$^d$ per cha. is the sum talked of and proposed. That Mr. Cotesworth be desired to go forthwith to London to negotiate and solicite the coal trade depending before the Parliament and that the moneys to be

raised as in the article above, be either lodged with him in specie or otherwise notes for the parties concerned payable on demand.

The 'Five' decided to meet a week later at Mrs. Hutchinson's to settle all accounts and Messrs. Poyen and Grey were instructed to come prepared with them. In theory, 'the Chamber' was to close down—a shrewd move, as it proved. We know that the 'Five' met, as arranged, on the 21st and discussed the clauses of the Coal Bill of which they had now received precise information from London. Cotesworth was present at this meeting but no minutes were recorded. Thereafter the scene shifts to London. There were no more 'official' meetings of the 'Five' until July, though they continued to meet in informal 'conferences'.

## III

### THE LONDON MARKET

In the eighteenth century the trading interest, especially the City of London, to quote Walpole, 'resembled a hog whom if you attempt to touch, though you was only to pluck a bristle, he would certainly cry out loud enough to alarm all the neighbours'.[1] This was certainly true of the capital's attitude to the coal trade. The eighteenth-century Londoner would not starve in silence. Had not Jonathan Swift in this very year told Stella of the great convenience of coal fires? With unfailing regularity in every decade the government was forced to intervene. The first occasion with which we are concerned was in 1711 when a bill to prevent unlawful combinations in the trade was passed.[2] We have first to inquire where and how the London clamour against an alleged monopoly of producers originated. Where did the consumers' squeal really come from? Generally speaking, the two ends of the economic process—the producer and consumer—are known quantities: it is the elusive middleman who completes the equation.[3] But contemporaries and

[1] Quoted in my *Studies*, 304.
[2] Ashton & Sykes, *The Coal Industry of the Eighteenth Century*, 211.
[3] Westerfield, *Middlemen in English Business*, *passim*. 'There is abundant evidence that

historians alike are often ignorant of his mole-like activities. It is therefore a piece of great good fortune to have the weekly letters of Henry Liddell, the principal London agent of the Tyne 'Regulation', to his friend Cotesworth to supplement our story at this point.

From the first, the 'Regulation' established direct contacts with 'the Dealers at the Gate' and employed certain officials, Bowman and Gilroy, to negotiate sales and expedite the clearing and turn-round of ships in the Thames. Mr. Henry Liddell, known to his intimate circle of friends as 'the Governor', was himself a mine-owner and trustee for his nephew, the future baronet, and he had taken a leading part in organizing the combine 'when he was in the countrey'. He was now something of a self-appointed, higher co-ordinating authority in London. We cannot do better than to quote from his correspondence:

August 15, 1710. . . . I am and always was of opinion that a Bank of £500 should be raised and kept for extraordinary uses. I proposed it before I came out of the Countrey, but no notice was taken of itt. Nay when I came to Town I mention'd it to young Wortley who seemed to approve. I can't imagin the Reason why the last year's groats are not yet collected. Are they affraid of trusting itt? Sure a safe hand might be found out to lodge itt in. Indeed, I apprehend, as I formerly wrote and of late to Mr. Poyen, that the Consequences of not keeping Touch with the Dealers would prove very dangerous and occasion such a Confusion as would shake the Agreement more than all other Artifices that our Enemys could practice. I design for the Gate to-morrow to see if I can stopp their mouths by fair promises, but I doubt I shall not succeed since they are a sort of people that will not be fed with words only. 'Tis worth the consideration of the Five, and that speedily too; therefore, desire you will earnestly recommend this matter to them.

It will be recalled that a month later a decision of the 'Five' to break off all correspondence 'at the Gate' was only to come into effect '*if Mr. Liddell approved*' and from what we know of him it is safe to assume that he did not.

London was seldom free from some sort of a coal ring during the seventeenth century.' Nef, ii. 107.

December 4. . . . The two objections you raised in your last are the chief that can affect the Contractors[1]. . . . I believe it will be thought convenient to cancell it, for in effect if the Dealers should make a breach, I dont see that the owners ever durst venture to sue their Covenant, least it be thought an illegal one and then it turn upon themselves.

December 21. . . . The Dealers have bin with Uncle[2] and me and are dissatisfied that the Notes promised to be given them last Mich[ael-mas] are not yet come: they desire the Gentlemen would take into consideration the last letter they wrote to Mr. Poyen, so as they may have an answer to their demands one way or other. This must be don or I shall have no Peace. Let the answer be sent to some of their body.

December 30. . . . I must tell you that the Dealers were promised that Daniel [Poyen] should give them Notes att Mich'mas for the last sumer's premium, they are very uneasy and believe would gladly be att Liberty; some answer must be given them by order of the Five and till that be don we can't pretend to treat with the Oldners in private for advancing the Creditt of our Stella, I should say 'retrieving' but that is a word that has not rellished with me for many years.

On the back of this letter Cotesworth added a note, dated 4 January, of an informal meeting of the 'Five' at War-riner's: 'that I write to the Governor that Mr. Poyen had no letter from any of the Dealers'. On the same day 'the Governor' himself wrote, 'If the Dealers are not gratyfied, you will see a strange disorder att the Gate this next year. I know they deserve little but it ought to be well weighed what confusion they can bring the Trade in.' And again a week later,

January 11. . . . You would doe well to write to some of your Correspondents to treat about an interest att the Gate without loss of time. I may assure you that till matters be settl'd for this last year's praemium I can't pretend to discourse them about Clav[ering] Stella. Tis to be own'd that coals from severall Steaths have bin sent so very bad that it laid them under great difficultys; however I tell them they might have kept the prices more upon an Equallity, if they would have exerted themselves, lett their pretences to the contrary be never such. After all, 'tis worth the Gentlemen's [i.e. the Five] while to consider

---

[1] i.e. the 'Regulation'.       [2] Thomas Liddell.

if the Contract can be upheld, if these people be not gratifyed. Can their Opposition distress us? I am of opinion they can and even to a degree bring us into confusion and a breaking among ourselves, by giving an Extravagant preference in price to one or two concerns. We must consider what we sell for 11ˢ/-, that is allowing their praemiums etc, is about 9ˢ/4ᵈ neat and [it] can't be imagin'd this price can be upheld but by our unanimous agreement among ourselves and a friendly correspondence with those *necessary Evils* att the Gate. This ought to be well weighed and an answer must be given the Dealers without loss of time. 'Twixt you and me they told me that Mr. M[ontague's] Agent had promis'd that his share should be paid them tho' others did not. Don't take direct notice of this, but by way of supposition the question may be putt. I think ye Dealers in strictness meritt a — but the only quaery is if we can subsist and keep together without their assistance.

Throughout February he constantly reiterated this theme. Early in the month he pressed Cotesworth to come to London.

February 6. . . . Is itt not possible for you to contrive your business so as to accompany Mr. Barnes to Town: it might on severall occasions be worth your while I should think, especially you would have opportunity of settling an interest att the Gate, while they will not allow a Contractor to speak to them on such an account till their past year's demands be satisfied.

February 8. . . . You know every Additional Duty is a burthen upon a Trade and this laid on [the Candle duty] will make the Dealers more absolutely necessary to us than otherwise, who must exert themselves in the Regulation and for that service only, to make things goe smoothly on, the only way to free us from generall complaints which the last year had like to have brought us into Troubles, which, where they would have ended, God knows. Should you quarrel with the Dealers att this time, you may guess att the disturbance and interruption they would unanimously give to the Trade and though you were to ingage all the other Dealers in your interest, yet they are most of them people of little or no substance for which reason they can't force a Trade, if they doe, it must be by the Credit you give them and what sort of Reck'ning you will have with them att the making up your accounts, you may judge. When an answer is given to the Dealers it must be don with great Caution, least if they be discarded, their naturall Malice and Spirit of Revenge will readily prompt them to produce the

Letter and probably bring us into Trouble. For instance, were it expressed that some of the Ten had received £50 for the sale of Fieldhouse coals contrary to the stipulation, if this Letter were exposed, as certainly it would be by them, if disobliged, the *Review* would lay hold of itt and handle us as last year, that it was a plain proof of a design'd Monopoly, so that what now seems to sleep would be raised up against us and a prosecution would certainly be sett on foot. What then, you will say, can be don? We think a Cautious Letter to them must be framed, but particular instances of their false Dealing should be represented to my Uncle in a Letter to him and that he may charge them with by word of mouth. I think it would not be improper, if the general Answer to the Dealers be first inclosed to him that we may peruse and alter if thought necessary. Believe me we can't be too cautious as the world seems disposed. . . . I doubt the proposal of £2000 at Mich[aelmas] and £1000 after, will scarce goe down, but when the Five have come to a generall Result lett it be dispatched as above. As to an interest for your own att Gate, 'tis time it should be looked after and you must employ some friend of yours to transact, for I must not appear, nor can be of any service. It seems necessary Mr. Ord must keep back his Leadings whether we keep up our interest with the Dealers or not.

February 13. This Evening both Mr. Wortleys were here and it was agreed I should write to desire that upon Receipt of it you would gett Mr. White, Mr. Ord, and Mr. Barnes and who other you think necessary. . . . You will consider and draw up such a clause as may be thought of most use for adjusting ye Sunderland River and naming ye Commissioners. It must be return'd by ye first post or 2$^{nd}$ at furthest, least it come too late. You will give your opinion of what Mr. Hedworth communicated to you. We can't so much as guess in what Respect ye Union must be or what Tendency. Your Thoughts are ye best turn'd and most capable of diving into ye Mystery. We again press ye Determination of ye 5 and that with Speed. If they dont agree to satisfie ye Dealers w$^{ch}$ is ye unanimous opinion of all here concern'd that they should, they will send their Reasons. But I pronounce a bad Trade, if they be not complimented to their minds. . . .

February 20. . . . It is ye Opinion of Mr. Wortleyes, my father, and Uncle that if you came up to Town with discretionary power the Dealers might be brought to reason. I beg of you not to refuse in case ye 5 propose it to you. . . .

March 6. . . . I must own it were not seasonable at this juncture to appear with ye people of the Gate. . . . What is design'd by ye Bill is kept a secrett among those that bring itt in, so that we can learn nothing of itt, till we gett a copy which can't be till it be presented, yet I think ye real intent is to call in Question ye partys at Newcastle. A few days will discover and then we shall move as upon consultation may be thought most expedient. I foresee plainly there will be a breach and then ye fitters will obtain their ends and ye London Markett will be supplyed with a worse commodity and on Dearer Terms. . . .

On 19 March Mr. Edward Wortley at last got a copy of the 'designed bill' and Cotesworth was again urged to come up 'without loss of time' by 'the cleaverest Conveyance'. 'We think that itt will be about 3 weeks from ye first bringing in of ye bill and ye last reading.'

Who were these dealers, or rather the 'Ten' referred to in the letter of 8 February, 'whose natural Malice and Spirit of Revenge' was expected would cause trouble 'if they be not complimented to their minds'? They were members of the London Lighterman's Company—Sir Richard and George Oldner ('the fat Oldners', Liddell called them), John Dawson, Coltman, Bennett, Blunkett, Roberts, the Ryalls, Scott, Spencer, Webb, and Williams. Whether any of the following, Arrington, Godfrey, Hartley, Wren, and Robert Watts should also be included I cannot determine. It is clear that the 'Ten', thanks to their control over the Thames lighters and their marketing facilities, had practically a monopoly of the London retail coal trade.[1] Both before and after the crisis of 1711 Liddell remained convinced that an accommodation with these 'necessary Evils at the Gate', 'Masters of Impudence'—a new degree—was indispensable. We know, too, that the late Sir William Blackett of Newcastle had assisted in securing them their

---

[1] In 1692 the Commissioners of Customs supported a petition of the London Wharfingers 'that a competent number of Lightermen is essential for the ease and accommodation of Trade'. Treasury Papers, xviii, § 28. None of the signatories, however—some eighteen wharfingers and thirty-five lightermen—were members of the later 'Ten'. For the earlier importance of the Woodmongers' Company in the retail trade, see Nef, ii. 107 seq; Dale, *The Fellowship of Woodmongers.*

charter in the late reign.[1] The well-informed author of *The Reflections on the Coal Trade* states that they had in the past received 'premiums' from the coal-owners but evidently those promised by the 'Five' for 1710 had not yet been paid and they were highly incensed. They knew perfectly well of the existence of the Newcastle 'Regulation' and their own attitude to it at this juncture may be summed up in the phrase 'No Peace without Premiums', to vary slightly the wording of the Earl of Nottingham's famous resolution of that year. At the beginning of March Liddell correctly divined that 'the real intent' of the designed bill 'is to call in question the parties at Newcastle', and if the dealers had the slightest 'inclin' of the overtures being made to the Sunderland owners, their fears would be so much the greater. Cotesworth afterwards stated bluntly that the bill 'was intended to Break the Contract and to ly the Coal owners under difficulty'. It is not inconceivable, then, that the dealers had dropped a hint to the city fathers which resulted in the petition to the queen and privy council complaining of the high prices of coal and of a combination in restraint of trade. On the other hand, the 'Ten', no less than the 'Five', knew well enough that any hint of a monopoly must be avoided at all costs as it might lead to a prosecution under the act of 5 and 6 Edward VI, or, what was to be equally avoided, a parliamentary inquiry. However much they feared a producers' monopoly, it was scarcely in the 'Ten's' interest to force the issue by bringing it on to the public stage, unless indeed we must credit them with the cunning of a chased fox which tries to shake off the hounds by crossing the scent. The two events which brought on the crisis—the rise in the wholesale price of coal in the late summer of 1710 and the strike of ships' masters at Harwich—had both occurred in the previous year.[2] A war-weary London forced the government to take action.

Professor T. S. Ashton has already discussed the provisions of the Coal Act of 1711 which made illegal all

[1] Cotesworth MSS.  [2] *Infra.*

combinations of mine-owners, ships' masters, and lightermen and forbade the activities of 'crimps' and the mixing of coals, and there would be no occasion to dwell on the subject further but for the discovery, among the papers of the Newcastle 'Regulation', of the coal-owners' reaction to the bill and their line of defence in the House of Commons Committee. In a paper of rough notes and in another headed 'Questions that are to be ask't W. C. by friends', we can see how the defence began to take shape in Cotesworth's mind, when he was persuaded by the combine 'to solicit the bill depending in Parliament'. In due course he received a summons from Richard Ferrier, chairman of the committee, to attend 'at the Speaker's Chamber on Monday morning next (14 April) at 8 of the clock'. In his evidence he frankly 'owned the agreement' among the owners and admitted that he was their salaried officer 'appointed to review the Collieries to see that they worked fair'. He gave a brief historical account of the origin of the 'Contract', as he called it, 'two years ago gone Michaelmas': 'The reason of the Gentleman coming into the Regulation [was] occasioned by a complaint of masters and dealers of base mixtures discovered by the Consumers.' But the 'Contract' was no monopoly: 'I have heard them often say they did not think anybody bound by it, but it was a memo of some agreements.' He denied that there had been any 'obstruction' in the trade: 'When the agreement was made the Partners computed what coals might be spent in London in one year that their Collieries might work.' He denied that all coals in the 'Regulation' were sold at one price; for instance, Mr. White's coals were sold at a lower rate, though he agreed 'that fewer keels are employed than formerly'. He admitted that the 'Regulation' had appointed certain officers 'to see that the kelemen did not imbezzle the coals from the staith to the ship . . . and that the keles belonging to these Gentlemen did not carry any coals for any but themselves'. In brief, the 'Contract' was most emphatically not a monopoly in restraint of trade—he had statistics to hand to prove that it accounted for rather less than half the total output of Tyne and Wear. In any case, 'that upon complaint and clamour made against a contract and a Coal Chamber being kept', so runs a note, 'the Gentleman concerned gave orders for discharging the same chamber and cancelling the agreements and which I believe was done for the servants were paid and discharged'. How wise had the 'Five' been in their decision of 12 March!

Even more important was Cotesworth's justification of the slight rise in the price of coal. 'It was not raised till the second voadg of last year and that only sixpence whereas the additional charge [i.e. the cost of production] may be made appear above double.' The paper 'Reflections on the Coal Trade since its first rise' was almost certainly penned by Cotesworth for this occasion.[1] Notwithstanding the additional cost of the land carriage and the greater depths at which coal was 'dug'd', he proved that it was 'delivered into the keel at eleven shillings per chaldron of fifty three cwts', out of which the owner pays the fitter 'for sallerys, kele rent, and carrying the empty keles back at least 18$^d$ per cha.' and a like amount needed to be deducted 'for keeping the framed ways': 'Remains 8$^s$/- per chaldron which is not above 3$^s$/6$^d$ per tenn', he concluded. In any case, Sunderland owners, who were admittedly outside the 'Contract', had raised the price 'double'.

It is clear from the minutes of evidence which he kept and from the paper 'Questions to be ask't W. C. by his friends' that he was expecting to have to face hostile witnesses in the committee. And so it proved. Thomas Brumell was examined. He stated that he himself had seen the agreement among the coal-owners which was 'to raise the price'. He alleged that 'the Partners obstruct other very good collieries from working', that he himself had a colliery 'but does not work it for want of wayleave' and that 'Mr. Pitts' cannot work his for the same reason, with the result 'that for want of sufficient good coals the ships cannot be dispatched as

---

[1] *Supra.* It seems likely that this is the tract which Nef failed to find in answer to Povey's *Discovery of Indirect Practices in the Coal Trade.*

soon as they ought'. 'He believed the Combination is still subsisting, and is possitive the writings are in force for the managers had a meeting at Newcastle a little before he came away which was about the 21st of March last.' (Did he in fact know, or suspect, that there had been a meeting of the 'Five' on that very day?) He further alleged that 'gift coals have been sometimes allowed'. On the question of way-leaves, Cotesworth was well prepared. Among 'the Questions to be ask't' were what way-leaves he had taken for the 'Regulation'; 'whether Mr. Bromell and my Lady [Clavering] were as free now to bring down their coals to the river as they had been previously'; and whether such way-leaves were 'paid for by moneys [i.e. the groats] raised by the coal owners'. It is clear that the gravamen of the charge on this head concerned not what he had done in a personal capacity but on instructions from the 'Five'. On the question of 'gift coals' Cotesworth noted that they were 'never practised but in a slack trade and masters takeing advantadge got one, and from that to four in the score, but that was but very seldom and very rare from the best collierys'. His fellow delegate, John Ord, admitted that 'guift coals were sometimes on and sometimes off again, but Mr. Montague himselfe was always against it'. For the rest, Mr. Ord stated in evidence that 'he believes there was an agreement made by the several owners of collierys', which he proceeded to name, including Mr. Fenwick; that although he himself was present when the owners 'were chose', he had nothing to do with it save in his capacity 'as Cashire for Mr. Montague'. It would be difficult to match this piece of legal chicanery or understatement for Ord had in fact attended nearly all the meetings of the 'Five'.

It will have been observed that nothing had yet been said about the London lightermen who may well have been flattering themselves with the way things were going. But here Cotesworth held a trump card: 'That the Lightermen in January last was twelve month had £1250 for unlading the Contractors' coals and for dispatching their business the

quicker when they came to London.' This evidence, produced at the right moment, laid the lightermen 'on their
backs'—a feat for which Cotesworth became deservedly
famous.[1] If the 'Great Dons' had imagined that 'their' bill
would effectively dispose of 'the partys at Newcastle' and
'ly the Coal owners under difficulty' they were quickly dis-
illusioned. The resulting bill condemned combinations
among lightermen no less than among coal-owners so that
Cotesworth's final comment on the proceedings was 'but
we found means to obviate thes difficulties and procure a
good bill' (9 Anne, § 28).

The damaging disclosure that the lightermen had received
premiums from the coal-owners might well have had more
serious consequences had not the committee been deflected
by the evidence of another witness whose identity has not
been established. This was to the effect 'that the Mutiny
arose at Newcastle by the combinations of Masters of Ships'.
Mr. Herle, Sword Bearer to the City of London, stated:

That in May last, Sir Gilbert Heathcott, now Lord Mayor, told
him he heard there was a combination among the Masters of Shipps.
That the number of ships being very scarce in the River, [on the]
17th of May he was commanded to go to Harwich where he found
lying at anchor about 600 or 700 sail of colliers and found out there
their combination, for notes were given from one to another in a penalty
of £50 against those that broke away first and that the Reason of their
Stay was to raise the Price at market for if they had come sooner they
should have got nothing by their voyage by the reason of the Combination of the Coal owners of Newcastle and the Lightermen at London.

It will be remembered that the summer coal fleet did not
arrive in the Tyne in 1710 before July. Mr. Haw, master
of a ship, declared:

That the reason they lay at Harwich was because of the abuses they
received at Newcastle in the false measure, and to raise the price at
market. Said notes were given as aforesaid and that coals cost more now
by £18 in his ship load than formerly which was occasioned by short
measure and not according to Act of Parliament and the duty laid on

[1] In 1712 Sir Henry Liddell, Bt., expected him to lay the Chief Justice 'on his back'.

them by the Coal owners and formerly they could buy of any fitter but now they cannot.

Another master, Mr. Bowell,

Owned the Contract at Harwich and that the reason of their stay there was by the ill-usage of the Coale Owners at Newcastle and Lightermen at London for at Newcastle the language was 'You will load in the Contract or out', and if they buy out of the Contract the Lightermen will not come on board them at London by reason of the Large premiums they have from the Coal Owners at Newcastle and that the coals out of the Contract are as good as theirs, except Hutton and Benwell coals.

Captain Bowyer 'said the price of coals are advanced ten to twelve per cent. more than formerly; that formerly they [i.e. the ships' masters] had guift coals but none now'.

In view of this evidence, the ships' masters were regarded as the prime offenders and legal proceedings were started against them. 'The Town Clerk attended with the Presentments against the Masters of shipps and gave the Committee an account of the reasons of the same, as he apprehended a punishment for their Combination for never were [they] indicted before.' So it came about that ships' masters were also comprehended in the resulting act. This incident raises the large and complex question as to who owned, or controlled, the ships engaged in the coal trade— a matter on which the minutes of the coal-owners' cartel are strangely silent. We shall return to this subject later.

The coal-owners' chief delegate, having now the satisfaction of seeing the legal hounds chasing another fox, concentrated on another matter; the question of 'gift coals'. There was an old-established practice of coal-owners to allow 'gift coals' to masters of ships. Edward Grey, an ex-hostman, lately in the service of the combine, had a record of what allowances had been made since the year 1682, to which he was prepared to depose on oath. From this it appears that usually one or two chaldrons in the score were allowed—in 1689 there was none—but when trade was bad, as in 1690 and 1692, some owners gave 'five and six' in the score. It will be recalled that ships' masters had complained of inadequate measure and that they were forced to buy within the combine. Another paper, 'Answers to Mr. Ferrier's objections for taking off ye Gift Coal, 1711', shows that the chairman of the parliamentary committee was himself championing the ships' masters in this matter. He was M.P. for Yarmouth. In this document it was contended that the mine-owner 'gets but four shillings per London chaldron for his mine and adventure'. 'Now let ye world judge, if ye price of coals were 10$^s$/- then one in the score would be sixpence and consequently six in the score would amount to 3$^s$/- which reduces ye neat price to ye Owner to little more than 2$^s$/6$^d$ per London chaldron which is 27 to 28 hundred weight.'

And can any imagin that a Trade can be carried on at that Rate so manifestly to the ruin of every undertaker? But suppose they should be willing to sacrifice their last penny and struggle with it, ye consequences seem plain. All parties would be injured, most intirely ruin'd and then ye Trade would fall into ye hands of a few who have ye deepest purses, who having stood ye shock will find ye whole Trade of the River center in themselves and ye market making a greater demand than they can furnish and can't be supplyed elsewhere, is it not then naturall for those partyes that had suffer'd so much, when ye ball is att their feet to sett such a price on their commodity, which must be had, that will reimburse them, nay even if they took interest for their money that had bin so squander'd away, I believe none can blame ym.

It was a familiar argument. Cotesworth used it again in an interview he had at the House of Commons with Sir Richard Hoare, one of the City members, to prove that the clause in the bill which forbade mixing of coals would work in the same way in the long run. The anti-mixing clause also caused the coal-owners some concern, especially if it meant— and it was by no means clear on this point—that different seams from the same colliery could not be mixed at the staithes. Here legislative intention, as often, was not abreast of the facts of the case. Alderman Matthew White did not share his colleagues' fears as to the effects of the anti-mixing clause, contending 'that it had ever been allowed that all the coals from one pit were reckoned as one colliery'. For the rest, Cotesworth considered the act of 1711 unnecessary, claiming that the existing law against combinations in restraint of trade was both well known and effective.

He had every reason to be pleased with his performance. The more discerning among the coal-owners recognized their great debt to him at this critical juncture, though some of them were in no hurry to contribute towards the expenses of his London journey. What he and they thought of the act may be judged from the fact that early in July, when he had returned from London, the meetings of the 'Five' started up again and continued for another four years. The combination broke up from internal strains and stresses not because of legislative action.

What these strains and stresses were may now be briefly examined. By August 1711 all hope of a uniform price, or even of several prices for different grades of coal, was abandoned. Mr. Wilkinson was given leave to sell his Blaydon coals 'as he pleases and for what he sells them for more than 8$^s$/6$^d$ per chaldron . . . to be accomptable for to the Regulation'. Moreover, it was agreed that 'the Regulation fitters are to ly them aboard for which Mr. Wilkinson pay no fittage'. It was this problem of the differences in quality, and therefore of sales, which constituted a major difficulty for it soon made meaningless the original assignment of 'proportions' to the several proprietors. Accordingly, when the contract was renewed in October 1711 it was agreed:

That the whole vend shall be cast up of all coals in the Regulation for this present year at Christmas next and the dificiencies shall be made good either in money or by vend of coals in the next spring before those that are found to have vended their proportions shall vend any, and that such as are to pay money or stand still in vend shall make their option.

Hitherto, owners with 'short coals', i.e. deficient sales in any one year, had been allowed to add the equivalent amount to their quota for the ensuing year. But here was a new principle which was not likely to commend itself to the big proprietors, like the Wortleys, who had no difficulty in disposing of their quota and more, by reason of the superior quality of their coals. It was therefore further agreed at the same meeting

That Mr. Ord shall receive as soon as possibly he can, directions from Mr. Wortley in relation to the renewal of the agreement for next year that no time may be lost to determine the point.

This brought up the two 'Principals', the elder Wortley and his son, who attended the meeting of the 'Five' a fortnight later. It was then agreed to renew the contract for a further year; 'that Mr. Wortley shall have 4000 tens certain for Hutton and Benwell for the ensuing year, except before Lady Day next, he desires to be in proportion according to the quantities stipulated in the last agreement'. It was further agreed that all deficiencies *in this year's vend* to be made good either in coals or money, and 'that all extraordinary charges in the Regulation shall be proportionably paid according to the quantities'. But there were not to be money payments on 'deficiencies' for the ensuing year. Instead it was agreed

In regard Mr. Wilkinson has been some £1000 out of pocket by Stella Grand Lease and that he now only keeps her to prevent mischief to the Regulation, . . . that the Regulation shall undertake Stella from Martinmas next and shall have and bear profit and loss according to each gentleman's proportion in the Regulation.

In this particular, the 'Regulation' was becoming a real joint-stock undertaking as indeed it was in other matters, e.g. the taking of common way-leaves in Gateshead and Whickham and at Redheugh, and in authorizing common legal action against Brumell and Sir John Clavering.

At a meeting at Cotesworth's house three months later it was agreed that 'the deficiencies for the last year (1711) be made good in proportion and these to be settled and to be taken in coles'. A year later, however, this policy was reversed when it was agreed that the deficiencies for 1710 and 1711 'be thrown into an averidge . . . and shall be paid for at 15 shillings per tenn', the accounts to be made up and presented at the next meeting a month later. Ord was not present at this second meeting, having gone to London to consult his chief. It was agreed that,

> Mr. Wilkinson having in the account made up this day received 15s/- per ten for 314 tens for deficient vend for the years 1710 and 1711 from Bladon. It is agreed that what he vends in succeeding years above the yearly stipulated quantity of 200 tens, he shall repay to the Regulation 15s/- per ten for each ten so over-vended.

It was admittedly a reversal of a previous decision and threatened to split the 'Regulation'. In February 1713 Edward Wortley broke silence in a letter to Ord.

> I hope you will take care to set right the mistake that was made by some Gentlemen that seemed to expect we should bear a proportion in making amends for what had not been sold by others in the past years. I remember very well that when it was agreed we should have such a quantity certaine, it was understood by myself and every one I heard mention it that those who had sold short should have their quantities made up by selling so much more than their proportion as they had sold less in the other years. I remember particularly Mr. Wilkinson said it was hard upon them that we only should not abate of our sale, however he would not break with us upon it, and I would fain know how we could possibly be supposed to have a certain quantity if we were to abate and make a stop if others did not sell so much as they should. The thing in my opinion is so clear that it wants no explaining. If it had ever been intended we should contribute towards makeing up what they wanted no doubt but it must have been put in writing. What I say of Mr. Wilkinson's complaining was at your house and I believe most of the Gentlemen complained at the meeting at the Bowling Green when the matter was settled. I am sure for my part I always took it for a part of that agreement that we were wholly exempt from makeing up any deficiencies of past years. I hope the Gentlemen could not but be sensible how much we denyed our vend last year to keep our promise. . . .
>
> P.S. Had the peace been declared last summer, as it was expected, the other Gentlemen had gained sufficiently by their bargain and if we are to keep to a certain quantity this year you will find we shall be great loosers.

On the 'Regulation' bowling green, it must be confessed, the Wortley ball had a disproportionate amount of bias. Cotesworth who was 'the jack' in the game had increasing difficulty in holding the 'Five' together. His friend Henry Liddell feared the 'Regulation' would break up unless they 'cotton better together than at present they seem to do'. As early as October 1711 he had written,

I expect little from the meeting of the 5. If some must think of adding to their quantity while all others lessen, is what I never expect will be complied with and methinks an understanding is not cordially searched after: there needs no further argument than Wortley's supineness in lying at Durham when he should be upon the spott to assist and promote. You remark right he is puff'd up with a notion of ye wonderfull feats the people at Gate will doe for him, but after all I should not be sorry to see them drop his honor's sayle in the dirt.

A paper shows the kind of financial issue involved: '1266 tens over-vended [by Wortley] in 1712 to raise £949/12/7—Mr. Wilkinson to get £385/16/6, Bensham owners £287/19/6, Clavering Stella £246/3/-', and so on. Alderman Matthew White was to get £70 'for a recompense'. Conversely, the 'levy' on Wortley originally assessed at £266 had gone up to more than £1,647. At the meeting at Spurn's on 11 February 1714 it was agreed

That Mr. Alderman White shall have £50 allowed him in his account for his good services in the Regulation in consideration whereof he agrees to continue till Xmas next in the Regulation for both his part of Jesmond and Stella and to expect no other allowances for Stella more than the other partners have.

In other words, the 'Regulation' was threatened with secession at both ends—by those who under-vended as well as by those who exceeded their quota. The following resolution indicates the probable destination of the one talent.

On consideration that Mr. Wortley and Sir Harry [Liddell] agree that Blackburn shall be laid in for this year of 1713–14 they shall have their proportions of Blackburn added to Main Team and Hutton and Benwell, that is to say, Sir Harry shall have liberty to work his stipulated quantity of 2400 tennes out of Main Team and that Mr. Wortley shall have the quantity of 460 tennes which was stipulated for Blackburn be added to his stipulated proportion for Hutton and Benwell.

On this basis, the 'lying in' of redundant pits became largely meaningless.

The minutes of only two further meetings—and those out of series and by a different hand—have survived. At Shepherd's on 26 February 1715 it was agreed 'by the majority that Cotesworth acquaint Mr. Ledgard that these gentlemen are willing to give him £2,100 to be paid him annually on condition that he (and his partner Royle) shall not carry on, nor assist in carrying on Elswick Colliery for 4 years, the said term to commence at Christmas last'. To this resolution the following note was added: 'Mr. Ord desires to make a memorandum that he desents from the 1st Order.' This was apparently the last meeting of the 'Five': the good ship 'Regulation' subsequently floundered.

A letter from Ord to Cotesworth written a week before this meeting and endorsed by the latter 'About Elswick's lying' throws some light on Wortley's views on the matter.

First as to the time, the longer the better for Mr. Wortley, but he is not to be convinced that it's his intrest nor really otherwise than his very great loss to enlarge the time longer than for three years from last Christmas. The sum he will inevitably be out of purse in that time he says he can and will demonstrate (to you only) will be above £1800, besides the losse of what he might have gained wch he proposed if guift coals and confusion insue will be 30ˢ/- a tenn. And that the more [coals] he works, his water charge will be less. I should be sorry to find your labours and designs to which I have always been ready to contribute should have that effect. You know the reason of his self denyall, for if there were nothing but the general good of the trade, would he refuse £1000 or £1500 a year which he reckons at least his present profit would be. I have used all my arguments and I am firmly persuaded its not possible to bring him to a longer term. As to the sum, I am of opinion though we pay the greatest share of it, we had better give it than be drawn into the will of our fitters and the old confusion and though he [Ledgard] cannot be agreed with for more than he justly deserves if we could critically adjust it, yet we had better let him have more than run the hazard of the losse. I am sure your advantage by keeping us together is nothing with his own. . . .

That was not quite the end of the business. It is clear that Cotesworth strove manfully to keep the 'Regulation' afloat. 'We long to hear the issue of your two dark conferences', his friend Henry Liddell wrote from Ravensworth, 'your last still confirms me that we are harbouring a dangerous snake in our breast.' As early as December 1711 Cotesworth had suspected treachery in a certain quarter, for the 'Governor' replied to one of his letters 'I wish with all my hart ye principal foundation you build on may not fail, I won't say, as you do, through treachery'. We know some of the grounds for this suspicion and it turned on Elswick. In January 1716 the 'Governor' reported that 'Old Wortley's opinion of Elswick is that that coal will answer in every respect that of Benwell'; he added that 'J. Ord is a partner [in Elswick] and wrote him word he would not take £1000 a year for his share which is an $\frac{1}{8}$th [eighth] part, I think'. Lady Bowes, who was not in the habit of mincing her words, remarked in that year 'that old Wortley and J. Ord are two of the greatest R[ogues] that ever a County was blessed withall. They will by right or wrong, come at means to purchase estates, but at last must go to the D——l.' One or both of them were 'the dangerous snake that we are harbouring in our breast'. It is not without significance that when a 'Regulation' was next mooted (in 1725), Mr. Wortley was put down as owning 'all Elswick, all Blackburn, all Causey, all Tanfield and all Grand Lease Stella'. Moreover, his son was to repeat the role by breaking up a second 'Regulation' in the thirties. After all, meteors do not originate from a fixed constellation.

Other factors had contributed to the break-up. A paper which Cotesworth took with him to London in 1711 containing the names of the concerns in the 'Contract' with 'their supposed yearly Quantity', a total of 127,000 chaldrons, states that the 'non-contracting' collieries on Tyneside had an estimated output of 62,500 chaldron, Sunderland another 65,000, and Cullercoats, Blyth, and Seaton a further 15,000. In other words, the combination accounted for not quite half the total output of the region. Such men as Alderman Richard Ridley, the stormy petrel of the industry, Bowes, Fenwick, Pitt, Rudston, besides Sir John Clavering, remained outside. Undercutting by 'interlopers' was, therefore, a serious consideration. Then, in 1713, James Clavering of Lamesley, 'the Governor's' brother-in-law, deserted. It is a curious story. The Clavering family was a house divided against itself: James was at variance with Sir John and his Lady of Axwell Park. Not only was he a convinced believer in some form of regulation of the trade, he was one of the five 'Directors' and indeed in November 1712, along with Alderman White and Mr. Wilkinson, was one of an inner managerial junto 'who shall determine anything relating to the publick that William Cotesworth applies to them for and when they apprehend themselves under difficulty that they call a General Meeting'. Indeed, he was present at the meeting of the 'Five' on 29 April 1712 when it was agreed to encourage the copyholders to 'cut-up' the controverted Brumell–Clavering wagon-way 'and if they are opposed that then a joint force be raised to pull it up by force'; and he was apparently a consenting party to the subsequent legal proceedings against Sir John at York. But, thereafter, the family pull—his sister, the 'Governor's' wife, was no friend of Cotesworth—began to reassert itself. In the summer of 1713 his attendance at the meetings of the 'Five' became irregular and after November it ceased altogether. The meeting in December asked the secretary to write to Mr. Liddell 'that he will please to prevail with Mr. Clavering to attend the coal meeting and to acquaint him with the present state of affairs'. But the hope dwindled and the place of the meetings came to be varied 'in case Mr. Clavering comes not'. Domestic tragedy—the loss of his entire stock of children in 1714—and the death of the baronet completed the estrangement. He can hardly have approved of the arrest of his kinswoman in her own house, at Cotesworth's instigation, in April 1716, and the threat to carry her up to the Fleet if she did not give bond in a penalty of £1,000, to live at peace with her opponent. 'I do believe he has a mind by this quarrel to expose not only us as much as he can, but the Regulation in general', wrote his brother-in-law to Cotesworth in the following October. That is almost the last we hear of the 'Regulation'. Alderman White died in that year and the 'Governor' in the following January. By 1718 the 'Regulation' was no more than a memory. The initiative in the attempt at regulation in that year came, not from the coal-owners, but from the ships' masters.

Before turning to consider the complicated question of shipping, a word must be said about marketing, or what, in Sir Henry Liddell's phrase, 'the French call the Foible of the trade'. It is clear that to a point masters of ships were free to sell their cargoes how and where they liked. Matthew Ridley stated in 1764 that 'the Masters of Ships are in effect the Merchants and sell as high as they can'.[1] But, thanks to the overwhelming preponderance of the London market, the great bulk of the coastwise shipments went there. Before a coal was unloaded into a lighter there was hard bargaining between master and crimps 'at the Gate'.

I have bin twice down att ye Gate where I found poor John Walker att his witts' end, he could not dispose of his Clavering Stella tho' offer'd 6<sup>d</sup> under ye Markett [wrote Henry Liddell in March 1711]. Pray will you acquaint Mr. Clavering of this and tell him that my opinion is that the Master ought to have some consideration for ye loss of this voyage and lett him have a bulk of ye best this next if he can be persuaded to load.

In fact masters were often at the mercy of the dealers. 'Shippers have overglutted the market', wrote Liddell again in June 1711, 'and their customers finding they can be served at any time put off the evil hour of parting with money as long as they can.' Indeed he was then of opinion that 'you will be better served by the petty dealers such as

[1] Letter Book (Ridley MSS.).

Godfrey etc., than by the great Dons'. 'There is no dependence on any of the great men at the Gate', he wrote a month later, 'their promises are like syllibubs, seemingly great and yet nothing in them.' 'What damn'd fellows are these! I was provoked with them beyond measure', he exclaimed of the Oldners. 'I am perfectly plagued and distracted with the masters on the one hand and the dealers of another that I have not a peace-able hour', he told his friend in 1712, 'and what adds to it there is no prospect of better days. You observe right that these vermin will prove in some measure worse than gift, were it only on this account that they squeeze the poor masters as well as the owners. I wish, therefore, that any expedient could be thought of to bring them within bounds. Sure I am that Clavering Stella where we give them an unconscionable premium yet they do oppress our masters beyond any concern in the River. . . .' Words failed him to describe 'those vile wretches', 'vermin', 'masters of impudence', who 'hang in a clan much firmer than the coal-owners' and 'insist on full pay' of their 'unconscionable' premium. 'Indeed', he declared in August 1712, 'some expedient must be thought of to break into the measures of these great men, otherwise we shall be slaves with a witness and this without loss of time.' And what was more, three of the 'Ten'—Bennett, Blunkett, and Coltman—were known to be 'deeply soused' in financing the ventures of opponents of the 'Regulation'.

Among the expedients proposed by Daniel Poyen was 'to lay aside ye Dealers intirely, to allow ye Masters 2s/- per Newcastle chaldron and lett them fight their way', but Liddell was 'sure it will be ye worst of presidents that ever was brought on the trade'. Alternatively, it was proposed to play off 'ye Great Dons with the middling ones who are greater in number though not in bulk', but as Liddell pointed out, not only could the smaller men not take off 'the quantity' but they would require longer credit and at the end of the season coal-owners and ships' masters alike would not know what sort of reckoning they would get and might well find that they had incurred bad debts. After some experience, Liddell was emphatically opposed to this expedient. In November 1713 Cotesworth addressed himself to the problem, with particular reference to disposing of the coals from Clavering Stella, and he reduced it to two heads 'either (i) by menaging the Gate or (ii) giving way to the Fitters'.

One had better fall into the hands of the Dealers than those of the Fitters [Liddell replied] they have scrap'd all the Flesh off and left us to pick the bare bone, besides when we come into their clutches we never know the expence of the Trade, till the year ends and then 'tis too late to redress. Gift grows apace by their crafty and false representations and still under a pretence of acting as our neighbours do, which makes me call to mind when I went to school at Sir J. Kay's,[1] we used to attend upon the warren keeper to see the diversion of cony catching. He happen'd to catch a couple of Poll cats in his trapps one night, summons us boys to be witnesses to the execution which was after this manner. He got a Riddle, put their tails through, and after got a cloven stick and by that means pinch'd ym cruelly: the poor creatures fell to fighting as long as they had breath and after return'd till they scratch'd their eyes out and at last lost their lives. Dont you think that the man who had his hand on the other side of the Riddle with his two sticks was not something related to a certain generation of people who sport at the ruin of those they get their daily food by, besides what some of them hord up? Therefore, I had rather throw myself into the hands of the Gate, which though they be not of the same species, yet not unlike in qualifications, with this distinction only, that they pick your pocket but they tell you aforehand whereabouts the sum will be, whereas the other slides his hand into your purse, takes and takes again, and yet will not bear a reproof. I own that of the two evils, the least ought to be chose and therefore agrees with his good friend (i) is the more preferable. But then how will this matter be compass'd? Not so easily as one would imagine. We have so oft crack't our words with them in relation to the quality of our coals.

It was decided that Liddell should 'try the Dealers seperately, for they refuse to treat jointly with or for any concern'. It continued to be an article of his family's policy to achieve and maintain a *modus vivendi* with 'these necessary evils'

---

[1] In Yorkshire.

and that meant paying them a premium of at least 6*d.* per London chaldron.[1]

I could say more on this head [wrote Liddell in 1716] but will only mention this, that Blunkett, Watt, Coltman, Bennett when I paid ym ye Praemium att Christmas, which was 6ᵈ a London cha, told me that if they had suspected I would have paid ym as I did, that concern instead of vending 17,000 London cha, would have sold 40,000 and upbraided ye two Oldners and Godfrey for not letting ym into the secrett. . . .

But other people had other views, as we shall see. Besides, the day-to-day wrangling over prices and measure fell to the ships' masters. 'The Masters run about the Gate like so many craz'd people', wrote Liddell in 1713, 'they bellow, swear and foreswear every voyage that they will not be slaves to their fitters that they will be damm'd before they will load again.' How long would men of such notorious tempers continue to be 'slaves' to either fitters or dealers?

## IV

### SHIPPING

The crisis of 1711, along with other evidence, affords conclusive proof that the coal-owners neither owned nor had a controlling interest in the fleet of colliers plying between the Tyne and the Thames. It is necessary to state this at the outset for many contemporaries, including M.P.s, believed that they did. Lists have survived of all the ships which cleared from Cotesworth's staiths from May to September 1710 and for the following six months. Out of a total of 46 in the first period, 16 were Yarmouth-owned, 12 came from Scarborough, 4 from Sandwich, and 1 each from the following ten ports—Shields, Sunderland, Stockton, Bridlington, Aldborough, London, Rochester, Broadstairs, Margate, and Poole. Only 2 were Newcastle-owned, though Alderman

---

[1] *Infra.* 'The Dealers will grow yearly in their demands of praemium', wrote Liddell in February 1716, 'there is not one concern in ye River, save Team, that gives them less than 12ᵈ per cha & that I think is H[utton] and B[enwell] and theirs is about 9ᵈ. Had I apprehended that they would not have accepted att a reasonable rate, I should have [closed?] with Nᵒ 10 who were eager about her after our meeting at ye King's Head. . . . I must publish to all Dealers, little and great, that they shall have 12ᵈ per cha. This seems unavoidable.'

Rudston, a prominent merchant-shipper of the port, had another, the *Sant Simon*, possibly a prize. Of the 32 which cleared in the second period, 12 came from Scarborough, 9 from Yarmouth, 2 from London, while other 'south ports', Lowestoft, Colchester, Dover, and Sandwich contributed 1 each. The distribution suggested by these figures may not be fully representative but it is none the less highly significant especially when taken with other evidence. Brand published in an appendix a list of ships 'useing the Coale Trade at Newcastle' in the years 1702–4.[1] Yarmouth heads the list with a total of 211, followed by London with 168, Whitby 98, Lynn 74, Newcastle 71, Scarborough 54, Bridlington 48, Ramsgate 42, and Ipswich 40. This accords roughly with what Nef found for the seventeenth century, viz. that Newcastle occupied only fourth place in point of shipping.

'The coal trade has answered better in quantity vended than I expected', wrote Liddell in 1713, 'but after all masters and owners of ships will have the most reason to boast.' This is not to say that prominent coal-owners, like the Claverings or the Liddells, did not have an interest in shipping, even in ships belonging to other ports. We know, in fact, that they did and, what is more, we know in some cases how such part or full ownership came to be acquired, viz. the failure of a once independent master-owner to pay for the coals he had loaded during the shipping season. In this way George Liddell came to own parts in five or six of William Dove's ships in 1717 and John Binks's ship a decade later. Conversely, he was quite ready to dispose of his share in a ship whose master was not entirely satisfactory. Nor were coal-owners blind to the obvious advantages of having such an interest in a ship that they could oblige its master, under bond, to load at their staiths. This explains a

---

[1] *History of Newcastle*, ii. 677. The list was compiled by Edward Grey. *Supra.* Willan, *The English Coasting Trade*, 217–19 discusses the question of ownership and registration of shipping. There is a list of ships clearing from Sunderland from March to June 1750 in Durham Palatinate Records (P.R.O.), E. 122. 198/10. The number of coal ships clearing from Sunderland in 1783–4 was as follows: 1st quarter 502; 2nd 1638; 3rd 1946; 4th (ending Christmas) 771. Ibid. 232/1. N.B.—By that date the seasonal character of coal shipments was tending to disappear.

letter which 'Governor' Liddell wrote on Christmas Day, 1716, 'that he had instructed John Walker of Whitby to take an inventory and appraise our shipping as soon as they come in . . . perhaps some of them may unrigg in your River', i.e. the Tyne. Altogether the Liddells had an interest in about twelve ships at that time though the colonel confessed in 1717 that his family had lost £3,200 in shipping 'but most of it was my Grandfather's and uncle's, not above £300 since I came down'. It is known too, that the big London dealers, the Oldners and Blunkett, owned some of the ships engaged in the trade. But the great bulk of the fleet, amounting perhaps to six or seven hundred sail, were owned or controlled by masters from ports south of the Tyne. Indeed, in 1729, John Hedworth, M.P., a prominent Sunderland coal-owner, proposed that the coal-owners of both rivers should form a fund for the purchase of shipping and there is incontestable evidence that at that date the shipping interest was quite distinct from the coal-owners. Moreover, so far as shipbuilding was concerned, there had lately been a marked decline at Newcastle. In 1722, seven Tyne skippers of from thirty to fifty years' standing stated in evidence 'that formerly the business of shipbuilding was very considerable and flourishing in Newcastle, but of late years few are built and many of the Ship Carpenters who commonly when employed in their own business earned above 4ˢ/- a day and several of the Smiths are now obliged for want of Employ to get Bread for their familys to undertake the hard and dangerous work of Rowing in the Keels'.[1]

During the Spanish Succession War and in the immediate post-war period, the trade was liable to be dislocated because of the demands of the government on shipping for the requirements of military transport.

Trade is in great confusion beyond all dispute [wrote Liddell in June 1713]. I draw my inference chiefly from the number of large ships

---

[1] Minutes of Evidence (1723), ff. 49–50, the evidence of Thomas Gibson, Robert Dunkin, David Leech, Andrew Stephenson, John Paterson, Andrew Mathews, and David Saunders, senior and junior. For later shipbuilding figures at Sunderland, see *V.C.H. Durham*, ii. 302.

that are taken up by the Government at this juncture for transporting our forces from Ostend to Ireland, at least 40 sail, some say 50, which one can't expect to return to the coal trade again before September. Again, I apprehend that our oversea trade is knock't on the head, if true what I heard this day that the French have stopp'd 15 of our merchant ships in Roan River and will not suffer them to unload nor return.

And although seamen, keelmen, and coblemen engaged in the coal trade were exempt from the press, if an emergency threatened, ships tended to stay in harbour until the 'protections' had actually come down from the Admiralty.[1] It can perhaps be assumed that conditions had returned to normal by the spring of 1718, when a second attempt at concerted action among the masters was made.

Ordinarily, the great bulk of the ships engaged in the trade were laid up during the winter months. 'I should wish the ships would likewise cease running for they spoil the trade and make nothing to themselves', Liddell wrote towards the end of November 1716. That is what many of the ships' masters believed and wished to see adopted as a general policy. The Whitby men were the first to move in the matter.

*To the Ship owners of Newcastle from the Ship owners of Whitby*

December 30. 1717.

Gentlemen,

The season of the year requiring that joynt measures should be concerted for the future Regulation of the coale trade and remedying as far as we can the inconveniences that attended our last projects, occasions the trouble hereof with our sentiments how it may be managed the next year (we hope more regular than this last).[2] We beg you'll

---

[1] 'I received your list of the coblemen', wrote Colonel Liddell, M.P., in 1730, 'and spoke to Sir Charles Wager and Mʳ Cockburn [two Lords of the Admiralty] and Mʳ Burchet in the House who all told me that the Man of War was to leave his station as yesterday and assured me that there would be no more press, except something extraordinary, which there was no prospect of, should happen. However, as I pressed it, they promised me a general protection—that for the coblemen to be included with the keelmen.'

[2] There had clearly been some concerted action in the previous years. *Supra*. In June 1715 Henry Liddell wrote from London, 'The [Ship] Masters here talk of making two voyages . . .

favour us with your thoughts on the Articles below to which if you please to add any conducive to the General Good you may at all times depend on a ready complyance from

Gentlemen,

Your most humble servants.

1st That no ships begin to load coales before the 10th day of March, those laid by in any other places than Tinmouth and the other loading ports may sayle the 1st of March and so have ten days time to get downe thither and none begin any voyage after the 29th day of September.

2nd Coales of 12s/- not to be sold at London under 26s/- per cha. nor of 11s/- under 25s/- the fore part of the sumer (except it's thought to have them 12d higher the first voyage) and for the encouragement of small ships, we propose Boston, Lynn and Yarmouth at 20s/- per cha, from thence to Gravesend 23s/- (except Ipswich and Weavney 24s/-). Rotterdam and other ports in Holland, Newcastle coales 12½ guilders, and Sunderland 13 guilders.

3. All ships to deliver in turn according to the several sorts they are loaded with, but to lay after delivery till all that came up before them be dispatcht and none to be excused delivery in turn on pretence of taking freight.

4. To make agents privy to the sale of all coals and have the prices of every ship's loading registered by them.

5. Masters and men to be paid by the month: their wages to be made good as in other preceeding years.

6. Every Master to be obliged (by charter party or otherwise as may be found safe by law) to some particular owner or owners to a strict observance of the above articles or others that from time to time may be agreed on for the general benefit of the Trade.

There were no signatories to this letter which was addressed to Francis Rudston, Mayor of Newcastle, himself a

no longer than the middle of August, about wch time it is suppos'd ye greatest part of their stocks will be sunk, ye City will be supply'd with a Quantity to answer till next year's Trade put in, by help of ye Warehouses, wch were scarce touch'd when ye Spring Trade open'd. Upwards of 100,000 [chaldrons] appear by the Meter's Office to have bin already imported, Old Stock 40,000 [chaldrons] so that at most 140,000 more will be in, wch will be soon fetch'd up considering ye Numbers of ships in ye trade & ye dispatch they make. Both Yarmouth and Whitby seem fond of calling in all their craft.'

merchant-shipper. Colonel George Liddell received a copy of it and of another written two days earlier which was also enclosed.

December 28. 1717.

Since the above, in a conference with the Agents and some Masters from Scarborough, it's been adjudged expedient to offer the following proposal viz, that a person be sent to each port to you and other loading ports to endeavour to engage the Coal owners and fitters not to load any ships before or after the time agreed on by us. As this would be an effectual means to perfect all our other designs by preventing the Interlopers and all other ill-designing persons from loading and consequently feeding the market at the season the coal buyers should have for vending their stocks, we hope you'll be aiding and assisting to us and the rest of our brethren when they come over to you in so materiall an article which will give fresh life to the coal trade.

P.S. We've written to Ipswich, Yarmouth, Lyn, and Scarboro to the effect above.

It is obvious that this was not the first occasion the Whitby masters had combined. Liddell promptly forwarded both letters to Cotesworth in London and asked his and the baronet's advice whether, as a coal-owner, he should comply. Should he, in effect, refuse to load an interloper who came 'contrary to this agreement'? When he wrote to Cotesworth again, a month later, the matter had been taken a stage farther:

February 12th.

I have been this day with the Ship owners' ambassadors. They propose to have double coal ascertained;[1] that no ships shall sail before Lady day, nay not the neutral ships fraighted by dealers. I opposed the first as what was not reasonable and recommended the winking at the latter and not only so but that they should oblige all the ships in the contract not to load before Midsummer in Sunderland Road. They were for settling proportions between the two rivers, but that we referred till they had consulted Mr. Ord and the rest of the coal owners.

[1] i.e. that each lading (Newcastle measure) should yield double the number of chaldrons, London measure.

At the end of the month he wrote again,

. . . Forgot to mention agreement come to with the Ship owners' plenipos. . . . It was absolutely necessary and very fortunate we did it for had the ships gone they had brought down the Market and not only so but Numbers of them would have perisht this terrible stormy weather. The Dealers, at least such as have no coals laid up, will fire at it, but what is hitherto done is no more than common friendship obliged us to. The Sunderland owners pretend they did not refuse coals—and that to ingratiate themselves with ye Dealers—but that is known to be notoriously false.

March 5.

Encloses the agreement with the Plenipos concerning shipping. I fenced off all that possibly I could and told them that as we were so greatly concerned in shipping they could not but believe we were more desirous than any of our neighbours that shipping should be encouraged, but then I told them that all agreements of this nature should be so calculated as not to bear hard on any one particular set of men. That this seem'd entyrely calculated for Sunderland and, as they proposed it, to the manifest disadvantage of this port, so that the advantages we had by nature was to be given away by us. However, I told them they should apply to the cole owners not concerned in shipping and to the Cheif first and to make them speak out for they would find several that would perhaps speak smoothly, though not at all to the purpose. This I spoke to one of them who I could trust.

They insisted strenuously on double coal, but I told them that if that was their intention I would advise them to go home again without giving themselves any further trouble for I was satisfied it would not be complyed with, so they dropt that.

Two days after I, by accident, fell in with them again and one of them told me they had great encouragement both from cole owners and fitters, not one having opposed them; and in the afternoon I found it confirmed by several of our fraternity[1] and fitters who were to a man for it.

The Sunderland people, though they had refused to load any ships till Lady day, yet when the Plenipos came there in their way down they treated them in a very insolent manner, as they told me, and declared they would resent it to a degree.

As it was the general inclination of this port to come to an Agree-

---

[1] i.e. the Hostmen's Company.

ment to lye till the 20th inst, it was not my business to oppose it and, therefore, I told them that if they wave insisting upon some things which I thought unreasonable, relating to double coal and also to the selling at London, that I would readily agree to lye provided they would undertake that the port should not be sufferers thereby. They assured me they would engage that their ships should use our port much more than they had done and that we should be their darling. This they promist also publicly very solemnly.

*My good friend*, I perceive, tells you the Dealers are enraged at me as a principal. You know I was as much an agent as any there and the only one my father has to treat for his concerns. I will be bold to say that I argued more with the Plenipos in the Dealers' behalf than all the cole owners or their agents did. I would have had them given leave to have loaden up those ships that had then begun, but they would not consent to it, for they said some had offer'd to forbear and as I had none then loading, I had the less to say against it. Indeed, when some offer'd it at the meeting that they would not load up, I then joyned with others that as some did not load up their ships, we thought others ought not. Besides, I recommended to them never to sell 12$^s$/- coals above 26$^s$/-, nor 11$^s$/- above 25$^s$/6$^d$, except the first or last voyages and then not above 12$^d$ [more]. I further advised them to let the masters sell their own coals and not to do it by Agents for that would cause clamour. The great motive that induced me to comply, next to the consideration of those that had estates in shipping, was the General Complaint that the ships already come up had put such a damp upon the trade that several that had laid up coales last summer had not yet open'd their warehouses, and of this my uncle[1] complained as well as the rest.

The ships that went up since Xmas were generally trash coales from Bladon upon frieght and not much better than pan coals. Then there were others with Cully's [i.e. Cullercoats] and Blythe coales and these mixt with the other trash made them merchantable. Are we to encourage other people to trade in direct opposition to us? No surely! Your author, I doubt not, threw in his word against me and made what was said much worse than those that spoke it meant, but I will know the bottom of it. He cannot, I suppose, forgive me going into the fitting trade[2] and therefore is doing what he can to trip up my heeles. . . .

I think it a very great providence that we did comply with the earnest

---

[1] Thomas Liddell, M.P.
[2] George Liddell was himself a member of the Hostmen's Company.

solicitions of the ship owners and if I had a hand in it I have reason, I think, to rejoice that I contributed to so good a work what[ever] a few mercenary creatures may say. Had the coal trade begun as early this year as usual what a melancholy account should we have had of them. It was impossible for a loaden ship to have lived, so that numbers of them must have perisht and the light ones, if they had escapt must have been much shatterd.

It is perhaps not surprising in view of what we know of the combination among ships' masters in 1710–11 that they should again have taken the lead. What kind of response came from the south ports, Yarmouth, Ipswich, and Lynn, is not known for certain and can only be inferred from other letters. Liddell's cautious approach to the masters' proposals is very characteristic. His fear that the project was 'entyrely calculated for Sunderland to the manifest disadvantage of this port, so that the advantages we had by nature was to be given away by us' was not unfounded. Edward Grey, the Newcastle hostman, who prepared an analysis of the coal ships trading to the Tyne in 1705 added this note to his list: 'The reason why Sunderland ships load at this port is that it is dangerous in winter both for the ships to lye in the roads there and for the keels to go out to them.' The act passed in 1717 to improve the harbour at Sunderland was intended to minimize these dangers. But if ships were 'to deliver and sail in turn', then clearly, once they unloaded, they would tend to use the nearer port in order to dash back to catch the market. 'Sailing in turn' would have to be more narrowly defined before the Newcastle men would accept it. Then again, the subsequent attitude of Cotesworth and Liddell to the scheme shows that the former at any rate had not forgotten the events of 1710–11.

March 30.
... The shipowners have writ to us about refusing to load without certificates [i.e. of having delivered in turn] but I am of your mind it may be of dangerous consequence. Our lying to the 20th March has something to justify it, but to lye at this time of the year or to refuse to load coales would be condemned by all the world.

April 6.

. . . The masters are plying us about not loading without certificates or at least to make such as come without, pay 2ˢ/- a cha. more than others. . . . Mr. Ord and the Alderman[1] incline to it and so do the fitters in general. As to my own part, I should be sorry the Masters should again fall into the hands of the Dealers and except something of this kind be done they infallibly will and then both coal owners and masters will be slaves. The Masters have been very easy this fleet and seem very staunch towards this port, so that I would not have them baffled. They are full of fair promises and I hope will perform; and, if so, I cannot see any better expedient can be thought of than making ye interlopers suffer who would not own us but when the price is inviting. I say to make them and the headstrong Masters belonging to the Trade pay 2ˢ/- a cha. extraordinary would satisfy such as laid for price and would not be lyable to any public censure, as stopping by refusing to load would be if it were practised.

April 18.

. . . It is the opinion of most here that the Masters' project or Regulation ought to be encouraged. The way of doing it will not, as we take it, subject us to any censure from superior powers. It is, what I must own, I should be very glad to have supported for, if not, we return again into servitude and our Task masters will be the more severe upon us. I think the Masters laying their injunctions on the fitters will be a means to make them much more observant than they would otherwise be and is taking the odium a good deale off the coal owner. Your merry Andrew Dick has been at Alderman Ridley to desire that he would nominate him for an Agent for the Masters here to hold correspondence with their Agents above [i.e. in London] and to give lists of ships delivered out of turne. The Alderman ask't him if he had your consent or recommendation: he said 'No'. The Alderman told him he must excuse him, which gave Andrew much offence.

It is clear that the coal-owners generally welcomed this latest attempt at 'Regulation'. Indeed the colonel reported on the 20th that 'all others are mad to joyne with the Masters . . . Sunderland, as we are told, declare they will act as the Masters have desired', i.e. not to load without certificates. He pressed for final instructions from London

---

[1] Richard Ridley. In 1786 Matthew White Ridley stated it as his opinion 'that no one can work her [Bedlington colliery?] to advantage, without many ships of their own'. Ridley MSS.

by return of post 'either to come in with the Masters or Dealers and not hang in the equilibrium till we disoblige both'.

Ravensworth Castle.<br>April.

(Copy)

. . . On Monday at 8 a.m. came here six of the *Top Masters* in the harbour . . . and stayed until 4 o'clock. We talk'd over the whole affair of the trade and I was quite exhausted answering them one after another. They were very earnest either for us to absolutely deny loading interlopers and such as delivered out of turn, or to make them pay 2ˢ/- a cha. extraordinary. I told them in general that you and all your Agents were perfectly well disposed to promote the interest of Navigation and the Coal Trade so that there was nothing they could reasonably ask that you would refuse, but that their present demand for the Coal owner to agree (as above) was obliging them to act what we were of opinion was contrary to law. I told them that was what I could not think either fit for you to consent to or me to advise; but that I wisht they could find out some other expedient. They told me the Alderman was very ready to comply with it and so was Mr. Ord and all the fitters, coleowners and agents they had talkt with and, therefore, would oblige me to go to town yesterday and give the coleowners a meeting and they doubted [not] but we should find an expedient. Whilst we were talking a messenger from Alderman Ridley with one enclosed from the London agents to him wherein they give an account of some refractory masters who would not lye for turn and that they conjur'd us by the friendship we have for Navigation that we would nip it in the bud by refusing the loading them. . . . Upon this I fenc'd off as well as I could and promist to go to town yesterday. . . . Meeting with the Alderman at Mr. Ord's at 2 oc.—I got there a little before the Alderman to have a little free Conference with Mr. Ord before he came— Ord told me he had orders to act in compliance with me and read me part of Mr. Wortley's letter. He agreed with me that the scheme would be lookt upon as an unlawful combination, but to act and support the Masters as much as we could 'without breach of the law'.

He told me he thought if the ships that were now coming down and had delivered out of turne were loaden by any of us there would be an end of the Shipowners' project and then we should bring both them and the coalowner into severer bondage than before. That he designed to tell Charles Atkinson [his fitter] either to refuse them coals, as having constant oasts of his own that would take off all the coals that could be led for his share, or to make them pay 2$^s$/- extraordinary as the thing best suited and that Charles should communicate this to the rest of the fitters: this, says he, [Ord] I will not promise nor agree with either Coleowner or shipowner to do. But this I design to do, and if any of our fitters act otherwise, the masters will know it and may shew their resentment to such fitter. I found the Alderman of the same mind.

Mr. Ord is very clear that no law can touch him for what he shall do in his case, any more than it would a Master that should come to London and demand 2$^s$/- more, or that should refuse to sell his coals to any dealer (that was my own and the Alderman's opinion also). For though it might be a crime to come to an agreement to do this, yet every man, without any agreement, doing the same thing might not, I think, be criminal in the eye of the law. I proposed that the Masters should be told that in short we could not come into any agreement with them, but at the same time to give them a hint to exclaim against the usage they had from us by not agreeing and therefore they come to some of the leading fitters in each concerne and tell them that though the coleowners had not the friendship for them they expected, yet they hop't to find it among the fitters and therefore they would make the same proposal to them and enjoyned them not to load any. This naturally will make the fitters apply to and request leave of the coleowners to comply. The coleowner may assent by leaving them to their liberty to act as they shall see fit. This, I thought, was laying it upon the fitter. Mr. Ord and the Alderman agreed it much the best expedient and accordingly the Masters had notice as above who immediately went on the key in seeming wrath exclaiming against the Coleowners and design two or three to attack each considerable fitter this day, so that tomorrow we shall hear what turn it takes.

Jack Johnson declared (in my hearing) before the Masters that he would not load one of these refractory blades.

The Masters were with Mr. Hedworth in town yesterday and he declared he would not load one of these ships for the coals were his own and he would sell to whom he pleased and his fitters should sell as he ordered.

I did all in my power to gain time but could not, nor could I act otherwise than as above without exposing your interest. I have been greatly perplext in this affair and it has given me many an anxious

thought and broke me many an hour's rest. It is of too great a weight
for me and really above my capacity. I have acted with all ye caution
that possibly I could for your interest.

The Sunderland owners are grown a little reasty on a rumour that the
shipowners had made an agreement with this port that none of their
ships should load in their roads, but on being convinced it was not fact,
I believe, they will come in to a man.

I told the Masters that the Dealers were taking great pains to possess
the consumers with a good opinion of the Sunderland coals, so that if
we should incline to refuse loading ye Interlopers, they would order
them, as well as the refractory, to load all in that Road and by that
means increase their quantity and lessen ours. To which they assure
me that if there be the least prospect of Sunderland breaking measures
or any other way increasing their quantity, on notice thereof they will
not allow one ship, great or small, to load either in their road or Harbour.

They have had a great deal said to them, I mean the Masters, and
they promise very fair and seem perfectly friendly and I hope will
maintain their agreement and they do assure us if we do hold it we
shall save all our premium another year.

Thus the coal-owners decided to sail close to the legal wind
by 'laying it on the fitters'.

April 20.
... Received yours by which I perceive the Sunderland ships have
not acted as if they were under such engagements as those of other
towns nor can the agents say the coleowners are. The Masters here
assured us the fitters engaged not to load till the 20<sup>th</sup> ult° and after that
gave it under their hands not to load any ships that delivered out of
turn. Whether they will perform that or no I know not, but if these
ships that delivered out of turn came away out of turne it will soon be
known whether the fitters load them or not.

I have had a very difficult part to act, least by opposing the measure
the Masters were concerting when others were for coming into them
I should disoblige them, or on the other hand, by coming into those
measures to incense the Dealers and perhaps make you or myself lyable
to the censure of Council or Parliament.

Mr. Ord, Alderman Ridley and some others of the owners, though
they would not come to any engagement so to do, yet were resolved to
give orders as I told you in my last to their fitters, not to load any of

the transgressors and the fitters were very desirous that it might be so. What was I then to do? I could think of no way to keep myselfe loose, but by proposing that the Masters should apply to the fitters and tell them that the coleowners would not come into measures as they expected and, therefore, they expected the fitters should comply with their request or otherwise they should find their Resentment. This Mr. Ord highly approved as a very good thought and so did the Alderman etc. and the Masters were satisfied with it and went next day to the fitters in seeming wrath against us.

Yesterday I went again to town and had a consultation with the above Gentlemen and Robin Wright. They all agree that if Sunderland cannot be brought in, then the project must cease in course, but they are of opinion that if Sunderland do come into measures, the trade may be kept in a good decorum, without bringing ourselves into any premunire.

Sir Edward Northey's[1] opinion is undoubtedly very just as the case is stated but perhaps it might be a good deale different were the query otherwise put, for I suppose we do not come to any agreement with the ship owners to observe any rules, but the fitters of their own accords hear that such and such ships delivered out of turn. If they are not constant oasts, the fitter tells them that he expects every tyde ships that are his constant customers who will take off more than his share will be at the staith and he must not disoblige them. This answer serves likewise for interlopers. Now may not this be done without incurring a premunire?

Such as are constant customers we generally have some parts in and in such case you or the fitter or who ever has parts in them may withdraw your parts and arrest for profit or for a faire account and so hamper only three or four and the work might be done very easily afterwards.

Supposing Sunderland were hearty, we think this method or something of this kind would keep the Masters' agreement on foot and we would hope without being lyable to be called to any account for it.

Some of the refractory masters are come in, as Coates and Goddard. Coates loads generally with young Robinson and I hear he resolves not to load him. Goddard loads with me and is the only one among them that does load with me. I have ordered Tom Airey to put two keeles on board him and then to tell him that he has orders not to load him up

---

[1] Attorney-general. He had been consulted on a previous occasion. Dendy, *Hostmen's Company*, 162–3.

because he has not reckoned and paid me his profit. This will delay him some time till I shall hear and see what others do. If others do not load, I think to make Goddard buy my parts for I have but an ill account of him and that I can do safely and the doing that will retard him sufficiently.

I am in great perplexity how to behave the most to your advantage for it is nothing to me whether the agreement goes on or not. I would not disoblige the Masters nor, if practicable, have the project defeated. Please to give as speedy an answer as may be to this: whether if Sunderland give assurances of their zeal and, by their actions, answer it, whether, I say, in such case we may proceed in the method abovesaid or in what other. If we do not proceed in this way in my opinion shipping is ruined and, if so, the coal owner will feel the effects of it in a little time. It is not my own interest I am seeking but that of Navigation and the coal trade in both which you are greatly concerned and, therefore, if I happen to be mistaken in my notions, I hope you'll pardon my zeal, it being calculated chiefly for your service and I shall act as you direct: but I doubt it will not be possible so to act betwixt the two as not to offend either masters or dealers: nay in case we do not strike with one side early, perhaps may disoblige both. I shall, however, according to my best judgement, follow your directions and therefore desire you may be full and plain.

Mr. Ord has already full power to act with discretion. Alderman Ridley and Mr. Wright incline to what is above mentioned, provided the Sunderland owners give assurance of being steady, as I believe they did the other day. This makes the burden lye heavier upon me, who dare not consent or yet dare not refuse.

Legal subterfuge could scarcely go farther. An 'article' of agreement as to prices between the coal-owners and the shippers was actually signed but the onus of decision on 'delivering in turns' was to be thrown on to the dependent fitters. Of course, from the masters' point of view the success of the whole scheme depended on their getting better prices at the Gate. And this is precisely what happened. On 4 May Liddell was 'not a little provoked at the Agents above for setting so high a price . . . which has done great disservice to the trade by making them deliver slowly so that all our staiths are now full and our keelmen presented a petition to the Mayor and were ready for a mutiny but that care was taken by the Magistrates and fitters. If they do not lower their price, they must break of course for as all staiths are full the whole country would be in a Rebellion if ships should not be dispatched as soon as they come in.' A repetition of 1710–11 was threatened with the added danger of another Jacobite attempt in the north. Cotesworth was asked to give the masters 'an intimation of it that there might be better dispatch', and we may depend upon it that he did. He not only strove 'towards a comprehension at the Gate', but took the precaution of having an interview with the leading minister, Lord Sunderland, and serious trouble was avoided.

It is clear that the masters produced a similar scheme in the following year though our knowledge of how it was received by the coal-owners is confined to Sunderland where the six principal proprietors agreed on 29 February (*sic*):

That no coals shall be delivered from any staith on board any keel before the 27th March, except shifting keels which shall be certified as such from the fitter to the staithman, except 30 keels off Mr. Lambton's staith. And as for the keeles already loaden and to be loaden as above they shall not be cast on board any ship so as to be loaden above ⅔ of her burthen.

And in case any fitter shall lay any coales on board any ship more than is above mentioned, he or she shall be excluded from having any coals from any staith on the River Wear for the space of one whole year next ensuing.

Mr. Hedworth's boast that 'his fitters should sell as he ordered' was no idle threat. It was further agreed that 'no ship load coals unless she passes Gravesend loaden on or before 26th September next, provided the City of London be sufficiently supplied and that no ship on her last voyage be suffered to lay loaden in the River Thames one month after she passes Gravesend'. Best coals were not to sell in London under 27s. per chaldron. If other coal-ports agreed, before 28 March, not to load ships 'without certificates' of having delivered in turn, the Sunderland owners would follow suit.

We do not know how long the 1719 shipping regulation lasted or what measure of success it achieved though it is evident that some kind of 'contract' persisted. Ten years later trouble flared up again.[1] As before, the initiative came from Whitby and Scarborough where local committees were set up. The principal agents or 'plenipos' were William Ward and James Huston. Committees and agents were also appointed at other ports—Hull, Yarmouth, Rochester, for example—for when the agents from the latter port were examined by a parliamentary committee in May 1729 they said 'that they were appointed to see that ships kept turns and if they did not, were to write to Mr. Francis Armorer, attorney at Newcastle, Agent, not to load them if they had no certificate'. Moreover, they 'produced a letter from the Committee at Whitby appointing them agents, and for which they were to have 1[d] per chaldron'. This interesting piece of evidence, besides confirming the lead taken by the men from the Yorkshire port, suggests that the movement in the 'south ports' was not altogether spontaneous. We know, however, that the Yarmouth men were deeply involved. Thomas Airey, Liddell's principal agent, wrote from Newcastle on 11 February 1729.

The Yarmouth Masters have wrote their agent, Spanton, that they insist upon coming to sea five days before the Scarboro' and Whitby ships, but he has written them that they must either stand to the first agreement of all to sail upon a day i.e. the 3rd of March, or all that had been done would be undone.

Spanton was already in the north. 'I find they are at a stand what to do, whether to stay till the day, 3rd March, or begin

---

[1] In August 1728 George Bowes wrote from London: 'I am now informed that those ships that does not get up to be in the Contract List by the first of October will not be allowed to make another voiage this year by their Rules. But those ships that are up by the 1st [October] are allowed to make one voiage more. I hear M[r] G[ibson] intends the latter end of this winter to go to Yarmouth and the several Towns that are seaports.' At the end of November he wrote again, 'It was given out by Gibson that he would visit all the Sea Ports northwards amongst the masters in the Coal Trade and indeavour to corroborate the Famous Contract he and Horn has hatched to the great destruction of the Tine Trade, but others say he'll have business enough nigher home.' Bowes MSS. 40748, §§ 51, 55. Gibson had lately left the Custom House and formed a partnership with Furze.

to load directly', wrote Airey ten days later, 'Spanton has gone to Shields intending to get the Masters together and see if they will desist loading till the time before agreed.' A meeting was held at Shields on 22 February when 'all agreed to send for no coals till the 3rd of March'. The meeting sent an express to Whitby and Scarborough to 'desire they would continue in harbour till that time'. On the 25th, Airey reported that 'the Masters all lye very quietly, resolved not to load till the day'.

The masters had got the bit properly between their teeth on this occasion and they now had a powerful champion in Sir William Strickland, member of parliament for Scarborough. In addition to insisting on a closed season for shipping and that ships should 'deliver and sail in turn', they demanded that the London Lightermen's Company be thrown open, that they be forbidden to act as crimps, and that the masters themselves be allowed to appoint factors to sell their own coals. The master mind behind this concerted movement was William Ward, a Newcastle hostman.[1] Colonel George Liddell who was now member of parliament for Berwick, had an outline of the plan by the middle of January and immediately subjected it to close scrutiny. The five or six weeks' loss in 'leading' and shipping time, he submitted, would gravely prejudice both wagon-men and keelmen besides causing further deterioration and therefore increased cost of maintenance of keels and wagon-ways. He was of the opinion that 'lying for turns' would clearly favour Sunderland at the expense of Newcastle.

The Masters may of themselves agree to have an Agent at each port to sell their coals without the assistance of the Coale owner. But it is not reasonable for a Newcastle cole owner to agree that ships loaden there shall deliver in turn with those loaden at Sunderland, that being a great encouragement to ships to load in Sunderland Road in hopes of getting back into the River of Thames before ym that load in Tinmouth Haven; as we were fully convinced last year.

[1] Dendy, 275–8. Cf. Willan, op. cit. 38–39. Sir William Strickland was a Lord of the Treasury from 1725 to 1727. Add. MSS. 36125–6, *passim*: he was Secretary at War and Treasurer to the Queen in 1730. Treasury Books and Papers (1729–30), *passim.*

'The Masters, I think, might at least endeavour to find out some more Naturall expedient for the relief of the Navigation employed in the Coal Trade', he continued. 'They Rayle with great violence at the Dealers as the only means of beating down the price of coales, whereas 'tis greatly owing to their being too many Ships in the Trade and many of those ships having Masters of great passions and little Reason. They should, therefore, endeavour to reduce the number of their Ships, rather than raise the price of coales too high, by which means they will get more profit and the consumer be less aggrieved. Whenever coales are dear, Interlopers will come in.' 'So that upon the whole', he concluded, 'I think the article impracticable to be complied with, especially this year when we had so many coals of last year's working left upon our hands, though if others on our River agree not to deliver, I doubt we must do so too, but I think it highly unreasonable for us to tye up our hands and lye still when Sunderland can do little or nothing.' Many of the coal-owners on Tyneside, however, were disposed to come into the scheme.

A week later news of it leaked out in London. 'Today', wrote Liddell on the 23rd, 'I asked Alderman Bernard who told me that there was great complaints in the City that the Masters had by their combination and delivering in turns not only stopped the ships and hindered them bringing so many coals and thereby raised the price and obstructed the navigation of this River by making warehouses of their ships, but had lessened the Revenue and which will cause a complaint when it comes to be observed that of the £70,000 assigned out of that duty, there will be so considerable a deficiency. . . .' 'The City design to bring it into Parliament', he added. On the 1st of February, Bernard, who was one of the members for the City, 'told me that he was informed that not only the coalowners and masters and fitters had come to an agreement, but that the keelmen were in a combination not to load coals and had at Newcastle refused to load a ship that went down. . . . A complaint seems to him unavoidable.'

That night the *St. James' Evening Post* published news of the combination. 'I think the Masters that are here as well as their Agents use us very ill', wrote Liddell, 'the first in publishing to all the world as a reason for raising the price of coals that the coalowners have agreed that no ships be loaden till March 3rd and Ward uses us ill that instead of coming up direct he takes a tour along the coast to spin out the time.' 'I am very apprehensive we shall have a complaint in parliament against us though it was done without any direction of ours.' Hedworth, one of the members for County Durham, retorted that there could be no such agreement as alleged among the coal-owners at Newcastle for the principal ones were then in London, which was true enough. For all that, 'the *Evening Post* had last Tuesday put it into a very bad light and it made a good deal of noise in the House yesterday'. Could a parliamentary committee be avoided? Mr. Wortley declared that he would not have a complaint in the House for £10,000.

Liddell took upon himself to damp down the clamour. Towards the end of January and during the first half of February he had talks with both Strickland and two of the City members, Alderman Bernard and Sir William Thompson. He found the former 'a zealous advocate for the Masters and inveterate against the Dealers': he declared that he had 'instructions at large from the town of Scarborough' and had received a petition from the ships' masters desiring that the Lightermen's Company be laid open and such other relief as the House shall think fit: 'he told me the premium given to the Dealers was abominable, that Mr. Bowes told him he himself paid them £3,000 a year and the whole was £15,000'; further that Mr. Hedworth told him 'he should be glad if ye Dealers were broke'. But after 'two quiet free conferences, I entirely softened him', Liddell reported. At the same time he won the confidence of Alderman Bernard and arranged an informal meeting at the House of the principal coal-owners and the City members.

We convinced them pretty well that we have not so agreed and that 'twas to our prejudice. They owned the masters had traded to no profit, but that this method of proceeding must not be allowed. And that the only thing to clear ourselves would be to write this post to Newcastle to load the ships, for otherwise it must come into parliament and both masters and fitters would be sent for up immediately. We instead of that agreed to attend the Court of Aldermen next Tuesday. Whilst we were in Conference, Sir Robert Walpole came by us in the Low Gallery, behind the Speaker's Chair and Bernard told him what we were upon. He said they had had it before ym (meaning the Treasury) and they found that by the Masters' Contract last year the Revenue fell short about £15,000. He spoke it in a pleasant manner. I told him that for five preceeding years there had every year been more coals imported [into London] than were consumed which was the chief occasion of that. . . . This morning, Alderman Parsons was shewing a letter of complaint against Mr. Ridley for refusing to load.

At this joint meeting the City members, it transpired, were also 'for breaking the Lightermen's Company and for complaining against them for taking ye premium'. Meanwhile, they insisted that the coal-owners meet the lord mayor and aldermen at the Guildhall a week later.

In preparation for this second meeting Liddell arranged 'a breakfast conference' of the principal coal-owners of both rivers at his London house.

We unanimously agreed that we must assure them that we would write in the strongest terms to our Agents and Fitters to load all ships that demanded coales. This will convince them that we do not encourage it, but I much question whether they will not complain against the Masters in parliament and also against Ward who they are highly irritated at as the Contriver of these schemes. And indeed, among Friends, I could wish he were mumbled for 'tis all owing to him for had he come directly up, ye affair might have been so Concerted as to have prevented any Complaints.

'The Masters have by their own indiscretions made the agreement so public that it cannot be complied with', he wrote later. Much depended on the conference at the Guildhall appointed for noon on 18 February. Seven distinguished representatives of the Tyne owners, including four M.P.s, were present, and Mr. Hedworth and Baron Hilton for the Wear owners. Colonel Liddell was the principal spokesman. 'We assured them that we were in no combination nor knew of none: that the Masters every year gave their Fitters notice when they designed to open the Trade which must be at Spring Tydes to bring them out: that it happened to be a late moon this year and that as the Season was bad, the Masters had probably insisted with their Fitters not to dispose of their dry Coales on the Staithes till they came least they should otherwise have none, at least only wet ones, and to oblige their Customers probably the Fitters had promised them, but that, I was satisfied, that was the most'. The Court of Aldermen appeared satisfied with this explanation but 'insisted upon it that we would write by this post to our Fitters to begin to load all ships that demanded Coales and that without delay'. Accordingly, Liddell ordered his agent, Thomas Airey, to inform all his fitters of this forthwith 'and tell them I desire they will pursue it for their own Sakes as well as mine'. 'I hope we have stopped it going to Parliament', he added, 'but it is got into all Public Companys and the Coale Owners [are] ill-treated.'

'The City are at present quieted as to the Coale Trade in expectation of ships speedily coming up', he wrote on the 22nd, 'but they may be deceived for I believe the Agents have writ to the shipping not to stir till the time is expired.' The colonel's labours were by no means finished. At the end of the month, the shippers' 'plenipos', Ward and Huston, arrived in town and desired a conference with the coal-owners. Two meetings were held at Liddell's house early in March.

They pressed for our giving orders to our Fitters not to load any ships that did not bring down Certificates of their having delivered in Turn, that is, the ships in each Concern or Colliery to deliver in turn with the ships of that Colliery. Mr. Hedworth was very forward for it. I must own I thought it not proper for us to come into. First, as I did not know but it might prove prejudicial to ye River Tyne. And in the next place, as I was suspicious that if we had come into it, the Masters would have been so imprudent as to have raised Coales so high as that there would have been Complaints against them, as also against us, and we should have Entirely disobliged the Dealers and played the power too much into the Masters' hands. However, we at last consented in the following words 'Whereas application has been made to the Cole owners by several persons interested in the Navigation not to load any ships without Certificates. It is referred to the Respective Fitters to do therein as they shall see fit for the Benefit of the Trade.' You are to take notice that none of the Fitters are expected to comply with what is above [he added] except Blythe and Hartley do Comply. And if they do come in, we see no Objection to the Fitters coming into it; except they among themselves have any. And in case we find any Inconveniences in it, we reserve a Liberty of giving our Fitters contrary Orders. And in case any Fitter shall attempt to corrupt any Master by giving or offering them money, or any Master demand money, they will look upon it as an ill behaviour and Resent it.

After the 'Gentlemen' were gone, Liddell had some further talk with Ward and Huston who explained

that instead of certifying that they have deliver'd in Turne by the Directions of their Owners, the Certificate will only be that they made out so many chaldrons and he that has not that, will be supposed to be a Transgressor. I then told them that there would be several ships from the South, that is from this port or hereabouts that probably would not take Certificates from them, as some Dealers had an interest in them or in some of their Friends. That I did not see how the Fitters could refuse them if they did not at London undersell and they seemed to yield to that. Then we talked of the price to be set for this Fleet and agreed it to be 26s/-, and the next 25s/- or 25s/6d and not higher till about August and then 26s/- and perhaps the last voyage 27s/-.

Thus did 'the wise man of the North' try to safeguard the London consumer and so avoid clamour that was bound to lead to parliamentary intervention. Besides, he had largely drawn the sting from the shippers' proposal concerning loading by certificates and had hinted at a possible rift between the Yorkshire men and those from the 'south' ports. 'There are about 60 or 70 saile that I beleive will not lye and ye greatest part of them Yarmouth men', he wrote later in the month. At their meeting he also discussed with Huston the selling price of his own 'Teame' coals which, being somewhat better than the second grade, deserved a slightly higher price at the Gate and an understanding was reached. When, therefore, he discovered later that they had, in fact, been sold at the same price as second-grade coals, he made representations in the proper quarter. Huston replied that 'we must make it up in measure'. 'I did not expect such an Answer and have desired Gilroy to speak to him from me again for I shall not take such usage patiently. If the Masters can carry their point, you will find them very Tyrannical. Some of them have given out, that they would be loaded for so many keeles.'[1]

Both Bowes and Hedworth, the county members, were in favour of dissolving the Lightermen's Company and taking off the premium. 'I wish the Dealers may be broke. I think it would be a great advantage to us all', wrote Ralph Fetherston, Wortley's principal agent in the north. Liddell, however, was of a different opinion. 'I do not think that breaking them will do us any good, perhaps a good deal of harme', he wrote, 'for we by having a greater number of small chaps shall, I doubt, make more bad debts and it may be a means of putting too much power into the Masters' hands which will be Tyrannically used. Tis certainly the Coleowners' Interest to preserve the Balance of power in their own hands and not to let either of the contending partyes oppress the other. But this *sub Rosa*.' This, as we have seen, had been his family's attitude to the middlemen for many years. In the end, his valiant efforts to avoid clamour were unavailing. We can follow the subsequent course of events in his letters to his nephew, Henry Ellison.

March 27.
. . . As to the Coale Trade it is in great Confusion. The plenipos feed the market slowly and the ships lye dispersed as low as the Nore. The price they fix at 27s/- and say they will not abate a farthing. On

---

[1] i.e. for a ship to make out so many chaldrons at the unloading port—something approaching 'double coals'. Gilroy was Liddell's representative 'at the Gate'.

the other hand, the Dealers buy no more than of necessity they must. The Great Consumers, as Brewers, would have given 25ˢ/ currant, but as the price is so high set, they are extremely Enraged. They own the Cole Owners are clear, but the Masters according to their Usual Simplicity give out that the Fitters will not load any ship without Certificates. You must think the Dealers know whatever is done below[1] and make their own uses of it to blow up the Consumers. The Brewers, Distillers etc were to have a meeting last night to agree to buy ships and send down and so discover whether the Fitters will refuse them coals. If they do, and the Coale Owner to whom they belong hath plenty of coales upon their staiths, they will make proof of that and then endeavour to get the Hostmen's Charter dissolved. For, say they, the Crown granted them a charter to supply all the King's Subjects, not to deny any. I think the Fitters at Newcastle should consider well how far they may be affected by having the Trade laid open. When we were before the Lord Mayor etc. Mr. Bowes said that the Coal owners at Sunderland could command their Fitters, but that at Newcastle they were a Corporate company and not under the Command of the coal owner, so that they make use of that to make them more Obnoxious.

James Huston promised to come and talk with me before the fleet came up, but he has not and now talks in a high strain. He sayes the measure at Newcastle is not to be Endured and that he has ordered the master of his ship to load where he can have the best Measure. What he now says they will all say when they are a little stronger. . . . All that I aim at is to preserve the ballance in the Coal Owner's hand.

April 15.

. . Nothing in my opinion but long Easterly winds and the present press could have preserved the Masters' agreement so long, for abundance of the Masters dislike it and think the price too high. There would have several Foreland men (who are freighted by the Great Consumers) been down 'ere this had not the press prevented. . . .

April 17.

This day Mr. Bowes sent to desire me to meet him at the House for he wanted to speak with me on Extra-ordinary business. I met him accordingly and he told me that Sir Wᵐ Thompson yesterday informed him that ye Court of Aldermen last Tuesday took under their Con-

[1] i.e. at Newcastle.

sideration the Combination in the Coale Trade and resolved upon petitioning ye Parliament this next week. They say 'tis plain that the Fitters and Masters are in Combination; for not only the Masters own it, but the thing Speaks itself, for the Fitters had refused severall Masters because they did not bring Certificates, and among the rest say, that one of the Spantons went to all the Fitters and none of them would load him. They also say, that they cannot think that the coal owners would suffer the Fitters (who are but their Agents) to do such things if they did not approve of it and wink at it.

They talk of a design against the Oastman's Charter and to lay open Wayleaves. But of this more as soon as I can inform you. Mr. Wortley sayes he did not give any orders to any of his Agents since he writ to them to load any that demanded coals and that he does not know that any were refused. Mr. Bowes sayes he has no command over his Fitters. I wish Inconveniencys, and those great ones, do not fall upon the Trade, as well as Reflexions upon us.

April 24.

. . . The City complained against a Combination of the Masters and Fitters and with great warmth. A Committee was appointed who meet tomorrow morning where we shall attend. They would have complained against the Oastmen, but I set them right and got them to call them fitters as it comprehended Sunderland and the outports. I am sorry it comes into the House as we often cramps trade but they cannot affect the Cole owner and the Oastmen I hope to defend so as not to be sent for.

April 26.

. . . On Friday Morning the Ctee met where all that come have Voices. The charge made by Bernard, Perry, Sir John Eyles and Sir W^m Thompson was very heavy on the Masters and Fitters and bitter against Ward. They had laid it against the Company of Oastmen, but that I told them whatever was done was to be sure as much by the Sunderland Fitters as by them. They seem'd very intent upon breaking the Oastmen's Charter and laying open wayleaves; and Alderman Bernard had some schemes for that purpose which were sent him. I told him I was satisfied in my own opinion it would not appear that the Oastmen were in a combination to deny all ships that did not bring certificates for I employed 9 of ym and had not heard, nor did I believe, that one of them had denyed one ship. That there was not the least reason for Invading property by laying open Way leaves, for the

Coal Owners had not raised ye price of their coales one penny, nor was there the least grounds to surmize that the Coal Owners were in a Combination. We had a great deal of talk, after having order'd several to be summoned and adjourned till Tuesday morning. Mr. Bowes and I had a great deal of talk in behalf of Fitters and Masters and hope we shall excuse the Fitters being sent for. Sir W^m Strickland who is Member for Scarbrough, and a great advocate for the Masters, laid the Dealers thick on for receiving a premium and oppressing the Masters.

In short, the Aldermen have affidavits and know every thing that has been done. We left them in good humour and at our next meeting shall see more of the complexion of the C^tee and be better able to judge.

Mr. Wortley was not there, nor was Mr. Hedworth, tho' Mr. Bowes writ to him at Bath and he received it 'ere he set out Northward.

Two nights this week till near 8 and two till 10 is eno' to kill a horse. . . .

April 29.

. . This Morning the Committee met at Ten when Maltis Ryall[1] and young Williford were examined and Ward in part, the Speaker sending for us to come into the House. Maltis said Charles Atkinson and Simpson and Mr. Rudston and Reed[2] all owned that they had come into an agreement not to load any coals till the 3^rd of March: that he was told by a Master at Hull that Ward and Huston had made an Agreement with the Coal Owners and Fitters. We cleared the former and hope to set the latter in a good light before the C^tee. . . .

May day.

This Morning we had nothing material at the Committee but sit de die in diem. . . . I had yesterday some of the Masters and this day George Oldner and Blunket (who are with me at Ten) to see if I could prevent their exposing each other to the prejudice of all parties and hope with good effect.

May 3.

. . . Goodchild examined . . . [stated] That Mr. Sympson writ him that they would load the first ships but if after that they came without Certificates could not be loaden.

This is the substance of what passed. The Committee are as warm

---

[1] A prominent London dealer.      [2] Hostmen and shippers.

one against another as the Masters and Lightermen are against one another. Mr. Bowes, Mr. Fenwick and Mr. Carr are strong for the Masters. I am for neither but to see that neither be misrepresented. ...

May 4.

... This Morning we had a great deal of Wrangle at the Committee and a great deale of Dirt thrown and among the rest by Mr. Carr's[1] means the premium brought upon the stage and it made a great noise. John Kitchingman was then examining, who, by the way, is a man of very little probity. The Dealers are exasperated and say they will produce severall of the Fitters' letters to show that they were in the Combination and at the instance of the Masters, I hope to prevent it. I cannot yet be certain when I can leave this place but hope to be at a certainty in a week's time or less. I am quite jaded.

May 10.

... Yesterday after about 4 hours' wrangling we finished our Report in the C$^{tee}$ and I believe it will be Reported on Monday. The Fitters have been kept clear and as some ships have been loaded without Certificates, they may keep clear. The Coale Owner is charged with giving a premium of 6$^d$ per London cha, of making Masters pay but 11$^s$/- to the Coast for better coales than they send to London for 12$^s$/-. Lightermen charged as great oppressors, and I think Masters many of them are unreasonable, unthinking Creatures. I am quite sunk with 8 mornings' attendance on this Trade, so that I cannot enlarge this post.

P.S. I am glad Tom Airey did not refuse the *Prince Frederick*,[2] nor I hope our Fitters will not any, except others do. Nay, I should not advise it even then, except they would have their Company laid open which is aimed at. I just now saw Alderman and N. Ridley's letter to G. Oldner full of compliments and tell him that J. Crow (in their hearing) offer'd to load their ship before the Master had seen T. Airey, so that their Fitters, they say, would have been as ready as any to have loaded without Certificates.

May 13.

... Yesterday the Report was made from the Coale Committee when The City Members spoke smartly to the Combination among the Masters and Agents and perticularly against Ward. Sir W$^m$ Strickland and some others defended the Masters with great Zeale and Charged

[1] M.P. for Newcastle.      [2] A ship owned or chartered by the London dealers.

the Lightermen with much more than they ought to bear. Some would have brought in both Fitters and Coal Owners but the first was prevented and the C^tee declared that nothing appeared to them that the Coal Owner was any way concerned in any Combination. Many of our Members do not distinguish between Ship Owners and Coal Owners which was the occasion of that mistake. The House came to the Resolve which you will see in the Votes: the Masters and Dealers were in Combination to enhance the price of Coales which were illegall. Bernard moved for taking perticular notice of Ward and his Assistants and to address the King to order all of them viz, Masters and Agents to be prosecuted by the Attorney General, but that was overruled, as if any one of them should offend, they would be taken notice of the beginning of next Sessions. Tis an Extraordinary Resolution that the lightermen should be in a Combination to enhance the price of coales, when all the evidence in the Report is against them for depreciating coales.

Mr. Wortley and I thought in one way that there were faults on both sides but that the Dealers were not near so Culpable as the Masters represented them.

The Masters were very Shye of me as not their friend and run into corners with Sir W^m Strickland, Mr. Bowes, Mr. Carr (who was a very busy man against the Lightermen and in detecting the premium) and Mr. Fenwick. I endeavoured to soften both partyes and whenever I found any thing charged on either in the C^tee which was wrong, I endeavoured to set it right. Tho' I own myself against delivering in Turns and when ships are so deliver'd to lye in Turne, that being a discouragement to good and an encouragement to those that are Dealers in bad.

In short, the prudent part of the Masters I beleive think me their friend, the Lightermen do not think me their Enemy and the City Members and great Consumers, I have reason to beleive, are not displeased with my behaviour in this affair, by the freedom we have since it begun in Conversation which we had not before.

We can begin to see why Sir Robert Walpole should call him 'the wise man of the North'. On 6 May Tom Airey informed him that 'the Agents[1] write to Francis Armorer to write no more letters and is not to own himself an agent, nor make any disputes with any Masters. So you see they now

---

[1] i.e. of the ships' masters.

think as we do.' The masters had caved in. At no time during
the crisis do they appear to have considered the suggestion
to reduce the number of ships engaged in the trade advocated
by the more far-seeing men like Liddell and Hedworth.
They were too independent and headstrong to contemplate
such a step. Moreover, the shipping interest was clearly not
unanimous; the men from Yarmouth and the 'south ports'
did not see eye to eye with those from Yorkshire and the
north.

The dogged Yorkshiremen did not accept the setback of
1729 as final. In the following spring they came forward
again with their demands that the lightermen be 'laid open',
that ships' masters appoint factors to sell their own coals,
that ships sail in turn and that premium be abolished. Their
spokesman, Sir William Strickland, presented a petition on
their behalf to the House and early in March yet another
'Coal Committee' was set up under his chairmanship.
Colonel Liddell was again called into service, though his
views had changed but little. As to the first demand he
thought 'the Masters will make more bad debts by it and
I think it will not answer their end'. He was opposed to their
appointing their own factors and to sailing in turn 'for then
they will set what prices they please on coals and I think
have a greater power over Coal owner and Consumer than
such a Giddy set of people are to be trusted with'. He
thought that lightermen should not be 'hindered from being
crimps to such ships as they are owners in. But I wish there
were no crimps and that every master should do his own
business: that would do the Trade a good deale of service.'
In the evidence before the committee it was stated that half
the coals sold in London were bought by twelve lightermen
and half by forty more; that the lightermen acted as crimps
to more than a third of the ships and if ships' masters did not
sell to them they had a mark set on their ships and the delivery
of their coals was delayed.[1]

[1] Quoted in Willan, op. cit. 41–42. *Case of the Watermen and Lightermen* (1730), Ashton and Sykes, 203.

March 19.

Yesterday morning we closed the committee. . . . By the Resolutions we came to, you will see we bear hard upon the Lightermen and I wish they do not return us our Compliment. We examined Masters, Crimps, and Woodmongers; but did not call in any Lightermen nor suffer them to be in the room. If we take off the premium it is to be supposed we should save it, but I doubt the Lightermen will be for the Customers. And, also, I doubt the Masters will be for having it abated at Newcastle and so to pay but 11ˢ/- (per cha.), but that must not be yeilded to, as all the Cole owners here agree. But if we continue them at 12ˢ/- and they pay only 11ˢ/- Coastwise; then all masters will clear for the coast and go to London and so save or get 12ᵈ per chaldron. On the other hand, if we raise our Coales Coastwise to 12ˢ/- per cha, we shall send a good deal of our Coast trade to Sunderland, for tho' they sell at the same price now to the Coast, as they say they do to London, they have a great deale of the Coast trade. Whenever we raise 12ᵈ per cha they will considerably encrease in their Coast Trade. We have made a law against Bribery and Corruption, you know, and yet I doubt it will be practised. And if we make one against premium, I am satisfied it will be evaded by some or other. I wish we are not in a way of making the Trade worse, both for Navigation and the Coal owner.

March 22.

. . . Sends a copy of the Report of the Coal Committee which was made yesterday. Alderman Bernard charged the Committee with having condemned the Lightermen without so much as hearing them and was very Warme. The House agreed with the Committee and leave is given to bring in a Bill. The Lightermen and Watermen's Company, 'tis said, will petition and I believe the City will espouse them. . . .

In April a bill to dissolve the Lightermen's Company, to limit their activities as crimps and to forbid the taking of any premium or gratuity, was brought in.

April 16.

. . . Tomorrow we go upon the Coal Bill when the Lightermen are to be heard by Counsel. The bill, I discover, was drawn by Gil

Dawson, so that it may be known from what quarter it came. I believe it will pass tho' I do not think it will answer the end the Masters designed by it; if it does, I doubt the Cole owners will be in worse hands than before. But this only to yourself. There are some clauses which I cannot well judge of till tomorrow morning that we shall get copys of them.

The House certainly dealt brusquely with the lightermen on this occasion, 'their witnesses . . . being freemen of their company' were refused a hearing and a request to be heard by themselves was rejected. The resulting bill restricting their activities and allowing masters to act as their own factors passed into law though Liddell was 'satisfied it will not answer the Masters' expectations and I wish that the Coal Owners may find more good than harm from it.[1] An agreement among the Coal Owners is not only the most desirable but the only thing that can put the Trade upon a good foot.' Within a year the principal coal-owners were exercising their minds as to how they could get round the ban on giving any premium or reward, while Bowes, its greatest critic, was intriguing with the 'new lightermen' and woodmongers, for this species of 'vermin' proved to be hydra-headed. 'M$^r$ B[owe]s continues as unreasonable as heretofore', wrote Sir Henry Liddell later, 'but I hope tomorrow will bring us to some final resolutions, though probably most disadvantagious to myself.'

Liddell was right in thinking that the lightermen 'would return the compliment' at the first opportunity. In 1731, the City again petitioned against the ships' masters acting in combination for enhancing the price of coals by delivering in turns and a short bill was brought in 'which will pass', thought Liddell, 'to oblige them to deliver their cocketts

---

[1] 3 Geo. II, c. 26. In July 1730 John Lawton petitioned the Lords of the Treasury to enforce the act 'passed last session' for a standard [bushel] measure for coal and for sealing and marking sacks. The Commissioners of Customs and certain Exchequer officials pointed out that they had never had 'a coal bushel according to the act of 12 Anne', but had used the Winchester bushel. Accordingly, Drs. E. Halley, 'Astronomical Observator at Christ's Hospital', and Desaqualiers were called in to establish the dimensions of the standard 'vessel'. Treasury Books and Papers (1729–30), 410 seq.

[i.e. certificates] into the Custom House instead of to Mr. Ward as they do now'. The sequel is not without interest. Shortly afterwards Ward dined with the principal lightermen and the masters and dealers arrived at a *modus vivendi*, under which the latter were allowed a discount of 2 per cent. for prompt payment—the old premium, 'bribery and corruption', as Liddell had feared, had returned under a new guise. 'This day Mr. Ward agreed that the Dealers might have what coals they desired and out of what ships and not be obliged to take Mr. Bowes or Sunderland because in turn, so that all is easy', he wrote. But peace did not last for long. In 1738 and 1739 fresh trouble broke out and the coal-owners were again made to appear 'as black as their coals'.[1] 'A Bill passes the Lords this day and a severe one on Coal owner and fitter but the clamour from the city came with so great rapidity that it was not possible at this time to have a better', wrote Sir Henry Liddell. The result on this occasion was the re-enactment of an earlier statute empowering the City authorities to fix the price of coals. So far legislative intervention had been singularly unsuccessful in correcting the ailments of the trade, and, as yet, the shipping interest had shown a greater power of organization for common ends than had the coal-owners. A generation later the Customs authorities reported 'that almost the whole overseas' trade from thence [the Tyne and Sunderland] has been carried on by one continued scene of wilful perjury of the ships' masters'.[2] And certainly the Wear port had grown at the expense of Newcastle: by 1784, there were no fewer than 136 owners and masters of colliers registered there.[3] Was Liddell right in thinking that only an agreement among the coal-owners could 'put the Trade upon a good foot'? To his efforts in that direction we must now turn.

[1] 11 Geo. II, c. 15. An Order of Privy Council, 14 February 1739, pointed out that the statute 7 & 8 William III 'being still in force, yet for want of due and effectual execution thereof, the prices of coals are now unreasonably and excessively heightened...'. Add. MSS. 32693, § 74.

[2] Hoon, *English Customs' System*, 268.

[3] Palatinate Records (P.R.O.), 3/5 quoted in my article in *History* (1940).

## V

### 'THE GRAND ALLIANCE'

When Colonel Liddell was asked in 1718 about the former 'Regulation' in the coal trade he replied that it was so long ago that he had forgotten the details but it was his opinion that every one who had been concerned in it considered that they had profited by it. Four years later the subject was again on the *tapis*. It was first broached by Cotesworth in a letter to the colonel who replied from Eslington,

I think it very necessary (if not absolutely so) to have a Confederacy formed to save the coal trade from destruction and the neighbourhood of the River of Tyne from oppression. Next to yourself, I assure you I desire to give Mr. Edward Wortley and Mr. J. Montagu the preference of all others, there being scarce any besides a man can engage with in my opinion. . . . By your assistance and good judgement I think the coale trade may be set on such a foot at this time as may make it more flourishing then ever, and you, Mr. Wortley, and ourselves have a greater weight in it than ever and be able to defeat ye design of such as would confound both it and us. . . . I have not that readiness of thought, nor clearness of judgement so peculiar to yourself so as to descend into particulars but from what I have said you may believe, and I give you assurance, that I like your scheme and shall contribute all that I really can to promote it.

When this letter was written Cotesworth had already set out for London, little realizing that legal business and the inquiry into the 'Town Affair' would keep him there for more than twelve months. The time was certainly unpropitious for any arrangement between the principal proprietors: half a dozen important lawsuits were pending in Chancery in which one or another of them was involved. The very selectiveness of Liddell's list of possible collaborators speaks for itself: all the owners or lessees of the valuable 'Western collieries', Lady Clavering, Mr. Pitt, George Bowes, Gilbert Spearman, Alderman Ridley, and their satellites were omitted. Moreover, the colonel's father, Sir Henry Liddell, Bt., was now a

very old man—he died in the following year—and was
naturally unwilling to commit himself too deeply to any
scheme that would tie the hands of his young grandson and
successor. Above all, the corporation of Newcastle, at the
instigation of Alderman Ridley, had steadily refused to
grant way-leave to Cotesworth and his partners for his colliery at Heaton and the relations between the 'town' and the
gentlemen owners south of the river were bedevilled in
consequence.

These difficulties, however, did not deter Cotesworth and
during the next twelve months he had many informal conferences and discussions in town. 'If I prevail we shall make
the coal trade what it never was either to the proprietors
or the Country', he wrote in January 1723. 'The money that
the Trade now brings into the River produces for the necessaries of life of such as are concerned in carrying it on and by
my scheem I would leave at least £20,000 per an. on the
Banks of Tine more than now remains and no man should
say he is hurt by paying it.' But no appreciable progress was
made. 'People that are aptest to be slow in the disbursement
are the forwardest in the gain when it comes, as I and some
of my best friends find it', he observed. 'This year's trade
will partly convince the proprietors in the Trade that understand it, the necessity there is of a perfect Harmony among
those chiefly concerned', he wrote again in June 1723. 'I am
very sure there are some very busie to turn the Trade into a
channel that will be ruinous to the proprietors and only
profitable to such as gain by their master's misfortunes.'
When he returned to the north that summer he was already
a sick man.

In the last year of his life some progress was made towards the goal he had so much in mind. On 17 June 1725,
'at a meeting at Mr. Hodshon's in the Flesh Market,
George Liddell, George Bowes and Charles Atkinson
(present) to regulate the coal trade, the within-mentioned
persons and collieries were proposed to be partners to the
agreement'.

The following list was appended:

| | | |
|---|---|---|
| George Bowes: | : | Gibside and all collierys with Mr. Emerson. |
| Sir James Clavering. Bart. | : | Beckley. |
| Edward Wortley | : | All Blackburn, all Causey, all Tanfield, Elswick, all Grand Lease Stella. |
| Sir Henry Liddell. Bart. | : | Team and Eighton: All Heaton. |
| George Liddell | : | Farnacres, Bensham. |
| William Cotesworth | : | Park. |
| Richard Ridley | : | Byker: Dipton. |
| Matthew White & partners | : | Jesmond. |
| George Pitt | : | Tanfield Moor. Bucksnook. |
| Francis Rudston | : | Birkley. |
| Mr. John Wilkinson | : | Gateshead Fell and Heweth. |

The scheme was clearly based on the precedent of 1709 but the matter got no farther. In the following April articles of agreement were signed between George Bowes and Cotesworth for a term of fifty-one years; they agreed to drop all suits against each other and not to promote or encourage suits by third parties where one or other was involved and they came to an agreement on way-leave over Whickham Fell that had bedevilled their relations for the past dozen years. More important, this preliminary agreement paved the way for a larger settlement between the Wortleys, Liddells, Bowes, and Cotesworth which was reached after conferences in London in the summer of 1726. This was the origin of the so-called 'Grand Alliance'. The three principals signed articles of partnership for a term of ninety-nine years. They agreed to drop all suits in which any of the others were involved, to grant each other mutual way-leave rights, including the joint use and maintenance of existing wagon-ways, to work agreed quantities at the 'partnership' collieries, not to buy or lease any new collieries or way-leaves without the consent of the other partners and all such to be worked strictly as a joint concern.[1] Common sense had at last

---

[1] Copies of the agreement are in the Cotesworth MSS. In 1735 the 'Grand Allies' obtained a ninety-nine-year way-leave lease from the Earl of Carlisle at a 'dead-rent' of £400 per annum.

triumphed over fierce and mutually destructive rivalries. Cotesworth came in as a subsidiary and although the agreement did less than justice to him and his heirs, he accepted it almost as his last act. He died within a month of its coming into force. It was entirely fitting that the preliminary discussions which led up to this agreement should have taken place at his son's chambers in London for it was what Cotesworth had striven to achieve for fifteen years and more. At last, there was a grouping of principal proprietors, strong enough in the long run to compel the most powerful rivals to come to terms, and which could serve as a nucleus for a larger 'Regulation'. As such, the 'partnership' or 'alliance' was destined to dominate the trade for the rest of the century. Unfortunately, at first, as Colonel Liddell observed, the 'Grand Allies' 'seem to act more like adversaryes' than allies; the headstrong Bowes, in particular, throwing the trade in confusion in 1730 first by refusing to pay 'premium' to the London dealers and then by threatening to embark on a policy of price-cutting.

His more perspicacious partners recognized that the malady in the trade sprang from the cut-throat competition of Sunderland, Blyth, and of independent proprietors on the Tyne, like Alderman Ridley. Colonel Liddell, as he travelled up for the opening of the parliamentary session in the winter of 1729–30, made a point of seeing the Earl of Scarborough near Grantham. They discussed the coal trade and Liddell remarked that, in his opinion, 'nothing but a Regulation could cure it';

The Earl was of the same opinion and asked me if there were any hopes of one. I told him I doubted not, for I thought his River's [i.e. Wear] demands were too high and so were some Gentlemen of our River.

It was decided to discuss the matter with the principal coal-

Ashton and Sykes, 190. 'The Lords of Coal seldom exceeded twenty', writes Nef, op. cit. ii. 120. The 'Grand Alliance' represented a considerable contraction. Cf. 115. In 1742 the 'Grand Allies' decided to develop the colliery at Long Benton in preference to that at the Park, Gateshead. Ellison MSS.

owners in London, though at first this was done in a curious hole-in-the-corner fashion.

I had like to have forgot to tell you [wrote Liddell to his nephew on 13 March] that yesterday Mr. W[ortley] and Mr. Bowes without saying one word to me, either before or after, empowered Mr. Hedworth to propose to Mr. Ridley that there was a necessity to set on foot a Treaty for a Regulation among the Cole Owners to preserve the coal Trade. 'Tis true he was to say it as from himself but I think it had looked better that any proposal should have been made by us all or that we should all have been privy to it who were in Allyance before it was proposed. Mr. Hedworth could not but remark when he found that I did not know it.

'Whatever causes a Jealousy or Shyness among Allyes weakens that Allyance', he commented. A month later half a dozen of the principal owners met at his house to consider Ridley's reply.

Mr. Bowes has been very dry and very morose ever since he came to Town and was remarkably so with me then. He was very full of discourse, and in a positive way, so that not to be contradicted. He declares for a Regulation and said he would abate $\frac{1}{2}$ of his quantity rather than not have one. I told the Company I was glad to find we could not faile of an Agreement for Mr. Bowes would abate more than the whole partnership needed. 'Tis too disagreeable to repeat and I am sure very prejudiciall it must be to the partnership.

The prospects were not good. Nothing tangible was achieved in 1730 though Liddell was not discouraged. 'Time will show', he wrote later, 'whether the Method I proposed . . . of settling without parliament had not been more beneficial to Navigation and the Coale Trade.'[1] The motto on his seal above a snake which had been severed, *Rejoindre ou Mourir*, had a particular relevance for the coal trade.

In the summer of 1730 the situation got worse. 'I am concerned to find the Coale Trade is going into the utmost Confusion', he wrote from Eslington late in August. His ally, Bowes, without any kind of prior consultation, had given out that he intended to cut prices.

[1] *Supra*, 225.

I cannot think any person concern'd in the Coale Trade, except perhaps Meab Smith[1] [wrote Liddell], has come into so wild Measures and I cannot think if he had, that it was fit to be Copied after. Were the fact as it is stated (which I cannot by any means agree that it is) and that Bowes had acquainted his partners therewith and that he did intend to abate and given them time to have replyed, nobody, then, would have said he had acted unlike a partner, tho' perhaps much to the prejudice of the partnership.

Any person in the Way of Trade must act as the Generality that are in the same trade do, or he cannot expect to trade in so Considerable a Manner as they do. And he must have a Stock in Trade answerable to it, so as to support his own Credit and to give Credit to those he deales with. When we Enter'd into partnership, tho' Mr. Wortley and we had been at very great Expences which Mr. Bowes did not contribute to, we had nevertheless many Expensive undertakings to go on with after that, which occasion'd me to take up large sums as you know. Mr. Bowes was in the same Necessitous Circumstance that I was, but I think did not take up money to make his affairs Easy and so was considerably in arrear to Severall. As he had not for a long time discharged his premium, it swelled to a great sum and I imagine his Schiemist, T. Hall (who never did well for any he was concerned [for]) advised him not to pay the Dealers; and instead of promoting that Gent's vend, they would not buy his Coales but under the Market price, so that from their first apprehending they should not be paid, they stopt the premium in the price and made him fall greatly short in his quantity. This blew him up into Resentment, the Consequence of which now appears.

The Schiemist finding himself wrong has, I presume, thought this Expedient of Abating in price the way to fetch him up what he is short; which is paying the premium with a witness. Tis true it may Answer his End, in putting him into better circumstances this year, provided no others abate, but how shall he raise his price again?

I observe what he sayes of having long weaned himself from Expectations of profit and will for the future leave the care of his affairs to Agents as some other of his partnership have done. And I think I understand him what he means. I wish he had at first Chosen good Agents and left the Management of his Affairs to them: it had been much better for the partnership as well as himself.

[1] A London coal-crimp.

Bowes had fairly put the cat among the pigeons. 'This wild project of Mr. Bowes will probably bring about a Regulation', wrote Liddell a month later.

Bowes himself now became a leading advocate of 'Regulation'. 'I am of Mr. Bowes' opinion', wrote Liddell in the following November, 'that nothing but a Regulation will heale the Coale Trade, but I am not for trying so dangerous an Experiment as lowering coales to 10$^s$/6$^d$, nor protesting a Certain Coale Owner's Bills. The first may be of very ill Consequence, as I doubt we should not be able to raise y$^m$ againe. And the other would make that Gentlemen an Inveterate Enemy.'

Mr. Bowes, I find, says here that the Dealers use him ill on Account of the New Act[1] and people seem to think we ought (I mean the Coale Owners in General) to bear a proportion of what he Suffers for his Zeal for the Trade. I convinced some that it was not the Occasion.

As to his Contracting for 3 years at 10$^s$/6$^d$ with the great Consumers, that will not answer his purpose, for they must have a long Credit. I wish, however, an Agreement could be made and that we were as likely to come into reasonable Measures as that Gent$^{man}$ he complains of.

The nigger in the woodpile was Alderman Ridley against whom Bowes vented his spleen and whose bills he proposed to protest. Ridley's credit just then was certainly 'at a stretch' but he could not as yet be coaxed into a 'Regulation'.[2] Indeed, some sixteen years were to elapse before the Ridleys capitulated to the facts. And until the 'Grand Alliance' itself could show to the world a more united front who could blame him? So the price-cutting war was waged to its relentless end. Liddell was never in doubt as to what it would cost. We can follow the course of events in his singularly frank and outspoken weekly letters.

February 13. 1731.
. . . After pressing it very hard, at 2 o clock this day, Mr. Wortley, Mr. Bowes, Mr. Ord and myself had a meeting on the Coale Trade. . . .

---

[1] Throwing open the Lightermen's Company and making 'premiums' illegal. *Supra.*
[2] Ellison MSS.

Could I have prevailed for it a month ago, I do not know but something might have come of it, but as 'tis drove so late, that the Trade is just opening, I do not see that there can be anything done, but to lower Tanfield coales to 11ˢ/-, and Teame to 10ˢ/6ᵈ, for Mr. Bowes will not agree to raise his: and if he does not, we must do it or loose our Trade both here and coastwise. We pressed him to pay the Dealers the Arrear due to them, but that he swore he would not. We told him then we must lower to 11ˢ/- and that would oblige him to 10ˢ/- — and as he lower'd we must do so too; for we must not loose our Trade. He own'd he beleived we must do so. He said if a Regulation could be brought about, he would pay up his premium to us, so as to be all upon a Level but he would not pay it to them. I told him if he would have said so much when we pressed it above a month ago at his own house, perhaps something might have been done, but it was now too late, for the ships were beginning to load, and we could not disoblige our Customers the first voyage, and by that loose ym for the whole year, perhaps for longer time.

I then proposed that we should mend the Measure, by giving what we thought would make out 15 [cha.] of a keele, as Lady Clavering and Mr. Ridley did it, and so did the Sunderland Owners. To that he would not comply, but said he would prosecute any that did.

As I remember we gave the latter end of the year to the top of the plate and as the water at Teame is the worst, we gave something over it.[1] What is to be done now. . . I must leave to you.

February 20.

. . . Mr. Wortley and Mr. Ord came hither and he told me some of the Dealers came to him and that they were very pressing that he and we should keep our Coales here up at 12ˢ/- and that they would trust to our Honours. Also that to preserve our Coast Trade, we might sell at 11ˢ/- or as cheap as Mr. Bowes sold there. That the Woodmongers should not be able with the Assistance of the New Lightermen to do Mr. Bowes' business, tho' he would sell his Coals at 10ˢ/- when we sold at 12ˢ/-. Mr. Wortley was therefore for having us both write this night.

I told him that I could not think that upon so slight a Conversation we should give orders for raising our Coales, but see our Letters on Monday and perhaps have a Conference with some more of the Dealers. I told Mr. Wortley that I would make no promise to ye

[1] Keels had marking-plates to indicate a full load. *Supra*, 170.

Dealers of any Gratuity, but as I hope if we could keep up our Coales, Mr. Bowes would be convinced of his Mistake and do the Dealers Justice and then all would be friends.

February 25.

This Morning Lord Scarboro' sent me word he would be glad to see me. I went to him before Ten. . . . I saw both my Lord Scarborough and Mr. Hedworth: The Orders they have given is, when we fall either for London or the Coast, to do the same but not till then. They are both for a Regulation and say their Body is more united than it was.

My Lord would be content with 125,000 [tens] to our 300,000, but Mr. Hedworth says they cannot start under 130,000 to our 315,000. This I take to be the same as we offer'd them last Year, but would be more agreeable to them, I find. I told them if we were to encrease in proportion and abate in proportion, for my own part I should come into it. This must not be said but among friends, because they have put Harry Lambton at their Head, and he will be drawn but not ledd. We parted very friendly and promised each other to use our Interests on each River.

Afterwards I met Nich. Ridley and we talked over the affair. I told him except a Regulation could be had, we must run into the utmost distraction, I thought I might say destruction. That we thought severall of both Rivers were out of the way, but I beleived the River Weare would be more reasonable, being Sensible of the folly of being otherwise. That we thought his brother and some others, were out of the way and therefore I should recommend there to be a meeting of the Gentlemen at Newcastle and that he would recommend Moderation. That this night's letters would reach Newcastle on Sunday, that you might have two Meetings and write by Tuesday's post. That if there were a probability of an Agreement we would wait for your letters to come from you on Friday which will be here on Monday. That, till then, we would not order the lowering ye price but I would not be bound a post longer.

The owners on Weare are Alarmed and Stunned and so ought those of our River. If they will not, as the Disease is desperate, so must be the remedy. 'Tis true many Thousand pounds will be lost, and for which nobody will thank you; but when that is done, as a great many Collierys will be laid in and many of their Owners Shaken, it will make people a little more Cautious for the future how they burn their Fingers by meddling with Collierys.

We think that it may be very proper to lower to 11ˢ/- to the Coast, but if we can, in your opinions save our Customers without it, we leave it to you and Mr. Fetherston to act in conjunction what you think best. But if you think it Necessary, give notice to the other Gentlemen that you will lower.

Pray observe the Measure at Mr. Bowes' and other staiths and conform in it. . . .

February 27.

. . . Mr. Wortley seems so much inclined to keep up the price of our Coales and seem'd to give those Dealers that were with him so much Expectations of having the surplus of what we sold for more than Mr. Bowes for the last half year as well as to come, that he has laid me under great difficulty. This day they were with me for two hours, most part of which time I talk'd as if we resolv'd to lower for London Market, after the first voyage, and I beleived had already for the Coast. I was at last obliged to tell them that if we did not lower we would Endeavour to contribute to their loss in keeping up our Coales and keeping up our Vend. But they must not think of above 3ᵈ a London chaldron. If we could find a way of doing it, I think it would be better than lowering ye price for that not only will have no End, but 'twill be difficult to get them up again, after they are once Sunk.

March 13.

I am glad that you and Mr. Fetherston approve of our Conference with the Dealers. But I am sorry to see Mr. Ridley seems to put on the great man and as if he did not incline to a Regulation. I am of opinion that for all his Bounce to Mr. F[etherston], were Coales to be lower'd, he must shut up shop. The lowering the price of coales Coastwise would make the world beleive that we do pay a premium at London, till they are informed of the reason, viz, their Resentment to Mr. Bowes. 'Tis therefore to be delayed and avoided if we possibly can do it without loosing our Customers. . . . The Dealers promise they [Team coals] shall have as good price and dispatch as any in the River. If we abate 6ᵈ that reduces them to 10ˢ/9ᵈ. Were it not better if an Expedient could be found out to employ 6ᵈ well; Then they would be 11ˢ/-.

April 1.

. . . Mr. Bowes and Mr. Wortley . . . insist on keeping to Statute Measure and are for lowering the price to 10ˢ/- or under for they say that till that is done Mr. Ridley and others will not be brought to Reasonable terms.

April 3.

... Mr. Wortley and I are together every day and he and Mr. Bowes are very pressing for lowering Coales to 10ˢ/-. 'Tis not yet resolved ... and in all probability it will come to that in a post or two: for 'tis said Currantly, that Tully and Selby sell at 10ˢ/6ᵈ and I beleive others do give to both Masters and Dealers, so that it puts me to all the Confusion Imaginable which way to determine. There are, I doubt, Severall Inconveniencys will attend lowering. As the vast sum of money that will be thrown away by each Coal owner. Then I doubt we shall by it loose our North Biddick debt and I wish we may not Mr. Rudston's.[1] Also, as we now pay our Rents and Agents ill, I doubt we shall pay worse. And except we lower so as to break half the Trade, I doubt we shall be many years in Recovering what we waste in one or two.

There is one thing indeed to be said which is, that whilst the Masters can Continue to deliver in Turns, which whilst they give the Dealers the 2 per cent they may, I do not find the Dealers can serve us, as they would pretend to do and now instead of threepence pretend to sixpence per chaldron [premium].

April 7.

... I am a good deale of your Cosen Ellison and Tom Airey's opinion that we are like to be Sufferers in our Quantitys by the underhand dealings that there is by such as can worst afford it. That till we have a Regulation we shall grow worse and worse. That there are but two ways of Curing it. Either by giving Gratuitys and Measure: or by Sinking to 10ˢ/- at once and keeping at Statute Measure. The latter, I own, tho' a desperate Remedy, I think Eligible. Mr. Bowes has been long of that Opinion, I even think before 'twas necessary (or perhaps would have been) would he have paid his premium. Mr. Wortley is now as pressing for it as may be and will scarce let me lye in bed, for he gets here every morning by 7. He resolved to write to Mr. Fetherston to desire his and Mr. Atkinson's opinion before we fall, and desires yours, Mr. Ellison's, and Tom Airey's for our Justification. Tho' it seems so much the opinion of our partners, that I do not know whether we may not by next [post] give Orders for Lowering.

[1] Liddell instructed Ellison to insist on weekly payments from Alderman Rudston: his household effects were sold two years later.

Mr. Bowes would lower first and by that means seem to be the whole Conductor of the Affair; but that neither Mr. Wortley nor I think proper. We are either for having the Sunderland Owners lower first, or else together, but rather the latter.

Teame should be lowered to 11ˢ/- imediately to get a little vend before the fall, but would not have the Fitters discover it to anybody till they treat with the Masters. . . .

One thing emerges from this correspondence. Although the 'principals' were in London, the onus of decision was thrown on their representatives in Newcastle as was the case in the negotiations with the ships' masters. This procedure was doubtless dictated in part by the need to confer with the respective fitters, but there was some danger of it becoming a convenient habit. The Newcastle representatives eventually reported that in their opinion 'it is not yet necessary to lower the price' because three of Ridley's Byker pits 'are laid in by the rising of the water and that he cannot work above two-thirds of what he did last year'. It was thought that he would need a new steam-engine to cure the trouble. 'He still seems unreasonable in his demands and seeming to carry it with a high hand', wrote Liddell, 'we think that [a price cut] the only way to distress him to a degree and make him and others glad to accept of such terms.'

April 12.

. . . Not only so, but as Mr. Bowes will not pay his premium without Either a Regulation or that we fall our Coales to 10ˢ/-. If we for any time go on to sell at 12ˢ/- Tanfield, and Teame at 11ˢ/-, whilst he sells Tanfield at 11ˢ/- and Mr. Ridley under pretence of mixing Byker with Jesmond sells to the Coast so as to cut out Fellon at Lynn; they will cut us out of all the Coast Trade. For Mr. Ridley at least will out do us with Measure; and in Time Mr. Bowes by selling 1ˢ/- below us at London and Mr. Ridley by his Clandestine Dealing will cut us out of that market also.

The price being fallen now, would not, I think, have the Effect which Mr. Fetherston and Charles Atkinson think they will. We think it will (with putting his [Ridley's] Bills in Suite) sink his Credit, so that he must Either come into a Regulation in twelve Months or blow up—and that instead of Encouraging any to let him collierys at Easy rates so as to lye by; nobody that are Clear of him, will dare engage with him. Mr. Rudston must sue for peace on any terms and Lady Clavering will never come into Measures to throw away her Myne for perhaps less than the expense it lyes in bringing to the River. 'Tis true to Effect this may cost Each of the partners £10,000 or £12,000, and the Remedy is a desperate one; but what way is there to do better? By doing this, we think it will in a little time not only oblige Several Collierys to lye in, and thereby encrease our own Quantitys, but make others very Cautious how they Engage in New Undertakings.

The Masters . . . have orders to endeavour to get double coale but, if not, then to get such measure as will make 15 of a keele. Harry Walker is to trye his three ships at different staiths to see where is the best usage.

April 13.

Tho' I have writ to you to Acquaint Mr. Ridley etc that if they give Large Measure, or freight, that you must sink the price of Coales and which Mr. Wortley agrees to. Yet both he and I leave it to you to deliver that message or not, as you shall Judge best; and tho' you do acquaint them therewith, to do as you see fit in lowering the price of coales. Nay, perhaps it may be better not to do it. However, I would not have any body privy to this, except Mr. Fetherston. That so, if Mr. Ridley be afraid of lowering, it may Awe him a little at least as to measure and make him the [more] reasonable if we come to treat.

We think if he does not pay his Bills when due, Mr. F. and we should put ym in Suite. Teame must be 11s/-.

April 17.

. . . On Thurday I proposed for the present two things to the Commissioners of the Customs, towards Regulating the measure. One is that the officers shall be present at the Measuring of keels: and not to suffer any new or repaired keele to go a voyage unmeasured; nor any keel above statute measure to cast the same Tyde that she comes down. This [order] will, I believe, come down as soon as this.

And I have promised them that I will make Enquiry as soon as I come down and acquaint them with all the Inconveniencys the Trade labours under.

I went to Billingsgate to take leave of my friends. Mr. Bowes was at the Gun when I came there and it being a house he does not use, made the Dealers and Masters positive that it was concerted. But he cleared up that, for I spoke to several on the Gate and as I was coming in at one door, he went out at the other without so much as seeing each other. He had not one Dealer nor many Masters with him. I had near 40 of both sorts and all in good humour; only the Masters complain of Measure and the price at Teame. To quiet them I promised to lower Teame to 11s/- which Engaged some and pleased others. I hope for the reasons you give we shall not have occasion to lower the price of coales in General till we meet in the Country.

The moral is clear. In effect, Liddell had called in the state in the persons of the Commissioners of the Customs to intervene in the question of measure and before the decade closed it intervened indirectly in the matter of price. That some form of 'Regulation' was achieved in the early seventeen-thirties is certain. We know that Wortley stood outside it, or 'out of the way', as the phrase went. We know, too, that its policy was to close down redundant pits.

I am concerned that the Regulation should have so little Regard for their own Interest [wrote Liddell on New Year's Day, 1736] as tacitly to lett down two Collierys or to be so unreasonable as to Expect that our Partnership should singly bear that burden.

Indeed, in 1739 a well-informed Billingsgate pamphlet, by one George Nixon, openly accused the coal-owners of 'locking up collieries' and 'painted them as black as their coals'.[1] And to make matters worse, the winter of 1739–40 was the hardest of the century. The price of coals went up as the thermometer fell. Once again the consumers' squeal was heard in the land and led to the setting up of a parliamentary committee of inquiry. For a time the men of Newcastle expected to be called up for examination. 'There will be a fine posse', one lady reported. In the end the storm blew over. Parliament contented itself with re-enacting a forty-year-old statute which empowered the lord mayor to fix the price of coals but which had never yet been effective. It is of some interest to know that Bowes had completely estranged the dealers by refusing to pay the arrears of pre-

[1] Nixon's pamphlet was answered by Robert Ellison.

mium and that Nixon was known to 'hold a correspondence with a great man in the North' [Ridley].[1] In fact the coal-owners had critics in their own ranks for a venerable lady, *née* Clavering, did not scruple to declare in public that 'every word of Nixon's book is true' and that 'coals use to be sold at 9ˢ/- to the Masters and now they pay thirteen'. The great George Liddell died in 1740 and with him our main source of information ends. Fortunately, however, the Letter Books of Matthew Ridley for the seventeen-forties have survived and they enable us to trace the progress of his conversion.[2] The letters are mainly addressed to his creditors, Henry Norris, John Dobson, and Dean Sayer, and they have an added piquancy because of what Colonel Liddell had predicted years before.

I am drove to a necessity to trespass a little longer upon you [he wrote to Dr. Sayer in October 1744] for in truth we have had so terrible a summer for the Coal Trade that we are all put to great Difficulties to raise cash to carry on our works . . . my staith is full of your coals,[3] nor have I made a shilling of the Colliery this year, this is the case with everybody, so hope for your indulgence this dead season and shall make it up when the Trade puts in in the Spring.

January 1745.[4]

. . . But in Truth this has been the worst year I ever saw, the Coal Trade having met with many repeated Obstructions and the ugly Differences among the persons concern'd here has occasioned lowering of prices or advance of Measure which has been great Drawbacks from the profits, in so much that we have been glad to keep our works on foot within themselves and wait for advantages till the Times mend which we are in hopes will not be long of coming to pass, as every body is sick by this time of throwing away their money.

---

[1] Earlier in the century, one Nixon had been some kind of agent at Jarrow colliery. In 1715 he was associated with Brumell, Clavering, and the Bucksnooke owners.

[2] Ridley MSS. Matthew Ridley's Copy Book, unfortunately, only begins in 1741. Richard Ridley obtained a lease of the manor and colliery of Byker, including certain farms and wayleave rights, from Sir John Lawson (a papist) before 1726. Sir Henry Lawson renewed it for twenty-one years at a rent of £300 a year in 1729. *Northumberland Documents*, 94–96. Richard Ridley was Mayor of Newcastle in 1732 and his son, Matthew, in the next year. Brand, ii. 518.

[3] i.e. Sayer's lease of Tanfield Moor colliery.

[4] To Henry Norris.

June 1746.[1]

... You may depend I will pay you a handsom sum, but till we get the Coal Trade put upon a better footing, it is entirely impossible for me without selling the Estates; we are upon the Scheme of pursuing our own Interests and have had some meetings upon it. I flatter myself it will be brought to bear; in this time of lowering prices, I have suffered several £1000 which would have gone to pay off debts. . . .

December 1746.[2]

... Yet as the Case now stands, that the profits of the Coal Trade are little more than to carry on the works, I cannot be justified in Honour and common prudence in distressing the Affairs in general for the Sake of a particular Creditor . . . if a Regulation happens, which I think must take Effect in a very short time, I may be able in the next half year's payment to make you an Additional Remittance, but now I cannot do more than send a Bill for the half year's Interest. . . .

At last, in 1747, the desired 'Regulation' was achieved:

In order to bring the several Persons concern'd in the Coal Trade into a Regulation as to Price and Measure [he told Henry Norris in April 1747] it was necessary that every one should fix a settled proportion for his Share of the Delivery, which Delivery should always be in proportion, so that when any one exceeded what was set to him and another fell short, the person over, agreed to forbear selling any more till the short was brought up; at the beginning of January my Staiths were full and I loaded several ships, which threw me so far forward that I have been obliged to stop three weeks entirely and for other three weeks have delivered only between 3 and 400 cha weekly.

At last Ridley was beginning to learn the alphabet of 'Regulation'. Not that his troubles were over.

May 1747.[3]

... I requested it might be after May, on account of the Stagnation

---

[1] To John Dobson.

[2] Ibid. Matthew Ridley married Elizabeth, daughter and heiress of Matthew White of Blagdon who died in 1750. He thus succeeded to Blagdon and to White's extensive interests in collieries and glassworks; his share in the latter was said to be £600 in 1746. Ridley MSS. In 1746 Matthew White, Robert Roddam, Thomas Wilson, Thomas Dennison, Tyzack, Dagnia, and Hanzell petitioned against the recent heavy duties on white flint glass. Excise Minute Books (London Customs House). Cookson and Jeffreys who had set up a glassworks at South Shields did not sign.                    [3] To Dean Sayer.

in the Coal Trade which reduced our Income to be very small, and that still continues from a Humour of the Coal Buyers in order to distress us here but that will, I hope, soon be over. . . .

July 1747.[1]

I some time ago mentioned to you an Agreement in the Coal Trade here, which will turn out of considerable Advantage, but as yet Masters of Ships hold off from taking ye usual Quantities, but go to Sunderland which has kept us very bare, but that will be over in a little time, as Sunderland has no more Coals and the Season is not suitable for ym.

Unhappily, when trade was 'bad' from the owners' point of view it often appeared to be good from the point of view of the pitmen and keelmen engaged in it, and conversely 'Regulation' seemed to the latter to be a remedy worse than the disease. It often happened, therefore, that recurring crises in the trade coincided with labour troubles. 'Mutinies' of keelmen and pitmen were endemic in the eighteenth century. The following letter from Captain Gomeldon to George Bowes, M.P., is of special interest as showing how the keelmen enforced a stoppage among their fellow workmen as also for the glimpse it affords of Mr. Scott, the father of Lord Chancellor Eldon, who broke the 'mutiny' on this occasion.

There is no doubt but you'll have many letters this post to acquaint you of the Keelmen going to work again which was last Wednesday at noon Tide. In justice to Mr. Scot to whoes Merit and Courage it was principally owing & whoes modesty perhaps will oblige him to be silent is the reason of my troubling you with the Recital of this extraordinary and unexpected Change.

The few Skippers who were willing to work but dost not for fear of the Rest, were excited to atempt a Trial. At least a 1000 or 1500 People were assembled upon the Key to see the Event of this atempt, amongst whome were most (if not all) the Fitters in the Town. The Mutiners having man'd out several Keels, as they had done a few days before with success, to prevent the others from going, when Mr. Scot said to the rest of the Fitters. 'What shall we stand here as though we

[1] To John Dobson.

had nothing to do! Let us behave ourselves like men & assist those who are willing to work' & immediately called several of the Keelmen that were prepared to Board the working Keels, some by their names, others by the blue Bonnet Hat or habit they wore, Threateing them at the same time, which was seconded by the Rest of the Fitters, whilst some of the working Keels got by. This gave such a turn, & so suddenly, that the others who were for stopping their Brethren & Countrymen, set sail also crying one to another 'What shall we be forced to this without Soldiers, sure there never was such a thing before' & in less than an hour there were 200 Keels under sail & not one left on the key. Perhaps there never was so great a Body of Men, after the Magistrates had used their utmost endeavours & to no purpose, brought to their Duty by so lucky a turn & without the least mischief committed to anyone.

'It is very happy so early a stop was put to the mutiny among the keelmen', wrote Sir Henry Liddell, 'and I think we are much obliged to the Mayor and our Agents for their prudent conduct during the affair.' The events of 1740 showed that they were living on the edge of an industrial volcano.[1]

## VI

### LABOUR CONDITIONS IN THE INDUSTRY

Unfortunately, evidence as to the conditions of the men who worked in or about the mines is scanty for the early years of the century. The main reason for this is that many of the pits were still worked on a 'tentale' or output basis by family partnerships, so that it is impossible to discover the actual earnings of the skilled hewers and barrowmen. The costs of 'working', that is, of getting, at a new pit at New-

[1] Bowes MSS. 40748, § 81, 12 May 1738. Matthew Ridley's report on the 'rebellion' of May 1740 when the rioters seized the town's treasure (£12,000). *H.M.C. Carlisle*, 195. There was further trouble in 1749, 1765, and 1784. Ridley reported 'a general stop' among the pitmen from 17 September to mid-November 1765. 'We have had a very warm conflict with our pitmen at Mountmoor and those on the River Wear', wrote Nicholas Walton from Ravensworth in March 1784, 'which I hope was put an end to yesterday by the Magistrates at a Petty Sessions at Gateshead. Mr Thorp [the Rector] has been very useful and active. We were obliged to call in Military Aid last Thursday and Monday from Newcastle and there are now 80 foot soldiers quartered at the Steath on Wear and at Birtley where they will remain till the men are quiet and at work.'

bottle in 1719 were put at 3s. 6d. a score. Only occasionally, as at Bucksnooke in 1722, do we get a glimpse of conditions in a pit under direct management. It is clear, however, that from the earliest years of the century all classes of labour, including keelmen, wagon-men, 'way-creasers', wagon-wrights, as well as pitmen proper, were 'bound' men, under covenant to work for a particular master for a working year. In the early years of the century the date of the binding time was from early December to Christmas, being governed by the conditions which prevailed in the trade at the time.[1] The object was to get the workings and wagon-ways in proper order and a stock of coals ready for the fleet which arrived with the March spring tides. Winter working and leading were as yet discouraged both because winter-wrought coals quickly deteriorated into 'trash' and were, therefore, difficult to sell and because it was more expensive to maintain roads and wagon-ways in repair during the wet months. Admittedly, seasonal 'lying off' caused hardship—for instance, it was stated in 1723 that formerly the corporation of Newcastle had employed keelmen during the slack winter months in taking sand and removing wrecks from the river with a view to improving navigation, but that in recent years this had been discontinued.[2] But if the opening of the shipping season was to be put back to the middle of March, as was repeatedly proposed by the shipping interest, all the work-people must have 'additional consideration'. Indeed, in the opinion of George Liddell, this constituted one of the chief objections to the scheme of the ships' masters. He wrote in 1729:

But what I had like to have forgot and is very materiall; what must become of the poor keelmen? They are a Sort of Unthinking people that spend their money as fast, nay generally before they get it. They give over work the beginning of November and many of them had not then a shilling before hand. They live upon their Credit and a little labouring work till they get their binding money at Christmas. That

[1] Examples of the Miners' Bond are given in Ashton and Sykes, op. cit. 88, 242–4.
[2] *Enquiry*, loc. cit.

money goes to their Creditors and then they borrow of their fitters to buy provisions and have credit with the Runners for a little Drink and so they put off till trade begins which is generally about Candlemas. Now, if they are not to begin till about Ladyday, half of them will be starved; for as their time of working will be so much shorter, trades' people will not trust them, there being no prospect of being repaid.

We can begin to understand why the keelmen were so prone to 'mutiny'. And if their working season was to be still further interrupted because ships had to 'sail in turn', or because of a producers' stint, trouble was likely. Apart from the awkward seasonal character of their employment they had other grievances. In the early years of the century their 'charity' was misappropriated and badly administered.[1] But more than that, the whole industrial 'set-up' was unhealthy. Their real masters were the coal-owners, but in practice the keelmen were engaged and paid by the fitters to whom they gave bond. The coal-owners readily accepted a system which gave them 'power without responsibility'. Any reduction in the number of keels was likely to occasion trouble.[2] There was already a seasonal migration of labour from places as far away as Perth and Falkirk for work in the keels during the shipping season. We learn this from a chance letter of Charles Elphinstone who was arranging with his friend, Henry Ellison of Gateshead, for the conveyance of some pedigree beagles.[3]

There are several of this country fellows who have been all summer at the keels [wrote Elphinstone in 1743], now about to come home [who] could bring the dogs alongest with them. There are particularly two young fellows, one John Ferguson, a day labourer and one James Milln who lives with Mr. Leaton, a Newcastle merchant.

He added in a postscript 'any Sterlingshire man that's coming down may bring the dogs'.

As early as 1722 it was stated that the 'put' at one Gates-

---

[1] *Hostmen's Company*, 172–80. In 1712 the Hostmen discontinued their contribution to the 'charity', alleging that the money had lately been spent in encouraging mutinies and disorders. Brand, i. 451–3.    [2] *Supra*, 172.

[3] Ellison MSS. As early as 1712 *A Further Case of the Poor Keelmen* had stated that the keelmen were 'drawn largely from Scotland'; quoted by Ashton and Sykes, 196–7.

head pit 'on the Whitehill' was 120 yards long, 'and is so farr run' that the proprietor 'cannot work hir any longer to profit', while at one pit at Bucksnooke it was stated that the output could not be stepped up because 'she would be 9 or 10 barrow men ranck'.[1] Already in 1716 an agreement between Brumell, Spearman, and partners and one George Nixon who contracted for sinking two new pits there included an allowance of £15 'in consideration of making an open cast to convey horses into the drift to draw or put the coals'. Horses were certainly being used for underground haulage well before the middle of the century and they, in turn, were the occasion for employing young boys of ten or under, earning 2s. a week as drivers or in opening and shutting 'bradishes', as the air trap-doors were called, to allow the passage of a convoy of corves. We have seen that in the lead-mines women were employed as washers of ore in the seventeenth century, and their employment as pickers on the pit heaps was perhaps a natural extension of this. Again, as early as 1722, a double shift was being worked in at least two pits at Bucksnooke, the most famous colliery of the day. In August of that year the men at one pit 'stuck'. The agent reported that 'the pittmen have laid idle three days together and Mr. Bell [the manager] was forced to promise them a penny a score advance for hewing and twopence a tram for putting more than they are bound to, to get them sett on work againe, which is hard that he should pay more than they bound themselves to worke for'. It seems that the strike was broken by the threat to bring in men from neighbouring pits. Evidently the yearly bond did not altogether preclude the possibility of strike action. For truth to tell, skilled hewers were in short supply and in course of time employers began to vie with each other in giving additional 'premiums' at binding time, inflated extensions of the modest 'earnest' or token formerly given and accepted on these occasions. Conversely, as the century

[1] Cotesworth MSS. Matthew Ridley's weekly wage-bill in 1747 amounted to £600. Letter Book, 25 April 1747.

advanced, the timing of the yearly bond and a marked tightening up of its legal obligations were so adjusted as to give maximum effect, and this in turn was to occasion frequent and bitter disputes in the following century.[1]

The shortage of labour extended also to wagon-men and even to the horses they drove. Indeed, it was reported in 1723 that George Bowes had 'sent his fine horses to the waggons' and there is evidence that oxen were occasionally used.

> Drivers cannot be got for we all find it scarce practicable to get eno' for our present carriage without taking a great many very bad ones and in a manner compelling many others who are our agents, tenants, and friends who have a dependance upon us [wrote Liddell in 1729].

So that if the shipping season was to open later, 'we must also pay our carriage men about one sixth greater prices for they cannot earn as much in seven months as in eight and a half'. In the previous century the copyholders of Gateshead and Whickham had regarded 'wain carriage' of coals as their special perquisite and if a 'foreigner' from another manor was brought in he was required to pay what was called 'a catch'. At Gateshead the Vestry appointed four 'Wainmen' each year to collect tolls on coal passing through the township.[2] This money was supposed to be applied towards relieving the local rates but, at Whickham, much of it was spent by the 'grieve' in 'entertainments' to the copyholders at the end of his year of office. In the eighteenth century each proprietor had his own set of wagon-men drawn in part from his tenants and 'those who have a dependance upon us'—it was a normal requirement in farming leases in the mining districts. But the numbers of dependent tenantry were insufficient for the demand and others, less eligible, had to be taken on. Here again, proprietors competed with each other. For instance, the Crowley iron firm because it paid

[1] Hylton Scott, 'The Miners' Bond in Northumberland and Durham' in *Proc. Soc. of Antiquaries of Newcastle* (4th series), xi. 55–78.

[2] Their appointment appears to have lapsed in the second quarter of the eighteenth century with the shift of scene in mining and the development of wagon-ways. Minute Book, *passim.*

wages each week had no difficulty in getting hands, whereas other proprietors made 'pays' at irregular intervals. 'To make a pay to the waggon-men' served, on occasion, as an excuse for dunning creditors.

Chambers saies most of the Carriage go to Esq Crowleys [wrote Sisson in 1722] for they give better prices and pay ready money i.e. they pay every weeke. I told him if paying Every weeke would be such an inducement, wee wou'd send him money to do that rather than be disappointed.

At Ravensworth, the number of wagon-men came to be fixed in advance according to the probable output for the ensuing year. Thus in 1728 they started with 160 and in the following year proposed to reduce the number to 150, 'but as all our staiths will be empty and all the northern ships will start early', wrote Liddell in December, 'I should rather 170 for, if not, you will in my opinion, all suffer in your spring trade'. We have seen that the 'Regulation' in 1710 restricted leadings at certain pits to two or three days a week with a specified number of wagons or 'gates', thereby giving wagon-men an inducement to make common cause with the distressed keelmen.

I am sorry to hear the Western Waggon-way have begun so indiscreet a president as giving Retainers to new carriage at their coming on and especially when corn is cheap [wrote Liddell in 1729]. But as they have done it, I do not know but it may be necessary for us to do it, tho' I own I do not see it. If you give a premium to such as either left you when corn was dear or were not in our carriage, will not such as were in our carriage and continued, think that they are not better entitled to it as well as the 40ˢ/-?[1] I doubt they will.

'Presidents' of this kind by one proprietor in one district spread faster than the cattle plague. Nominally, the wagonmen came under the orders of the 'staithman', an important salaried official who was responsible for supervising the loading of the keels and keeping a record of quantities sold. His was a thankless task exposed to the curses of keelmen and

[1] The earnest or bond money.

wagon-men alike; a false step might lead to his being censured by higher authority.

The liberties our carriage men took some time since at Beckley and in the wet day at Tanfield lately shows the negligence of our staithmen who in order to make them the better customers have made them their masters [wrote Liddell in 1730]. They have been often warned, and in my opinion by not redressing what is complained of will throw themselves out of their employments.

Originally the staithman was responsible also for the upkeep of the wagon-ways but not all were fit for this work so that it came to be entrusted to 'way creasers' and 'wagon-wrights'. As early as 1730, there were 'spouts' at the larger staiths down which coals were shot into the keels below.

Throughout the century there was constant wrangling over 'measure', the size of the bowl tub, corves, wagons, and keels.[1] Where pits were worked on a 'tentale' basis, the lessees were under a strong temptation to use large measure and frequent disputes arose. In the 'brogling' pits at Gateshead another evasive device came to be widely practised, the burning of 'cinders' at the pithead or 'in the back lane', which found a ready market in malt-making, smiths'-, and glassworks. At first, 'cinders' were not included in the 'tentale' rent.[2] This nascent coking industry clearly existed on a small scale from the earliest years of the century but it was greatly extended in the second quarter of it.[3] Landlords did not for long remain blind to the frauds that were being practised on them and lessees eventually found themselves faced with large claims for arrears. Indeed, by the middle of the century, George Claughton, a notable pioneer in the coking business, found himself in Morpeth gaol.[4] Uni-

---

[1] 'The usual bowl tub ought not to exceed 36 gallons: its general reputed measure was 35¾ gallons.' Mr. Humble, a viewer, 'reckoned eleven score and ten corves to a tenn'. The dean and chapter allowed 22 wagons to a ten (evidence in a dispute concerning measure at Gateshead Fell colliery, 1736).

[2] At Jarrow colliery they were included in the 'Landsale' account in 1740. Audit Book, 36.        [3] *Supra*, 40.

[4] Lessee of Low Fell colliery. In 1746 he had sixty-one 'fires for burning cinders'. His landlord charged his 'stack' of cinders at the staith at the rate of 5*s*. per chaldron.

formity in measures at all levels remained an ideal rather than the accepted practice.

The obligation of providing 'hovels' (*sic*) or dwelling-houses for the pitmen as new pits were opened up rested from the first with the coal-owner. Indeed, in new areas, it was customary for the owner or lessee to give an allowance 'for the pitmen's lodging till houses can be built for them'.[1] When Sir Henry Liddell tried to negotiate a lease of Urpeth colliery in 1712 he wrote,

We are to pay 40$^s$/- damage for heap room yearly, and to make ample satisfaction for wayleaves and all spoil of ground for building hovels, stables, cottages and all other necessarys for ye Colliery, *the like, I believe, never heard of.*

Living in London he was not quite conversant with the latest developments in these matters. The tied pitman's house and a special coal allowance—even the keelmen were allowed 'fireing coals'—go back to the earliest years of the century.

[1] e.g. Nixon's lease, 1716. Ashton and Sykes, 161.

## CHAPTER VI

# Politics

There are secret springs in all Governments which
are not to be fathom'd.    (*Henry Liddell*, 1716)

## I

THE *leit-motiv* of politics in all ages is power. In the eighteenth century power was called 'interest' and the men who wielded and enjoyed it tended to place the emphasis on the expressions of successful influence in their own localities. For this reason politics 'at the centre' were conditioned by, but in a sense strictly subordinate to, local considerations. Thus election to parliament, an advance in the peerage, the obtaining of a place in government service or a living in the church for a relative or dependant were taken as the outward and visible signs of successful 'interest', gratifying to patron and recipient alike. Nor was it simply that the prospect of life-long enjoyment of such things merited and frequently involved arduous and persistent application at all levels. A civilization that is based on land does not live merely for the present—ownership of land tends to confer length of vision. A great landowner like the Earl of Darlington or Sir James Lowther thought in terms of a permanent interest 'extending to latest posterity', as palpable and enduring as land itself. Now in this connexion there had already occurred in the north-east a notable shift of power. In 1675, after a struggle lasting over half a century, the County Palatine of Durham was given parliamentary representation.[1] After the death of Bishop Cosin the gentlemen and freeholders had at last triumphed. The question therefore arises, How soon did County Durham approximate to the norm whereby both county and borough seats were dominated by

---

[1] Surtees, *History of Durham*, i. p. cxlvii. The references to Bowes are all taken from Add. MSS. 40748.

certain powerful local landed families? Precisely how did the
quasi-feudal magnates, the dukes of Somerset, Richmond,
Portland, and Northumberland, the great earls of Carlisle,
Scarborough, Thanet, Darlington, and Lonsdale, and the
bishops of Durham and Carlisle control their dependent
tenantry at elections and so dominate the political scene?
What is the historical explanation of the traditional Whiggism of the north and to what extent can 'party' be identified
with economic interests—land-owning, coal-mining, or commerce?[1] Just how was a balance struck between the great
lords, the local M.P.s, and the government of the day in the
all-important matter of the disposal of patronage which has
been rightly called the cement of eighteenth-century politics?
Did any of the towns—Newcastle, Morpeth, Berwick,
Durham, Appleby, Cockermouth, and Carlisle—return local
merchants or did they tend 'to pay a compliment' to the
neighbouring gentry in the choice of their members? What
precisely was 'the government interest' at Berwick? Did
the northern M.P.s tend to act as a group at Westminster
and how far did they succeed in manipulating the political
machine in their own interests or in those of their locality?
These are some of the questions that will be discussed in the
present chapter.

An answer can readily be given to the first of the questions
posed above. An Eden of West Auckland, for example,
represented County Durham continuously from 1702 to
1727; John Hedworth of Chester deanery from 1713 to
1747; and George Bowes of Streatlam from 1727 to 1760.
In the reign of George III Sir Thomas Clavering of Axwell,
defeated in a freak election in 1760, had an unbroken run
from 1768 to 1790 and Sir John Eden of Windlestone, his
berth fellow, from 1774 to the same date. The same tendency
is observable in Northumberland where Algernon Seymour,
later Lord Percy, was member continuously from 1708 to

---

[1] As late as 1753 Lord Ravensworth caused considerable stir in parliamentary and government circles by accusing Stone, Murray, and Bishop Johnson of Gloucester, a former prebend
of Durham, of Jacobitism. Horace Walpole's *Letters* (ed. Toynbee), iii. 146.

1723, Ralph Jenison from 1723 to 1741, and Sir William Middleton from 1722 until his death in 1757. If we turn to the boroughs, a like continuity is evident. Thus Charles Montague, first elected for Durham city in 1685, was returned at four other general elections from 1694 to 1702; Thomas Conyers, first returned in 1698, at seven others (1702–22); a Shafto from 1727 to 1742; and Henry Lambton continuously from 1733 to 1761. Indeed, a Lambton represented the city in unbroken succession from 1733 to 1813, and a Tempest from 1742 to 1800, when the male line became extinct.[1] There is no case of a local tradesman being returned for the city during the century, although in 1747 Alderman Wharton, a local colliery proprietor, was a strong candidate. At Newcastle the picture is rather different. Sir Henry Liddell of Ravensworth was member from 1700 to 1710 (he still owned a family house in the town); William Wrightson, member from 1710 to 1722, had married a local merchant's daughter; while William Carr (1722–34), the Blacketts (1710–74), the Fenwicks (1727–47), and the Ridleys (1747–1836) all had long-established trading connexions in the town. Until 1729 the town was a Tory stronghold and the change-over was only effected by *force de rigueur*.[2] It is significant that the attempts of a powerful 'stranger' like George Bowes of Streatlam to insinuate himself into the borough by getting himself made a freeman were frustrated. By contrast, the city of Durham largely succumbed to this electoral device in the second half of the century.[3]

---

[1] Official Returns (1878). Blair, *Arch. Ael.* xxiii–xxiv. Sharpe, *Knights and Burgesses of the County and City of Durham*, gives the successive polls. Namier, *Structure of Politics*, i. 108–9. 118–23.

[2] Colonel George Liddell, M.P. for Berwick, wrote in March 1729 apropos of the disputed election at Newcastle. 'Mr Carr had no opposition [in Committee] yesterday so that by Tom Watson who disqualified by a list for bribery 310 and J. Stanley near as many . . . so that by disqualifying 605 he [Carr] had a majority of 23. I think there was scarce anybody believed the witnesses. However, Sir William [Blackett] was voted not duly elected and Mr Carr voted duly elected.'

[3] In the 1729 Durham election Henry Lambton, the defeated candidate, contended that the mayor, Robert Wharton, who was the returning officer, had admitted 'a great number' of Papists to vote for his opponent, John Shafto of Whitworth, who polled 577 votes to Lambton's 533. Gowland MSS. R. xviii, § 20. Lambton was returned unopposed in 1734. 'I am

According to Bishop Cosin the gentlemen freeholders of Durham had earlier offered the bishop 'the nomination of one Knight and one Burgess', if he would agree with their petition for representation. Actually, in Durham itself the influence of the dean and chapter, even more than of the bishop, was often a determining factor in the choice of member. In 1689 Sir John Sudbury of Mile End, Essex, heir of the late dean, 'had an inclination of offering my little service to the city of Durham', but was content to withdraw on learning that two stout churchmen 'Brother' Tempest and Mr. Morland were standing.[1] In 1722 Bishop Talbot, within a year of his translation to Durham, got his son returned for the city who continued as member until his elevation to the woolsack. 'A great Inquiry is made on all hands', wrote Lady Bowes to her son in 1727, 'to know whether or noe you have the Bishope and the Deane's Interest, for all the Chapter's Tenants refuse to doe anything either the one way or the other till they certainly know which way the Deane gives his Interest'. The following letter from Bishop Chandler to his patron, the Duke of Newcastle, gives some idea of the local ecclesiastical influence that was exerted on these occasions:[2]

*26 June* 1747.

If the friends of Gov^t· have set up Mr. Wharton it is more than I know. They did not concert it with me nor with the Dean and Chapter who have a better interest in the City by reason of their large property there than the Bishop hath. The enclosed printed paper will show *who* set *him* up and upon *what footing*, was sent by post from London to several in the City and gave the first occasion to his declaring himself.

The *service* mentioned to be done to the City of Durham was his opposing the Dean and Chapter to make the River Wear navigable as high as it could be made and in consequence thereof to the working of their collieries,[3] in direct violation of a contract made with the Church,

glad to hear M^r Lambton is not to have any opposition at Durham and that the Baron [Hylton] and M^r Clavering accompanied him on his perambulation.' Ellison MSS.
[1] Hunter MSS. xii, § 133.    [2] Add. MSS. 32711, § 554. The italics are the bishop's.
[3] Wharton had a lease of Rainton colliery from the dean and chapter. In 1715 Mrs. Wharton paid a fine of £1,500 on its renewal. Audit Book, loc. cit. The controversy over the Wear navigation figured prominently in the city election in 1760. Add. MSS. 33061, § 254.

in which however they miscarried last year in the Committee and *his promoting the trade* of ye City was by supporting a chimerical, impracticable scheme to make the River navigable to ye City (as it was proved in the committee) and carrying their goods by water at a *dearer rate,* than they could have them by land from Chester [-le-Street].

What his Political Principles really are I cannot say but for these 16 years past he never acted with me nor my friends on ye side of the Gov^t· as he did not in B^p Talbot's time with him. But was still encouraging one projector or other for depriving the B^p of those Privileges which are and always will be, while in proper hand, a check to their running riot in the City. For the reasons above, was I ever so well disposed to serve him, the Chapter I doubt would be very unwilling to espouse his interest, especially since he hath constantly and very lately been intriguing with an eccentrick member of their Body,[1] to the prejudice of their, and I might add, of my influence in the Place. But whether they will or not, all past conduct shall be forgot by me at Your Grace's desire; but having already given Mr. Lambton wholly what Interest I have, I think I cannot appear for Mr. Wharton without hurting him or without his leave. But if Mr. Lambton will signify to me, that he is willing to join Mr. Wharton, he shall be at liberty to use my interest for their Common Service as occasion shall require. Your Grace, I hope, will be pleased to allow me otherwise to continue steady to my word, without suffering in your good opinion where I shall always endeavor to stand well and to approve myself.

P.S. I have wrote thus much to my steward.

In the event the alderman was not returned. More than half a century was to pass before a Wharton was first returned for the city.[2] The city election in 1761 was the most controversial of the century. Major Gowland had the support of the powerful Earl of Darlington, a near relative of the Duke of Newcastle, who with the support of the bishop and the government had 'carried' the county. 'The poll of the City was closed this evening at 3 oclock when the majority was declared in favour of M^r Gowland 23', he wrote to Newcastle. 'A greater number would have appeared at the

[1] Dr. James Johnson, a reputed Jacobite; he was appointed Bishop of Gloucester in 1752. Sykes, *Church and State in the XVIIIth Century*, 36.

[2] Richard Wharton first returned in 1802 was later one of the secretaries to the Treasury. In 1747 the polling was Lambton 737, Tempest 581, Wharton 538. Surtees, op. cit. i. p. cxlix.

Poll but that General Lambton or his Friends had sent for
the Pittmen of Lambton which occasioned such a Riot that
no Business could be carried on in Court, nor the Major
chaired.' Gowland was subsequently unseated on petition
and the election gave rise to the Durham or Grenville Bill
on controverted elections.[1]

The influence exerted by the great peers, whether lay or
ecclesiastical, on elections is notorious. In the election of
1747 Lord Ravensworth wrote apropos of the fight in
Northumberland: 'I am clear His Grace of Somerset and
Lord Carlisle will never engage for Lord Ossulton.[2] Other
interests, except the Lords, may be guessed how they go.'
Peers had to be careful, however, not to appear too prominently: 'I thought it improper in my Situation to appear
personally at the Meeting [at Durham] very well remembering Lord Gage, then M$^r$ Gage, with two Brother Peers',
wrote Darlington in 1760, 'but my Brother Peer R[avens-
worth] scrupled not to shew himself.'[3] Bishop Chandler's
postscript provides a useful clue as to the 'efficient agent' on
these occasions, namely, the lord's steward or estate agent.
'Pray let me hear by the bearer about ye freehoulders who
you will have them to voit for', wrote Hugh Ridley, Mr.
Ramsay's sub-agent at Bellister, in January 1716 apropos of
the Northumberland election. And again a few days later,
'You give your freehoulders leave to voitt for who they please
which is well, but old Mr. Douglas was heare att my house
in Christenmas and tould me y$^t$ you had given your consent
that your freehoulders should voit for his son and wood a
had me to a sent a man for them jest then to bring them to
Haltwhistle to [meet] him that evening. I tould him that
could not be done but when [you] had given consent he

---

[1] Add. MSS. 32929, § 480; 32932, § 156. The Earl of Darlington had asked the duke to
excuse his non-attendance at the opening of the parliamentary session 'having engaged to
serve a Friend who stands for a contest for the City of Durham and whose affairs require my
presence. Whether he will succeed or not it is impossible to say as City Elections, you know,
are very precarious. He spends little or no money and his opponent a great deal.' The poll was
Gowland 775, Lambton 752. Included in Gowland's poll were 215 'occasional' *ad hoc* freeholders whose votes were disallowed on petition. Sharpe, op. cit. 44–45.

[2] The son of the Earl of Tankerville.      [3] Add. MSS. 32913, § 18.

needed not feare that they would searve him if you ordered it.'[1] At the same time Robert Coatsforth of Unthank, near Haltwhistle, sent the following letter to the candidate, John Douglas 'at the foote of Westgate in Newcastle'.

I prest him [Wallace] to know who he would be for. He told me he was not engaged to either but must consult his teanents before he came to any resilution and for his part he desired to goe along with his neighbours wch gave me great hopes he was our owne. . . . Writ him that the writs was out and desired to know when he thought it would be proper for Mr. Bacon and me to cum up and have the Teanents together to give them a drink and consult proper measures for conveying them safe to Anwick, but received the enclosed for answer wch blasted all my hopes. Mr. John Bacon came over to me on Tuesday morning . . . when he came here found him very wise but with some persuasions we prevailed to have the Teanents sent for to Hagaford. They seemed all willing to goe along with us if their lord would give them liberty. We stayed two neights and hopes we have not lost our labour.

N.B. There are Ten to Twelve Ramsay teanents in Hartleyburn as good as any we have and they will be either lost or left at home if care be not taken. If you have any further account when the election will be pray let us know by the first opportunity that we may prepare for a Jurney. I hear Mr. Delivall[2] has sent his letters to Knarsdale but I hope he is disappointed but must keep that to yourself for it is soe desired by Mr. Wallace.

It is evident, then, that the 'tenants' were usually quite prepared to 'sarve' their lord in such matters; but it was for the steward to issue directions. Above all, they had to be most assiduously 'solicited'. 'Parliamenteering' while it lasted was a very strenuous business, especially in a county election.

Yesterday at 10 in the morning I came to Darlington. Mr Bowes, Mr Allan, others & myself solicited the Town. Mr Hedworth had sent there before but I hope you have one vote through his Interest there [i.e. the second vote]. Mr Hedworth's plan is minutely compleat and he has sent his Circulars through the whole County according to

---

[1] Cotesworth MSS.

[2] Francis Delaval was returned in February 1716. The by-election had been caused by the expulsion of Thomas Forster, the Jacobite.

the method I have been often hinting. I called at Mallet of Gainford: your Tith Tenants are secured. Mʳ Lodge has been very diligent: he has secured one way or another, as he tells me, all sides there that can offer any way for your Interest. I writ this day about 30 letters and subscribed near 200 more in your name to the Neighbourhood.[1]

Again, 'from my pillow four in the morning':

From Darlington I sent the Letter . . . and took Mʳ Wilson & another Gentleman with me to pursue Sollicitation. We called in all Towns on the road to Hartlepool & had good success. I brought over Captain Davison of Red Marshall who solicits equally for you & Mʳ Hedworth: he brings in a great many little villages. At Gretham, Strantham and other Towns we had great success. . . . Mʳ Hedworth solicits night and day & nothing but a constant sollicitation must be used night and day till it is over. I am almost dead with fatigue.

'I have ordered my servants that are on the road for Cockermouth to declare to all that have any dependance on me to assist Mr. Lawson in this single election', wrote the Duke of Somerset from Petworth in 1700.[2] In 1722 Cotesworth instructed his steward, Thomas Sisson, to canvass the Gateshead freemen for Lord Vane and to order the tenants of the manors of Hartleyburn and Bellister to vote for Mr. Jenison in the Northumberland election. In 1747 Henry Carr wrote to his brother-in-law, 'I dont question you will be for supporting Sir Wᵐ Middleton. Would it not be right for Mr. Sill [the agent] to go about among the Freeholders to prevent their engaging themselves and would it not be a proper compliment to Sir Wᵐ to carry them down to the Election at our own expense?'

[1] George Bowes of Durham to his namesake, the candidate. Bowes MSS. 40748, § 45, June 1727.

[2] Carlisle MSS. (Castle Howard). In 1695 the duke wrote that the Earl of Carlisle and Sir William Blackett had 'named the very man, Mʳ Charles Montagu, to be one of our Knights, since we are all agreed he cannot fayle, but why should we not likewise think of one other and not let our interest be divided in their second votes'. But Montague was returned for Durham city in 1695. Again, in 1740, the Duke of Somerset wrote concerning the Cumberland election: 'As Sir James Lowther has represented the county in many parliaments [he] thinks there will be no occasion for him to devise a Public meeting, for he is here of my interest, but his colleague is moveable if your Lordship knows a better man to be in his stead.' The Public or county meeting of freeholders where candidates were formally adopted was not an empty formality in the north. *Infra*, 287.

A year later, on the death of Mr. Fenwick, the other member for Northumberland, he wrote:

> Our tenants [of the above manors] have been asked not to engage themselves. Mr. Algood has declared his intention of standing but was pretty well assured that you would be for Lord Ossulton. . . . Parliament had been adjourned for three weeks before the vacancy occurred so that you will be home in time to direct our Freeholders yourself for Lord Ossulton. I should certainly vote for Lord O. if he had been opposed by any Person reasonably suspected of Jacobitism, but considering Mr. Algood's good character and his zealous behaviour in the late Rebellion, I cannot bring myself to vote against him in favour of the son of a man who, though Lord Lieutenant of the County, deserted it so shamefully in the time of danger and who himself seems to have nothing said in his favour but that he is a Whig set up by the Whig Party, who I wish had made choice of a man of more merit, as I think we shall look a little too sour and shew ourselves too irreconcileable to the bare name of a Tory if we can't be so far soften'd and reconciled by Mr. Algood's behaviour as to look upon him almost as one of ourselves, but must to a man oppose him. And, if that should be the case I fear the consequence of it would be a reuniting of the Jacobites and Tories whom the latter at the time of the Rebellion separated themselves from, and which separation, I hoped, would continue and bring the moderate part of them over to us, if we show a reasonable moderation on our side and a readiness to receive them.[1]

Two days later he wrote again to explain that 'Mr. Sill having an opportunity of sending up to W^m Tinlin's [the sub-agent], this day I directed that your name should be made use of to secure our Tenants of Bellister and Hartleyburn Manors for Lord Ossulton, not intending that a private scruple of my own should be any check to the Engagement you may have entered into. As I have not been abroad, I don't hear at all how matters go among them, nor have I any

---

[1] Ellison MSS. There had been a suggestion that Lord Ossulton should contest the seat in 1747. Lord Ravensworth reported to the Duke of Newcastle that he had met Lord Tankerville in Newcastle 'when I found from him that no public motion had been made by his Lordship to declare his intention for Lord O and indeed almost as little done in private to come at a guess of the sense of the County, so that your Grace may see this affair which ought now to be near the end of its course, is yet to start'. 'As the experiment will be very expensive his Lordship only is proper to decide whether he should risque the tryal.' Add. MSS. 32711, § 275; 32707, § 304.

news to send you.' Sill, the steward, later reported that the majority of the freeholders at Hebburn would not promise their votes to Lord Ossulton, whereupon he wrote to each 'who had not made Lord O. a promise . . . and John Walton [the farm bailiff] was sent to bring them over for his Lordship'.

The methods of canvassing are well illustrated in another letter relating to the election in County Durham in 1747 consequent upon the death of Mr. Hedworth. 'Home from Raby where they were all much employed in dispatching Circular Letters, some of which you would be desired to dispose of in your neighbourhood', wrote Carr, 'but circulars have but small effect without you follow them.' He added that Mr. Vane was coming 'here [Cocken] for two or three days as his Headquarters to make his Rounds in this neighbourhood w$^{ch}$ will secure him from sitting up drinking at night after the hard duty he will have to go through in the day'.[1] Vane proposed to visit the gentlemen near Newcastle during Race Week and 'on Wednesday, being an idle day throughout, would be glad to pay his compliments to the Freeholders of Newcastle'. Similarly, Robert Ellison of Newcastle reported in 1748 that 'yesterday Lord Ossulton accompanied by Sir W$^{m.}$ Middleton and Mr. Liddell waited upon the Freeholders at this place' and had now gone to Shields. 'The general bent of the people's inclination', he added, 'is to Mr. Algood in preference to Lord O. and no less other circumstances give all the reason imaginable to fear all endeavours for his Lordship's success.' He explained that there was personal resentment against Lord Ossulton, 'he being a stranger in the Country and a Military Gent and son of a Peer are most industriously propagated'. Many of his friends are 'lookwarm or neutral and

---

[1] Ellison MSS. It was considered very important that a prospective candidate should be well supported on his 'Tour' by the influential gentry. Thus, in 1727, George Vane contrived that his friend Bowes, a candidate for Durham county, should visit Stockton on the day when the mayor of the town was to proclaim the accession of George II, so as to ensure a good concourse of freeholders. 'Sir John Eden's [the rival candidate] reception at Stockton was so far different from what he expected that I believe it has almost broke his heart.' Bowes MSS. 40748, § 25.

several of the Dissenters, nay some of the Ministers, are supporting a cause wch their greatest enemies are espousing with all their might', though he admitted that several of the Non-conformist ministers 'especially of Newcastle have been very active and done all in their power' for him. By the middle of January Ellison took a despairing view of Ossulton's prospects and reported that he had met with 'very rude treatment' at Hexham and what was 'very extraordinary' no one now knew his whereabouts or those of his agents. On the 19th of the month he wrote, 'Lords Tankerville and Ossulton have not yet received the Return of the Engagements of the Freeholders from the different parts' and, as for Bellister and Hartleyburn tenants, 'Tom Tinlin has either neglected that interest or his wishes are another way'. In the end Algood, not Ossulton, the official Whig candidate, was returned for Northumberland and Vane for County Durham. Clearly we must begin to allow for a sturdy independence among northern freeholders that transcended 'party'.

Carr's letters on the Northumberland election of 1748 furnish a clue to a change in political sympathies which had occurred since 1745. Hitherto 'the north parts' had vied with Oxfordshire as a region where 'Party prevails so much'. The reason is not far to seek. In the north, just because of the local strength of the Catholics and Non-Jurors, Whiggism was correspondingly strident and assertive. Men who were in their prime in 1715 had lived through one revolution and their fathers had doubtless told them of the 'troublous times' since 1639. They were in no doubt as to the political fruits of these two revolutions—greater personal freedom and security under the law, freedom of thought and opinion—and they clung tenaciously to them. In their address to George II in 1727 the freeholders of Durham declared that 'Our Fathers, by their arms and generous dangers' have won for us 'Our Trade, our Liberty, our Greatness and our Religion' and they resented the attempts 'to fetter us to the wretchedness and slavery of Popery'. 'I was in King Charles the Second's reign what was called a Whig and so have continued and am at this day', wrote Cotesworth in 1720. 'I think there are a set of men among us that are more than mad', he had written in 1715, adding prophetically, 'they will be subdued'.[1] For himself, he honestly believed that it was thoroughly justifiable to 'double-tax' the Papists and Non-Jurors who had caused the troubles and expense to the government by their sedition in 1715. For the same reason the men who had profited directly as a result of the Glorious Revolution tended to be Whigs—ecclesiastics, like Dean Montague of Durham who, after one remove, had succeeded the Jacobite Granville, and laymen beholden to government for office or commissions, or who had speculated in forfeited estates or invested in the funds. Whiggism for these people meant quite simply garnering the fruits of revolution, and these were best appreciated in precisely those regions where they were most immediately threatened. 'Pray tell Capt. Martin that if the Pretender lands I'll throw off my gown and accompany him in fighting against the cowardly fellow', wrote a young northern undergraduate from Cambridge in 1719. In Durham city in the Forty-Five the mob attacked the Roman Catholic chapel and the priest's house and were only restrained by the commander-in-chief. 'I shall be glad to hear the disorders in our Country are put a stop to', wrote Carr in 1746, 'for if the Roman Catholics had behaved in a much worse manner than they appeared to us to do, I should have been sorry to have had the Mob become Judges and Executioners too. . . . The Papists seem to have had reason to be alarmed and I suppose many of them have quitted the Countrey.'

By contrast, the conservative gentry and lesser squires of the remote valleys, the rank and file of the old parochial clergy, and the privileged freemen of old corporations like Newcastle harboured Tory, not to say Jacobite, sympathies. Thomas Forster of Bamborough, one of the members for Northumberland since 1705, was expelled the House in

---

[1] 'Mr Carr is Mayor [of Newcastle] in spight of Mr [Richard] Ridley and all the mad gang', he wrote in 1724. Bowes MSS. 40748, § 21.

1716;[1] William Wrightson, who was first returned for Newcastle in the Tory election of 1710, held the seat until 1722 when he was returned for the county but was unseated on petition. The elections of 1722 and 1727 were fiercely contested in the north and they set the seal to Whig as-cendancy. But, after 1745, as Mr. Carr hinted, party distinctions had become largely meaningless; it was time for a more realistic approach. Mr. Algood's success in 1748 was followed twelve years later by the defeat of the official Whig candidate for Durham county by an 'outsider' of suspected Tory affiliations.[2]

Moreover, in course of time, another and older tradition began to assert itself, the revival of what was termed the old 'Country Interest'.

I am very sorry for the bad Aspect the Publick affaires have [Dr. Lowther wrote on Christmas Day 1741], and indeed in some measure surprized, as Mr. Blackett writes word that only 208 had met upon the Country Interest and yet they told 242 upon chuseing the Chairman etc. It is to be hoped that the good cheer they will meet with this Christmas will open some of their eyes and bring them to the right side, ours I mean.

At that date Blackett, one of the members for Newcastle, 'was at the height of his popularity . . . styled . . . *the Patriot, the Opposer of the Court*'.[3] Besides the official Whigs there were the 'anti-ministerial Whigs'. One of Mr. Carr's most intimate friends, Dr. George Lee, member for Brackley, was one of the latter—'a stanch Whig but anti-ministerialist'; he had been appointed chairman of the Committee of Elections on the eve of Walpole's fall.[4] 'Cant help being solicitous about Public Affairs', wrote Carr in February 1742, 'and 'tis with great pleasure that I perceive the pre-

---

[1] In August 1701 Lady Chaytor wrote to her husband: 'Your cosen Forcster of Bawam-brough is killed at Newcastle Assizes in a duel with Fenwick about choosing a Parliament man.' Forster had remarked that there were 'too many such [i.e. Tories] in the House which displeast Fenwick'. She added that this Forster was 'the last of his family'. William Forster had represented Northumberland from 1689 to 1700 and Ferdinand, the victim of the duel, succeeded him. Thomas Forster, who was returned in 1705, had married the daughter of Sir William Forster. Blair, op. cit. xxiii. 120–2.    [2] *Infra.*

[3] Namier, *Structure*, i. 118.    [4] *Parl. Hist.* xv. 226, 333, *passim.*

sent change has not yet thrown us into the hands of the Tories. The Whigs who are promoted will, I hope, keep up the present balance between the Prerogatives of the Crown and the Liberties of the People and secure us the due enjoyment of our civil and religious rights without oppression or persecution wch Tory principles naturally would lead to.'

## II

The nexus of politics in the eighteenth century was the enjoyment or the prospect of places or pensions, but misconceptions existed at the time, which have not been completely dispelled, as to the amount of patronage at the disposal of a government and how it was administered. We now know that the amount of patronage directly at the disposal of the Treasury was strictly limited. Most heads of departments were jealous of their own patronage rights and resented any encroachment. The heads of the big revenue departments, for example, appointed their 'inferior officers' directly, under a rotation system; the nominees had to pass a proficiency test and were at first made 'supernumeraries' (i.e. additional to the regular establishment) and put 'under instruction'. 'People think it is an easy matter to get places and removes', wrote Cotesworth in 1723, 'but they have been so full at yᵗ Board [Excise] that they have let twenty members of Parliament away not satisfied.¹ They had so many young men certified for and unprovided for, that I could not get Jno Lidster in till it drew near his turn. I am not sure whether I can get him made supernumerary on Bell's quitting.' The unpublished correspondence of Colonel George Liddell, M.P. for Berwick (1727–40), not only confirms this conclusion but throws interesting light, more especially as Berwick was 'a Government borough', on how a conscientious member dealt with the numerous applications that reached him.²

¹ He told another correspondent 'that the Excise Board has the greatest number of certified appointment men on their hands that were ever known'. Cotesworth MSS. His friend Charles Sanderson's appointment as Distributor of Stamps was confirmed in 1715.
² 'Yesterday noon Mʳ Gibson came to me and told me I should be pleased with ye good

A few examples must suffice:

Sorry I cannot serve J. Sutton but there are so many people that have been long solliciting and yet unprovided for that I have not been able to succeed for Cosen W. Stockdale though I have the assistance of Sir Wm. Strickland and Mr. Gibson.

If you will send up Isaacson's Christian name . . . I will join with M^r Jenison and M^r Carr but I have so many solicitations that I have no credit left. He [Isaacson] should get up a case where and how long he has served and in what Regiments.

Sorry I could not serve Mr. Potts having two or three others upon my hands and besides have not the least interest in the Duke of Argyle. However, I forwarded [to] Jenison and Sir Wm. [Middleton] but have not heard who has got it. I believe the office will sink.

It is not practicable at this time to get your Bro. Robertson as a Surgeon as he had not been in the Navy before, there being so many old Mates; two that got in some years ago for Mates, I have got to be Surgeons and four for Mates (one my friend Wake's son) and I have two more will be in soon, so that I think I have my share of that sort.

I really have done all in my power and have had very high words with the [Salt] Commissioners for refusing to give me a promise to make him [W^m Grieve] a supervisor, alleging that he is not qualified for it. But if not, I doubt he is not qualified to be a Collector at Portsea, tho' if he be, I cannot pretend to get him it as I hope you will be so kind as to satisfy them in and assure them I am ready and willing to do him any service. I wish you and they would point out a way to do it, I would soon convince the World of my readiness.

I shall be very glad to serve any friend of yours but I doubt the Books for Instructions at ye Excise have been shut ever since Xmas. . . . I shall however endeavour to serve W^m Cotesworth.

He was even called upon to assist in passing the accounts

news he wrote me', wrote Charles Sanderson to Liddell in July 1727, 'he said he was just then come from Sir Robert Walpole and that you should have ye Government's Interest and the Duke of Argyle's & that they had fixed upon you and General Sabine and they recommend to you to Joyne with ye General in your Interest. Sir Robert had a very good Character of you.' 'You see', wrote Liddell to his friend, 'ye *Gov^t* are very desirous that General Sabine should be chose and I am sure so am I and should be very sorry y^t ye Corporation of Berwick from any Intestine Jarrs should oppose a Gentleman so capable of serving them and thereby disoblige ye Gov^t which may be of great disservice to every Member of ye Corporation who has occasion to ask their favour.' Ellison MSS.

of a military storekeeper at Berwick which showed small deficiencies in blankets, sheets, and flock beds.[1]

Much of the patronage at Berwick was military. In a letter to John Sibbit, one of his principal election agents, Liddell informed him that he had recommended his son for an ensign in Brigadier Kirk's regiment but the latter was 'prodigiously surly and told me he did not think his Regiment was to be filled up with Officers out of Berwick'. A month later he assured the mayor, Thomas Watson, that he was trying to get Captain Vaughan 'a Troop or a Company of Independents' and had been 'since twice after it but the great man [i.e. Walpole][2] is as much overlaid as we little ones'. It was partly to counteract the inconveniences of being 'overlaid' that Liddell hit upon a method of dealing with applications for local patronage 'irrespective of party'. 'As I had sometimes eight or ten letters for one place and perhaps after all provided for him that least deserved it', he explained to another of his election managers, 'I therefore insisted that all recommendations should be by the Magistrates who best knew and judged of the petitioners, and whoever were so recommended I thought it my duty to serve in turn and had never so much as enquired whether they were for me or against me.'[3] But troublesome difficulties persisted:

4 January 1737.

Mr. Townsend [Commissioner of Excise] told me he was sorry I had not put him in mind sooner of Rob[t]. Boyne for he was engaged for so many North Country youths that he could not serve him. I told him I was sorry he did not, when he writ, tell me so for then I should have applied elsewhere. He had forgot his promise but after a little talk he sat down and writ to Bradshaw, the Supervisor, and I send

---

[1] The weight of flock in some of the barrack beds was a few pounds below standard.

[2] 'So that we cannot get an opportunity of more than a word with him once in a week.'

[3] 'I thought the Magistrates knew best who wanted and who deserved places', he wrote, 'and that whoever came so recommended should be the first provided for, after those already so recommended. That I had never so much as enquired whether such as were so recommended had been my Friends at the last Election but had done the best to serve all as I thought it my Duty.'

it down this post. I would have acquainted Robin therewith but do not know how to direct. . . .

After ten years' experience Liddell summed up the matter thus:

It is a troublesome thing to have to do with Offices.[1]

Now it so happened that during all this time he was a great favourite with Sir Robert Walpole who called him 'the wise man of the North' and he had been returned for Berwick by what was known as the 'Government Interest'. This did not mean, he was careful to explain, that 'I could dispose of any place belonging to the Government and therefore cannot make any . . . unreasonable promise'. He has left a candid letter as to his method of approaching 'the great man'.

At the first opening of a Sessions 'tis as impracticable to have an hour's private conversation as 'tis to fly [he wrote in 1730].

The first thing I did this morning was to attend Sir Rob$^t$. before he came out of his Levee viz, at ½ past 8. Horatio was with him who I complimented with thanks for his civility to Sir Harry [Liddell] at Paris wch he took very kindly and said many good things of him. Sir Rob$^t$ asked me what commands I had. I first apologized for breaking in upon his retired hours and then told him it was for a Tidesman's place at Shields. He told me he doubted it was disposed of last week. I replied that it was not of half the value and that I was jockyed in that made me not loose a moment. He told me I should have it and had it been of much greater value as freely and that if I would order Sir Chas. Turner [the Chancellor of the Exchequer] he would put in his name wch I did immediately and 'tis done. At St. James' in the Public Room as soon as he saw me he himself spoke to Sir Chas. to do it and I told him it was done. From Sir Rob$^t$ I went to Lord Finch and settled the way of pursuing Wilkinson's affair, (the parson). We went in quest of the Lord Chancellor but missing him and the House of Lords not sitting till tomorrow, his Lordship promised to write to him not to engage for the living till we see him.

[1] *H.M.C. Carlisle MSS.* 157, 163, 174. In the thirties Walpole began to encroach on departmental patronage, especially the Customs. See my *Studies*, chap. vii. Lord North kept a Customs Book, arranged alphabetically, in which the applications of local M.P.s were entered in one column and the appointments, when vacancies occurred, in another. North MSS. c. 78.

In the event he found that the living at Long Horsley 'was given away before we applied', but Lord Finch was 'exceedingly zealous' and the Lord Chancellor 'vastly civil' and 'told me he should have been glad to have obliged me and hoped to do it another time and that I must come and see him'. Indeed, by 1731, reports were current that Colonel Liddell had been made a Commissioner of the Treasury or of the Customs.

As to my being made a Commissioner of the Treasury it has as much foundation as the Report of my being a Commissioner of the Customs and after that of the Excise. I neither asked nor so much as thought of any of them and there too many that are pressing for them to have them offer'd unasked and where they would not be accosted.

His reward was the support of 'the Government Interest' in elections at Berwick where a combination of military, ordnance, custom house, and post office officials tipped the balance. We must now see what this interest amounted to and how it was managed.

'It is no very agreable thing to have fresh candidates leading up the dance two years before the probable time of Election', wrote Liddell in 1732:[1] 'It will make it expensive but as I believe the contests all over England will be strong, I will not decline nor shall I doubt success.' In 1727 both the government candidates had been returned but in the election of 1734 Liddell was opposed by two strong candidates, Lords Barrington and Polwarth, and the contest was a stiff one.[2] Liddell divided those of his supposed supporters who were domiciled in London into three 'divisions' or groups of about thirty each and 'supped' them on successive

[1] Ravensworth MSS. (Family Book at Eslington).

[2] When Liddell arrived in London a few days before Christmas 1733 there was a strong report that Lord Barrington had got the government interest. 'On Thursday morning I saw Sir R. W. & asked him what was doing in relation to it', wrote Liddell. 'He told me that nobody had applyed to him, nor if they had, should he have disposed of the Govt's Interest to anybody without my Approbation, but especially not to Lord B——n, for he would have no Transaction with him on any account. That if no other person could be brought in, he must come in, but not by his means. That what was reported of the D of Argyle and Ld Isla's designing to get him the Govt's Interest, he was satisfied was not so, for neither of them like him. This latter part, I believe to be true for I had it from a good friend of mine, I mean Brigadier Russell of Berwick, who had it from the Duke's own mouth.'

nights at the Bedford Arms since they were too numerous
to entertain all at once. The other two candidates did the
same. At his first 'entertainment', Liddell reported, two of
Lord Polwarth's 'managers' came uninvited and other two
at the third; the company on the latter occasion was not as
large as had been expected because 'one of the Crosby's [a
rival agent] followed my Inviter and I believe prevented
them coming to me'. Even so, the 'entertainment' went on
until four in the morning. The other candidates were also
plagued with unwelcome guests for Lord Polwarth 'slaved'
one of his agents for having invited the Burnets and Crosbys,
the latter 'one of the most inveterate men I ever saw'.
Liddell himself had no delusions: 'in short, many of the
burgesses here are the vilest impertinent fellows that I ever
saw', he wrote.

In Berwick itself he had half a dozen agents at work
besides the governor, Brigadier Russell, the mayor, the collector of the Customs, and the commissary who supported
his interest.[1] As the election drew near all these were co-
ordinated by his confidential manager, Henry Ellison of
Gateshead, and his kinsman Robert, collector of the Customs
at Newcastle. 'I hope by having ye Government's Interest',
Liddell had written in 1727, 'I shall be so strong as that we
may leave out such of the Voters that take Premiums [i.e.
bribes] as may be suspected to be loose ones, but that I leave
to you and my friends to consider of.' But, in 1734, all hands
were at the pump. 'They have drunk hard these two days
and have had seven houses', wrote Sibbit, Liddell's most
active agent, of the opposition candidates, so that it would be
necessary 'to entertain our friends lest they should think
themselves neglected'. Accordingly, Liddell forwarded to
Ellison a thousand guineas: 'I hope 800 of them will pay
the premiums but of that you will be best able to judge who
are upon the spott.' Neither of the other candidates was

---

[1] The Sibbits, Sam Kettelby, Luke Nealson, George Temple, David Wake, and William
Armorer. Liddell reported that Brigadier Russell 'is most zealous for me'. The governorship
at Berwick was worth £600 a year. *Army Lists.*

wholly acceptable to the ministry and there was always the danger that they would join forces. In fact, the government was in a grave dilemma as to what attitude to adopt to the second candidate since Lord Polwarth was confidently expected to join the opposition and the objections to Lord Barrington on personal grounds—he championed the Dissenters—were almost equally weighty.[1] In the end, it came down in favour of the latter and gave instructions that single government votes, as distinct from 'plumpers', should be cast for him. Even so, Barrington was at the bottom of the poll.

Open bribery of electors was, of course, illegal, but it was practised none the less. Mr. Bowes was alleged to have spent £5,000, others put it as high as £10,000, on his unsuccessful candidature at Berwick in 1722.[2] But it was risky, as it might lead to the unseating of the candidate on an election petition. Discretion and subterfuge were essential. At Morpeth in 1727 the Earl of Carlisle paid £1,200 to the fifty-six burgesses, subject to the condition that there was no disputed election. 'This day', wrote Colonel Liddell in April 1734, 'Lord Barrington and Lord Polwarth did me the honour to meet at my house to settle the way of sending down the London burgesses so that neither they nor we would transgress the Law, in which we all agreed to summon them to supper tomorrow night where we shall be all together.' The three candidates then 'appointed one with all the Burgesses to explain the law to them and shew them that we could do no more than provide a ship and agree with the Master for so much a head for meat, drink and freight. Nor could they take money or promise without incurring the law. A master was to be treated with and I hope most will go down and trust to our generosity after the Election is over.' And accordingly that was done. At the same time, Liddell was able to make a firm forecast of the probable result.

[1] Diary of Dudley Ryder (ed. W. Matthews), 154.
[2] Cotesworth MSS. Bowes was returned for County Durham in 1727. In 1733 Lady Irwin reported that he 'goes with the Minority'. Carlisle MSS. 106. He was appointed Collector of Customs at Bridlington in 1730. Treasury Books, 608. Bowes MSS. *passim*.

'According to the best information I can get, the numbers of the several candidates stand thus:

|  | Barrington | Polwarth | Liddell |
|---|---|---|---|
| In Berwick, Govt, & Outlyers . | 203 | 227 | 300 |
| London & South . . . | 35 | 47 | 44 |
|  | 238 | 274 | 344 |

'I really think that tho' I can perhaps take off 5 or 10 votes from P, I really think he will push B hard.' And so it proved. Eighteenth-century election forecasts were nearer the mark than Gallup polls. After Liddell's death in 1740 'Intestine Jarrs' in the corporation of Berwick did not prevent the steady return of Thomas Watson, ex-mayor and government pensioner, until 1765. 'Sixteen years in Parliament I have never voted but with H.M. Ministry', he declared in 1755, though he continued to be plagued by the Barrington interest and the ill-disciplined Custom House officers. In course of time he learnt that the government interest was not one and indivisible.[1]

[1] Liddell died in 1740. 'If I do not mend', he wrote in the previous November, 'I cannot think of engaging for a new Parliament for I would not pretend to do the Corporation of Berwick so much Injustice as to offer my Service if I was not like to be able to attend my Duty, though they should be willing to choose me.' He advised his friend Ellison, however, not to make such a declaration at present 'for should I not be able to serve them, the Interest might be presented and transfered to some friend of the Government'. In the event, Mr. Grey offered to stand and the Colonel assured him of his friendship but 'Burnett and that party have abandon'd him, for they tell him he can but be their second man'. 'I doubt we shall break and sacrifice a good Interest.' Barrington came in in 1740, when Lord Polwarth became the Earl of Marchmont, and sat until 1754. Blair, op. cit. xxiv. 87. Thomas Watson's hold on Berwick began to break up in 1759 when the opposition party carried the election of the mayor. 'It is the 1st Election of any sort I lost for above 35 years I have been in the Magistracy of this Corporation', he wrote to Newcastle. 'I was in hopes I should have been honoured with your Grace's commands so as to have at least commanded the Collector [of Customs] of this town not to assist in an adverse way to my Interest both as a Candidate for the next General Election but likewise in respect to my friend Mr Hall for Mayor who lost it yesterday by 16 votes. The party that set Colonel Crawford up and supported his interest engaged him to exert everything by whatever influence against Mr Hall & no Person here were more violent than the Collector & most of the Custom House Officers : the election was carried with all possible heat of opposition & expence.—I have ever since Colonel Crawford appeared here declared, as have most of my best friends, not to take the least part in favour of Colonel Crawford, but nevertheless the Burgesses in general crowded to him & that in resentment of Mr Delaval's neglect of them ever since the last Election & to this hour I have no manner of connection with Col. C. but quite the reverse. I am under great concern that I am so unhappy as not to be able to silence Mr Temple, the Collector.' In the election of 1761 both Watson and Crawford

The provision of transport, whether horse hire or ship, to carry voters to the poll was permissible and entirely reasonable. 'It is reasonable to bear their charges', wrote the veteran Hedworth in 1729, 'but to make a positive bargain, I fear, will disqualify them from voting, if the oath be put to them.'[1] He must leave that 'to his Friends' Honour which I dare undertake for'. In 1747 Henry Carr thought it would be 'a proper compliment to Sir Wm. Middleton to carry them [our tenants] down to the Election at our own expence'. Trusting to a candidate's 'generosity after the Election is over' was a neat way round the law but it, too, might have its disadvantages. 'I am extremely concerned at my L$^d$ Vane's ill usage of the people', wrote Cotesworth to his steward in 1722, 'I wish I had a list of the debts; you may tell the people that I will not forsake them, tho' others do.' 'Learn what you can what the Town says of Mr. Carr and whether his Election Bills are all paid', he wrote later. There is a paper in the Cotesworth MSS. 'of sums owing by Lord Vane

---

were returned. Watson retired in 1765 in favour of John Vaughan whom he had long since canvassed for the borough. His last letter to Newcastle, 22 July 1765, speaks of the changed political situation. 'There is room I think for me to make my Election [at the next general election] though it must be attended with great Expence. Sir J. Delaval had secured his own seat by the most notorious Bribery of Five guineas a man in hand given & a promise of five more for the second vote & it has been reported his Brother, the Knight of Bath, is to be nominated by him as they are both Lord Northumberland's friends & too notorious to be doubted. His Lordship exertts himself in a most extraordinary manner, both promises, threats & even at a very great Expence. I thought it my duty to lay before you many very extra-ordinary exersions of power and influence of that administration which only enabled Sir J. Delaval to carry his election even at not less than £6 or £8000 & he was drove to every recourse & by L$^d$ Northumberland's Application letters were sent from the Board of Ordnance wrote in the strongest terms to the principal officer in this place in that Board's service to enjoyn every person in Employment under that Board to vote for Sir John Delaval, a copy of the letter I shewed L$^d$ Granby and wonder when his Lordship assured me he knew nothing of such letter or application, but said he supposed it had been ordered by the other Gentlemen at the Board at L$^d$ N's request. A person, one Freemantle, was sent down from London & applied to every officer under the Board of Customs, threatened the loss of their places immediately if they did not vote for Sir J. D. The officers of Excise were all ordered at a great distance; most of them had been appointed at my instance. Never was known such bare-faced means used with every voter that held an Employment, & out of 45 M$^r$ Vaughan had 43 promised to be for him. I fear to be too tedious & only beg to add that your Grace will do me the honour to mention me to L$^d$ Rockingham that I may have the appointing of whatever Employments belongs to Berwick. Am something [?] at a loss to know or be advised what steps to take to retain the Burough or at least to secure my seat.' Add. MSS. 32896,§ 180; 32968, § 174.                    [1] Ellison MSS.

to publick houses in Gateshead for procuring votes for him'
when he stood for the county in 1722.[1] Nearly £20 was
owing to a dozen of the leading publicans besides a variety
of incidental items:

|  | £ | s. | d. |
|---|---|---|---|
| Mr. Bulman for horse hire to Alnwick, Durham, Richmond, Long—[?]. | 1 | 10 | 2 |
| Abram Bunting's Note for procuring Hexham votes. |  | 16 | 0 |
| Horse hire and loss of time for Arthur Brown who came from near Morpeth and gave Ld. Vane a single vote, being five days abroad and horse hire. |  | 15 | 0 |
| Note of horse hire to carry freeholders to Durham who voted for Ld Vane. | 15 | 7 | 0 |
|  | 2 | 14 | 8 |
| Cash spent at Witton Gilbert paid by Mr. Shadford and Sisson when went there among the freeholders but were all engaged before. |  | 2 | 6 |
| Cash spent in going about Gateshead by Rch. Dobson and Thomas Sisson to see how the freeholders stood in their promise to my Lord. |  | 3 | 0 |
| To the same when they went through Gateshead to invit them to a treat the night before the day of election. |  | 3 | 3 |
| To a treat made at Roger Thompson's, 27th February 1721, among the Burrow jury when they were called together to procure their vots and interest for my Ld. Vane. |  | 18 | 2½ |
| To Benjamin Huitson, Baleff, for loss of time, 10 days, in going about the parish of Gateshead to invite the freeholders to my Ld. Vane's treates and seeking horses for the freeholders to ride to the Election upon. |  |  |  |
| Cash spent at the George the Saturday before the election when the Agents had instructions when to act. | 2 | 5 | 6 |
| Wm. Dent's Note for procuring and carrying in Swallwell votes. | 1 | 11 | 8 |

---

[1] Immediately after the poll, however, Cotesworth wrote: 'My Lord lost his election, but
no Credit: His behaviour being like a Compleat Gentleman. I wish I could say his competitors
and their agents had done the same. The difference between my Lord & M^r Hedworth lost
him his election for they both threw their loose votes on Sir J^no [Eden] who without that
accident could have had no share in the Election. My Lord gave Sir J^no 180 votes which were
to have been returned but were not.' The voting stood thus: Eden 1342, Hedworth 1204,
Vane 1060.

It was these debts to which Cotesworth referred for he had actively supported Lord Vane's candidature and it was his stewards, Sisson and Dent, who had acted as the local 'agents'.

My Lord Vane desires your Companys to meet his friends at Sherif's hill at 7 oc on Wednesday morning where there will be a Gent to receive and conduct you to Kedeshon from whence my Lord will accompany you to Durham to the place of Poll and from thence to dinner. The reason why they go so soon is that the Candidates all go into Durham about 10 oc. Those that want horses will be furnished upon your sending to Benj. Hewetson.

Hewetson's notebook with his pencil notes 'Go' or 'Not able' and some names crossed through has survived. But the excitement of the 'big day' when all the freeholders had ridden to the poll at Durham was soon a thing of the past.

Of even greater interest are the little notebooks used by the local canvassers, Thomas Sisson, Richard Dobson, and Roger Thompson. From these it is clear that they proceeded street by street. Here are a few entries:

*Bridge.*     Co. Stephenson will not pro[mise], yet believe he will.
            Robt. Grieve.    the same.
            Jno. Alderson.    Drunk in bed.

*Maine Street* Rch. Todd at sea but will vote as Mr. Row votes.
            Robt. Tindle    not within, but his wife promised.
            Geo. Robson    hides out at Birkley.
            John Craiston will not promise, (I will make him).
            Thos. Wilson    In his doteage.
            Thos. Gare    I believe he is a Papist. (He is a Papist.)

Others are recorded as 'will consider on't', 'almost consents', &c. William Harper evidently made a shrewd bargain; his house was 'purchased to serve this turn . . . is not worth 40ˢ/- per ann. and was bought within the time'. In the next election when Mr. Bowes was a candidate, 'Thos. Armstrong promises Mr. Bowes one [vote] but is a great man for a set of bells'; likewise against J. Robson and J. Craiston was entered 'a strong man for the bells'. Church bells and altar cloths at Gateshead and presents of pedigree dogs at Berwick were all part of the racket.[1] The entry against George Surtees's name in 1727 reveals another view-point: 'will not promise, saies Mr. Bowes never can pretend to stand that is such a stranger in Gateshead'. 'The push at Durham will be a strong one', wrote Carr in 1747, 'I think Mr. Tempest will be thrown out, his people having lost him a great many votes—an ill-judged step of the Old Colonel's (as they call him) by refusing to treat any longer.' Evidently a candidate's confession of a superior moral attitude towards bribery was as fatal as a failing purse.

## III

It is interesting to contrast this with Colonel Cuthbert Ellison's unsophisticated account of his own election for Shaftesbury in 1747 which had all the slickness of a military operation.[2] On 12 June he wrote that he had been 'employed these three days in walking from house to house solliciting votes for myself. If promises wou'd chose me, I should certainly be elected, but they are not to be relyed on especially when the electors are poor and vote on paying scot and lot.' His opponents were the two retiring members, George Pitt and Peter Walter.

These gentlemen are young and rich, therefore 'tis more than probable they will spare no expence to be re-elected; they have the advantage also of having great part of their fortunes in this neighbourhood but as I am supported by Lord Ilchester's interest and have the Returning Officer, most of the Magistrates and better sort of the people by that means in my favour, I may hope for success, but my election will

[1] Sure enough St. Mary's, Gateshead, got a set of six 'musical' bells installed in 1730. Robert Cotesworth and Nicholas Ridley are inscribed as 'principal benefactors'. Brand, i. 494. Hutchinson, *History of Durham*, ii. 467. Ralph Jenison, formerly member for Northumberland, applied to the Treasury in the election of 1754 for a contribution of £600 towards the cost of paving the streets of Newport, Isle of Wight, which the candidates were expected to bear. 'The people of that place', Jenison told Henry Pelham, 'have taken the opportunity of Paving their town against a General Election & M^r Holmes says the candidates are to pay for it.' Add. MSS. 32734, § 148–9, quoted by Namier, *Structure*, 160. Jenison of Walworth, County Durham, was duly returned: he was in receipt of a government pension. Ibid. 247, 269.

[2] Ellison MSS. For Lord Ilchester's interest at Shaftesbury, see Namier, op. cit. 203, 247, 283.

be dubious, troublesome and very expensive. We declare all upon separate interests but I am apprehensive there is a secret understanding between my opponents, but if that should appear I am told it may be of service to me as several people wou'd then fall off from them to me. Lord Ilchester is with me here; we shall continue till Monday next and then we shall return to town till about a week before the Election when we shall come down again unless we should think our game too desperate to pursue, but at present we think it a good one, if well played.

Back in London, he wrote again a week later,

When I came from thence [Shaftesbury] the Interest I set up upon seemed to be as good as either of my opponents and by letters from the Corporation since, believe an accession of strength . . . the fate of my election is uncertain at best, can only be carried by good management and great expense. My sole advantage is that my noble Conductor is active as well as experienced in operations of this sort.

On the 29th he wrote from Shaftesbury,

This morning I was (with Mr. Pitt) chose for this place. Our Election was a quiet one and I may say unanimous but wou'd not have been so but for Lord Ilchester's address and good management. The famous Peter Walter's heir was for some time a very formidable opponent till he declined some days ago. The rich Beckford of Jamaica then seemed inclined to enter the lists wch obliged us to take such measures as prevented his further engaging.[1] These however were expensive and effectual. The Elections in the Main go as the Govt. cou'd wish. Mine was a quiet one but attended with great expence.[2]

---

[1] Six months later William Beckford was returned for Shaftesbury since Pitt had elected to serve for the county of Dorset.

[2] Ellison did not stand in 1754. He was a close friend of Lord Ravensworth who tried to obtain a Customer's place at Newcastle for young Henry Ellison 'my near relation, one I value and love'. The Duke of Newcastle replied in 1761,' Both these offices [at Newcastle] are sinecures of £400 or £500 per ann. The one Sir Robert Walpole gave to his nephew, Mr Horace Townshend, the other Ld Wilmington gave to Mr Sharpe, First Clerk of the Council and one who had served long and been of particular use to my Ld Wilmington whilst he was President of the Council. *I have not given one sinecure to any one Relation I have ever since I was at the Treasury* and indeed there is but one of any value that has fallen in my Time. Your Lordship will judge whether I must not have Friends and Relations of my own who may expect such sinecures when they fall. But tho' it may not be in my Power to do this, I will find some way of providing for Mr E. as soon as I possibly can' (my italics). In his original letter Lord Ravensworth had remarked that Mr. Ellison is 'very capable of any Employment of Business & that is what we most wish him'. Add. MSS. 32930, § 327; 32931, §§ 216, 329. It is worth noting that leading Whigs, like Ravensworth, still looked to the Duke of Newcastle for patronage as late as the end of 1761. General Ellison, hearing a report in that year that

It was Ellison's military connexions which explain how it
came about that a Durham man represented a borough in
Dorset; in the next election, another Durham man, Sir
Thomas Clavering, succeeded him. The 1760 by-election
in County Durham, occasioned by the death of George
Bowes, was of unusual interest. In the first place, there is the
curious fact that one of the candidates, Sir Thomas Clavering,
was already in the House as member for Shaftesbury, and,
if successful, would have had to resign his seat by applying
for the stewardship of the Chiltern Hundreds. The explanation of his conduct is that, like his rival, the Vanes, he was
manœuvring for position in readiness for the general election
due to fall in 1761. Both sides in the fight were concerned
to establish a 'permanent' interest in the county. The situation presented a nice dilemma to the Duke of Newcastle.
On the one hand, Sir Thomas Clavering, the Whig candidate,
was backed by Lord Ravensworth, the Earl of Northumberland, and other notabilities, whereas the Vane candidate,
Robert Shafto, was a man little known in the country and
suspected of Tory associations. But it so happened that
the Earl of Darlington (Vane) was the Duke of Newcastle's
very near relation and connexion and had obtained a prior
promise from the minister of the government's steady support for his candidate. Nor was that all. Bishop Trevor of
Durham was the close personal friend and faithful henchman
of the Duke of Newcastle—he owed his appointment to

Lord Northumberland was going as Lord Lieutenant to Ireland, reviewed the prospects of
getting his nephew a place 'on that establishment'. 'Formerly the Lord Lieutenants had the
disposal of many employments which they have not now', he wrote. 'In the Civil branch very
few indeed are in their gift: in the Military they nominate their own Aid de Camps and
fill up the vacant commissions of Cornets and ensigns and sometimes *recommend* to those of
higher rank. The only good things in their gift are Church preferments. Their chaplains are
generally soon greatly provided for. The rest of their attendants, those designed for the Church
and Army excepted, are usually disappointed in their expectations, the Treasury here disposing
of the first Places in the Revenue there and the Commissioners who reside in Ireland do of
those of less value. The Secretary being out of the question, the place perhaps most to be
coveted in the Lord Lieutenant's gift is that of Usher of the Black Rod. 'Tis almost a
sinecure & worth £1000 each session. The face of Affairs are greatly changed in Ireland since
I first knew that country [*supra*, 84]. Those of Government were then easily conducted. But
'tis now totally different who ever goes from hence will be engaged in difficulty and his
measures, whatever they be, will meet with opposition' (31 January 1761). Ellison MSS.

his family's electoral services to the duke at Lewes and Chichester.[1] What side was the bishop to espouse? In 1727, a conjuncture of the Vane's with the bishop's 'interest' had 'laid the foundation' of Bowes's parliamentary fortunes, but the family connexion of the Vanes with the Duke of Newcastle had since greatly strengthened the 'Barnard interest', and the Earl of Darlington, now lord lieutenant, was out to capture both county seats and 'transmit his Interest to latest posterity'. The situation was not unlike that of pope and emperor, the north Italian cities, and the kingdom of Naples in medieval times.

Before George Bowes was dead the Earl of Darlington had apprised his kinsman of the impending demise and secured a promise of support in advance. Lord Ravensworth out of respect for his old friend waited until Bowes was buried, but, the ceremony over, wrote that same day to Newcastle urging the claims of Sir Thomas Clavering.[2] 'His is a very old Family in the County, it has been as true a one for the Protestant Succession and to the present Royal Family, I may say, without exception as any in it.' In reply the duke explained his close connexion with the Earl of Darlington, whom he had promised to support, and urged compromise 'among Friends'. Bishop Trevor was between the hammer and the anvil and we can best follow the developments in his correspondence:

[The Duke of Newcastle to Bishop Trevor].

September 29th, 1760.

I am sure your Lordship will forgive me for the trouble I am now giving you arises from my real regard for Ld. Darlington and from my desire (if possible) to preserve the peace of your County upon the present vacancy. I know how much I can depend on your Judgement . . . and am glad Ld. Darlington and you are united. . . . Desires you will do what, upon the most cool consideration you shall think most

---

[1] Add. MSS. 32688, § 606; 32988, § 216. The family seat was at Glynde near Lewes.
[2] Lord Ravensworth explained that his 'Friendship and Connection with Mr Bowes made me resolve to take no step till after his Funeral which was this Day'. Ibid. 32912, §§ 155, 207. In his reply the duke pointed out that he had promised 'any little Interest which I might be supposed to have in the County of Durham to my near relation . . . Lord Darlington'. The whole of the correspondence is in the Newcastle Papers.

conducive to the interest of the Publick . . . for the establishment of my Friend, Lord Darlington's interest. . . .[1]

Sends the letters which have passed upon the subject. You will see that in my letters to Sir Thomas Clavering and Ld. Ravensworth, I have declared my intention to support Ld. Darlington's interest if there should be a contest. But I do for the sake of the Publick, as well as for my Ld. Darlington's interest, deprecate an opposition if it can be avoided. . . . Lord Mansfield's opinion (on the subject) is as strong, if not stronger, than mine.

And for God's sake, my dear Lord, use all your credit and influence with my Ld. Darlington to prevent one. It is (as my Ld. Mansfield says) immaterial who comes in now, if everything can be settled to your satisfaction for a future Election. All Ld Ravensworth and Sir Thos. Clavering desire me to do is to recommend Sir Thos. to your Lordship and Ld Darlington. That I have refused, but to recommend Peace and Union I cannot refuse, for the sake of the Publick. Sir Thos. will certainly be supported by many considerable Whigs. The Tories will always take the side where they can do the most mischief and therefore, to be sure, the contest will be very great and very expensive. Whosoever shall get the better, which from what I have heard, I should think would most probably be Sir Thos. Clavering, and then we have lost Sir Thos. Clavering and given a triumph to his party and perhaps have endanger'd my Ld Darlington's Brother the next Election.

There is great weight in what Ld Ravensworth says: that in the present circumstances of the Nation it is very happy that everything seems so quiet, so near a General Election. For God's sake, therefore, let us keep it so wherever it depends upon us. If I was not convinced of the Advantage to the Publick in what I now recommend I should not so earnestly press it. When once opposition is on Foot in one County, it soon spreads and none at present is so likely to spread as amongst Friends and those esteemed to be of the same Party. I should also have more difficulty in writing thus freely if I had not declared that if there was an opposition, I had taken my Part which side to be for. . . . Hope I shall not be suspected of any private view or want of affection. I would not write thus to anybody else but to one on whose Judgement, Integrity and Friendship I entirely depend.

The answer which your Lordship and my Ld Darlington have returned to Sir Thos Clavering is to refer yourselves to the General

---

[1] Ibid. 32912, §§ 209, 303, 446, 493. The Earl of Darlington succeeded to the title in 1758. As Lord Barnard he had been a lord of the Treasury under Pelham.

Meeting (on Wednesday se'en night). You therefore are yet unengaged and at liberty to be for Sir Thos Clavering or to make any agreement with him and his Friends for the present vacancy and the General Election.

P.S. Since learnt that this Mr. Shaftoe [the rival candidate] is the son of a Gentleman who was formerly chose at Durham. I thought it was Mr. Jennison Shaftoe. The Father and Family of this Gentleman were always very violent Tories. This Gentleman I hear is not. But that circumstance will certainly incline the Tories for Mr. Shaftoe and, of consequence, the Whigs for Sir Thomas Clavering. This is a bad circumstance if there is to be an opposition and will work in favor of Sir Thomas.

Lord Mansfield who had great respect for the bishop's judgement assured Newcastle that he would 'follow, not force the Bent of the County' though, he added significantly, 'I know His opinion was that bringing in Raby might be rather too strong'—the Vanes already held one of the county seats. The bishop replied without delay.

Aukland.<br>October ye 2nd.

... Concurs in [Newcastle's] sentiments and informed Ld Darlington that I should have time by the General Meeting to feel the pulse of this County. I own I wish a candidate of more indisputable interest than either of these had appeared which had made peace at once, but no such could be found to accept it. I do not doubt success in making peace by a compromise for the General Election wherein I shall insist upon an explicit declaration. ...

P.S. It would be a shame not to be quiet here when Oxfordshire is so.

Much would depend on the county meeting, due to be held on Wednesday, the 8th instant, when the candidates would be nominated.

Durham.<br>October 7th, 1760

Found Ld Darlington at a further distance from agreeing with me than before and though I threatened to go my own way, could prevail no further than a faint neutrality. Ld Darlington is against any compromise with Sir Thomas Clavering and so are Sir Ralph Milbank and Mr. Norton Davison who have hitherto been disengaged and are both of great weight, especially the former. Shaftoe has been with me to declare his attachment to the Govt., in which I believe him sincere, but the Tories are certainly pleased with his standing and glad to join him. The run for him is certainly very great and he gets on much faster without expence than the other does with it, so that I feel myself reduced to the necessity either of going with the stream or running the torent of separating myself publickly from Ld Darlington and appearing at least on the weaker side. After the meeting, must take my part soon which is not yet known, though I am much sifted and beseiged. My opinion is clearly with your Grace but I have my doubt how far circumstances will let me follow it. A constant succession of people coming upon me has prevented my writing sooner.

It is clear that the bishop had misgivings about making the Vanes 'too strong' and that the Duke of Newcastle had cooled somewhat in his support. But the Earl of Darlington held to his course. 'I flatter myself you cannot condemn me for attending to my own Interests and that of the Numbers of Gentlemen whom I am strongly connected with for it is incumbent upon me to pay some Regard to them as a Security for one of my Family who I ever mean to offer, for it may not always happen hereafter to have so good a Man as well as Bishop.' Events justified him. On October 9th Bishop Trevor wrote:

After the meeting here yesterday in which Ld Darlington by his brother,[1] Sir R. Milbank and Mr. Davison had declared for Mr. Shaftoe, I also in the evening did the same, as the measure in my opinion, *as things are now circumstanced*, most agreable to my professions of following the sense and maintaining the peace of this country. . . . Will explain my motive more fully later.

The meeting did but little to shew the sense of the country, but the general appearance of it is for Shaftoe. Ld Ravensworth was let into a declaration against the Militia which did no good even with his own friends.[2] Chief Baron Ord is now with me who is attacked at Morpeth

---

[1] He scrupled to appear as a peer at the meeting. Add. MSS. 32913, § 18.

[2] Early in September Lord Darlington, as commander of the Durham Militia, protested against their being drafted to Sunderland where they might become involved in supporting the press-gang. Add. MSS. 32911, § 218. Lord Ravensworth had long had his own views on

by Ld. Garlies whose trust is in money and the disadvantage of Ld. Carlisle's minority.[1] The Chief Baron apprehends expence, but not much danger. Mr. Shaftoe in the meeting declared his atachment to the Govt. upon Whig principles as well as to your Grace in private to myself. Sir Thomas goes on with his canvass but I should think that upon once more feeling the pulse of the country, he will desist. I do not Imagine that expense will be now of any service to him; all, beyond his family connexions and the coal interest upon the River Tyne, is uphill work.

Sir Thomas was not deterred: he determined to pursue the matter to a poll and obtained the support of John Wesley. Wesley's 'circular' to Methodists of 20 November struck a new note in 'Parliamenteering'; 'I earnestly desire all who love me to assist him [Clavering]—to use the utmost of their power: what they do, let them do it with all their might: Let not sloth nor indolence hurt a good cause; only let them not rail at the other candidates. They may act earnestly and yet civilly. Let all your doings be done in charity and at the peril of your souls receive no bribe.'[2] The poll continued for five days but on the evening of 12 December, Sir Thomas 'declined polling any more votes'. In the event, Shafto was successful thanks to the support of the Darlington and Stockton wards—the north was solid for Clavering. That the result was something of a political freak is evidenced by the fact that Clavering was returned eight years later and continued to represent the county for over twenty years. The Vanes owed their success in 1760–1 to the fact that at that juncture they commanded the support both of the bishop and of the government. Yet it is clear that the powerful Whig magnates had 'to follow, not to force, the bent of the county'. 'Feeling the pulse of the country' at a county meeting was no empty formality in the north.[3]

the militia and the employment of foreign troops in this country. Horace Walpole's *Letters*, iii. 394.

1 Robert Ord had been member for Morpeth from 1741 to 1755 when he was appointed Chief Baron of the Scottish Exchequer. Colonel Liddell wrote in 1740: ''tis said and generally believed J. Ord is a Tory'. Lord Garlies was returned for Morpeth in 1761.

2 Sharpe, op. cit. 24. Clavering's main strength had always been in Chester ward, i.e. the northern half of the county. Surtees, *History of Durham*, i. p. cxlix.

3 Lord Mansfield to the Duke of Newcastle. Add. MSS. 32912, §§ 227, quoted in Namier,

IV

Professor Namier has discussed at length the question Why men went into Parliament.[1] What they did when they got there is no less important. Northern members tended to be taciturn—no speech of Colonel George Liddell is recorded and only one each, in their long parliamentary careers, of Lord Ravensworth, George Bowes, and Matthew Ridley. The early eighteenth century was the great age of parliamentary lobbying, a subject that has received less attention than it deserves. In Queen Anne's day, northerners frequently spoke of 'friends above' and 'friends below' and 'friends out of doors'. Behind the innocent phrase, 'all that come to have voices', that usually applied to House of Commons committees, lurked the possibility of a skilled hand, not necessarily himself a member, successfully manipulating a committee on an important local issue. All the arts of what Americans call 'rolling the pork barrel' were practised to perfection in Hanoverian England and the experience has left its mark on some famous Standing Orders of the House. Sir Henry Liddell, 3rd baronet, and his sons were adepts in this gentle art, which, as will be seen, transcended mere party alinements. In the spring of 1714 W. Wrightson, one of the Tory members for Newcastle, promoted a keelmen's petition to throw open colliery way-leaves. Political histories would have us believe that at the time the House was furiously divided and exclusively concerned with the succession issue. The following correspondence of Henry Liddell, junior, conjures up a very different picture.

This morning early my father and I went a visiting some members about rejecting that for ye way leaves; first went to Sir Wm. St. Quintin[2] whom we thoroughly apprized of the state of the case and thence to Mr. Hedworth where we found Cuddy Fenwick and another stranger wch prevented any discourse save what had passed in their house two days before. He frankly declared that he wou'd oppose it with might & Main. That Chief Justice [Parker] had like to have

*Structure*, 91. Frederick Vane and Robert Shafto were returned in the general election in 1761.    [1] *Structure of Politics*, i. 1–76.    [2] Member for Kingston-upon-Hull.

quarrell'd [with] him because he would not come into their measures.
... Thence we went to a Tory member near Golden Square where we
were disappointed as we had bin four times before, since the Gentleman happen'd to be always abroad. So we proceeded to the Court of
Requests. Ye first person that presented was James M[ontague][1] who
told us that his uncle Wortley had already ingaged all his friends and
even Sir P. K.,[2] but that we must not relye on. I thence proceeded to
ye Lobby, where the Company was very thin, ye House being upon
Business scarce a member to be seen. There I met with R. W[alpole?]
who had no mind to take notice of me but at last was pleased to inquire
after my father's health. I remov'd thence back to a Coffee Ho. where
I dropt my father. I sent for a friend or two who is acquainted with
some Tory members, for it is among them that we must carry our
point. I gave him a copy of the [keelmen's] Petition with some few
remarks of my own to refresh his memory, had his promise that he wld
make use of ym and hop'd to meet with success, so we return'd to
dinner at 3 a'clock. We have severall emissarys abroad who work
heartily for us. Att our coming away we met with a Gentleman who
will prove the best sollicitor agst the Keelmen's petition off any in
England. We hope to ingage him. But friend of mine, the case ought
to be stated, the Chief Grievances and inconveniencys displayed: this in
a few lines wou'd be very useful and as speedily as may be.

Three weeks later the baronet himself wrote:

My son Harry's indisposition deprived us of his assistance this day
agst the petition for waggon-ways from Newcastle. However, such
diligence was used in soliciting members to be early in the House by
Ld. Wm. [Poulett][3] particularly and many other friends that the Petition was not offer'd by Mr. Wrightson who gave out yesterday it
should be this day and by ye appearance of his friends no other was
expected. There was at least as good a one agst it wch I believe might
alter the Resolution taken yesterday of wch we had no notice till that
afternoon. Mr. James Clavering, Lambton and Seigneur [Henry
Liddell] were diligent and zealous sollicitors without Doors. Your
servant from whom you have this account was not idle from the 1st
notice of what was designed till 2 this afternoon when Mr. W[rightson]
declared he wou'd not deliver the petition this week. Besides Ld. Wm.
we were much obliged to Sir Joseph Jekyll[4] for his attendance, Lord

---

[1] Camelford.  [2] ? Sir P. King, member for Beeralston, Devon.
[3] New Lymington.  [4] New Lymington.

Lumley,[1] Sir Arthur Keye[2] and most of our Northern acquaintance and many others, even whom we cou'd hardly expect, were gained to oppose so extraordinary a petition. However, a Bill is prepared and printed of wch I am promist a copy. Mr. Headworth wishes it cou'd be so model'd as to secure such waggon-ways as cross highways from being pull'd up as he apprehends his may be the earlyest as any, but expresses himself so desirous to secure property that he wishes the best councell's advice and that a meeting may be had to consider of the Bill proposed. I did not oppose the motion from that ingenious Gent who has many to please. But am not fond of a Bill for this purpose least it lett in a greater mischief than that desired should be cured. For indeed I am not so apprehensive of ye danger our Knt of the shire suggests.

By the middle of May Henry Liddell, junior, was abroad again. 'I can assure you our friends High and Low in the House of Commons are pretty numerous insomuch that Mr. Wrightson and his party have not thought fit to make any motion as yet. . . . We dont apprehend their succeeding tho' they may give us trouble enough.'

J. H[edworth] and L[ambton] seems apprehensive that his way will be pulled up and several others, but I propose that those wch are not, should contribute to ye charge equally, being from a publick advantage. If such an offer was made him it wou'd induce him to remain firm in opposition.

Neville Ridley[3] was att ye Lobby the morning the petition was to be presented by his friends. I can tell you who exerts himself against us: that is Tom Gibson and were it not for his interest they wou'd be able to make but an indifferent figure.[4] I need to tell you no more of our interest with the Torys than that Ld. Lansdown told an acquaintance of mine lately that he was assured that if any member in the County of Cornwall shou'd be for the Petition he was certain they must never think of being chose again, for there, they were as choice of their propertyes and made as much by way-leave as any people whatever.[5]

The final result was reflected in Liddell's mood at the end of the month: 'Frank Baker and I melted down your token at

---

[1] Arundel.    [2] York county.    [3] Not a member.
[4] A city financier; he entered parliament in 1722 as member for Marlborough. *Supra.*
[5] Ellison MSS.

the King's Head last Wednesday hand to hand. My father, hearing the occasion of our meeting, came abt. 8 o'clock, smoaked half a pipe, drunk to your good health, ye Honest Alderman's, and some others of like stamp and then went to the Colledge, a frollick I have not known him guilty of for twelve month by past.' It seems not improbable that 'Uncle' Thomas Liddell owed his return for Lostwithiel in Cornwall at the ensuing election to the friendship of Lord Lansdowne.

Three years later a very different scene presented itself when the Wearmen, Hedworth and Conyers, promoted a bill to improve the harbour of Sunderland and to make the river navigable to Newbridge. Cotesworth first heard of the project towards the end of March and lost no time in working up an agitation to defeat it as, in his view, it would gravely prejudice the coal trade on the Tyne.[1]

Though I am of the Committee for bringing in this Bill [wrote Thomas Liddell, M.P. for Lostwithiel], yet it seems to me rather better to let them load their Bill with as many absurdities and things that cannot be supported as they please than to hinder them from it, because upon the debate in ye House it will be less likely to pass. The reasons you give against this Bill, I think, are unanswerable. Mr. Gibson is very busy in this affair, the success of which you will hear of in a little time.

Charles Sanderson of the Inner Temple, though no member himself, contrived to keep Cotesworth fully informed of the progress of the bill in Committee.

Inner Temple
March 28. 1717

Dear Freind,
The Committee on the Sunderland Bill met the first time this morning at ten. They made my Ld. Wm. Powlett Chairman. Mr. Hedworth gott all freinds there. There was about 18 and only Mr. Wrightson and Mr. Shippen[2] spoke for us: that is to say—Mr. Wrightson spoke for the Bishop of Durham—yt he was Conservator of Wear and yt his right and priviledge might not be taken away unheard. Mr.

---

[1] Cotesworth MSS. Newcastle had successfully opposed the project when it was first raised in 1705. Brand, ii. 507    [2] The famous Tory member for Saltash.

Hedworth said he doubted that right of the Bp̃p—but he had neglected it 42 years and noe injury to him if that right (if he had any) was taken away from him. Mr. Shippen insisted on that right, but Mr. Gilfrid Lawson[1] said it did not appear, the Bp̃p had given any orders to insist on that right or to oppose that Bill. Mr. Tom Conyers said the Bp̃p a year agoe agreed to this bill. Mr James Mountague said the Bp̃p had wrote to him last night to take care of his right and hoped the Committee would take care not to prejudice it. Other gentlemen insisted yt the Committee cou'd take no notice of it till the Bp̃p had peticioned the house and they had referred it to the Committee. Mr Shippen moved for a fortnight's time for the Bp̃p. Mr. Wrightson seconded that mocõn but it was carried by a great Majority in the Negative. Upon a consultacon w[ith] Mr. Wrightson, Mr. Pitt,[2] Mr. Gibson, Mr. Ridley etc. it was agreed Mr. Wrightson should goe down to the house and present the Newcastle peticon w[ch] he did accordingly, the Committee sitting this morning and the house referred it to the Committee with Liberty to be heard by Councell. The Committee have gone a quarter part through the Bill to folio 3 to the first ('And be it enacted'). They examined 3 wittnesses, Mr. Scarfe, Mr. Antony Ettrick[3] and another to prove the badnesse of the harbour. Mr. Hedworth has changed the word Conservators to Com[rs] throughout the Bill—and on the other side is a list of the Com[rs] inserted in the Bill w[ch] Mr. Hedworth delivered in, except that Mr. Wrightson named Geo. Liddell w[ch] Mr. Hedworth opposed, but my L[d] W[m] prevailed to lett him stand. I told my L[d] he had forgott you but he says he will putt you in. Mr. Wortley[4] never attended and on application to him sayes he is noe wayes concerned and Mr. James Mountague is as indifferent as him, at w[ch] wee are all surprized and know not the meaning of it. I see noe likelyhood but the Bill will passe currently the House of Commons and I find wee are so unconcerted and undisciplined among ourselves that wee shall doe noe good. Noe hopes but at the L[ds] Barr. Tomorrow morning wee are to gett as long a time as we cann for the town of Newcastle to send up their witnesses and to make their defence. Mr. Wrightson intends to move till this day 3 weeks but I expect onely till tomorrow fortnight at furthest and the Committee will adjorne to that time if they grant us soe long. I think you ought to send up

---

[1] Cockermouth.

[2] George Pitt, M.P. for Southampton. He owned collieries in County Durham. *Supra.*

[3] Leading Sunderland merchants.

[4] Edward Wortley, M.P. for Westminster: he and his nephew James Montague were leading coal-owners on the Tyne. *Supra.*

witnesses to prove Newcastle has allwayes had more Coales than London and the Coasts can demand and (if you can) at lower prices than Sunderland—or at least at the lowest prices that ever were known and to prove the great Quantityes of salt at Newcastle and the low price. Yt Sunderland cannot provide near such Quantity. To prove the Justice of the duty of 1ˢ/- per chaldron and yt it was not for a great debt due from Newcastle for some members' wages: that duty is an imposičion and illegal—to prove the allegačon of the Newcastle petičon.

If any Coalowners or Landowners upon Weare are aggreved by this bill they ought to peticon the House of Commons, for Newcastle cannot urge the Greivances of those Coale owners and Landowners but onely their own greivances by this bill. Perhaps it may be proper to have a petičon signed by the Coale owners on the River Tyne—to have it in their power to deliver it or not deliver it as they shall be advised. It may be proper to prove this bill calculated and will redound to the profitt of 4 or 5 particular persons and not of the whole coale trade on the river Wear. I think the Town of Newcastle should be makeing all their defence ready or at least be preparing agˢᵗ they have a more certain account of the time per next post.

The next letter is undated:

Dear Freind,
Yesterday morning the Committee satt about 11 o'Clock—Lord Lumley stickles very hard to gett all his freinds attend and soe does Mr. Hedworth. I attended the sitting of the Committee and Newcastle petičon and the House of Commons' order thereon was read.[1] Mr. Wrightson was not come and Mr. Nevile Ridley was walking below in the Court of Request. I gott him up. My Lᵈ Wᵐ acquainted him yt they had read that petičon and order. I prayed that they would indulge Mr. Wrightson, the Newcastle member, (who presented the petičon) and was expected every minute. Then the Committee layd the petičon on the table and proceeded on the Bill. In lesse than halfe an hour came Mr. Wrightson and Mr. Shippen. Mr. Wrightson moved till Thursday fortnight, but after many speeches the Question was putt—17 negatives and 3 affirmatives vizt., Lord Morpeth,[2] Mr. Eden,[3] and Mr. Wrightson. Then they moved for Thursday next and

---

[1] This affords clear proof that Sanderson was present in committee, though not himself a member of the House.
[2] Member for Morpeth.          [3] Durham county.

carryed it. It is observable that after Mr. Wrightson had mov'd and given his reasons for Thursday fortnight, my L<sup>d</sup> W<sup>m</sup> said his mo̅c̅on was not seconded and therefore could not be putt. Mr. Wrightson desired Mr. James Mountague who stood on his left hand again and again to second Mr. Wrightson's mo̅c̅on—My L<sup>d</sup> W<sup>m</sup> called upon Mr. Mountague to speak and I begged him to second the mo̅c̅on, but the devill a bitt would he say a word. Thereupon Mr. Shippen seconded the mo̅c̅on and it was carryed as above by 17 ag<sup>st</sup> 3 in the negative. After the Committee had fixt it for Thursday next, about 5 or 6 of Sir Henry's [Liddell] friends came—but Mr. Hedworth has gott soe many of his freinds in the Committee yt noe good is to be done. Mr. Wrightson, Mr. Ridley and Mr. Gibson and I mett last night at the Grecian. I advised that Mr. Wrightson move the house yt all members yt come to the Committee should have votes—especially it being made a publick bill as by the last Clause in the printed bill and being of a publick nature wherein London and the whole Kingdome is concerned. And if wee prevayl'd upon that mo̅c̅on then to move to enlarge the time to hear Newcastle by their Councill. But not to make the last mo̅c̅on unlesse we prevail'd on the first mo̅c̅on for all members who attend to have votes, for it is to noe manner of purpose for Councill to attend this select Committee of Mr. Hedworth's, but rather on Thursday next to tell the Committee, yt the shortnesse of the time rendered the Common's order for Newcastle to be heard ineffectuall and wee could not possibly have our witnesses ready and soe make the Committee ashamed of what they have done wch may be urged in the upper house. If wee succeed in both our mo̅c̅ons in the house, we shall gain time and be fully heard. The bill is soe popular yt I despair of successe and all Sir Henry's [Liddell] freinds say there is nothing can be said ag<sup>st</sup> it. The Committee have struck out the Clause wch makes the Com<sup>rs</sup> Judgement and decree finall from wch noe appeale lyes. They are come to the 5<sup>th</sup> folio to the clause how farr to make it navigable and they give out to Durham.[1] This I observed upon in my last. The Committee adjorned yesterday till Monday next at 10. They will go through the Bill in the Committee at two sittings more at furthest; on Tuesday next at furthest the Committee will have done it and ready to report it to the house but will stay till Thursday to hear Newcastle, but all at present seem not to trouble ym except the 2 mo̅c̅ons above mentioned be granted by the house. Sir Henry mett ym twice at the

---

[1] Cotesworth had urged that the river be made navigable to 'Shinckley Bridge' [Shincliffe], a mile beyond Durham.

Grecian—neither of the Newcastle Aldermen were there yesterday and none expect Mr. Carr's appearance.[1]

If the Town intend, they must have their petiĉon ready to the Lords and send it up in a week at furthest.

April 6, 1717.
Saturday.

Dear Freind,

Inclosed are the copyes of the four Clauses Mr. Conyers added to the Bill. This day being a Lesure day L$^d$ W$^m$ reported the Sunderland Bill, but before the house entered upon it, Mr. Wrightson informed the House the hardshipp and impossibility the Committee had putt upon the Town of Newcastle in giving them but 4 or 5 dayes to bring their witnesses from Newcastle and mov'd the Bill might be recommitted, soe that they might have a reasonable time to produce their witnesses before the Committee. L$^d$ Hertford[2] seconded the moĉon. L$^d$ W$^m$, Mr. Hedworth, Mr. Lawson and Mr. John Smith[3] spoke agst it, and upon the Ques$^n$ putt, not above 6 affirmatives and all the rest Noes, so that the universall sense of the house was agst us. The house proceeded then upon the report and about 5 this evening gott through it and ordered it to be engrossed. It being concerted and agreed between Mr. Liddell, Mr. Wrightson, and Mr. Lowther[4] in the house, Mr. Wrightson moved for Thursday fortnight for Newcastle to be heard at the Barr of the House. Mr. Thos. Liddell seconded it and spoke very well but short. Mr. Hedworth very long and warme and Mr. Conyers and L$^d$ W$^m$ very warme agst the moĉon. Mr. Lowther very artfully yt it was a good bill but he was for maintaining the Honour and Justice of the House and to hear everybody what they could say and yt thro' the distance of the place and badnesse of the weather and roads he thought a lesse time could not be given. Mr. Young[5] and Mr. Banks[6] spoke on the same side, he call'd it [the Bill] a Jobb. It being very late and a very thin house when the Speaker put the Quest$^n$. It was carryed in the Affirmative. I did not expect the successe today. This is the first turne wee have given them. Hedworth and Conyers are confounded madd. Thursday fortnight is the 25$^{th}$ inst and the Thursday in Easter week. Now you must pursue it for the Intrest

---

[1] The two members for Newcastle were William Wrightson and Sir William Blackett. W. Carr lost the seat in 1710 and was not returned again until 1722.

[2] Member for Northumberland.          [3] East Looe.

[4] Cumberland.          [5] ? William Younge, M.P. for Honiton.

[6] Joseph Banks (Grimsby)—a close friend of Cotesworth. *Supra.*

and creditt of Newcastle and for the creditt of our freinds to prove that we have what is materiall to offer agst the Bill and to prove by 4 or 5 Witnesses or what number you think proper the several facts I have wrote to you and what you (who know best) think proper to prove. I think if you can prove Sunderland trade is in 4 or 5 hands and none can bring coales but ym[1] to Sunderland, it will damm the Bill. The Agreement or contract with the Coasters not to come before Ladyday and after Michaelmas is materiall.[2] The 1s/- per chaldron must be read. To be considered how farr the provisions of this Bill may affect and damage the mouth of the River Tyne—some of your Trinity men are proper for this. Serjeant Darnell and Mr. Reeves are retained for us: they must have true copyes of this Act as modelled to inable ym to expose it as to the illegall part of the many absurdities and inconsistencyes in it. You ought to send us a map of the situacõn of these 2 Harbours from the sea.[3] You must send a breife setled among yourselves and your witnesses ought to be in town this day fortnight or Tuesday fortnight at furthest.

P.S. Lord Wm[4] added your name and James Clavering Junr Esq. to the Comrs' names.

On receipt of this letter Cotesworth instructed Sanderson to charter for him in town a special coach to come to Newcastle for him and he eventually agreed with one Joshua Perry for £27. A week later the Gateshead man was speeding to London. True, the Wear Bill eventually passed into law but only after it was shorn of its objectionable clauses and Cotesworth and his friends had been included in the list of commissioners who were to execute it. The incident affords an admirable illustration of how an astute and determined man, starting with an initial handicap, could yet whip up an opposition capable of modifying an important local project.

That substantially the same tactics were used to surmount

---

[1] i.e. the colliery-owners.      [2] *Supra*, 205.

[3] I have not found any map among the Cotesworth Papers.

[4] Lord William Poulett, a friend of Cotesworth. *Supra*. He had estates and lead-mines in north Yorkshire which doubtless explains his support of the Sunderland Bill. In 1728 George Bowes, a London merchant, wrote to his namesake, the M.P. for County Durham; 'I took leave to tell you that the Bishop [of Durham] should say to a Justice of the Peace of your County that dined with him that that day there would be as great a Contest for a Commissioner of the River Wear as if it had been an Election.' Bowes MSS. 40748, § 55.

the last constitutional hurdle, the house of peers, and that in respect of its appellate jurisdiction, is evident from what happened concerning an appeal in 1715. Certain coal-owners who were interested in a colliery at Tanfield Moor, G. Spearman and W. Wright in conjunction with George Pitt, M.P., and Lady Clavering, sought to reverse a verdict given at York concerning a disputed way-leave over Alderman Ramsay's 'liberty' at Whickham. Cotesworth, Ramsay's brother-in-law, proceeded to London in order to concert measures, and when it became clear that no agreement would be reached by private negotiations between the parties concerned, he set to work with a will. His weekly letters kept Ramsay fully informed:

August 11. Upon this subject he [George Pitt, M.P.] tormented me for 4 hours but I was deafe to all importunitie. This morning I rise at 5 and writ to all our Solicitors to appear at Westminster: at 8 I took coach and called on such as I could hope for any help from: at 12 I got to Westminster and at 2 Mr. Sanderson gave me the motion drawn up. I got it delivered to my L^d Rochester to move it to be heard on Monday sennet. Pitt went to him and desired he w^ld not move it as soon as I left. I brushed in to my L^d and Pitt and begg'd my Lord to hear me wch he did patiently . . . at last we have agreed to Hear the appeal by consent on this day fortnight.

August 18. Your case is printed and I herewith send you it. You may please to let Mr. Ord[1] see it and desire him to shew it to our friends and then he may send it to Capt. Liddell.[2] All hands are now at worke for the day of Battle draws on. I must own our friends seem Zealous in engageing their friends in the Lords' House to attend the Tryal wch is all I have to ask of any of them. I see no cause to fear the Success—Law and Reason seem both to be attached to your cause and I hope our adversaries will not be able to raise an Intrest to prevaile against both.

August 25. Your cause wch should have been heard this day was putt off till Tomorrow when I hope nothing will intervene. There is a Council held every morning on this great affaire of the French King's death . . . so that the Chancellor never gets to the House of Lords till 2 a clock: it was past 3 yesterday. . . . Our friends are all very Zealous

---

[1]  A Newcastle attorney.                    [2]  George Liddell, later colonel.

and after they had engaged as many Lords as each of them could to appear today, they were forced to give them Countermanding orders and solicit them to appear tomorrow. It is very fatigueing work. My Lord Scarb[orough] is very kind. He should have gone to Hansteed tomorrow and put off his journey on acc^t of this Cause. Sir Harry [Liddell] lay in Town last night y^t he might be near at hand this morning and is forced to ly in Town this night againe.[1] My L^d Scarb[orough] obliged me to be at his House this morning between 7 and 8 and I am just got to my Lodgeings at 7 this evening, but I hope it will be over and end well else it could not be endured. . . . I must entreat you send this to Mr. Ord and desire him to shew it to the rest for as soon as I have sealed this I must go to the Councel and be out Tomorrow at 7.

August 27. I can now send you the agreeble and long wished for Newes that that august Assembly, the Peers of Great Britain in Parliament, have affirmed the decree you had in the Court below so justlye and so equitably obtained. The Hearing of the Cause began yesterday att halfe an hour after one and lasted till halfe an hour after Three when we were ordered to withdraw & the Lords in about 10 minutes affirmed the decree not one Lord opened his mouth against so Righteous a Cause and so Just a decree, but several there were y^t Censured the appeal. Your Councel Sir Jos[eph Jeykell] exerted himself even beyond what is common and Mr. Cowper lashed a little the Chiefe Justice[2] for male-administration of his power in threatening to commit his client, a worthy Honest Gentleman and a man of fortune in his Country of wch he hoped proper notice wld be taken. Many a time was your name Repeated as was that of your Relation and assistant, W.C.,[3] a worthy man. My affidavit was Read wch Pinn'd the Basket. The Bishop of Carlisle[4] got twice up from his Bench and came to Mr. Cowper to desire him to remarke what he, the Bishop, thought was fit to be taken notice of. My Lord Scarborough put off his Journey till this morning to Hansteed y^t he might attend the Cause and obliged my Lord Lumley to attend also. He has been kind beyond measure. He has several days this weeke obliged me to attend him at his house before 8 a clock. He sent for me this morning before he tooke his Journey, raised my L^d Lumley y^t he might introduce me to him and ordered my Lord when

---

[1] He now lived in Kensington.

[2] Sir Thomas Parker, later Earl of Macclesfield. There is more than a hint that he had been biased. The Claverings who were parties in the suit were related, by marriage, to the Yorkes.

[3] i.e. Cotesworth himself.　　　　　　　　[4] Nicolson.

he wanted any advice in the north to apply to me and desired I wld advise his man White[1] in his affaires. . . .

I beleive there never was any Cause so powerfully solicited nor so attended to by the Lords. There were about 45 in the House who sat and heard the Councel on both sides with as much attention as I do my Curate when they say I sleep for there was not a word of moment I beleive yt slipt them. Poor Lord Sumers,[2] who cannot go over the Roome without being led, attended the whole time tho' it cost him 2 guineas to appointe a Proxy wch his Comeing to the House on your acct [on the previous day (?)] occasion'd. . . .

Sir Harry,[3] Mr. Carr and Mr. Wortley wrought hard for you. There were 7 Bishops attended you being a True Churchman *viz*, the Bishop of Oxford, Sarum, Carlile, Bangor, Litchfield and Chester and I know not who else. Mr. Pitt and I are just parted at 2 o'clock very good friends.

It is therefore irrelevant to count heads in an attempt to assess the strength of the coal interest in parliament or to discriminate finely between merchants and landowners. To do so is to miss the endless ramifications and electoral compromises of eighteenth-century politics.[4] 'I think it is verey hard yt out of 12 members for ye two countys there should be but two Coaleowners, for there never was a time yt ye Coale trade required more friends', wrote William Gilroy, a London coal-crimp, in 1727 by way of comment on the recent elections for Northumberland and Durham.[5] Moreover, as we have seen, the coal-owners were not so strong nor so well organized as the shipping interests engaged in the coal trade, and the wiser heads among them would have kept coal 'out of parliament'.[6] Besides, on occasion, the 'Grand Allies' had perforce to be self-effacing when high prices roused the fury of Londoners. In any case, the coal interests in the north-east were not one and indivisible for although

---

[1] Edward White, the steward at Lumley Castle.
[2] Somers, the Whig statesman.     [3] Liddell.
[4] For instance, part of the electoral compromise in County Durham in 1727 between the bishop, the Earl of Scarborough, Bowes, and the Vanes was that the latter should come in as member for Steyning ('A Court borough') in Sussex and that the Earl of Carlisle's candidate, Robinson, should come in for Morpeth. Bowes MSS. 40748, §§ 28–39.
[5] Ellison MSS.     [6] *Supra*.

temporary accommodations might be reached between owners on Tyne and Wear, the undercurrent of fierce rivalry persisted. As we have seen, Sir Thomas Clavering did not carry his election in County Durham in 1760 although he was backed by 'the Coal Trade'. But what they lacked in numbers they made up in astute parliamentary lobbying, for they knew well that landlords in every county of England in any way concerned with mining had certain basic interests and could be coaxed to coalesce, like globules of mercury, under gentle pressure. And when they found a worthy champion of the industry they were reluctant to dispense with his services; in 1802 they insisted on electing Rowland Burdon for a third term against his will.[1]

Local issues, then—the Wear navigation in 1747 and 1760, the threat to the time-honoured grazing rights of Newcastle freemen on the Town Moor in 1774[2]—were the staple of politics in the eighteenth century. This is reflected on the rare occasions when northern members ventured to open their mouths in the House. In 1749 George Bowes, in his one recorded speech, opposed a government proposal to grant the city of Glasgow £10,000 as compensation for the losses sustained in the late rebellion: Newcastle had been at least as loyal, he contended, and 'has a better plea for relief than Glasgow'.[3] Four years later, Matthew Ridley, member for Newcastle, opposed a bill on the third reading, for a national census and for an exact register of births, marriages, and deaths. He had at first approved the bill in principle but confessed that he had changed his mind on receiving numerous letters from 'the most eminent of his constituents'—he indulged in a little homily on the relations of a member to his constituents—and now feared 'riotous resistance' and a 'popular flame' if the bill was passed.[4] Besides, there was the question of the additional expense involved which would inevitably fall on the rates—an infinitely more important consideration than satisfying 'the

---

[1] Quoted in *History* (1940).   [2] Namier, *Structure*, 120.
[3] *Parl. Hist.* xiv. 497.   [4] Ibid. 1330–5.

curiosity of City gentlemen who love to deal in political arithmetic'. The bill passed the Commons but was thrown out by the Lords. There was one matter besides coal, however, on which northern members displayed a lively interest —the question of the corn-laws. In 1766 Lord Ravensworth 'earnestly applied to all the King's Ministers' for a bill to allow the importation of rye duty-free 'so necessary for the sustenance of the North'. Six years later Sir Thomas Clavering and Sir Edward Blackett moved resolutions to prohibit the exportation of home-grown rye when the price reached 28*s.* per quarter. Rye was a necessary ingredient of the 'geordie' loaf.[1] These men knew only too well the probable consequences in 'mutinies' and 'villainous riots' of distressed keelmen and colliers. Politically, the north was already marching on its stomach.[2]

---

[1] Ibid. xvii. 478. *Correspondence of George III* (ed. Fortescue), i. 428. *History*, loc. cit.

[2] See M. Ridley's report on the 'rebellion' of 1740. *H.M.C. Carlisle MSS.* 195. Brand, ii. 520. For later troubles, see Ashton and Sykes, *The Coal Industry of the Eighteenth Century* 111–33. In 1795 A. Mowbray wrote that 'the poor [in Durham] will not eat good rye bread except under the greatest necessity'. *Annals of Agriculture*, xxiv. 91, quoted in Salaman, *The History and Social Influence of the Potato*, 506.

## CHAPTER VII

# The Bishopric

It is a pleasure to those who have had any share
in placing great and deserving men in high stations
to see them make use of their power and influence
so much to their own honour and the public service.
(*The Duke of Newcastle to Bishop Trevor of Durham*,
1759)[1]

## I

IN the eighteenth century anyone crossing the Tees from
the north was said 'to come out of Bishopric', such was
the extraordinary dignity and repute of the prince bishops of
Durham. On first entering the diocese the bishop was met
'in the midst of the Tees' by a great bevy of his principal
tenants and freeholders. When Bishop Talbot came north
in the summer of 1722 Cotesworth, being himself obliged
to travel to London on important business, sent these instructions to his steward:

On receite of this, dispatch an express to Mr. Weatherby, Mr. Dent
and Mr. Rootherford to prepare themselves immediately in the most
decent manner to go with you to meet the Bishop in the midst of the
Tees where he will be on Thursday morning next. He lyes at Allerton
all night on Wednesday and intends to be in Durham on Thursday
early. You must send to Mr. Rootherford [at Shields] to meet you at
Whitesmocks which is the House on the left hand after you are come
in at the Gate off Durham Moor in the way from Gateshead Park to
Sunderland Briggs on Wednesday evening and you must send to
W. D.[ent] (at Swallwell) and J. Weatherby to come down to you and
dine on Wednesday and then set forward and if you have time you may
go on to Mrs. Howes at Ferryhill and ly all night: it will make ye
journey on Thursday morning to Teeside the easier. I have writ to
Mr. Rundell [the bishop's secretary] to let him know that you all four
belong to me that he may acquaint the Bishop.[2]

At Farewell Hall, on the outskirts of the city, the bishop
was met by the dean and chapter, where addresses of wel-

[1] Add. MSS. 32896, § 243.  [2] Cotesworth MSS.

come were read. In his address to young Bishop Trevor in 1753 Dr. Sharp, the sub-dean, remarked that the bishops of Durham were 'men illustrious in themselves, great in their abilities and repute', a proper match for 'the extraordinary Dignity and Powers' of the Palatinate.[1] His concluding wish, 'May you perpetuate the Family name in this Northern Climate', was sincere, if scarcely in the best taste. *Alia tempora!*

Cotesworth sent more instructions as to the bishop's reception at Park House when he came on his primary visitation: 'You must have the gardens clean, the walks well-rolled and the Court kept clean. . . . Tell Mr. Baker I hope the Bishop will be admitted into the Dining Room.' Others also made elaborate preparations to entertain his lordship on this occasion. George Bowes, 'the Count', was credibly reported to have laid in 'twenty dozen of marrow bones' for the occasion. 'The 20 doz of marrow bones was not a mistake in me', wrote Sisson to his master in London who had queried the statement, 'for Mr. Baker did tell me it and he said he see them lying in Mr. Armstrong's kitchen. I made a wonder at it, but he assured me it was true, he having seen them himself.'[2] Bowes knew well enough that, metaphorically speaking, the bishop might make a valley of dry bones suddenly spring to life.

The enormous power and prestige of the bishop rested on a solid foundation of property. Among the Cotesworth MSS. is a paper 'A Rentall of the Bpp of Durham's freehold and Copyhold Rents', clearly belonging to the early years of the century. Though it is incomplete it lists a total

---

[1] Add. MSS. 32732, § 240–2. 'I found it was thought requisite', wrote the bishop, 'that Dr Sharp's speech with my answer should be printed, so that I could not refuse it without displeasing the Chapter, whatever good reasons I might have for declining it.'

[2] Cotesworth MSS. In the summer of 1718 when Lady Bowes was expecting her eldest son from London she thought it proper that he should be met by his principal tenants. 'I wonder you should think me so soft', he replied, 'as to desire any of the Country Tenants to meet me: it is the surest sign of a little low spirit to be tickled with such nonsense. There is nobody shall know when I come but yourself. I desire you not to publish it.' Bowes MSS. 40747, § 169. 'Your hopes of my coming down soon are vain', he had written earlier, 'for surely you don't think me such a fool as to prefer ye charms of a stupid dull Country Life to ye pleasures of ye Town.'

of some 1,694 tenants and properties, widely dispersed throughout the county with particular concentrations at Darlington, Easington, Bishop Wearmouth, the Boldons, and Whitburn, and at Lanchester and the Aucklands. The tenants included lords Lonsdale, Scarborough, and Widdrington besides most of the local gentry, but the great bulk were small freeholders or copyholders. Only three collieries are mentioned specifically—Burnop and Hamstells at a rent of £11. 1s. 8d., Penfield at £5. 15s. 4d., and Buttifield Township at £8. 18s. 7d.—but the rental itself is incomplete; it does not include the Grand Lease of Gateshead and Whickham.

In order to appreciate what I shall term 'Episcopal Recovery' in the eighteenth century, we must go back to the Restoration period. Anyone who reads the unpublished correspondence of Sir Gilbert Gerard, Bishop Cosin's favourite son-in-law, with Miles Stapleton, the bishop's secretary and factotum, will quickly discover the grave perils to which the see was exposed.[1] The sole preoccupation of these two men was to obtain for themselves valuable leases of church lands, both episcopal and capitular, more especially if they were thought to have a rich mining potential. The barest summary of their loot will sufficiently demonstrate that the aged and well-meaning bishop had been quite unable to resist their insidious pressure. In addition to the Grand Lease itself, they obtained leases of Tanfield and Coundon collieries, the limekilns at Ferryhill and Merrington, all the so-called 'wastes' in the Palatinate, and the bishop's lands at Auckland save the demense, besides rich and extensive lands and water-mills, all rolled together in a single lease, at Northallerton, Brunton, Crake, and Darlington. 'I hope to God that thes Leases maie doe us some good', wrote Gerard. 'I am confidentt ther is nothing that ar off this kind that can be fownd out but my Lord will grant it us.

---

[1] Hunter MSS. vii, §§ 60–104. 'My Lord's years makes him uncertain but this is fixtt', wrote Gerard in 1671. 'Truly I would not have my Lord spoil a certon for two tries. . . . You know although it be but in small things it is uncertain to find my Lord in a humour to comply in it but oppertunitie may compas any resonabell thing.' *The Correspondence of Miles Stapleton* (Surtees Soc. cxxxi), *passim*.

Therefore, I pray be industerous to inform yourselfe of thes thinges.' Well might Gerard suggest that on occasion his collaborator should present a volume to 'the Liberary' at Durham 'to please my Lord'. So far as these men were concerned the term 'Restoration' is a sad misnomer. Rather were they the Parliamentary Committee for Sequestered Estates under new management, having as their text: 'Wheresoever the carcase is, there will the eagles be gathered together.' On at least three occasions the dean and chapter, to their credit, refused to confirm Cosin's leases.[1] 'I hope you will meet with better entertainment in the world than at first you had', wrote Stapleton's brother. 'Your beginning was difficult and somewhat entangled with various straits and varietys of accidents. It may please God you may see better times and enjoy a more plentiful and serene state.' His prayer was answered.

If we turn to the Registers of Leases of the dean and chapter a similar picture is presented. In 1687 Sir John Sudbury—nephew and heir of Dean Sudbury—had a Durham rent-roll of nearly £500 a year; his total receipts from the Palatinate—he himself resided at Mill Green in Essex—for principal and interest in that year amounted to £2,441. 6s. 3d.[2] By contrast, a junior prebend had to be content with a lease of the kelp rocks and 'sea ware' at Whitburn and other places for his portion.[3] In short, had this process continued with gathered momentum for another generation both the episcopal and capitular properties, vast as they were, would have been largely eroded away. The measure and methods of recovery form the central theme of the present chapter.

It would be wrong to suppose, however, that the process was suddenly halted. The main burden of Spearman's *An*

[1] S. P. Dom. Charles II, clxxviii, § 112. Viz. the Grand Lease of Gateshead and Whickham, and of the manors of Howden and Sadberge. The action of the chapter raised the question of confirmation of 'concurrent' leases. *Infra*, 315. Cosin protested and the chapter later confirmed the Grand Lease to Gerard and Stapleton. Register (1665–72), §§ 369, 419.

[2] Hunter MSS. xii, §§ 84, 87, 93. Surtees, *History of Durham*, ii. 373–4.

[3] Audit Books, *passim*. In 1722 Dr. Finney was granted this lease, paying no fine: ten years later, Dr. Hall obtained it paying an annual rent of 5s. and a fine of 2 guineas. Kelp was used extensively in the alum works at Staithes and Boulby.

*Enquiry into the Ancient and Present State of the County Palatine of Durham*, published in 1729, is that it was continuing unabated. In particular he cites the lease by Nathaniel, Lord Crewe, of the quarries in the manor of Easington 'to his nephew Charles Montague', Bishop Talbot's lease to his son-in-law, Dr. Sayer, of all the coal-mines within the enclosed copyholds at West Auckland, a joint lease of the rich coal-bearing manors of Houghton and Newbottle to Dr. Sayer and other members of the bishop's family and Mr. Stonehewer, the bishop's steward, and a third lease to Dr. Sayer who was his spiritual and temporal chancellor, of the rich colliery at Tanfield Western Lea. Indeed, the reputation of the misnamed and mercenary Nathaniel Crewe who enjoyed the see for close on half a century is unenviable. Colonel George Liddell, who had good reason for knowing, wrote: 'the Bishop's Information is an original. He is a buck of the first head. I could not have thought anyone living could ever from a pulpit have utter'd such base, false, malicious lyes.'[1] Spearman asserts that the Newbottle colliery lease was first granted by Bishop Crewe to Stonehewer, his steward, and that the bishop was 'ashamed of it and wrote to the Dean and Chapter not to confirm it', but that is perhaps not the whole story.

The underlyings of the late bishop [continued Spearman] prevailed upon his Lordship for great sums, secretly paid to them, to make grants or leases of commons belonging to the copyholders and which upon their coming to an agreement for the division [i.e. enclosure] they were entitled to canton among themselves and enjoy the inheritance thereof, yet such lessees under colour of such grants interrupt the tenants in the usage of the said Commons and their common highways along and over the same and vex them with multiplicity of litigious suits and

[1] Cotesworth MSS. The elder Spearman had held the office of under-sheriff under Bishop Crewe. Surtees, *Durham*, i. 95. The sheriff and under-sheriff were appointed by the bishop's letters-patent 'during pleasure', and Spearman had no legal grounds for complaint when Bishop Talbot's high sheriff appointed his own deputy. *Infra*, 329. Spearman also had interests in Tanfield Lea colliery but was unable to exploit it without way-leave rights over Whickham manor. He had therefore a double grievance. 'Spearman is such a rogue', wrote Cotesworth in 1721, 'that he'll pay nobody unless the utmost necessity obliges him and before that is he'll make and spend three times as much in the law.'

actions thereabout as in the case of Cotesworth and Ramsay, who having got leases of the manors of Whickham and Gateshead, play'd the tyrant over their neighbours and made themselves masters of the wayleaves and a great part of the collieries and thereby got near £3000 per annum for one colliery.

Here Spearman was writing as an aggrieved party having been worsted in a recent trial at York. We know that a suit was still pending in Chancery in 1726 between him and Cotesworth, Colonel Liddell, and others touching a colliery way-leave in Fawdonfield. What is not in dispute is that when Cotesworth, the tallow-chandler, obtained a renewal of the Grand Lease of the manors of Gateshead and Whickham for his brother-in-law, Alderman Ramsay, in 1712 he paid £1,050 to the bishop besides a douceur of 50 guineas to Mr. Stonehewer, the bishop's steward.[1]

What is equally significant for our present purpose is Cotesworth's cool-headed calculation in the previous year of the eminent worth whileness of the purchase of the two manors when they were ordered to be sold by Chancery decree.[2] A paper in his hand headed 'A Computation for the first purchase of the Two Manors wch cost £5850' has this covering note to Alderman Ramsay, 'You are not to shew this to any person whatever, Mrs. Ramsay excepted, nor allow any to have a Coppy, for it may loose the Bargain wch I am fond of. W. C.'[3]

Buying long-term leasehold land at seven and a half years' purchase, collieries at three years', and mills and other 'contingencies' at less than three, was, indeed, 'worth money': small wonder that he was 'fond of' the bargain. In short, the bishop's reserved rent of £235. 11s. 4d. was only a fraction of the annual profits of the lessee. In 1727 Cotesworth's heir sold one of the manors, Whickham, to Sir Henry Liddell for £22,000![4] But it was not to be expected that eighteenth-century bishops would for long be blind to such things or be content to see their own lessees making fortunes while their own revenues remained stationary, *au fond*.

---

[1] Cotesworth MSS. The payment to the bishop was a 'fine'. Cotesworth and Stonehewer became close friends.    [2] As a result of disputes between members of the Gerard family.    [3] Cotesworth MSS. (See next page.)    [4] Ibid.

Rents rec<sup>d</sup> for the Manors of Gateshead and Whickham at
Martinmas 1709

| | | | | | | |
|---|---|---|---|---|---|---|
| £642. | 9. | 6 | Coal rent at 4 years' purchase | = £2568. | 9. | 6.[1] |
| £511. | 18. | 0 | Bishop's land, in this sum | | | |
| £ 38. | 12. | 0 | is Copyhold rents out of wch the Bishop has annually | | | |
| £235. | 11. | 4 | paid him, so that the real Rent remaining is | | | |
| £276. | 6. | 8 | at 10 years' purchase | = £2763. | 6. | 8. |
| £ 40. | 0. | 0 | per ann. for Sir H. [Liddell's] steaths and way-leave at 4 years' purchase | = £ 160. | 0. | 0. |
| £ 40. | 0. | 0 | per ann. for the Montagu's steaths and way-leaves at 4 years' purchase | = £ 160. | 0. | 0. |
| £ 49. | 7. | 2 | per ann. houses, milns standing and other Contingencies at 3 years' purchase | = £ 148. | 1. | 6. |
| | | | | £5799. | 14. | 4. |

£7000 is the full purchase (including the moiety of News-
  ham) in which is included £141 per ann. freehold wch at 19
  years' purchase will amount to £2679 and that deducted from the
  whole purchase rests [for
  Gateshead and Whickham]   £4321
£4321 wch deducted from the £5799. 14. 4. it will abate the purchase
  £1478. 14. 4, wch is above ¼ and that will bring the Bishop's land
  to 7½ years' purchase and the Contingencies to 2¾ and Coal Rent
  etc. to 3 years' purchase.

The two [manorial] Courts are not mentioned nor are they of any real
advantage worth nameing, but the Park House is worth money.

*   *   *

The first indication of a change in policy is contained in a
letter from Cotesworth's son while he was an undergraduate
at Cambridge in 1718:

A pamphlet has by chance fall'n into my hands supposed to be writ
by the Bishop of Ely setting forth the value of Church and College

---

[1] *Sic* in MSS.

leases.[1] I hope it won't by chance fall into the Bishop of Durham's hands for fear it should persuade him to raise his fines, for he shews that 7 years being lapsed in a lease of 21 years, the interest of money being 6%, the tenant in such case ought to pay near two and a half years' value for the renewing of his lease up to 21 years. For 7 years lapsed in a lease of 21 years, if you take but one year's value for renewing it up to 21 years you give your tenant £11/11/8¼ᵈ% for his money, therefore, he says, leases sold at 6% inheritance according to that proportion ought to be sold at 16 or 17 years' purchase. The reasons and proofs of his calculations, he says, may be seen in a book entitled *Tables for renewing and purchasing leases of Cathedral Chapters and Colleges,* published about thirty years ago and printed at Cambridge. Mr. Button[2] may probably help you to the Book.

The 'tables' referred to were the work of Sir Isaac Newton.[3] If young Cotesworth was right in attributing the pamphlet to Bishop Fleetwood, author of *Chronicon Precosium,* then Bishop of Ely, the debt which his ecclesiastical brethren and successors owed to Fleetwood is inestimable, for he was the first to draw attention to the uneconomic rents of church and college lands and to show how the rot could be stopped.[4]

In 1721, when the Cambridge undergraduate died, Cotesworth was able 'to put in another life' in the Grand Lease on paying the bishop £50, but it was the last time that renewal was effected at so cheap a rate. In 1728 Dr. Sayer, the bishop's secretary, asked Robert Cotesworth, the new lord, to submit accounts of the actual profits of the lease during the two years since his father's death so that the amount of the fine

---

[1] *The Value of Church and College Leases considered.* There is a second edition (1722) of this pamphlet in the British Museum (518, k. 4) from which it is clear that the original edition was dated 1 July 1718. The 'Tables' may well prove to be the work of Fleetwood himself. By 1704 he was advocating an adjustment in church and college rents in proportion to the increase in the price of corn. See G. N. Clark's article in *E. H. R.* li. 686.

[2] A Newcastle bookseller.      [3] British Museum, T. 1571 (8).

[4] Everard Fleetwood, *An Enquiry into the Customary Estates and Tenant Rights of those who hold lands of the Church* (1731). Also W. Derham, *A Defence of the Churche's Right in Leasehold Estates.* Roger Long, *The Rights of Churches and Colleges defended. The Reasonableness of Church and College Fines asserted,* all published in 1731. 'Their crime, as you call it, was that they had made a strict Enquiry into the value of their Estate and exacted from you somewhat more than one year's rent . . . for renewing a lease up to 21 years, whereof 7 were run out.' In 1740 the chapter at Durham bought a pamphlet on college leases for the library. Audit Book, 59.

on renewal might be determined. In reply Cotesworth pointed out that 'last year was a notoriously bad year for collieries', but the bishop signified his readiness 'to come to an agreement for an annual renewal for his life as well as a renewal for the present term expired', leaving the amount of the fine to be settled 'either by waiting some years longer before renewing or to venture on a computation by guess acceptable to both sides'. The young lord and his advisers, perhaps not yet fully aware of the new situation, somewhat unwisely, rejected this proposal. 'Remember your good Father had enemies', Dr. Sayer reminded him, 'and one, now a good friend of yours, was once most diligent in his representations. Your lease was represented much higher than any other ever gave countenance to and Blackburne Colliery not only called £5000 to £6000, but a pretended offer made of hiring it at £4000. You must imagine it was not unnatural for the Bishop to listen to news of such advantage to his See, nor had he reason to disbelieve the accounts when they came from a friend and a neighbour to the estates themselves.' Sayer, who declared that he had no sort of personal interest in the fine, added that 'he had acted a kind part in undeceiving the Bishop' and expressed the hope that 'Blackburne and yours are both settled as long as the Bishop is of the diocese'. The malicious tongue of George Bowes had been at work; the dead bones were beginning to move. But Bowes, after all, was merely the occasion through whom offence came.

The negotiations with Cotesworth were on the point of breaking down completely when Sayer addressed this final letter to Park House.[1]

Auckland.
Monday (Mem: this Monday was
Sept. 30th 1728).

Dear Sir,

I must own I was determin'd by the ill success I met with (when I had lately the Honour of seeing you at Gateshead) to intermeddle no

[1] Cotesworth MSS.

farther in the Affair of your Lease, but as it is my Lord's Inclination not only to treat but renew with his Tenants at reasonable and easy Terms, and I know Renewals are particularly of Consequence to you, I cou'd not so far forget my Friendship to your Father and his Family as to quit the Reference made to me without one attempt more towards an Agreement between you. I need not take Notice to you, that the present Bishop is singular in the Terms he insists upon with his Tenants, seldom taking above 2 thirds of what all other ecclesiastical Persons or Bodies take. Your Father was fully sensible of this and I am persuaded you yourself will be so, if it shou'd please God to remove the present Bishop. I did hope that as you mention'd several Considerations upon wch you put the Rent for Wayleave and staithroom, you wou'd have been so kind upon our Conference as to have distinguish'd and explain'd them (at least so far) as to have enabled me to have made some Proposal of a Fine wch might have been to the Satisfaction of both Parties. Whatever is held of the Bishoprick is (let it be under what circumstances it will) capable of some Valuation and tho' perhaps this of wayleave ec may not admit of one adequate and certain, yet some it undoubtedly may: indeed in such cases it is difficult for the Bishop to do himself, his See, I may say his Tenants too, Justice without an ingenuous Assistance on their Part, for there may be many Circumstances attending them wch they themselves alone are privy to, but where Tenants do not think proper to make this Compliance, my Lord can have no other method of proceeding but to rely on the Informations he receives from the Countrey and from those he engages to enquire. I must say in your particular Case that the Accounts my Lord receives do give the See a much higher Credit in your Wayleaves and staithroom than my Lord himself is inclin'd at present to apportion his Fine to: His Lordship thinks himself intitled to a Consideration for the Wayleaves etc., not only as it is a Rent dependant on and arising from the Lands held of the See and wch you will enjoy 19 years before any acknowledgement is paid for it (the term you are treating for being reversionary and not to take Place till after the expiration of the 17 stile in yr lease) but as your Father particularly engag'd upon the last Renewal, that my Lord shou'd upon the next have a Fine in Proportion to his own Benefit, in case he shou'd agree with the Collieries, and upon such assurance and with a Prospect of a Performance of it, the Fine at that Time was settled. However as the Advantage of a settled Rent has not been enjoy'd above 2 years and those years have prov'd less profitable than the future may be expected to be, His

Lordship has laid his Commands upon me to acquaint you that tho' the Valuation deliver'd to him is near £3000 per ann, Land etc together, he is pleas'd to offer to renew with you for the sum of eight hundred Pounds: and this he do's upon Condition that you in the method (you desire) of yearly Renewals do agree for the future to pay a Fine of two hundred Pounds each year for such Renewal. When you consider these Terms propos'd, you will allow, that as the present Fine of £800 bears no Sort of Proportion to the Account given in by others, so the future one of £200 will bear a very reasonable one to that given in by yourself. My Lord further orders me to desire your Answer within a week or 10 days time because it is with Difficulty he comes into this Proposal wch I have made to him and is not willing to bind himself for any longer time: so that if you do not accept it within that time, ye whole must come to a new Treaty, wch I shall beg leave to excuse myself from being concern'd in. It is certainly of advantage to both Parties to have quick and settled Renewals and on your Part it is evident that by the Payment of this Fine of £200 yearly (shou'd a Successor accept it too) you will in some Sort gain a Perpetuity of the remaining Income or Profit arising from your Lease. As my Lord is very positive with regard to the Terms offer'd and will not depart from them, I wou'd not enter again into canvassing those Considerations you mention for the Rent of the Way leave ec, but only observe in general that much of what is said to be given up in Respect to Collieries originally came from the See (if I may use that Expression) as your Father himself obtain'd them for Passage thro' the Lands held of it. My Lord leaves Auckland on Wednesday and will expect your answer at London.

I am,

Your most obedient Servant,

E. Sayer.

Cotesworth had no option but to capitulate. The bishop himself wrote from London on 15 October.

Sir,

I have received the favour of your letter of the 8th and will order a Lease and Articles to be drawn against your comeing to Town. As to the Dividing of the Manners into separate leases, I shall be ready, as far as I may doe it, to oblige you, but you will doe well to consult with your Lawyer, in what manner it may be done Legally and with security to the Lessees. The little mistakes between you and Dr. Sayer will be easily rectified when we meet.

> I am, Sir,
>> Your affectionate Humble servant,
>>> W. Duresme.

Cotesworth had decided on 'load-shedding'. Later in the year he sold Whickham to Sir Henry Liddell.

Before pursuing the subsequent developments in respect of 'fines' on renewals, we must notice a singular attempt by Bishop Talbot to unfetter himself and his fellow bishops in the disposal of leases. Under a statute of Henry VIII's reign, confirmed by Elizabeth on her accession, bishops were restrained from granting leases for terms longer than twenty-one years or three lives and all such leases were required to be confirmed by the appropriate dean and chapter.[1] 'Soon after the Bishop of Durham's [Talbot] accession to that See', wrote Spearman in his *Enquiry*, 'a Bill was brought into Parliament which the Bishop and his friends stickled very much to promote.'[2] Spearman called it a Mines' Bill because its operative clause dealt with 'mines which have not been accustomably letten'. As originally conceived, the bill was meant to apply to lands owned by colleges, hospitals, and parsonages as well as bishop's lands. In effect, it proposed to dispense with the need incumbent upon bishops to obtain capitular confirmation of such grants. The elder Cotesworth called the bill the 'Bishop's Bill' and, fearing that it would 'shake' his existing leases, consulted learned counsel and took appropriate steps to resist its passage.[3] He was not alone. Sir John Eden, the county member, Mr. Lambton, 'and abundance more' strenuously opposed it.

---

[1] 31 Henry VIII, § 17; 32 Henry VIII, § 13.

[2] *An Enquiry*, 57–80. Hutchinson, *History of Durham*, i. 566–72. 'This attempt alarmed the whole nation', wrote Spearman, 'and a vigorous opposition was made to it and particularly by the Dean and Chapter of Durham and the copyholders and leaseholders of this County, for it appeared to them that the Bill was calculated for the Bishop of Durham and his family only and not for his successors.'

[3] 'The Bishop's Bill wrights', he wrote, 'are the Archbishop of York, the Bishops of Lincoln & Durham, Lord Harcourt & Lord Carteret and the "scabb'd Prebendary of Durham".'

The sub-dean and chapter of Durham preferred a petition against it:

Most humbly sheweth that your Petitioners have lately been informed that there is an Ingrossed Bill sent down to this Honourable House from the House of Peers intitled An Act to enable Archbishops, Bishops, Colleges, Deans and Chapters, Hospitals, Parsons, Vicars and others having Spiritual Promoc̃ons to make leases of their mines which have not been accustomably letten not exceeding the term of one and twenty years and without taking any fine upon the granting or renewing of the same. And your Petitioners are also informed that such Bill hath been read a first and second time and is committed to a Committee of ye Whole House.

That your Petitioners are advised and humbly conceive that if the said Bill, as now framed, should pass into a law, it will not only be destructive of ye Ancient Rights of Deans and Chapters with respect to Confirmac̃ons, but may also be prejudiciall and dangerous to the Revenues and Possessions of Archbishops and Bishops. And therefore, your Petitioners most humbly pray this Hon'ble House that they may be heard by their Councell before the said Ctee in order to be relieved against the said Bill (before the same passes into law) in such manner as to this Hon'ble House in their great Wisdom and Justice shall seem meet.

[Signed by the Sub-Dean and 6 other prebends.]

Durham. 4th March 1722–3.[1]

The bill occasioned some verses in the following vein:

There was no more in't but my good Lord of Durham
Was to seize all our Mines and our Land to secure 'em
For himself and his Friends and to pay nothing for 'em.[2]

It would seem that shortly after his translation to Durham Bishop Talbot had had differences with the chapter. In December 1721 Sir Henry Liddell had written '. . . Knows not how the Bishop stands with the College and could not learn from Mr. Mountague, but believe him too wary to give just cause of offence, though many reports of that sort

[1] Register, § 203. The signatories were Drs. Watts, Wheeler, Finney, Hartwell, Eden, Mangey, and Hall.

[2] Add. MSS. 40836, § 48, in E. Vernon's *Commonplace Book*. Vernon corresponded with George Bowes.

fly abroad, I believe more invented than real'.[1] Spearman, a few years later, openly insinuated that the bishop had encountered resistance from the chapter in the matter of his mining leases. 'I have not seen the Bishop since you sent a copy of the act', wrote Cotesworth in 1723. 'People use him and his son[2] ill about the Bill; they both declare they intended no ill to anybody, though it seems some were so wicked as to send for Bowes up to take my lease of the Bishop which they said would be void by the Bill. The Bishop sent his Secretary to me to assure me he has not the least thought of any such thing, but he does not want his enemies that have done him all the mischief they can. I hope he will prove a very kind lord. . . .' In a postscript he added, 'The Bishop's Bill was debated today: he wou'd not appear at the Commons' barr. They go upon it tomorrow when they will use him as he deserves.' 'The Bishop's Bill is either new-modelled or dropt', Colonel Liddell reported later. 'The Bill was dropt or withdrawn and did not pass', wrote Spearman six years later, 'but many of the old Prebendaries of Durham soon after dying, the Bishop had the opportunity of prefering many of his friends in their places, he thereby hath a majority in the Chapter to confirm such leases as he thinks fit to grant.' Spearman likened the process to the odious contemporary practice of the king's ministers getting a majority in parliament by the corrupt distribution of places and pensions.

On the appointment of the kindly Bishop Chandler in 1730 the situation eased. 'On Tuesday last Mr. Carr and myself waited on the Bishop about our renewals', wrote Henry Ellison, 'he perused our article with great freedom and asked if we were willing to go on upon the same terms. We told him we were and he said so was he.' 'He made no inquiry at all into the value of the estate or its annual income', wrote Carr gleefully, 'and seems very ready to do

---

[1] Cotesworth MSS. Dr. Montague was dean.
[2] Charles Talbot, M.P. for Durham, later Lord Chancellor. *Parl. Hist.* viii. 22. Add. MSS. 40836, § 48.

everything his Predecessor has done in regard to this affair.'
On this occasion a fine of £100 was paid for Gateshead
manor alone. It will be recalled that two years earlier Robert
Cotesworth had made a suggestion to pay an annual fine
rather than a lump sum as one or more lives dropped out of
the lease. Recent events had suggested that the Cotesworths
were not 'long-livers' and the young heir may well have
thought it preferable to pay a modest annual fine rather than
a big sum 'at one chop', especially since, as Dr. Sayer suggested, the payment of a yearly fine gave the lessee 'a sort
of Perpetuity of the remaining Income or Profit'. Be that as
it may, we know that after 1728 an annual fine was paid,
though the lease itself still ran for the maximum period of
three lives.

A good illustration of the importance of cultivating
friendly relations with the reigning bishop is afforded by the
correspondence of Henry Thomas Carr with his brother-in-
law and joint lessee, Henry Ellison. In 1749 Carr hoped
that his friend Gilbert, of Salisbury, would be translated to
Durham on Bishop Chandler's death, but a year later he was
less sanguine. He wrote from Whitworth, near Bishop
Auckland:

I believe our Bishop now declines fast and I fear my friend will
scarce succeed him which will be a disappointment to me as the hopes
of that was a main inducement to me to fix where I now am in a convenient situation to have kept up my interest with him and by that
means have had it in my power now and then to have recommended a
worthy man to him. I'm glad, however, to hear that the Bishop of
Bristol is pitched upon who is a man of unexceptionable character in
private life and will be much loved in the County, though I think the
other [Sarum] in the case of any new troubles arising from the North
would have been a much more useful man to the Public. . . .[2]

---

[1] Ellison MSS. Hutchinson, op. cit. 574.

[2] Ibid. i.e. from the Jacobites—a significant reminder of the political and military importance of the bishops of Durham. In 1744 Bishop Chandler had been the first to report the
movements of suspected persons to the government. Add. MSS. 32702, §§ 92, 355. 'The
intended invasion by France in favour of a Popish Pretender . . . has inspired me with a fresh
spring of spiritts insomuch that I am determined not to be an Idle Spectator.' A report had
reached him that the French 'intended a descent at Blyth'.

Carr had deliberately moved from Cocken to Whitworth in order 'to keep up an interest' with the bishop; his younger son 'Ralphy', still a mere schoolboy, being designed for the Church. 'I see the Bishop of Bristol named in ye Newspaper to succeed to Durham', he wrote in August 1750 from Alderley in Cheshire, where he was staying with his friend Sir Edward Stanley, 'I wish it may be either him or the Bishop of Salisbury, but the latter seems very happy and easy where he is'.

Bishop Butler's reign at Durham was brief but long enough for him to leave his mark in the matter of fines. In September 1751, Carr wrote from Whitworth,

. . . Received from Mr. Sill[1] a fair copy of the Rental with remarks which I that day left with the Bishop who treated me with great civility but the trouble we took about our Observations seems to be to very little purpose for yesterday afternoon Mr. Johnson came to me from his Lordship who fixes his Rule absolutely upon the Rental and makes no Deduction even for the Sesses and Taxes; he has only deducted the expence of Court keeping.

The Neat Rental    £1139
Add sesses and taxes  £   75 which he [Ellison] had deducted.
               £1214

This being a yearly renewal, by Sir Isaac Newton's tables to be worth $\frac{1}{9}$th upon ye proportion of one year's Rent for a Fine at ye expiration of 7 years, his Lordship's demand, therefore, is £134.

I told Mr. Johnson that if that strict Rule was to be observed we should be in the worst situation of any Tenant of the See of Durham considering the losses and the expense of suits we were liable to. I also took notice to him of several of the remarks we had made on the Rental and said we could not think it worth our while to renew even with his Lordship upon those terms for his Life: that the chance was greatly against us, Park Colliery being the only thing in our favour that was not yet certain and when won effectually it would be some years before you and I could reap any benefit from it more than the present Rent, as the Lessees were entitled to work off a great Quantity of coals due to them:[2] that I could give no answer myself but would write to you about it: . . .

[1] The steward.     [2] The colliery, not yet 'won', was leased on a tentale basis. *Supra.*

Suppose we should continue to renew annually at present according to the circumstances of the Rental but without coming to any Agreement for the life of the Bishop and continue this method til the Partners have wrought off all their short coles etc. so as to keep our Lease full against that time when Profit will arise to us, if ever it does, I speak this upon a supposition that his Lordship should stick stiffly to his Rule which I can by no means think a good one as it makes no distinction between the best and the worst tenants, those that improve their estates and support the Rights of the See and those that trouble their heads about neither. . . .

Carr's fear that the bishop would 'stick stiffly' proved correct.

26 September 1751.

As we are entered into no agreement for an Annual Renewal, being punctual to the time seems no way necessary and the next lease would be best dated 12th November. The rule they go by is to consider the value of the present year for contingencies.

The more I think of this Agreement with the Bishop, the more I am perplexed about it. An annual renewal without any agreement to continue it might be fair enough on both sides, but the matter seems mightily against us if we are to tie up ourselves during the life of the Bishop to the same fine. The contingencies, I say, are greatly against us. There are many probable chances to lessen our Income much and but one to increase it and that at present seems a very precarious one, I mean Park Colliery, and with regard to that it ought not to be brought into the calculation at present, for considering the short coles the Lessees are entitled to, there is no probability even if the colliery goes on ever so well of our having any advance of Rent for it these 7 years. The Bishop's Agents, to curry favour, may endeavour to make slight of our Remarks as mere Glosses to answer the present purpose: we know they are founded on Truth and will stand the test of an Inquiry. But as you are a better judge of all these things than I am, I submit it entirely to you.

On 14 October he wrote again,[1]

I went this forenoon to Auckland and spent the day with the Bishop who received me very graciously, but his Secretary, Mr. Pearson, and also Mr. Hodgson being from home, nothing was reduced into writing, but he seemed to think of fixing the fine at £128 and would agree to

[1] Ellison MSS.

renew during his life. As to the altering the date of the lease he did not think it necessary as the first Rent might well enough be made payable at Martinmas, though the lease should bear date in this month, but if the alteration was necessary he should not insist upon anything for the month, nor did he expect anything for the House and Gardens though it was usual to take advantage of any improvements after the expiration of the first 7 years. He had indeed mentioned them . . . as in making a bargain of that sort it was common to take notice of everything. Upon the whole, I spent the day agreably enough and in the evening we walk'd together half way up the Outer Park in my way home, where we parted. His Lordship said he would give directions to have the lease etc. done soon but whether it could be before he left the country on Monday next, he could not tell, but if not, it should be sent down from London.

I left your memorandum with him, also a short sketch I had drawn by way of agreement to renew annually on the same terms during his life.

Before Bishop Butler died Carr had migrated to Mobberley in Cheshire in order to be near a more kindly ecclesiastical patron, his close friend, Sir Edward Stanley.

Mobberley Hall, Cheshire.
September 25. 1752.
. . . I wonder we have not a Bishop of Durham yet, if Trevor had been certainly fix'd upon I should have imagined it would before this have been fix'd up. It seems at present more indifferent to us upon our own account, as a new one can scarce demand more of us than the last did.

Three weeks later the Duke of Newcastle wrote from Hanover signifying that he had at last obtained the king's consent to the translation of Bishop Trevor to Durham.[1] The

---

[1] The king at first refused to nominate Trevor whom he stigmatized as 'a high Church fellow, a stiff, formal fellow and nothing else'; but he gave way in the end. Sykes, op. cit. 39. 'I have watched my opportunity', wrote the Duke of Newcastle, 'and have at last succeeded even better than I could well have flattered myself. Brother Pelham's early and continued zeal for your success in this great affair has been of the greatest service to you.' 'You will particularly connect yourself with the Archbishop to preserve that Union and Harmony under his Grace upon the Bench which is so necessary for the King's service and for the good of the Church.' In reply Trevor ascribed his promotion 'absolutely and wholly, under God, to the zealous and steady interposition of your Grace and your Brother on my behalf'. Add. MSS. 32730, §§ 138, 161. *H.M.C. Eglinton*, 292–309. There is a portrait of Trevor in Hutchinson, *History of Durham*, i. 580.

letter was sent by special courier. At the end of October Carr
wrote again to Ellison,

> Our new young Bishop you will treat with as you think most proper.
> An annual renewal might be right, but considering how soon the
> Colliery may be wrought out or given up, it may be a great doubt
> whether an Agreement for so high a fine during the life of so young
> a man would be a prudent thing with regard to our children, but I
> leave it to you to act entirely as you think proper.

'The Bishop agrees to renew your lease for the year ended
18th July last at the fine paid to Bishop Butler viz, £128',
wrote Nicholas Halhead, the steward, in August 1754, 'you
can send a London bill instead of cash if you wish, but need
not give yourself the trouble of procuring one, for his Lordship has lately laid out so much on his Castles and their
Furniture that I don't know that he will have any occasion
for remittances to London this year for his winter's subsistence. You need not doubt of my Lord's doing what
appears to him reasonable on future renewals as well as on
all other occasions.'

Bishop Trevor's reign at Durham lasted for nearly twenty
years. The most notable thing about him was his constancy
and affection for his patron, the Duke of Newcastle, which
continued unbroken until the latter's death. 'Your desires
will always have the force of commands with me', he assured
him.[1] His letters give an impression of an amiable and
business-like man whose main preoccupation was with
ecclesiastical patronage and politics, as indeed was expected
of a good eighteenth-century bishop.[2] It seems probable that
much of the furniture at Durham Castle dates from his time.
There was no marked increase in fines during his episcopate

---

[1] 'Nothing gives me such inward comfort', wrote Newcastle, 'as to find that when I am
deserted by some, from views, I suppose, of interest . . . and from whom I could least suspect
it from all sorts of Ties of Relation, Friendship and Connection, ever since they came into
the World; others, my Oldest and Best Friends redouble their attention and Goodness to
me.' Add. MSS. 32979, § 201. Sykes, op. cit. 179–80.

[2] In his very first letter from Durham, Trevor reported on the electoral prospects in the
north. Add. MSS. 32732, § 240.

though he greatly furthered the trend towards short-term leases.

Our Bishop is changing his leases for lives into years as fast as renewals of them are applied for [wrote Joseph Dixon to Ellison in 1756] at which great complaints are made, though to no purpose. In Bishop Chandler's time he never asked more for a new life but one year's value and for two lives he had four years' value. . . . I doubt as there is but one life in being they will expect a large fine and perhaps insist upon your acceptance of a lease for years, instead of lives.

Certain it is that by 1771 the great bulk of the episcopal leases at Durham were for terms of seven years.

Before turning to consider the steep increase in fines under bishops Egerton and Shute Barrington, we must first note the developments in the policy of the dean and chapter in respect of fines. We have already seen that capitular farming rentals remained stationary throughout the century.[1] Since 1680 the Ellisons had held the manor of Wardley, near Hebburn-on-Tyne, with Heworth mill and other small properties under lease from the dean and chapter.[2] Major Ellison's younger brother, Henry of Gateshead Park, looked after the estate while he was away in the army.

Upon looking over our Books [wrote William Pye, clerk to the chapter, in 1738] I find that seven years of your Brother's lease are expired 15th November last. I thought it proper to give you this intimation because the fines run high after 7 years: if a lease runs eight years, it is a year and a $\frac{1}{5}$th; if 9 a year and a half, by which you see how they rise after seven. I send this out of respect to your brother.

Accordingly, John Airey of Newcastle, the family attorney, was instructed to negotiate a renewal of the lease:

I attended the Chapter yesterday [he wrote]. Dr. Johnson, Dr. Sharp and Mr. Bland present. They asked £500 for the fine. I bid them the old fine and gave reasons. After a good deal of debate, I withdrew. . . . Again called in: the fine set at £440. I did all I could to have the old fine but they would go no lower.[3]

Now in the original lease to Robert Ellison in 1680 the

---

[1] *Supra*, 131.     [2] Register of Leases, § 157.     [3] Ellison MSS.

fine was fixed at £130, but was increased to £160 on the first septennial renewal in 1687, at which figure it remained, subject to small adjustments consequent upon irregular renewals, until 1731 when it jumped to £400.[1] The reserved yearly rent remained at £13. 9s. 4d. The sharp increase in the fine caused the new owner seriously to consider selling part of his 'patrimony'—a step to which he was reduced thirty years later.[2] Before the lease was due for renewal in 1752 Pye wrote again,

> At a meeting of the Chapter last Saturday they had come to a resolution not to renew or contract for the renewal of any lease under four years or above four years and under seven, but to renew at the end of four years and at the end of seven, unless upon cases of necessity.

And a year later, after an unsuccessful attempt by Ellison to reduce the fine:

> At the two last renewals when the Fine at each was set at £440, there might be as much reason to abate, for they deduct only the reserved rent and nothing for taxes or tithes. They said they would not recede from their last fine; so set the same for 7 years, to wit, £440.

Robert Swinburne, the steward at Hebburn, stated in 1753 that Dr. Chapman, one of the Durham prebendaries, was reported 'to be very intent on raising the Fines to more than a year's value for seven years, giving as his reason 'the high rates at which lessees sold their interest in the lands'.[3] 'In most estates in this neighbourhood the Fines have hitherto been so much under the real yearly value that the Purchaser buys both the ignorance and lenity of the Lessors', though he confessed that this did not apply to the dean and chapter of Durham who 'know the value'. 'Fines never go back, even if rents fall', he concluded.

It is clear, then, that the policy of the dean and chapter in this matter had proceeded *pari passu*, if it had not actually anticipated, that of the bishops. The result was reflected in greatly swollen 'dividends', though, thanks to the uneven

---

[1] Audit Books, *passim*, 'Contracts'.
[2] In 1765 he paid a fine of only £69. 8s. 8d. on the remainder.
[3] Ellison MSS.

incidence of renewals, these fluctuated from year to year whereas the allowance for residence remained unchanged at £100 per annum to the dean and £50 to each prebend.[1] The following tables, chosen more or less at random, give the net payments of 'dividends', exclusive of the residence allowance and the 'corps' of lands attached to each prebend.[2]

| 1687 | | 1766 | |
|---|---|---|---|
| The Dean | £78/12/4½ | The Dean | £562/8/1½ |
|  | [Gross £158/9/-][3] | Bishop of | |
| Dr. Graham | £87/2/1½ | Gloucester | £295/6/8½ |
| Sir George Wheler | £83/12/6½ | Dr. Markham | £264/7/6½ |
| Mr. Cave | £62/11/6½ | Dr. Murray | £278/7/5¾ |
| Dr. Mountagu | £90/11/5½ | Dr. Douglas | £305/14/7¾ |
| Dr. Adams | £76/1/5 | Dr. Moore | £282/18/11 |
| Mr. Knightley | £77/8/2 | Dr. Bland | £303/13/10¼ |
| Dr. Grey | £83/11/4½ | Mr. Spence | £279/7/9¼ |
| Dr. Bagshaw | £84/6/6 | Bishop of Oxford | £294/16/2½ |
| Dr. Brevint | £77/-/10 | Mr. Weston | £281/11/10¼ |
| Mr. Morton | £114/19/10[4] | Dr. Vane | £279/12/7¼ |
|  |  | Dr. Dickens | £282/5/7¾ |
|  |  | Dr. Burton | £288/17/2¼ |

In 1764 Bishop Trevor told the Duke of Newcastle that at Durham 'he had but one prebend of so little value as £350 per annum, and that is no small thing; all the rest are £500 per ann and upwards'.[5] No other profession could show an average increase of between three and four hundred per cent. between the Revolution and the accession of George III. By contrast the salaries of the great bulk of civil servants had

[1] Audit Books, *passim*.
[2] Each prebend at Durham had certain lands 'assigned . . . for the increase of their Residences' since the foundation statutes. *Durham Cathedral Statutes* (Surtees Soc.), cxliii. 121, 232–59.
[3] Dean Granville had unusually heavy deductions in this year; e.g. 'his rent to the Church', £106. 1s. 4d. In the following year he had 'noe dividend so that there is nothing out of which to deduct his Perditions'. Audit Book.
[4] There were no deductions in this case.
[5] Quoted by Sykes, op. cit. 182.

remained stationary.[1] Dr. Smith, treasurer to the chapter in 1679, wrote on the cover of the first Audit Book:

> A Caveat for ye Treasurer at his Perill.
> Write before you Pay.
> Receive before you Write.

Later treasurers were kept too busy to indulge in such moralizing.

From the Book of Temporal Acts, which contains a summary of Bishop Egerton's leases (1771–86) we can get a bird's-eye view of the situation.[2] Seven-year leases were now the rule.

### Fines on Renewal of Leases

| | Totals | Fine paid by Ellison for the Manor of Gateshead |
|---|---|---|
| 1771 | £2686/1/1 | £159 |
| 1772 | £6254/9/- | £222 |
| 1773 | £1901/10/11 | £248/8/- |
| 1774 | £3398/10/4 | £241/10/- |
| 1775 | £4243/4/- | £235/16/- |
| 1776 | £4208/1/7½ | £263/8/- |
| 1777 | £4102/9/6 | £274 |
| 1778 | £4004/1/10 | £283 |
| 1779 | £3025/16/11 | £264 |
| 1780 | £2104/12/1 | £249/8/4 |
| 1781 | £2827/18/2 | £249/8/4 |
| 1782 | £6166/1/4 | £288 |
| 1783 | £6142/4/9 | £267 |
| 1784 | £3115/13/- | £260 |
| 1785 | £3005/1/5 | £298/17/9 |
| 1786 | returns | £389/15/- |
| 1787 | incomplete | £434/9/9 |
| 1788 | | £470/14/- |

These tables tell their own tale, but worse was to come. The fines paid by Ellison for the manor of Gateshead to Bishop

---

[1] See my *Studies in Administration*, 218.

[2] The Bishop of Durham kindly placed the Episcopal Registers at Bishop Auckland at my disposal.

Shute Barrington were: 1791 £511. 8*s*. 6*d*., 1792 £499. 15*s*. 8*d*., 1793 £509. 2*s*. 2*d*. The method used for calculating the amount of the fine was explained by William Emm, the bishop's secretary.

Wm. Emm to Henry Ellison[1]

July 16. 1789.

. . . Desired to present the Bishop's compliments and to inform you that the fine for the renewal of your lease of Gateshead Manor is fixt as under: His Lordship places an implicit confidence in the account you have sent of the Rent and the fine is fixt in proportion to it but with the addition of one fourth (¼) which His Lordship has adopted the resolution of taking of all his tenants and therefore I must beg leave to add that no abatement will be made.

| | | | |
|---|---:|---:|---:|
| Rental 1787–88 with contingencies | £3465. | 15. | 2 |
| Deduct the reserved rent | £ 117. | 15. | 8 |
| Divide this sum by Number 7 | £3347. | 19. | 6 |
| | £ 478. | 5. | 7 |
| Add one fourth | £ 119. | 11. | 4 |
| Fine | £ 597. | 16. | 11 |
| Fees | £ 11. | 2. | 0 |
| Total | £ 608. | 18. | 11 |

The method of calculation has all the slickness of the modern income-tax. The lessee ventured a protest:

*Henry Ellison to Wm. Emm*

July 20. 1789.

I understand the rule adopted for setting the Fines is that his Lordship has determined to take one year and a ¼ Rent for the renewal of 7 years and, of course, one seventh of the annual rent and ¼ of that ⅐ for the renewal of one year which puts the tenant who renews every year not upon an equal footing with him who renews once in seven years, for calculating at simple interest only, his fine will at the end of seven years much exceed that of the other.

The Manor of Gateshead consists principally of a great Number of contingent articles, in particular of collieries which form the largest portion of its income and are of a very uncertain and precarious nature.

---

[1] Ellison MSS.

The colliery at Gateshead Park which can last but a few years unless the lessees undertake a new winning and go to a lower seam. . . . This estate, also, beside the ordinary expense of management requires a viewer, to whom a fixed salary is given, to inspect the workings of the Mines to see that they are properly conducted. . . .

A great advance in the fine took place at the accession of the present Bishop. For many years the lease has been annually renewed but the position is now much worse than that of newer lessees who renew only every seven years.

We know, for example, that for the twin manor of Whickham Lord Ravensworth paid a fine of only £1,500 every seven years.[1] Ellison proceeded to a detailed analysis of the rental pointing out that he had always given a faithful account of the 'profits arising' and that the 'contingencies' were a very uncertain quantity.

We need not take the story farther. In effect, with the 'ingenuous assistance' of the lessees, the bishops had hit upon a system of 'Pay as you Earn' while the standard rate could be increased at will. Clearly, before the end of the century, a notable recovery had occurred in their financial position largely, if not entirely, as a result of increased fines and shorter leases. Whether this was part of a general episcopal or landlord policy, common in varying degree to the whole country, it is too soon to say. As early as 1750 a writer in the *Gentleman's Magazine*, who subscribed himself 'a True Briton', stigmatized the increase in fines as a prime cause of the oppression of tenants and attributed it in turn to the stewards or estate agents.[2] Certainly where mining leases were common, as in Durham, the new policy brought a rich harvest. But it is clear that its success must be attributed in part to a new type of ecclesiastical official and to the principle of continuity of service. Richard Stonehewer and Dr. Sayer were already vastly different from Miles Stapleton, Bishop Cosin's secretary and factotum: Nicholas Halhead was steward of the Halmoot Court for nearly twenty years before Bishop Trevor appointed him principal

---

[1] Book of Temporal Acts.    [2] *Gentleman's Magazine*, xxi. 13.

registrar and rewarded him with the mastership of Greatham Hospital.[1] William Pye was chapter clerk for nearly as long. William Emm had acted as proxy in a vacant living as early as 1755 thirty years before he became secretary first to Bishop Thurlow and later to Shute Barrington.[2] To compare the impersonal and efficient service of these men with the unashamed carcase-pickings of a Gerard or a Stapleton a century earlier is to step into a different age. The contrast is as great as that between the reformed civil service and the corrupt revenue farmers of the Restoration period. Yet just as the 'oppressions' resulting from the shameless nepotism of the Caroline bishops led to an attack on Palatinate jurisdiction in 1689 so, in time, the new chastisement with scorpions raised up the 'Radical Jack' Lambtons of the nineteenth century.[3]

## II

Apart from losing control over the office of lord lieutenant which passed to the Crown in 1689—Bishop Crewe recovered control for a short time towards the end of Queen Anne's reign—and allowing the appointment of a bailiff at Gateshead to lapse and the conservatorship of the River Wear to go by default in 1717, the shell of Palatinate jurisdiction remained intact throughout the eighteenth century.[4] The bishop still appointed both the sheriff and the chairman of Quarter Sessions. For example, on his appointment in 1721, Bishop Talbot invited Sir Henry Liddell to fill the office of sheriff.[5] On the death of Bishop Chandler in July

[1] Book of Temporal Acts (1769), §§ 131–3.

[2] Bishop Trevor's Register, § 29, at Embleton vicarage. In 1799 Emm stated that the bishop's 'agent' was Richard Burn of Dean's Yard, Westminster. Add. MSS. 36901, § 178.

[3] 'At the beginning of the late Revolution', wrote Spearman, 'an attempt was made in Parliament to take away this County Palatine, but did not succeed.' *Enquiry*, 38. See my article, 'The Bishops & Reform', *E.H.R.* lvi. 459.

[4] Surtees, i. p. cxlvii. When the bishop ceased to be lord lieutenant he lost control over the appointment of the J.P.s; e.g. Cotesworth submitted lists to the Secretary of State of suitable (and unsuitable) candidates. Robert Delaval, gent., of Durham city had been appointed bailiff of Gateshead in 1681. Register of Leases, § 79.

[5] A nice gesture in view of his expensive lawsuit with the late bishop. 'They look upon the grant of under-sheriff to be void and absurd', wrote Colonel Liddell, 'and offer the said High Sheriff liberty of choosing his own under-sheriff.'

1750 a delicate situation arose. The Assizes were due to be held in August, but the sheriff's patent had lapsed on the death of the bishop. The two county members promptly pointed out the grave inconveniences of postponing for another year the Assizes which were then held only once a year in Durham, and urged the Crown to appoint a new sheriff *sede vacante*.[1] And this was done. In Trevor's day the bishop still presided in person at sittings of the Durham Court of Chancery as Bishop Crewe had regularly done, according to Spearman, until one day he remarked 'that *John Dee* and *Richard Roe* were very litigious persons and accordingly he summoned them to appear before him to be censured' and thus betrayed his woeful ignorance.[2] Bishop Egerton still appointed by letters-patent not only the sheriff but his own attorney- and solicitor-general, the auditor and the clerk of court, bailiffs and seneschalls, coroners and apparitors, constables and gaolers, masters of hospitals and of the schools on Palace Green, besides a score or more of gamekeepers and rangers in the *Alta Foresta* in Weardale, Howdenshire, and throughout the Palatinate.[3] Not that nepotism ceased, but nepotism which, in the main, did not touch the 'efficient offices' and was confined to those with salaries under £5 a year is comparatively innocuous.[4]

What of the spiritual side? How far do the Spiritual Acta Books for the half century from 1730 to 1786 reveal successive bishops faithfully discharging the standard duties of visitation, public ordination, and confirmation? Bishop

---

[1] There were precedents for this, e.g. the appointment of Sir Gilbert Gerard as sheriff and of Richard Neile as under-sheriff on the death of Bishop Cosin in 1672. Add. MSS. 35603, §§ 244–5. The county members, Bowes and Vane, pointed out that a year's delay in holding the Assizes 'must produce great misery to the prisoners of which there are at present great numbers crowded into a very narrow compass, great expense to the County which is obliged to maintain the criminals and a great danger of a contagious distemper by their long confinement in a disagreeable place'.

[2] *Enquiry*, 95–102. 'I shall be kept here with the Chancery sittings till the middle of this week', wrote Bishop Trevor in October 1759. Add. MSS. 32896, § 340.

[3] *Temporal Acts, passim.* N.B. Bedlingtonshire, Islandshire, and Norhamshire remained in the County Palatine until 1844. *Northumberland Documents*, xviii.

[4] The fees and salaries of these officials were now largely nominal, e.g. the auditor £20; the attorney-general £5.

Chandler held ten 'General' ordinations in the first ten years of his episcopate, but none apparently after 1741. All save one were at Durham. In his short episcopate Bishop Butler held one. Bishop Trevor held yearly general ordinations in his private chapel at Bishop Auckland throughout his eighteen-year episcopate as did Egerton his successor. These were invariably held about the third week in September before the bishop went south for the opening of parliament. In addition Bishop Trevor held five 'Private' or 'Special' ordinations and Bishop Egerton three, usually for single individuals; for instance, in 1780 Francis Henry Egerton, the bishop's son, aged twenty-four, was admitted priest within six weeks of being made deacon. It is interesting to note that the total number of priests ordained in the thirties and again two decades later was practically the same—an average of about five a year, not many considering the size of the diocese and the fact that a proportion were Scots who were not instituted to livings in the Palatinate. But whereas in the period 1731–41, the proportion of priests to deacons was more than four to one, in the fifties it was almost exactly equal. In eighteen years Bishop Trevor ordained eighty-two deacons and ninety-six priests and Bishop Egerton seventy-seven and ninety-nine respectively in thirteen years, which represents an appreciable increase. On three occasions, orders were received barring unsuitable candidates.[1] In 1748 Archbishop Hutton sent instructions not to ordain or institute Bernard Tournier, curate in the isle of Jersey, without first acquainting the Bishop of Winchester or the Primate. In 1759 the Archbishop of York sent notice not to ordain Edward Mountenay, William Tetlow, and Jonathan Nixon, and in the following year the

---

[1] 'I am much obliged to you', wrote Trevor when he was Bishop of St. Davids, 'and particularly for ye good advice you gave me in it which arrived very seasonably, while I was engaged in examining the candidates for Orders. I will not be so partial to my own sagacity, as to attempt assuring you, that no unworthy persons have passed thro' my hands into the ministry; I can only answer for my doing my utmost to prevent it, as far as the miserable circumstances of my poor diocese wou'd allow me.' *H.M.C. Eglinton*, 281–2. There is no evidence that he examined candidates at Durham.

bishop was instructed not to proceed with the ordination of one Williams without notifying the Archbishop of Canterbury. No reasons were given for the action taken though it is easy to understand the reason in Tournier's case. Were the other candidates unsatisfactory? The figures given above do not include candidates for whom 'Letters Dimissory' were granted to other bishops: we know, for example, that successive bishops of Carlisle regularly performed such service for Durham candidates in the first half of the century.[1]

Evidence on visitations and confirmations is scanty. Bishop Chandler held an 'Ordinary' visitation in 1736 and again in 1740: that of 1746 was held by Bishop Samson Benson 'who confirmed at Newcastle deanery but wav'd all the other parts'. Bishop Trevor held visitations every four years during his episcopate (1753–70) but unfortunately there is no indication of his practice on such occasions. His successor, Egerton, held his 'Primary' visitation in the summer of 1774, beginning at Morpeth on 12 July and proceeding to Berwick, Bamborough, Alnwick, Newcastle, Durham, Stockton, and Darlington and ending at Staindrop a month later, confirming young people in the afternoons of the same day or on the following day. But no evidence of numbers has survived. Four years later he followed almost exactly the same itinerary. In 1782 he issued a commission to the Bishop of Clonfert to visit the archdeaconry of Northumberland, Egerton himself doing the Durham archdeaconry. It was this Irish bishop who consecrated new burial-grounds at Berwick and Sunderland. In June 1776 the bishop himself 'at the Chapel Royal of St. James after morning service confirmed the Lady ——, daughter of the Earl and Countess of Gower and the two daughters of Admiral and Lady Mary Forbes'. In 1784, in failing health, he

---

[1] Between 1702 and 1718 Bishop Nicolson of Carlisle ordained 142 candidates, 25 of whom were Scots graduates and 19 were from the diocese of Durham. Bishop Waugh (1723–34) a total of 140, including eight from Durham. (Information, by kind permission of the author, from Anthony Armstrong's unpublished thesis on 'Episcopal Administration in the Diocese of Carlisle 1702–47'.) For Bishop Chandler's practice when he was at Lichfield, see Sykes, op. cit. 104, 112, 120. Bishop Nicolson's *Diaries*, Cumberland and Westmorland Arch. Soc. (N.S.), ii–iv.

granted a commission to Mr. George Harris, his 'Vicar-General and Principal Official', with power 'to admit and institute' during his lordship's absence 'all and singular clerks . . . and to license such as should be nominated, affixing the bishop's seal to all instruments'. Fortunately, on Bishop Chandler's visitations, there have survived the 'Presentments'. These include the usual items of the fabric needing repair, e.g. St. Margaret's, Durham, 'the chancel is so ruinous and out of repair that the Inhabitants who assemble at the Altar to receive the Holy Sacrament (which is administered monthly as well as at the great festivals of the year) and others who constantly sit in the Chancel to hear Divine Service are not only incommoded by pieces of the wall or plastering falling on their Seats and the Altar Table, but in rainy and wet weather are exposed to the danger of catching cold by the drops which fall in great abundance from the roof: and that those Inconveniences have been urged by persons who have not been constant Communicants as reasons why they have not been more frequent than they are'. The dean and chapter as impropriators who had leased out the tithes &c. were accordingly presented. At Haydon a bell was 'wanting', while at Embleton Dr. Tovey was presented in 1740 'for not having the vicarage house in repair and for not residing in the parish these eight years, only two times staying a short time each'. At St. Hild's, George Middleton Esq., Mr. John Cookson, and Richard Ridley Esq., were presented for refusing to pay Church sess; and Mr. Joseph Cookson 'for audaciously and profanely ordering the Church Bell to be rung for the death of one of his servants, which when the matter came to be known was for a Dog of his', an incident reminiscent of George Selwyn's famous story. At Whittingham James Hargrave Esq. of Shawden, John Walker, and Mrs. Catherine Proctor were presented for 'going to no place of Worship on the Lord's Day'; at Tweedmouth, William Atkinson 'for fishing on the Sabbath Day'; at Stamfordham Edward Wilkinson 'for working on the Lord's Day'; and Joseph Nicholson of Heddon 'for disorderly Behaviour in time of Divine Service'. Mary Patterson of Holy Island was presented 'for teaching school without licence' and the Rector of Kirkhaugh for keeping £30 of the School Charity 'which he will not allow the use of to a schoolmaster'. But the great bulk of cases presented were for moral offences—adultery, 'ante-nuptial' fornication, 'lying under a common fame of living in a Criminal conversation', &c. In the case of Katherine Key of the parish of Middleton St. George, 'the penance to be performed' was as follows:[1]

> She was to present herself in the parish church . . . on some Sunday before 21st April 1732 where being in her penetential habit viz<sup>t</sup>. Bareheaded, barefoot and bare legged, having a white sheet on and a Rodd in her hand, and standing upon some Forme or other high place so as the whole Congregation may see her, immediately after the Nicene Creed shall, with a distinct and audible voice, say after the Minister as follows vizt, 'Whereas I . . . (Good Neighbours) forgetting and neglecting my Duty towards Almighty God and the care I ought to have had of my own Soule, have committed ye Grievous and detestable sin of Fornication with John Arrasmith in the parish of Haughton to the great danger of my own soul and the Evil and pernitious Example of others, I am now heartily sorry for the same, desiring you and all other sober Christians offended thereby to bear witness to this my hearty Sorrow and Repentance and to pray with me and for me to Almighty God that he will pardon this and all other my sins and offences and so assist me with the Grace of His Holy Spirit that I may never commit the like hereafter, saying after me, 'Our Father which art in Heaven . . .'.

The rector and churchwarden duly certified that the said penance was performed on 12 March.

More important, the Acta Books reveal a parochial clergy mostly serving on a bare pittance of from £20 to £40 a year—the average is nearer £30 than £40—for whom Goldsmith's *Vicar of Wakefield* might have been specially written. The bulk had degrees—after 1720 there was a steady infiltration of Scots graduates—the rest were *literati*. They were effectively denied all hope of promotion to the

[1] Bowes MSS. 40748, § 61.

plum rectories which were held in plurality by the cathedral prebendaries, who took part in a sort of general post whenever any vacancy occurred in their own ranks. Yet I have found no instance of deprivation for moral depravity or other offences and only two cases of sequestration, consequent upon legal proceedings for the recovery of debts, in a period of over half a century.[1] Moreover, where, as at Brancepeth, there were disputes between an incumbent and his parishioners over increased demands for tithe or Easter offerings, these were occasioned by high-placed or well-connected clergy. For instance, the novel demands in the thirties of Mr. Wicket, Rector of Brancepeth—a rich living, reputed to be worth £400 a year[2]—for Easter 'reckonings' alienated all the substantial farmers at West Park, who appealed to their landlord for assistance.[3] Wicket was the bishop's ordinary, who, according to Spearman, was 'ordained priest and deacon in three days' time, though never admitted a member of any university . . . the flagrancy of that fact, of his life and conversation being matters only fit to come under consideration of a Convocation'.[4] At Bishop Chandler's visitation in 1740, James Wilkinson, the curate at Brancepeth, 'being called and producing his orders, My Lord Bishop inquiring for his nomination, who having nothing to show his Lordship monished M<sup>r</sup> Wekett ye Rector to give him some nomination. Whereupon M<sup>r</sup> Wekett instantly nominated him as his Curate and accepted and approved of by his Lordship.' In October 1760 there was another irregularity at Brancepeth. Thomas Goodfellow Shafto was appointed rector in succession to William Forster though he was only made deacon at a 'private' ordination on the 7th

---

[1] In 1762 a sequestration of the rectory of Whitfield was issued to John Heron, gent., and William Alexander, yeoman, 'for the levying of £30 debt and 50 ⁸/- costs which Robert Lowes recovered in the Court of Common Pleas at Westminster against John Verty, rector of Whitfield'. Likewise, in 1766, the vicarage of Alnham, Rev. Thomas Wrangham, was sequestered.  [2] Valued in the King's Book at £60. 10s. 5d.

[3] Ellison MSS. Wicket pointed out that he had taken the opinion of 'that great civilian, D<sup>r</sup> Strahan' and of Mr. Fazackerley and 'both concur that all ecclesiastical dues at Easter are payable . . . and cannot be included in any prescript rent'.

[4] *Enquiry*, 120.

of September of that year and ordained priest a fortnight later.[1] The explanation is that the patronage was vested in his brother, Robert Shafto of Whitworth, who was on the point of winning a notable parliamentary by-election for Durham county.

This affords a good illustration of the patronage system which had come to be largely controlled by the local gentry, though the bishop retained the nomination to some thirty-seven livings and six chapelries in the diocese, including the rich rectories of Stanhope, Sedgefield, Monkwearmouth, and Ryton, and the dean and chapter of nearly as many more. Thus, the Earl of Northumberland nominated to the livings of Elsdon and Alnham, the Delavals to Ford, Matthew Ridley to Cramlington, Lord Ravensworth to Lamesley and Tanfield, Rowland Burdon to Castle Eden, and the Tempests to St. Nicholas, Durham. The same church in Newcastle was in the gift of the Bishop of Carlisle, as were (and still are) the rectory of Rothbury, and the vicarages of Corbridge and Newburn. Gainsford was in the gift of Trinity College, Cambridge, in 1782; Benton in Northumberland of Balliol College, and Embleton and Ponteland of Merton College. The non-residence of Dr. Tovey at Embleton has already been noted while the appointment of Dr. Sainsbury to Ponteland in 1779 scarcely does the college credit. Four years later he obtained a dispensation from the bishop 'from reading the Common Prayer . . . until the impediment of his ill health should be removed'.[2] In 1768 the curate at Earsden was 'nominated by a majority in number and value of the proprietors of lands in the said parish . . . and of the voluntary contributors to the support of the curate there, the true and undoubted patrons'—an interesting case, presumably, of a new curacy. Patronage might change hands by agreement or it might be divided and patrons take their 'turns' in nominating. Thus, in 1757, Ann Jefferson nominated to the rectory

---

[1] Bishop Trevor's Register, § 58.
[2] Bishop Egerton's Register, § 139. He remained at Ponteland until his death in 1787. Foster, *Alumni Oxonienses*. For the value of these livings, see *Arch. Ael.* (N.S.), xvii, 244–62.

THOMAS HENRY, 1ST BARON RAVENSWORTH

of Elton 'for this turn, being one third right of patronage', and there were other instances. The monarch also enjoyed some ecclesiastical patronage in the diocese.[1] In 1760 George III nominated James Douglas, Vicar of Kelloe, to the rectory of Stainton-in-Strata, and in the following year George Smalridge to Bothal and Thomas Dockwray to the vicarage of Stamfordham: ten years later he appointed also to Bolam, Hart-cum-Hartlepool, and in 1771 to the rich rectory of Stanhope 'for this turn'. The same phrase was used when the king appointed Dr. Richard Kaye a prebendary at Durham in succession to Dr. Lowth, promoted to the bishopric of Oxford. In 1777 Dr. William Digby was presented by His Majesty 'in full right' to the deanery of Durham in succession to Dr. Dampier who had owed his appointment three years earlier to Lord North, his former pupil.[2] Similarly, in 1769, John Ross was presented to the twelfth stall vacant by the promotion of Edmund Law to the see of Carlisle, 'by His Majesty George III the true and undoubted patron for this turn by virtue of his prerogative Royal'.[3]

The following correspondence between Sir Henry Liddell, later first Baron Ravensworth, and his close friend Henry Ellison concerning the living at Whittingham reveals patronage at its best and is of special interest to *alumni* of Durham.

January 21. 1743/4. ('past ten')

Last night's post brought me the news of Mr. Nevison's death and as the living is the Parish of my residence I have taken some pains to secure it and do at least stand as good a chance as any competitor of doing so. As I hope to pass a good deal of my time there, I would covet an honest man and such a one as I could always be pleased with as a companion. Under these wishes I now stand, but who to pitch upon to secure 'em me, I know not. I beg your sentiments on this matter which to myself I look upon as one of moment. To live on the living is a claim I shall most certainly make. I thought of Dr. Baker as a

[1] Registers, *passim*.    [2] At Eton.
[3] Law's appointment to Carlisle was due to the collaboration of Bishop Trevor and the Duke of Newcastle. Sykes, loc. cit.

debt due to him but he dwells his thoughts on a sinecure and it is the proper rest for him.[1] Dear Harry, think well for me and let me have your answer by Monday seven night.

January 31. ('past 9')

I received your friendly letter yesterday and the objections to the two persons you have named are real ones and their being so have left me entirely at a loss for a proper person in case my solicitation to nominate should succeed. I should be absolutely averse to name a person but of Northumberland or Durham by birth or one who has so long resided in one of those Counties as to be looked on as a native. When I say I am an absolute stranger to the young Clergy of both, it is really so. Wolfal is an honest man, an excellent scholar but a low and too quiet creature.[2] I would have one not to bring reflection upon myself, one who would be quiet in his office but no so far as to render himself contemptible. I have been casting about the two countys and of my own knowledge cannot guess at one unless it be Thorpe of Chillingham. What I have seen of him makes me imagine him a civilized, cheerful, man. If you cannot think of a better, I should be glad if you by some means, quite privately, would find his character. I shall be unwilling if I carry the point, to loose the opportunity of obliging some one. By what you say of Mr. E[llison] of Whelpington, I fear he would scarcely justifye me naming him, even to the Parish and the character he would carry in the neighbourhood.[3] Mr. Swinburne is a man I should like, barring his determined way of thinking. One of my own principle is undoubtedly a thing to be coveted, as it avoids some shyness which costs trouble to set upon a right footing between people who may be much together and not upon an equal footing. You see, Dear Sir, what I want is a person of our own country, not above residing at a place distant from the busy amusing part of the world, nor one who shall set himself above those he will be to live with, and in principle a Whig. I have thought if Dr. Sharp[4] had a son in orders he would have been a proper person, but I think he has not a child of age to be in orders. He or Harry Wastell[5] are likely to know the deserving young men of

[1] Dr. James Baker, a mutual friend, formerly Liddell's private tutor at Cambridge. In 1749 Liddell, now Lord Ravensworth, tried to obtain for him a sinecure in Cleveland, formerly enjoyed by Dr. Hayter, a prebendary at York. 'It would give me real satisfaction to know that I had obtained it for him.' Add. MSS. 32719, § 259.

[2] William Wolfall was a lecturer at Berwick and curate at Tweedmouth and Ancroft. Bishop Chandler's Register.

[3] Nathaniel Ellison had been vicar at Kirkwhelpington since 1734. He was later appointed Vicar of Bolam.    [4] Prebendary of Durham.

[5] Rector of Simonburn 1723–71. Venn, loc. cit.

their own profession. What you are so good to do for me will be an entire secret. I waited on Lord Carlisle to know if he had heard from one or two he has wrote to me for. . . .

P.S. I expect next post I may tell you whether I am to carry this point or not and as it is uncertain, dont let it get abroad.

(P.P.S.) ('past 10') Since 9 o.c. I have had notice of the necessity to write to the Bishop and two Prebends of Carlisle with interest, I was till now a stranger to. I am fairly laid in, but whether shall succeed is very uncertain. Whoever has it, if I name, must hold no other living of which he is now possessed. I have warning of this and am glad it comes in time to prevent any one taking that ill.

March 8.

I have this day wrote to Mr. Thorp of Chillingham to know if he will accept the living of Whittingham, in case I at last do nominate, and quit the preferment he has. If he does not, I am at a loss who to name and must beg you will pitch upon a person for me if you know one better than Middleton or the parson who lives at Edlingham[1] this last I name only for the sake of naming as I never heard ill of him. . . . You will see it has been in my power to nominate, however it may end.

P.S. I wish you and Delaval could pitch on some one thing, least nothing for your purpose happens at Newcastle.[2] The persons you name I must know of what university they were and what degree they took. It is a good living and one would have a creditable person. . . . I have desired Mr. Thorpe's Resolution by the first post.

For some reason, not yet clear, Erasmus Head was appointed to Whittingham and Thomas Thorp remained at Chillingham until his death in 1767, when he was succeeded by his son Robert.[3] In 1763, and again in 1782, the bishop himself nominated to Whittingham 'for this turn by lapse of time', though Lord Ravensworth was still alive.[4] What matters is

---

[1] Michael Mitford was vicar there in 1746.

[2] Lord Ravensworth eventually obtained a sinecure appointment, joint customer in the port of Newcastle, for his friend Ellison.

[3] After 1747 Thomas Thorp was Vicar of Berwick as well as Chillingham. John Fell was appointed curate at the latter in 1751 at a salary of £25 per annum, plus surplice fees, although he was not formally licensed until 1754. Bishop Trevor's Register, § 13.

[4] In 1782 Dr. John Law resigned the living at Whittingham and Bishop Egerton appointed Dr. George Owen to it. Register, § 124. Lord Ravensworth had considerable influence at Cambridge. There is some truth in the Earl of Darlington's charge that he was 'a Schemer'. Add. MSS. 32726, § 252; 32958, § 196.

that the Thorps had caught the eye of the Liddells and possibly of others: in the second half of the century members of this family were appointed to rich livings at Houghton, Gateshead, and Ryton.[1] Archdeacon Charles Thorp, cofounder and first warden of Durham University, had two generations of outstanding clerics behind him.

In the same year that Sir Henry Liddell invited Thorp to accept the living of Whittingham, John Nelson of Birstall, a foreman mason who in the late seventeen-thirties had helped to build the new Treasury in Whitehall and another Yorkshireman, Thomas Beard, came to Durham as military conscripts *en route* for Sunderland.[2] They were the first Methodist lay preachers in the north. 'Of truth, in word mightier than they in arms', said John Wesley of them.[3] The fervour and seriousness of the new religious movement made a strong and abiding appeal to the Durham miners. The social and political consequences of the evangelical revival over the intervening two centuries are inestimable.

[1] Robert Thorp, formerly Vicar of Chillingham, was collated to the rectory of Gateshead in 1782 in succession to Dr. Richard Fawcett. Egerton Register, § 122. There is a memorial tablet to him there.

[2] Nelson, *Journal* (1820), 21–22, 156–7.

[3] Wesley, *Journal*, iii. 141.

## CHAPTER VIII

# Schools and Colleges

Give me leave my Lord to make one Observation
more and I have Don—and that is when you peruse
Admiral Pye's Letters you will please not to scruti-
nise too close either to the speling or to the Gram-
matical Part as I allow my Self to be no proficient
in either. I had the Mortification to be neglected in
my education, went to sea at 14 without any, and
a Man of War was my University.

(*Admiral Pye*, 1773)[1]

## I

THE preamble of Law No. 97 of the famous Crowley ironworks at Winlaton which dates from the early years of
the eighteenth century, reads as follows:[2] 'the raising and
continued supporting of a stock to relieve such of my workmen and their families as may be by sickness or other means
reduced to that poverty as not to be able to support themselves without some assistance, *the teaching of Youth* and
other matters of so great concern, are so incumbent upon us
that there is no avoiding of a General Contribution for the
same.' It proceeded to arrange for the appointment, and to prescribe the duties, of 'the Clerk for the Poor'. 'He is carefully to
teach and instruct the workmen's children and to be constantly
in his school', from 8 a.m. to 12 a.m. and from 1 p.m. to 4 p.m.
during the winter months and from 6 a.m. to 11 a.m. and from
1 p.m. to 5 p.m. in summer. 'He shall not upon any account
of Races, Cock fightings, Rope dancers or Stage Players
dismiss his scholars but constantly attend school'; 'he shall
not without the consent of the Governors give his scholars . . .
leave to play or absent himself for more than half an hour in
any one day in school hours; he shall carefully teach all his
scholars that are capable of learning the Catechism of the
Church of England . . .' and on Court days 'he shall, upon

---

[1] *Sandwich Papers*, i. 36.     [2] Add. MSS. 34555, § 97, headed 'Clerk for the Poor'.

demand, bring two or three lines of the writing of such of the workmen's children as are under his care to lay the same before the Governors that his conduct may be the better judged of', and in association with the works chaplain 'shall bring such scholars to be examined in public in the Catechism'. Finally, 'he is to take care to make his scholars shew due respect to their superiors and especially aged persons and to correct lying, swearing and such-like horrid crimes', setting a good example himself in these things since 'example availeth more than precept'. Here we have a characteristic conception of education in an age which saw the founding of hundreds of charity schools in what was probably the most remarkable educational renascence in this country since the Middle Ages.[1] In the present chapter, however, we shall not be concerned with that kind of education which in Crowley's view called for 'a General Contribution' and which for so long was intimately associated, as here, with pauperism, but rather with education as a self-imposed responsibility of parents.

Concern for the children's well-being reached its climax in the matter of their education. Chaytor and Cotesworth were agreed on that if on nothing else, though the latter having had little or no schooling himself, was disposed to attach the greater importance to it. 'I am not so much for Richmond school as formerly', wrote Lady Chaytor, 'being their is such guifts given to the master and usher, more than my purs will allow; it would trouble me to have my boys dispiest or neglected.' She proposed, therefore, to send them to 'Darnton' [Darlington] until such time as her husband could make arrangements at Westminster or Charterhouse but he soon found that it was difficult to get a place at the latter 'without great interest'. Cotesworth's two boys, aged fifteen and fourteen respectively, were transferred from the Royal Grammar School, Newcastle, to Sedbergh in the Easter term 1716. This move, I fancy, was determined by two con-

---

[1] Jones, *The Charity School Movement in the Eighteenth Century.* Cotesworth bequeathed £50 to the one at Gateshead.

siderations. First, his nephew from Egglesburn had been at
Sedbergh before going up to Cambridge in 1712; secondly,
Dr. Jurin, Cotesworth's cousin, until recently headmaster of
the Royal Grammar School at Newcastle, had lately resigned
that post to take up a medical career. It was rumoured that
he had not been too well appreciated by the authorities there;[1]
at least Cotesworth's friends, the Liddells, had a poor opinion
of the place and sent young Harry Liddell, the future baron,
to Hackney School. Hugh Moises, the great headmaster at
Newcastle, to whom Eldon paid tribute, came later.

Cotesworth himself conceived of education quite simply
as fitting his children for the stern business of life and he
would have agreed that, like war, it was too serious a matter
to hand over to pedagogic generals. Certainly he had no mistaken or exalted expectations, still less any thought of
abdicating or relinquishing final control and he himself
remained incomparably their greatest educator. He liked
to hear of his children's progress and was anxious that they
should become 'complete scholars', but he was much more
concerned that they should not be 'puzzled by over-much
study' and that they should not impair their health. To this
end he provided each of them when they went to Sedbergh
with 'a galloway' that they might take regular recreation.
For the rest, he seems to have conceived of 'grammar school
learning' as the first stage towards a career that he had
already mapped out for them—law for the elder and commerce for the younger son. 'There is great beauty and
harmony in exact reading', wrote this self-made man; 'you
know', he told William, the elder boy, 'that Bob was much

[1] 'Your Town was unworthy of so honest a man as Jurin', wrote Henry Liddell in January
1716. 'Posterity will have occasion to curse those who have had any hand in making him
uneasy in ye Post he was possessed of. But what other can be expected from such a sett of
governors and to be succeeded by such a wretch who is not worthy of wiping his shoes is no
less admirable. By this they seem resolved that the next generation shall continue in ye same
obscurity. Ignorance is the Mother of Devotion. Oh Blessed Mother Church, you have
named that Person that poysons all and yet I wish he can be outed.' Edmund Lodge, Jurin's
successor, continued as headmaster until 1733. Brand, i. 96. Tom and George Bowes were
transferred from Newcastle to Mr. Hiff's school in London in 1717 and when their elder
brother examined them he found them 'but backward in their learning'. Bowes MSS. 40747,
§ 150.

fallen off his reading at home'; he was therefore to get the usher, the second-master, at Sedbergh to instruct him privately in it as occasion offered. And when the elder boy sent some of his own poetry home, the father wrote: 'my knowledge of poetry was never much, but I believe you have done very well. I wish you do not labour too much in them and the rest of your learning.' For his own part he wanted his sons to be instructed in the four rules of arithmetic and he made no objection to their suggestion that they should begin to learn French which would be useful for their legal studies later, provided always that 'it did not hurry or oppress them': 'I would not have your health impaired by too much puzzle.' The staple subject in the curriculum at Sedbergh was, of course, the classics but Cotesworth made no comment upon it. We can leave the boys to speak for themselves in their weekly letters home.

Sedbergh.

April 7, 1716.

Honoured Father,

We arrived here on Wednesday night between 6 and 7 o'clock where we found Mr. Sutton waiting for us at Jacob Holme's, who received us very kindly. Mr. Rose was there when we lighted and having got into his cups he called for a Bottle of wine, three pennyworth of apples and three pennyworth of Ginger Bread to give us our welcome to Sedbergh.

Our Landlady is a very neat woman, and as far as we have tried, does very well by us. We have always 2 Dishes of meat to dinner and there are three sorts of Bread set upon the table, and we have liberty to choose of which we will. As for our breakfasts, we have butter and bread and cheese, and as much milk as we desire, and if we be hungry betwixt meals she bids us call for what we want. We have a little room entire to ourselves where we have shelves for our books, and pins for our cloths, and there's a room almost as large as the Hall[1] which we have liberty to walk in. Mr. Saunders [the Headmaster][2] seems to be a very civil man and calls every day to see us. We gave him everyone a Guinea

---

[1] i.e. at Gateshead Park.

[2] Samuel Saunders, headmaster from 1709–41, formerly Fellow of St. John's, Cambridge. Venn, *Alumni Cantab.* iii. 15.

and my Uncle (according to the custom of the School) gave the Usher half as much. There is one Mr. Holt, a young Gentleman taller than Neddie,[1] lodges here. He is on the second seat and seems to be a very well disposed young man; he's the only one that we have got acquaintance with yet.

My uncle has taken Mr. Cramphorn's field for a Guinea a year and he thinks that if we keep in the Gallaways til the middle, or latter end of May with a little few oats now and then, it may serve them. Mr. Sutton is to buy us a Gallaway when he can meet with one that pleases him.

Jack Bright[2] is not yet come. My Uncle will write you how much affraid Dr. Allinson[3] is of meeting with trouble from the Government.

Your Dutyful son,
William Cotesworth.

The next week's letter was written by the younger boy, Robert.

April 15.

. . . My Landlady does very well by us and is very civil as likewise is every Body else. Mr. Sanders is not at all severe, but on ye contrary very good humour'd. Mr. Sutton has not yet pickt upon a Gallaway for me but has 2 or 3 in view, the one of which is a Welsh one but hard to take when it is at grass.

My brother gives his duty to you and my Aunt, his love to Hannah and service to all friends. . . .

P.S. [by William] I have been forced to buy several Books since I came here which I never learned before. I desire that you would let Neddie buy me Madam Dacier's Homer, it's in either 2 octavo volumes or 5 twelves: it is a very good Book and will be a means to make me understand Homer perfectly. Mr. Sanders bought it very lately. Our seat is to-day making Latin verses upon one of our Scholars who is dead of the small pox; they are to be pinn'd upon the Pall.

The fear of getting the Itch[4] has quite cured me of handling things. Mr. Sanders takes a great deal of pains and teaches exactly after Mr. Jurin's method, so that I hope we'll make good improvement under him. We were not found at all deficient when he examin'd us. I hope this will find all friends well which concludes me in haste.

---

[1] Edward Mawson, Cotesworth's clerk.　　　[2] Of Badsworth.
[3] Vicar of Middleton-in-Teesdale: he was apparently suspected of Non-Juror sympathies.
[4] Dudley Ryder got the itch in Scotland in this same year. Diary, op. cit. 259.

April 21.

Hon'd. Father,

We are sorry to hear by Neddie's of the 13th inst that my Uncle's rather worse than better. We stil continue very easie here. Mr. Saunders is very kind to us and I hope we perform on our part. Bob is the best scholar in his seat and Mr. Saunders is pleas'd to give me a Character not much inferior to any in the School, whether I deserve it or not I cannot tell. However, I shall always endeavour to do what I can. We for the most part have the news at our Landlord's and when we have it not there we can read it for a Dish of Coffee at Jacob Holme's. I was at Firbank last Thursday. Mr. Sutton has not yet met with a Gallaway but he hopes to get one at Kendal Fair next Wednesday. We are both very well and desire that you'll give our dutys to my Aunt and Love to Hannah w^ch concludes me.

P.S. We have never yet got our Ginger Bread.

Saturday, April 28.

Hon'd. Father,

We received the unwelcome news of my Uncle's [Ramsay] death last Monday night and that which makes it ye more unacceptable to us is ye loss you have of a companion with whom you used to spend your vacant hours so agreeably. We took particular notice of the excellent admonition he gave us at parting which was 'Fear God, Honour your Father, Love your Relations and be Gracious', all which we hope by ye Grace of God to put in execution. He gave us 2 Jacobus's when we parted which, if you have no exception to it, we design to keep. Mr. Holme writes that you bid Tommie Richardson[1] get what money he wanted of us, if we don't change ye 2 Jacobus's we can let him have none for fear we run out ourselves. Our Ginger Bread is at last casten up. Mr. Sutton had it from Mrs. Farrington of Kendal that my Uncle had left you £1,000 per annum and had left my Cousin Suttons, but £1,000 amongst 'em. I forgot to tell you in my last that Mr. Hunter came to see us on Monday gone a seven-night. We stil like both our School and Lodgings very well. The watch is of no use at all to us; we have a great want of her. Mr. Sutton has not yet bought a Gallaway. He has seen one yt goes extraordinarily well and he believes is a very good one, but the man asks 4 Guineas and ½ for it and we dare not venture to give yt price.

---

[1] A relation of Mr. Stonehewer, the Bishop of Durham's steward, who was a friend of Cotesworth. Surtees, *History of Durham*, iv. 145.

We shall have time enough at Whitsuntide to go to Preston and Leverpool if you'll please to let us. . . .

P.S. Bob will write next week.

Saturday, May the 5th.

Hon'd. Father,

My Brother has writ so largely to you that I will not trouble you with a long one this week. We are about ten in our Latin class (which is the 4th) among which is one Pepploe, the parson of Preston's son, a very sober lad; but I can scarce give another in the seat the same character, except those we brought along with us.[1] We are but four in our Greek class (which is third) of which the man's son where you us'd to light when you came to Sedbergh is head. I read the same books I did when I was Mr. Lodge's schollar.[2]

I like my gallaway very well and I hope when you see it it will prove to your satisfaction.

Your Dutifull son,
Robert Cotesworth.

P.S. I want a new everyday coat.

[Enclosure from the Headmaster                May 1st, 1716.
     to Mr. Cotesworth]

Sir,

I can't omitt so good an opportunity of letting you know that your Sons are very well and very good, and heartily congratulate you upon so comfortable a prospect of yr well doing in ye world. I understand you desire they should visit some parts of Lancashire at Whitsuntide wch I shall not be against and will take care for a sober, carefull man to go along with them.

The Bearer (Mr. Taylor) is a Gentleman of very good merit and is so kind as to undertake ye gathering Subscriptions for Building a New School here. I am ashamed to ask any assistance from you but yet, if you can inform him of any that you know to have been Sedbergh Scholars, and are likely to be contributors, I daresay you will do it and thereby add to ye favours wch must always be gratefully acknowledged by

Your most obliged humble Servant
S. Saunders.

[1] i.e. Richardson and Bright.
[2] Edmund Lodge, who succeeded Dr. Jurin as headmaster of the Grammar School, Newcastle, in 1715. Brand, i. 96.

Sedbergh.

[To their Aunt, Mrs. Ramsay]. May 5, 1716.

Hon'd. Madam,

My Brother and I are very sensibly afflicted at ye Malancholy newes my father's brought us of ye death of my Dear Uncle, by which you are deprived of ye kindest husband and we of one of ye most valuable Friends; but we will always (as it is our Duty) bear a gratefull remembrance of him and will, as we are bound by maney Ties, pray for your Health and prosperity, and remember with gratitude ye maney Favours which you were pleased to heap upon us and on all occations that offer give due proofs of it.[1]

That your immoderate greife for ye Death of so dear a Husband, may not impair your Health, which will be a second great affliction to us will be ye Hearty prayers of

Hon'd. Madam,

Your most obedient and much obliged nephews

Wm. Cotesworth
Robt. Cotesworth

Saturday, May 12.

Hon'd. Father,

We received yours for which we thank you. We design to set forward for Lancashire on Tuesday next, Mr. Saunders has taken a great deal of pains in providing a man to goe with us. He has at last pitched upon Mr. Baker, Master's Brother, who is very well acquainted with ye country and is a very sober young man. Tom Richardson will not go into Lancashire with us; I do not know his reason for it. I wish he may not fall into bad Company. Jack Bright is very well and sticks close to his Book. Mr. Saunders heard that you design'd to be over here this Whitsuntide. I believe we would be all very glad to see you. If ye subscriptions towards the building of the new School do not answer our Master will be a considerable loser, they are forced to fetch their Freestone above 10 mile.

P.S. Wednesday was my Birthday.[2]

Saturday Night, May 19.

Mr. Taylor got home last Saturday night, I believe ye Subscriptions have answered pretty well. Mr. Saunders took ours very kindly

---

[1] Cotesworth, senior, had sent a draft letter for the occasion.

[2] He was born in 1700 and christened on 20 May. Robert, the younger boy, was born in August 1702. St. Mary's Parish Register, Gateshead.

and bid us return you his thanks. We set forward for Lancashire last Tuesday morning and we have got safe home again ys night. We went to Liverpool which is three score mile; I shall without fail send you an account of our expences next week. I would have done it now but it is pretty late and I am almost tired with my Journey, so I hope you'll excuse me. I cannot omit ye extraordinary Civilities we had shewn us at Preston by Parson Peploe, ye Vicar. We carried him a letter from his son. He gave us a glass of wine and set a Nephew of his about ye Town with us who gave us an excellent Description of the Battle.[1] When we went home to our Lodgings at night he sent his nephew to invite us to Dinner, and accordingly we went. Our dinner was a Salmon and a Pudding, a Quarter of Lamb and Rasp Cream, and a glass of wine. We were never so much made on at any place in our Lives. We do not know how we shall be able to make ye least return. I believe there is not a Priest within an hundred mile round better affected to ye Government than he. He has 2 sermons publish'd that he preached before ye Judges. I fancy a letter from you as an acknowledgement of his Favour would oblige him. If you'll please to send it to me I'll get it forwarded.

We will give you a full account of all that we saw in our Journey next week. Jack Pearson[2] is gone from Lancaster to Liverpool in order to be ship'd for Carolina; we could not be admitted to see him. Tom Richardson could not be persuaded to goe with us but he's gone to Penrith with some of ye Town's People without Mr. Saunders' full consent. We received our Money in due time. We design'd to ride in our Coloured Cloths before you writ. We are pretty well after so long a Journey. Pray present our Loves to my Sisters. I did not know yt Bettie was come home. My arms ake very sore so I hope you'll excuse ye writing. J.B.[3] is pretty well but a little tired. He presents his service to you. We are in great hopes of seeing you at Sedbergh ys summer.

P.S. Mr. Saunders continues his civilities to us. He came to see us ye night before we went away where he gave us a charge to behave ourselves modestly where e're we came and to be sure to take care we did not ride too fast. We hear nothing yet of Dacier's Homers.

The father had also sent some final instructions about the Lancashire journey. 'Be sure you ride no waters in the least hazard: make the man always go first. Especially be sure

---

[1] i.e. the Fifteen.   [2] A local young man who had joined the Jacobites. *Infra.*
[3] Bright.

you make not too great journeys. Be careful you lye every night in dry and clean sheets and feed your horses prudently. Want nothing that is necessary, consider every one you give trouble to in a reasonable way. Leave no reproach behind you of being extravagant and simple disposers and scatterers of money, nor of being sordid. Your aunt would have you ride in your coloured cloaths and I am of this same mind, so keep your mourning fresh.'

[From Robert]. Saturday, May 26.

According to my Brother's promise in his last we would have sent you an account of our expences but Anthony Bindless (the man that went along with us) being abroad we cou'd not get to pay him so we were willing to omit all til next week, till we cou'd pay him, that we might not come on with after reckonings.

Fearing you shou'd give me a reprimand for not telling you what Towns we saw and how I like them I send you the following account of our Journey: on Tuesday morning the 15th of this instant May, between 5 and 6 of the clock we set out from this place and got to Lancaster about 12 (which is 20 miles)[1] and an acquaintance of Jack Bright's shew'd us the town; but I don't at all fancy the place. About 4 in the afternoon we set out of Lancaster and got to Garstang about 6 (10 mile from Lancaster): I like not that place neither. About 7 next morning we set out of Garstang and got to Preston at 10 (ten miles from Garstang) but Preston being a place where much was to be seen and it proving an ill afternoon we went no further that day and I fancy that [town] before any we went through. On Thursday about 6 in the morning we set out of Preston to Liverpool (20 as long miles as ever I rid)[2] and got there at 12. Mr. Sanders writ to a Quaker in Liverpool about some business and at the same time he desired him to show us the town, wch he did, and we thanked him; we staid all night at Liverpool and on ye next morning (which was Friday) we set out thence and got to Garstang that night and laid there, and on Saturday morning we came from Garstang to Sedbergh.

All the rebells were gone from Lancaster Castle to Liverpool to be transported and Jack Pearson among the rest, but when I came there the Serjeant that kept guard told me no body was suffered to go and see any of the rebels; the Souldier that went along with me to ask the Serjeant to go and see Jack Pearson told me that he was very generous

---

[1] Actually 26 miles. The boys frequently underestimated the distances.    [2] Thirty miles.

to him, for he never let him want either for drink or money which I wonder one of his circumstances shou'd do. His Sister is in town but is not admitted to see him.

The rebels as they went through Liverpool to be transported cried, 'Never fear but we'll come together again and appear for Jemmy'. We saw a great many going to the change to be bound to trades in the plantations and were very lusty fellows.

I want a new everyday coat very soar. I desire therefore you would hasten a new one as fast as you can. . . .

On the receipt of this letter the father replied: 'I am afraid you have too nice a taist for Country towns and villages. The hurry you put yourselves to is contrary to my mind and order. I fancy the transient view you took gave you not time to see the beauty of those retired country places.' And then this rebuke for the elder boy! 'Your brother's usual shyness shuffles off all difficulties off his own shoulders and lays the burthen upon my willing and undesigning Bobby.' William was duly shaken and made amends a week later.

June 2nd.

Hon'd. Father,

We hope this will find you safe arrived from Egglesburne. Wee were in great expectation that you wou'd have cheated us as you used to do and surprized us here, but since your affaire did not allow you we are very well Content. We have not yet got Arthur Bindless paid nor know when we shall and we being at present held a little busie, we desire that you wou'd not expect our Account til it come—which will be as soon as we can conveniently. We'l be sure to send it by Ned at latest. Bob gave you an account of ye Journey last week so that I have very little to say about it. We saw ye greatest misery at Lancaster that ever we saw before. All [the rebels] yt ever could go in cartes or Ride on horse back they carryed to ship off at Leverpoole, ye rest wch were about 34 (most of 'em Scotchmen) lie in a kind of a Dark hole underground and are so weak that they cannot help one another. Some of them are spotted with ye fever. We saw one of them lying dead wrapt in his Plad wch is sold to buy them a Coffin with. There is not one Roman Catholick left in Lancaster. We past by Squire Carris's seat about a mile before we came to Lancaster. Ye old Gentleman dyed in prison: one of his sons made his escape and joyned Marr and it's said his other son was executed. His was a mighty pretty seat. There was Gallow-sayes and heads put up at Every Towne we came at. There were about 12 gentlemen that kept Coaches at Preston before ye Rebellion, about six of 'em are fled nobody knowes where to and there is not one Roman Catholick left at Preston, tho' ye Towne swarmed with them before. We see a great many fine Scotts all our Journey thro' which belonged to ye Rebells. Preston is not so much damaged as to ye outward appearance of the Houses as one might have reasonably expected. We saw a great number of ye Gentlemen Rebells at Liverpool. They have money in abundance and are not at all daunted and are drunck every night. We saw my Lord Mullinex, who is prisoner at large in Liverpool,—by all that I can learne my Lord Derwent[water] was straingly mislead in ye Rebellion. He was exerciseing his men upon a Marsh when he heard the King's forces were just upon 'em. He seemed very joyfull, put off his hatt and Shouted they are all for us. He immediately put spurrs to his horse, comanded his men into ye Towne and Rid to meet 'em. He met them with their swords drawne a little before they came to Ribbald Bridge which is a short mile out of Towne in a great Consternation and Cryed 'we are undone, they are against us'. He commanded in ye Church yard and was observed to be pretty active ye whole action through till he submitted. The Maids of Generall Foster's Lodgings will take their oathes on't that he was in Bedd with a sack possett in the hottest time of ye action. The Highlanders were very fond of fighting and wou'd faine have sallied out of the Towne but ye valient Generall Foster swore he wou'd stick ye first man that offered it, whether he wou'd have had the courage to have done so or not, I know not. If they had got so farr as Leverpool I was very Credibly informed a great many hundred more wou'd have joyned 'em. This is the Cheife thing of what we saw—a Discription of ye battle unless you know the Towne wou'd be needless. I am glad to hear my Aunt Hannah got safe to Unthank—we thank you for your care about Homer. I writ to Alderman Bowes ye first opportunity I had. Bobb's Gallaway is an Excellent good one, it did not give one Trip in ye six score miles. J. Bright presents his service to you. I am very easy in my Greek Authors as I am in everything else. Mr. Saunders is very carefull and kind to us all; he presents his service to you. I writ to my Uncle as also to my sister Bette to make up my former Neglect. Bobb's well and gives his duty to you and service to all that askes for him as does

Your obedient son,
William Cotesworth.

The father was highly pleased with this effort: 'It was writ with judgement in an easie style', he commented. 'Mr. Baker carried it to the Mayor [of Newcastle] and Mr. Ellison would needs carry it to Hebburn; the original went last post to Mr. Liddell who it is likely will read it to my L$^d$ Chancellor. You had need to be circumspect for you see how I expose you for talking of your father's cheating you.' The letter was eventually circulated in London. Mr. Liddell's comment was doubly flattering; 'it is wrote with so much good judgement and observation that one may readily guess at whose feet he had bin bred. In short, I shew'd it to several of our friends who were so taken with it that they seem'd to question my veracity in affirming that it was wrote and penned by a North Country Schoolboy not above fourteen years of age.'

On the following week the boys had a different event to relate.

Saturday Night, June 9.

Hon'd. Father,

We are just returned from Kendall where we have been confirm'd by Dr. Gastrel, Bishop of Chester. Mr. Saunders made us thoroughly understand what we were going to do before we went. . . . You are afraid we hurried ourselves too much in our Lancashire journey, but we saw all we could see and it proving a wett week we were glad to get home again. I fancy I answer'd most of Bob's deficiencies before I received yours. Bob perhaps left out some things that I might have something to say too of the Journey. As for Ribbald Bridge there was no action at it. We saw it. Liverpool is a town of great Trade very finely built and increasing every day: there are three new streets a building in it. The greatest shock that ye King's Forces received was from the Rebels lying under a Garden Wall: about 20 fell at one shott. We gave ye Quaker that Shew'd us the Town a bottle of wine. Fothergill forgot the watch at Kirby but we will receive it on Monday. We have received Homers, which please very well. We are with our Loves to my Sister. . . .

June 16th, 1716.

We received the watch last Monday, which goes eight minutes too slow every day, but my Brother is for getting her figure encreased and then he thinks she'll goe well enough. . .

July 6.

Hon'd. Father,

    . . . Mr. Saunders has now begun our Seat in making English Verse now and then, so that I shall want some Books of Poetry to learn me the handsome Turns and Flights that are necessary in that kind of Exercise; I have made enquiry and find that Dryden's Fables, Mr. Steel's Collection, and the Works of the Famous Tom Brown are the newest. State Poems by The greatest Wits of the Age, are the best, but they are so dear that I am affraid I must not meddle with 'em. If I could get a List of my Uncle Ramsey's Books there are some useful ones perhaps among them that would save us buying. If You'll please to employ Mr. Fothergill in the buying of 'em he understands them best. He desir'd that I would send to him for any book I wanted. We desire that you would send us Money the first opportunity. We are both very well and easy and want nothing but Good Company, but as we have our Gallaways we make the better shift.

July 14.

    We have received the 10 Guineas, for which we thank you. Our Account amounted to more than my Aunt expected in a place she us'd to despise so, but as there was not one Farthing unnecessarily spent I know it will be excused. Mr. Saunders has just left me. He has seen several of my Books which he approves very well of. We are the best pleas'd with our Change[1] that ever was. Mr. Saunders says he'll lend me Mr. Pope's Homer which is a favour he shews to few. He approves very well of my reading French and has order'd me the books I here enclose a note of for Mr. Button. We ride as often as we conveniently can. I hope Mr. Saunders does not think we make an ill use of our Gallaways. Mrs. Cramphorn thanks you for the sugar which is rather too good. Mr. Sutton takes as much care of us as you could do were you here yourself. We send the old watch in the Box the new one came in. Mr. Saunders has set my new one right. Everybody's very civil to us. We are both well and desire to be remembr'd to all Friends wch concludes me.

The father had sent a stone of 'the best 8ᵈ souger to present to your landlady that she may make Bob Large puddings'.

---

[1] Of school.

July 28.

I have received the Books which please all very well, but the State Poems which are so badly bound and have been so much used that they'll scarce bide handling. Mr. Button sets them down £1 and I am informed that they cost but so much at the first hand. Paradise Lost which he sets down the full price for is a Second handed Book though not very much abus'd. I return it, having had one before. I have informed Mr. Saunders of the dearness of Dacier's Horace, he says it is not to be had in fewer volumes nor cheaper than the price Neddie talks of, but its very necessary for me if I learn French. He desires that I may have Terence and Telemachus with all convenient speed. We have got all our Hay very well in. Jackie Bright is very well. We were never better nor easier in all respects. Mr. Saunders has begun me in the French Grammar.

It is surprising to find that there was no summer holiday: the letters continued throughout August, though in attenuated form.

August 5.

We have received little these two weeks past, so have little to write. Mr. Saunders has begun me in my French Gramar. I learn it at no certain time but any hour yt I am at leisure. The Watch has never gone a minuit wrong since Mr. Saunders encreased her Figure, wch is about a month since. We are very well and easy in all respects.

August 12.

We have received Neddie's with the Hood and Apron for Mrs. Sutton, which we will give her the first opportunity. We received the ten Guineas you sent us last in due time. We have got our Night Gowns made. We got one of Wm. Burton and the other of Mr. Rhonsone of Kendal. Mine wch was bought of Mr. Rhonsone was the cheaper. We are both very well.

[To Mr. Edward Mawson at Mr. Cotesworth's          August 12.
        Shop in Gateshead.]
Neddie,
    We have received yours and will send the book that wants binding next week. You must desire Mr. Button to give us two or three Poems into the bargain of the Books we have got of late. I would have the Rape of the Lock for one and Young's Poem on the Last Day if you

can get 'em. We have a great want of our Account. I would have you to endeavour to get me it.

August 20.

Hon'd. Father,

We have received yours with the box and the paper of Poems. I had all the Poems that Mr. Button charged except the Petticoat which I keep in my own hand, the other two I have sold for the same price yt Mr. Button charged them at. We will send the Account next week. We are sorry to hear of yours and my Aunt's Indisposition. There are a great many loose people stragling about these parts, nobody knows their business but they are well mounted and well armed. We are very easie and well.

August [26?]

We have received yours which was very acceptable. We are very glad to hear that Mr. Russell is like to make so good a man. Mr. Bright is very glad to hear of his grandfather's success at York.[1] I am sorry yt I am forced to run the hazard of disobliging him by accusing him of eating Trash; his late sickness was occasioned by three pints of Black Currins, he has been very sufficiently cautioned against Fruit and I believe he eats little or none at present. He lay four hours in most violent Fits, there were six to hold him and they all prov'd too weak. His teeth were several times set and Mr. Saunders was out of all hopes of his recovery. He is now very well. . . . We commonly ride twice a week. We are still very easy and never better in our Lives.

P.S. I am very easy in my French.

September 9.

. . . As to the Gentlemen, about 3 weeks agoe 4 of 'em came through this Town very well mounted with swords by their sides, but had but very ordinary Cloths, no Body knew what they were or where they came from, they did not light in town and I have enquir'd of several but cannot learn where they did. There has none been since. Sergeant Cuthbert[2] came through yesterday from Lancaster Assizes in his way home, he sent for us and Tommy Richardson. I went, but Bob had got a little cold which made his eyes run so he stay'd at home. He gave us a glass of wine and forced a shilling upon me and promis'd to call and acquaint you that we were well. We enclose my Aunt the measures of

---

[1] Sir Henry Liddell's suit with the Bishop of Durham.
[2] John Cuthbert, Recorder of Newcastle 1708–24. Brand, ii. 216.

our Necks and Right Hand Wrists, tho' we have more shirts at present than we will wear out as long as we shall have Occasion to stay at Sedbergh. We have got all the books we sent for except Madam Dacier's French Terence which I fancy Mr. Button has forgot. I have a great want of a Latin Bible. I believe there is one amongst my Uncle's books. Bob is very well again.

P.S. The Tape is the measure of our Necks and the paper of our Wrists.

September 16.

. . . Bob has made a considerable progress in Horace and has begun Themes and Verses which he does very well for a Beginner. His Seat gets a whole Greek chapter to construe and decline every morning so that I fancy he's before Bob Sutton in everything. Our Riding Coats are both grown bare and over little so that we have a very great want of new ones—if my Aunt thinks fit we would have 'em after the long fashion for I believe they'll best suit Sedbergh air and Christmas Travellers. We are much oblig'd to my Sister for her kindness but if we make her abate Luxury we hope it will be a benefit to herself as well as us. Pray is Hannah come home or will she stay till we see her at Unthank?[1] We are sorry to hear of Ald[erman] White's illness.

P.S. I believe all our Seat goes to the College at the beginning of the Spring and some at Christmas. I fancy I may go conveniently about Shrove Tide which is ye cocking time.

[? September 23.]

. . . I should be very glad to have a Latin Bible; we translate Job into Latin verse every Saturday so that I have a great want of it. Bob's was only a Snotty cold, he was very well again the next day.

P.S. Two of Mr. Craister's sons of Chester came here last week, they are lodged with us.

October 6.

We received Neddie's dated ye 28th of the last Month with a Latin Bible and our wide Coats which fit pretty well all but to the length: if they had been—inches longer we could have dispens'd with them. We send enclosed both our accounts. We would be glad if Ned could spare the money to have it by the return of the Carrier that we may pay Mrs. Cramphorn.

---

[1] Near Haltwhistle, the seat of 'Uncle Coatsforth'.

Sunday, October 21

... I am sorry that Bob has acquitted himself so ill in his last to you but I will be bound for his better performance by the next Carrier. I send enclosed a copy of an Epistle that I have translated out of Horace, which, with several other such like pieces serve to divert me at my leisure hours. Mr. Saunders never read it so that I hope you will not expose it too much.

I parted with my Companion (who was as much diverted with this kind of exercise as myself) last week. He is since gone to Oxford. His name was Noble. We have together gone through most of a Coppy book. We were in hopes to have seen Hannah at Unthank next Christmas. . . . Mr. Sutton's Daughter has been here most of this week upon an invitation of my Landlady's.

In his letter of 17 October the father had written: 'I am not perfectly satisfied of your letter being very correct English. I hope for a better performance from you the next opportunity for I had not sent you to Sedbergh but for your improvement wch my dim sight cannot discern at this distance any other ways than by your letters.' But the younger boy knew how to turn the tables.

October 28.

Hon'd. Father,

I received yours of the 17th of this instant, wherein I find you are most justly displeas'd at the scantiness of the paper and the mean stile of my letter, for wch I hope to make amends by my future diligence, but being favoured with more of yours I shall be more exact in observing both the stile and the method. . . .

P.S. My Brother received the 5 guineas and having paid my Landlady £4 for our board, find that the rest of our Gallaways' winter provision comes to more than is left, so we will be obliged to you if you'll order Ned to send us more money.

November 3.

. . . The longness of our accounts shows a downright simplicity and a Paternal Honesty; however for the Future we shall put several little expences in one article. As to the Writing Master he's only a Kendal man that comes over a Month every summer so yt we have no opportunity of learning Arithmetick. Some Lumps yt rise in Bob's neck was

the reason of his taking Physick, but he's now very well again. I believe
he meddles not with Fruit at all. We are sorry yt you should suffer
by the complaint of our wide Coats.

I have not an opportunity to follow my French so closely as it
requires, however tho' I get the less, yet I hope it will make it easier
to me when I come to read it at Cambridge. The Seat yt I am in is the
first in the School and has been so ever since Easter. Two or three have
gone out of it above a year since to Cambridge, one of which got a
Scholarship, so yt I find by those that stay yt I might have passed
tolerably well with. Here, however, since I have had the Fortune to
light of so good a Master I hope my time so far is not mispent. As to
the leaving off my School-Authors at College I hope I shall be very
well qualified to do yt by Christmas for I have already read through
most of Latin Virgil, and with moderate study I shall goe through
Horace before Christmas. Terence I have at my finger Ends, so that
after I have finished Horace and Virgil I shall have got all that I can
at Sedbergh. Very few of our Class expect to come after Xmas; however they all goe at the beginning of the spring at the latest. The longer
I stay after Xmas I will be so much the more behind hand in the profession yt I am like to get my living by. My Companion's parents live
at Penrith. He was examined by a Fellow of Queen's College in
Oxford. The Fellow said yt he had lost his time for he might have
passed very well last Easter. I was generally reckoned his equal. I hope
I have fully answered this Article.

We go to bed constantly at 9 and rise at 6; as for our Diversion, we
take it any Afternoon. We both thrive very well and have never had
anything like the Itch. Bob has grown the best yt ever was known in
so little a time. I am affraid if he goes on the House will never hold him.
I am affraid we must not trouble the Usher with his reading for he's
held very throng at present so yt he has seldom a leisure hour to himself.
I am in hopes that he is much improved. Mr. Saunders gives him a
mighty character for a good Scholar. I believe the Peak would be
very acceptable, tho' Miss does not wear 'em at present, yet she designs
it next spring. As to the Gold, Mr. Saunders is so very careful of us that
it cannot be mispent. We are both as well and easy as we can wish to
be. We are very sorry to hear that my Aunt's eyes are so ill. . . . We
are very well served as to our Diet. I hope Bob continues perfectly well
disposed and may very safely be trusted with himself at Sedbergh after
my departure to Cambridge. I am sure that he makes a very considerable progress in his Learning. . .

We have schemed our Unthank Journey and we hope to the best Advantage. It's 17 mile betwixt here and Penrith to wch place we could hire a man. Now if we could hit of P. Mawson's day he might carry us to Brampton where we should be very glad to meet a man of my Uncle's if he could spare one for a day's time. We are in great hopes (if your health will allow it) to see you at Unthank.

But that plan had to be abandoned.

November 17.

. . . We are very well pleased with the Prospect of seeing Newcastle again at Christmas. We desire you to inform us by the next Carrier what Cloths you would have us bring home. We have a spare box that we could send our black Suits in by the carrier. And we think our brown cloths would be as suitable to ride in. We shall put up all Books and Linnen before we leave Sedbergh so yt if we do not return they may send 'em to us without any trouble, but these things we refer to my Aunt. We break up on the 6th of Xber, which falls on a Thursday, so that if we can meet my Uncle at Brough that day betwixt 10 and 11 o'clock we can reach Egglesburne yt night, rest there Friday and so be with you on Saturday. I shall not fail writing to my Uncle, but lest my Letter should miscarry I hope Neddie will inform him by Dickie Dowson. We are both very well and shall be very glad to find all Friends so at our arrival.

November 25.

. . . My Uncle Sutton when he came through here gave all our Boarders dinner at his Host House. We are both very well and are preparing everything for a Newcastle Journey. We hope to bring you the next letter ourselves.

Unfortunately no more Sedbergh letters appear to have survived. It is probable that the elder boy left at Christmas 1716; when next we hear of him he was settled at Trinity College, Cambridge.[1] Early in 1718 the younger brother was in London at Mr. Wright's, a writing master 'at the Hand and Pen in St. Mary Axe, near Leadenhall Street', having then a business career in mind; he began to learn 'High German' and Spanish. By that time, boys from the northern counties had begun to attend famous schools in

---

[1] Admitted May 1717. Venn, *Alumni Cantab.* i. 401.

the south. 'Jacky' Clavering was at Eton in 1714–15—the inclusive cost was stated to be £43. 11*s*. 6*d*. per annum.[1] Two of Cotesworth's grandchildren, the Ellisons, were there from 1745 to 1753 and two Durham Whartons later in the century, while Mr. Carr of Cocken's eldest boy went to school at Fulham with Master Stanley of Alderley. At the beginning of the century, the school at Hackney held pride of place.[2] Henry Ellison, and his cousin Charles Sanderson, the London lawyer, had been pupils there. In 1724 they were commissioned by Colonel Liddell to make inquiries about it with a view to placing his nephew, the young baronet, 'to finish him in his school learning'.[3] 'You'll see what youth of fashion are there and make what observations you can.' The decision was unanimous. 'All agree Hackney must be the place' and lodgings were promptly found near the school for the boy and his tutor. Twenty years later when Henry Ellison, junior, was designed for Eton, his uncle, Major Cuthbert Ellison, made the preliminary arrangements with the 'Dame', Mrs. Mary Young, widow of a former master.[4] 'If the young gentleman shifts but twice a week, which is the allowance unless paid for extraordinary, 8 or 9 shirts will be sufficient; if he changes three times a week, he should have a dozen.' For the present she could offer only 'a half bed', and added that a payment 'extraordinary' was usual if a boy had a room to himself.

I can't say at present who will be his bedfellow, but I assure you it shall be one who is healthy. As there are some things to be bought at Master's first coming [she continued] I shall take the liberty to give you now a list of them viz., a silver porringer and cup and spoon, a knife and fork, a pair of sheets and pillow bears, a dozen of napkins, 'do' of towels, half a dozen plates, a chamber pot, bason and candlestick.

'We sometimes have money in lein of the above things',

[1] *Eton College Register (1698–1753)* (ed. R. A. Austen-Leigh), xxiv. 'We infer that from £20 to £30 was the annual charge made by a Dame for board', though sons of peers paid more.
[2] Mr. Newcome, headmaster. Philip Yorke, eldest son of Lord Chancellor Hardwicke, and Dudley Ryder, another lawyer, went there. *Diary of Dudley Ryder*, 66, 180.
[3] He had formerly been at a school at 'Sennocks' (Sevenoaks).
[4] *Eton Register*, xxviii. Mrs. Young lived at the Manor House until 1775.

she added, 'but the things would at present be much more agreable to me, my stock of them being pretty much exhausted.' It was the middle of the War of the Austrian Succession. Eton already had a school doctor in attendance. We have seen how he handled a case of what he called a 'bastard pleurasy'.[1] The reports of Mr. R. Purt, young Ellison's 'tutor' or housemaster, at Eton have survived. 'He is very well and proceeds very regularly and diligently in his learning', the first reads. 'He is very far from being deficient either in apprehension or memory and is as much inclined to industry, attention and application as any child of his age can be.' Two years later he wrote enthusiastically that the boy was 'not inferior to any with whom I am concerned in capacity and far superior to most in Diligence and Application'—an admirably terse and candid report. Mr. Ellison paid an entrance fee of £12. 6s. 0d. and the half-yearly bills came to just over £26. The boy had his own tea-kettle and cups but the father ordered him 'to drink tea only once a week' as it was not good for his health. Shortly afterwards Mr. Purt left Eton 'that he might give up his time wholly to the Duke of Bridgewater'.[2]

The local grammar schools in County Durham had a fair reputation and were still attended by the sons of the neighbouring gentry.[3] Young Henry Ellison was at Houghton before going to Eton; his cousin Ralph Carr and Sir John Gresham were at Durham in the fifties under Mr. Dongworth. The headmaster of Houghton, the Rev. T. Griffith, described Ellison on leaving as 'one of the flowers of the school, a favourite both of himself and of Mr. Munton', the usher. His last half-year's bill amounted to only £7. 19s. 11d., made up as follows, board £6, learning 1 guinea, writing master 3s. a quarter, 2s. 6d. 'order money', 2s. barber, 1s. for shoe-blacking (besides numerous items, '8d for repairs'),

---

[1] *Supra*, 101.    [2] Ellison MSS.

[3] At Morpeth Grammar School in 1717 it was stated that 'only three boys in the school could make any exercise and those made it for all the rest for so much per week or quarter'. The headmaster, Mr. Salkeld (a Jacobite), was said to be 'ignorant beyond belief'. Cotesworth MSS.

8*d*. for exercise books, and 3*d*. for 'school-sweeping'. Clearly, it was not the question of cost which explains the decline of the local grammar schools. In 1748 Ellison's brother-in-law, Mr. Carr of Whitworth, sent his younger son, Ralphy, 'to a very private school at Craike to wear off the Newcastle tone which he learned at Houghton', and at the same time his elder brother was fixed up at Heath Academy. Later he inquired about the cost at Eton but decided to send the younger boy to Durham, only to change his mind again later.

> You will be surprised to hear that instead of sending my son Ralphy from hence to Eton, I have let him go back with my nephew to Durham [the father wrote in 1754]. As to the point of learning I think he can be nowhere so well as under Mr. Dongworth. I was only afraid of his getting a taste for company and dress by too frequent attending the Assembly and the Concerts in Durham, but upon a little conversation with him, [i.e. Mr. Dongworth] he in a great measure dissipated our fears and he is so much of a man and so good a scholar that I thought it too late to remove him to another school and at the upper end of Eton School he would be intitled to as much liberty as he can have at Durham where I now shall continue him til the time of his going to Cambridge, from whence I have had a letter from your son which shews me that the discipline and lectures at Clare Hall are still kept up as they were in my time and there I shall most probably send him next Year. Sir John Gresham, I fancy, will leave Durham before Whitsuntide.

A day later, Mr. Carr had changed his mind again: 'I think Ralphy too young to be trusted to the management of himself there [at Durham]. I am come to a sudden resolution of sending him for a year and a half to Eton School where he will be under much greater restraint than at Durham which may teach him to submit the more readily to the strict discipline of Clare Hall when I send him to Cambridge.'

Nor was the education of girls neglected. Cotesworth's two daughters were sent to school in London—indeed, he claimed to have spent more on their education 'than many high personages'. Hannah Ellison, in turn, sent her own daughter to a boarding-school at Chelsea and Mr. Carr sent his youngest daughter 'Peg' 'to a boarding school at Chester'. 'Young girls must be allowed to be taught their graces', Sir William Chaytor wrote in 1700, 'but for old wives and foolish widdows to turn hobby horses, I would have bells hung at their ears.' 'Music and dancing seem to me not to deserve much time or expense, they are little better than amusements at best and at matrimony they are generally superseded', wrote one, Gilbert Michell, apropos of the education of Miss Saville, a future Lady Scarborough.[1] Cotesworth bluntly declared that his intention in spending so much on his daughters' education was 'to bring them home marriageable'.

Unfortunately, little is known of the technical schools which existed in the north at this time. In the seventeen-thirties the scientist, Thomas Wright of Durham, taught mathematics and navigation to seamen in Sunderland during the winter months when shipping was practically discontinued.[2] The conditions laid down by Dr. Theophilus Pickering, a Durham prebendary who founded the Free School at Gateshead in 1701, were that the master should teach all the children of the parish the Latin and Greek tongues, to write and cast up accounts, 'and also the Art of Navigation or Plaine Sailing'.[3] Were these practical subjects, though remaining nominally in the curriculum, in fact crowded out by the classical cuckoo? And were the schools too closely geared to the universities for these subjects to thrive? We cannot say.

## II

One of the most remarkable educational phenomena of the closing years of the century was the rise of the fashionable 'prep' school. In the Easter term 1789, two Ellison boys from Gateshead were sent to one at Bradenham, near High

---

[1] Benham, *Records of the Lumleys*, 217. In 1710 A. Barnes of Newcastle went to London to arrange for his daughter's education. 'A publick school I know he would avoid', wrote his friend, Henry Liddell.

[2] Wright, 'Journal' in *Annals of Science* (1951), 1–24.    [3] Brand, i. 669–71.

Wycombe, at so early an age—the eldest was under nine—
that the master, Rev. Thomas Lloyd, felt considerable concern about the long journey home by coach for their first
Christmas vacation. Mrs. Lloyd took the precaution of packing some salve for the journey but they got chilblains badly
none the less. When they returned to school it was found that
they had a rash 'the same as our little brother had'. Mr.
Norris, the school doctor, 'calls it the blisters, not the
chicken pox and says that the chicken pox, the watry jags,
the Blisters and swine Pox are all the same Disorder under
different names'. 'Nobody has caught the chicken pox from
us but Mr. Lloyd's little girl', they wrote cheerfully. When
the father suggested that his sons be inoculated, Mr. Lloyd
hesitated on account of their tender years and only consented
under pressure. 'If you are resolved upon inoculation at so
early an age, we heartily wish you success.' Nor was that all;
on one occasion the younger boy, 'Cuddy', aged six, had
violent toothache and since applications of hot flannel failed
to cure he went 'to a very good dentist at Wycombe' and had
two of the offenders out. 'I bore the operation very courage-
ously and made not the least noise', he wrote bravely. 'I am
very glad they are out Papa for they teased me much.' After
four terms at the school, the father animadverted on the boys'
accent—apparently the north country tendency to raise the
voice on the last syllable had not been eradicated. The headmaster replied:

It was impossible their manner of Reading should have escaped you;
it has been long a subject of conversation here, sometimes of mirth, at
other times we have treated it very seriously particularly to Master
Ellison. He can inform you that he has hardly ever said a lesson or
read an English book to me without my talking a great deal to him
about it. I have only observed that he generally spake the last syllable
in a sentence nearly a third above the last but one. I have made him
repeat the concluding syllables after me and have sunk my voice which
he exactly imitated and therefore (I) doubt not but we shall acquire a
proper cadence in time.

We can begin to see what genteel parents were about in

sending their children to schools so far away. 'Being in London, I hope, will correct their language', wrote Admiral Collingwood of his daughters' schooling. Society was becoming more sophisticated. Besides, Mr. Lloyd knew his job. On the subject of Latin, he wrote:

> I do not expect boys to take the order of construction at first by intuition and therefore I give it them, but as soon as I think they are able to go at all alone, I wish them to exercise their powers. [He expected that] pretty soon they will begin to turn English into Latin and that regularly every evening. If contrary to ancient usage you would wish it should be done oftener, I have not a single objection and will exercise them in it twice a day. As far as my observations and acquaintance extends in public schools (and I have a little) their Recommendations do not depend much upon prose Latin, chiefly, as I have always found, upon Latin verses.

Thus early were the 'prep' schools geared to the classical mill of the public schools and universities.

Normally there were only six lessons a day at Bradenham, the rest of the time being given over to games, the school garden, or visits in company with parents or friends to places of historic interest in the vicinity. 'I can play at cricket and trap and Cuddy also', wrote the elder boy in his first term. 'Bradenham Fair will be soon and my companions say it is a very pretty one and there will be a great deal of fine cricket playing.' Six months later the boys' aunt wrote that 'the dowager Lady Ravensworth talks of giving them a sight of Eton at the time the Boys are likely to be in the Playing Fields'. In April 1790 the headmaster himself wrote that he had taken 'a very pleasant commodious house in Bradenham Green, a very pretty spot, within fifty yards of the Church and where the young gentlemen may qualify themselves for Eton in the manly game of cricket'. It was this generation which later fought at Waterloo. 'We are all going to have a nice garden made in the Cherry Walk and Cuddy and I have got a rake, Mr. Lloyd sent to Wycombe for them.' 'You cannot think, Papa, how pretty this fine weather makes our garden look and what a number of flowers we have in it', they wrote at the beginning of March 1790. But the boys' minds were still much on horses, and at Bradenham Fair they bought a toy one for 6*d.* and 'a whip which cost but a penny'. Besides sightseeing visits to Windsor and Eton they saw Sir Samuel Dashwood's famous house at High Wycombe. Some time later they asked if they might have dancing lessons from a man who 'comes to Bradenham twice a week to attend the Ladies' Boarding School'; but this was an extra. In Michaelmas term, 1790, they were joined by another boy from Newcastle, Master Peareth, whom they quickly reported to be as 'gay and happy as any of us'. That parents were prepared to send such young children so far away from home and to pay such heavy school fees may well cause surprise. The composition fee at Bradenham in 1790 was £60 a year, Mr. Lloyd having found that the device of an inclusive fee was preferable to charging for each single item as board, tuition, postage of letters, tips to servants, &c.

## III

It would be true to say that more importance was attached to schools than to universities in the eighteenth century. 'We must not think of the university', wrote Sir William Chaytor in 1701, when discussing his sons' education,[1] 'unless they will study divinity and except Tom could get to Trinity Hall' (from Charterhouse). He added that Sir John Saville 'will scarce send his eldest son to the University for fear of debauching him'. Dr. G. M. Trevelyan has shown that student numbers at Trinity College reached their lowest ebb in the first half of the century and he reminds us that for the most part the notable advances in knowledge in that age took place outside what Dr. Johnson called 'academic bowers'. This was the age when a professor at Oxford

---

[1] Chaytor MSS. W. Blakiston Bowes was at Trinity College, Cambridge, 1710–13. Several of his college letters and some of those of his tutor Nicholas Claget have survived. He took his own footman with him to whom he paid £5 and allowed a livery every year—'he can shave and take care of my wigs'—but he soon disgraced himself by attacking his master with a poker in a drunken bout.

wished 'to emancipate himself from the slavery of pupils'.[1] The contemporary attitude to universities is further reflected in a letter from Lord Ravensworth to his close friend Henry Ellison of Gateshead. They were discussing the next stage in the career of Henry Ellison II—later the father of the Bradenham boys. He had been six years at Eton and 'his time of life will soon call for some remove'. 'A University might be made the properest step after school', wrote Ravensworth,[2] 'and in one we have lately heard of many new Regulations, but at the same time of various irregularities; some think it a necessary part of education taken with its faults, others are absolutely adverse to it.' After due inquiry the decision in this case was favourable; the young man went up to Clare Hall 'where I believe the method which was established there by my old worthy tutor, Dr. Laughton, is still pursued', wrote the boy's uncle, Mr. Carr.[3] 'I have often heard Mr. Courtail greatly commended', he added. Fortunately we have the reports of the master, the Rev. John Courtail, on Ellison's progress.

May 26. 1752. He seems to be a youth of good parts and abilities, of a sweet temper and a sober and studious disposition. He has been perfectly regular and conformable to College Rules, nor does he seem fond of contracting too large an acquaintance, which is the bane of most young men in this place. A hopeful pupil [he concluded], as I make no doubt but he will pass his time here much to his own credit and the satisfaction of his friends.

Three years later after notice had been given of the intention to leave college at the end of term, the master reported again:

[1] Wooll, *Biographical Memoirs of S. Warton*, 305. Compare the attitude of Henry Vane, a fellow of Trinity College, Cambridge. 'Setting aside all considerations of Professions, as well as that of the pleasure which generally attends a studious life, I think one must look upon a man as a very great criminal who entirely neglects the pursuit of knowledge, for ye Mind should have nourishment as well as ye Body and Knowledge should be reckoned amongst the Necessarys of Life.'

[2] As Sir Henry Liddell he entered Peterhouse in November 1725 and took his master's degree four years later. Venn, *Alumni Cantab.*, s.n. Later in life he exerted considerable influence in elections at Cambridge. Add. MSS. 32726, § 252; 32958, § 196, *passim*.

[3] Henry Thomas Carr was admitted to Clare in 1716. Venn, op. cit. 295. For Richard Laughton's great reputation see Winstanley, *Unreformed Cambridge*, 188, 193.

Behaviour pretty even and uniform. He has most applied himself to the Classics in which he has acquired a good and critical taste. He has also gone through the elements of Geometry and Algebra. . . . I was in hopes he would have applied himself to Philosophical Learning, at least to so much of it as is generally taught in this place. But he has been greatly deficient in this respect (possibly) thinking it would be of no use to him or from imagining it would break in upon his other and more favourite studies.

The master agreed, however, that if only one subject was to be pursued 'he had made choice of the most useful and the best'. 'He had been regular and sober, nor have I any reason to suspect him addicted to any vice. He is, I believe, pretty fond of tennis and other exercises, but I never heard that he had any inclination for Gameing. He seems to be prudent and frugal in his expenses and always appears sensible and manly in his behaviour.' Evidently, undergraduates were still treated rather like schoolboys. In his last term the bills amounted to £21. 7s. 3¼d.—it was arranged that he pay them himself 'as it will teach him economy'—made up as follows, buttery bill 9 guineas, 'cash' (i.e. pocket-money) 6 guineas, tuition £3, bedmaker 14s. 6d., sizar 10s., coals 1s. 6d. This figure should be compared with the fees charged at Bradenham and with the estimated cost of a student at the Middle Temple or with the premium of £600, plus £30 stamp duty, demanded by a London banker for an apprentice in 1755. The father was evidently very well satisfied for he made the college a present of plate.

Undoubtedly, one of the causes tending to discredit the universities earlier in the century was that they were hot-beds of High Church and Tory principles. 'They are bred up there in the most narrow, confined, ungenerous principles in the world and go out from thence possessed with the notion that religion and good sense is to be found nowhere but among their own party or sect', wrote Dudley Ryder of Oxford in 1715, adding, 'that the Whig gentry and nobility are afraid of sending their sons there and begin to take them from thence and send them to foreign parts, particularly to

Holland, for education'.[1] This is clear, too, from the correspondence of Cotesworth's nephew who was at Peterhouse from 1712 to 1716.[2] Mr. Saunders, the headmaster of Sedbergh, wrote in June 1712.

Sir,

Your son being just setting forward to see you, I ought not to omitt so good an opportunity of doing him that justice which will at the same time encrease your satisfaction and make him a more welcome guest to you. His behaviour, ever since he came under my care, has been such as I cou'd wish. He has all along shewn himself a youth of strict sobriety, modesty and diligence and his Improvements are such as (I doubt not) render him capable of being admitted in ye University with credit. I wou'd advise your sending him to St. John's in Cambridge, it being a College, where he may have the best opportunitys of making considerable advancements in Learning of any I know and where it may be in my power to do him some kindness and shew how ready and glad I shall be to encourage and reward so good behaviour as his, even after he has left me. I design to visit Cambridge myself this Whitsuntide and if I knew you was resolved [on] St. John's, I daresay I cou'd procure some considerable help towards his maintenance there before he goes. If you don't send him this month before ye commencement it will be full as well for him to stay till November; and if you continue him till then under my care, I'll endeavour it shall be for his advantage.

P.S. I ought here to do justice to his late Master who had taken care to ground him very well.

By the end of the month the boy was at Cambridge. He wrote from Peterhouse,

Dear Uncle,

I got well to Cambridge on Friday last where after having refreshed myself a little I went to Mr. Allen who took care to see me with my Tutor, but it being about 4 in the afternoon, my tutor told us it was so late that the Master of the College would scarce take the trouble to examin me then, so I was not admitted till Saturday, being examined by the Master, my tutor and two Deacons. I find the hiring of beds very dear in this place, I cannot have one under 6s/- a quarter which will soon run up the price of a little bed; wherefore I have writ by this post

---

[1]  *Diary of Dudley Ryder*, 74.    [2]  Cotesworth MSS. Venn, *Alumni Cantab.* i. 401.

into the country to have one against this quarter's end. As to my diet, I think I can live for £7 or £8 per annum, then there will be £3/10/- per ann for tuition and a Chamber and £2 to a washer and bed maker, besides many other smaller matters, but I hope the first quarter will be ye worst. . . .

The question of fees can scarcely have been a decisive factor in a university education. This young man's bill for his last term before graduating was made up as follows: 'To present Quarter £4/10/-; to ye College £3/10/-; to ye Lecturer £1/2/6; to ye Proctor £2/2/6; to treat ye Junior Fellows 10ˢ/-; to ye Cook and Butler's Men 2ˢ/-.' 'All these are required to be cleared before we can sit for a degree', he wrote. There were further items, £5 for a gown and 10s. for a hood. The next quarter's bill was as follows: 'Bursar £1/14/8¼; Cook £2/-/4; Coals 9ˢ/-; Butler 6ˢ/-; Laundress 9ˢ/-; Bedmaker 5ˢ/-; Shoemaker 11ˢ/-; Tuition £1/-/-; Pocket Money 13ˢ/-; Sizars 6ˢ/-½ᵈ; Chamber 10ˢ/-; Millener bands 9ˢ/-', a total of £8. 13s. 0¾d. 'I do not much fear but that I shall at Midsummer be Scholar-Butler wch will in some measure ease you of the now burthen', he told his uncle who was paying for his education. He was eventually awarded a scholarship worth 3 guineas a quarter, though he explained that items for salt, pepper, fire, &c., 'about 13ˢ/- by the Quarter', were deducted from it.

Meanwhile Uncle Cotesworth had written to inquire about other matters.

St. Peter's College.

April 15. 1715.

Dear Uncle,

I have since my last to you, as far as I cou'd conveniently, informed myself what influence the Bishop of Ely has in this University. I find he has the disposal of one fellowship in St. John's and one fellowship with ye Mastership of Jesus; who now holds those fellowships I am yet to learn.[1]

I need not tell you our master, Dr. Richardson, is made Chaplain

---

[1] Winstanley, op. cit. 168, 283–4.

to the King, nor what party he holds to, tho' he has always been a professed, yet a moderate party-man.

I shall shortly, I hope, see Cousin W^m[1] at Cambridge. If, as I presume, he is designed for law, Trinity Hall is the most proper place. That Hall may, as it was supposed when I was admitted, be so stocked as not to admitt of one more; but whether such a thing ever happened in Cambridge since it was a University, I leave others to determine. As for Logick, 'tis almost banished the University and but rarely, except in the Studies and heads of the old fellows, to be met with. . . .

[The same.]
July 12. 1715.

Though I have not, as I expected, had the satisfaction to see Cosin W^m a member of this university before the commencement, yet I hope he is not detained because as some perhaps vainly fear the lawn sleeves are growing obsolete and out of fashion. If he designs to take a degree I shall not expect him before next Spring; if not, 'tis all one what time he comes.

Whether blind zeal, generally destructive to its admirers, has not precipitated some gentlemen as well in this as other universities to actions of wch they may, tho' too late, repent, is, I think not to be doubted.

On the pretender's birthday, some too warmly zealous gownsmen of this University met at a tavern, illuminated ye house, drank ye health of K. J[ames] 3 and gave money to ye mob to do ye same, but being apprehended by the Vice-Chancellor in action have suffered condign punishment, one Batchellour being expelled, one more, with two Sophisters rusticated for one year. We have lived in quiet, I will not say content, since.

I have sent you my Quarter's bill of March 25 1715 and should, if my tutor had been in college have sent midsummer's, but fearing lest by waiting his return I might miss of an opportunity of having money returned by our Cook who is about to pay for his coal at Lynn, I desire you wou'd send me a bill to clear the two last Q^rs, wch will make due to my tutor about £7: the caution (£6) lays dead in his hand.

A year later there was more trouble.

It would be strange, every day affording fresh matter for speculation, should Cambridge, ye learned body, act no part on the publick stage

---

[1] The Sedbergh schoolboy.

to the advancement of its honour or the improvement of society: but how much it has contributed to either let it's last week's behaviour speak.

It being proposed by the Vice-Chancellor to address ye King upon ye quelling of the rebellion, the Sen^r Regent, such is his extravagant power,[1] did, without producing his reasons, put a stop to that proceeding and having as it may be supposed, without reason, rejected cannot, by reason, be prevailed with to let pass the address. . . .

[2 June] On Monday and Tuesday night last the Mob led on by blind unbridled zeal, a distemper not more epidemical or destructive in former than the present times, run very high, Wigg and Tory exercising their furie upon each other, the windows and meeting-house; but this brutish proved no long lived satisfaction; the names of severall scholars engaged in these disturbances being taken and carried to the Vice Chancellour, who with the heads of the University has spent two days in examining these busie gentlemen: this being the 3^rd [day] will, I suppose, put an end both to their tryal and stay in this University.

In December 1716 he wrote 'there have been lately six scholars expelled this University for a year for drinking downfall to B[isho]pps, P[reben]ds and D[ea]ns and damnation to those [that] wou'd not defend Oliver; whether ye punishment be not too easie for such an offence is not for me to determine'. Clearly, at Cambridge, Puritanism and Non-Jurism could not lie down together.

Meanwhile, our north country undergraduate had been suspected, indeed accused, of 'favouring the Pretender's cause'. The occasion was his supposed reflection on the Vice-Chancellor and the Bishop of Ely. In a letter of 6 September he had written:

The Bishop of Ely designing, I suppose, to make all the Fellows and Scholars in Cambridge and the neighbouring Clergy, if there's any occasion for 't, converts, has published his Charge lately given here at the Visitation, which being a political composition, knowing Newcastle tho' not delivered as perhaps 'twas agreed into the hands of the Rebells, still labouring under the too epidemical distemper, State-ruining

---

[1] Winstanley, op. cit. 22, 24.

discontent, I wou'd willingly send, if I cou'd tell what way to be administered by way of purgation.

He had little difficulty in rebutting the charge though in the process it appeared he was not one of the master's favourites. Albeit, he gave his uncle an assurance that he was 'well affected to and satisfied of King George's right': 'I think any one who doubts of, and I am persuaded none ever yet was satisfied of, the P[retend]er's right may very safely adhere to K[ing] G[eorge].'

After graduating, and until he had finally decided on a career, he stayed up at college, resolved 'to get acquainted with some old Moralizer and for that end singled out Plutarch, a companion neither unpleasant nor unprofitable'; he also proposed to learn French 'not because this language is in vogue among the Beau Monde, or from any satisfaction I can propose to myself by reading a language so effeminate, so small spun as scarce to bear anything that's grand . . . but because there are some things sent into the world not to be despised because of their French dress; with these I wou'd not willingly be unacquainted'. Meanwhile, he awaited his uncle's instructions whether he should take orders and surveyed his chances of a fellowship.

The expectation of a fellowship in our College where there are only 14 foundation Fellows and no one after he is M.A. can sit for one there. All from the time they commence A.B. till M.A. have a propriety, except their country be full, to sit. Every fellow being free to vote as he pleased 'tis not very easy to secure their interest, except by a general acquaintance with ym.

In the end he took orders: unhappily nothing is known of his subsequent career.[1]

Clearly then, as now, the popularity or otherwise of the universities was closely bound up with the question of careers. Since law and medicine were largely catered for elsewhere and entry into the civil service was a lottery, dependent largely upon patronage, and since, as yet, the

---

[1] Venn, op. cit. s.n. He was ordained deacon in London in March 1718.

universities taught little science, there were few avenues besides the Church and ancillary schoolmastering that a university could offer in the way of a career. And even in these the openings were strictly limited thanks to the working of patronage and the fact that the clergy were notoriously 'good lives'. The tradition had not yet been established that a university career was socially the correct thing for a gentleman.

William Cotesworth was made of better stuff than his Peterhouse cousin. At the end of his first year at Cambridge he wrote to his brother Robert who had just gone to a commercial school in London.

I would recommend to you the reading of as much English as you can possibly find time for without neglecting French and those studies wch you live in London purposely to learn and not only to observe the thread of the story or any other matter contained in what you read, but read carefully and slowly and endeavour to understand the beauty of the Language and tho' you may not judge very nicely at first, yet you may depend upon it that by constant observing and practice, you will in time understand it truly. The writing of Letters would be a very proper exercise for your leisure hours and if you have nobody to write to, invent someone . . . ; then you must labour that subject very diligently for a man that would compose nicely must reject many more thoughts than he inserts. Never be weary nor think you compose too slowly but if you write one letter in the week, if you do it nicely, think you have done enough. To read all the letters that you can lay your hands upon is the best way to stock you with subjects and to read letters wch you meet with by chance wou'd please me better than any Collection that is printed for in print there is always something aim'd at wch often runs the author into a necessity of being bombast, whereas between Friends a letter is commonly free and unconfined wch is certainly the most acceptable way of writing. It is often a great ornament to conclude a letter handsomely, wch particular, I fancy, is best learnt by a printed collection.

I hope that you'll have been in a dancing master's hand before I see you at Cambridge. If your vacation at school happens when my Father and Aunt leave London, I fancy that will be a convenient time. Pray present my love to my sister and my little lass[1] who I hope by this

---

[1] His sister Hannah?

time understands the Spinnet better than her master. I shall expect to hear from you very frequently and you may depend upon a constant correspondence on my side for you may believe me, Dear Brother, to hear of your welfare and improvement is very much the wish of

Your most affectionate brother.

We can 'readily guess at whose feet he had bin bred'. 'I desire and heartily wish', he wrote on another occasion, 'that we could settle a good correspondence for we are all young and at a great distance from our Friends so that we need all the comfort and advice we can give one another at this distance.' He had some advice, too, about clothes—the younger boy had objected to wearing his north country 'wide-coat' in London; it was apparently not smart enough. 'The less noise you make about your cloths the better it will be for you and you may depend upon it my father will be as fond as you can be of seeing you decent and what that decency is, he's the best judge.'

From time to time the younger brother was commissioned to buy things in town for the Cantabrigian—tea, coffee, a coloured china milk-pot, snuff (plain Spanish), and 'ye incomparable powder for the teeth sold at Mr. Halsey's in St. Michael's, Cornhill'; also, to see Mr. Benazeek, the fashionable jeweller, about his watch and at the same time to drop a timely hint to the father about his promise of a pair of silver spurs.[1] Along with these commissions went more fraternal advice:

Pray take care how you venture upon the Thames or in any other place to bathe and how you walk the streets when its dark. There are so many accidents that may happen, that you cannot be too careful.

Robert was also to make a point of visiting his kinsman, Dr. Jurin, now in London,[2] 'for his conversation must be a great spur to quicken your desire of knowledge and make you endeavour to have a general taste of all things that lie in

---

[1] Isaac Cookson in the Side, Newcastle, made silver spurs.

[2] He lived at Garlick Hill. On the death of the elder Cotesworth, he wrote to Robert 'I sincerely join in your sorrow for the loss of him who we had both of us many reasons to love and honour.'

your way wch may make you acceptable in the world'. In the summer of 1718 it was arranged that the younger boy should visit Cambridge and stay at Trinity. 'Come as soon as ever you break up and if you would send me word what day you intend to come I or somebody from me shall meet you at the Coach House and conduct you safe into the second court at Trinity College.' 'I would without jesting', the letter continued, 'have you take a little care of your hair before you come because you'll be taken notice of . . . and I would have you bring as much linen with you as may serve you a fortnight for I intend to give you Quarter so long.'

In the following spring a farther move was contemplated. 'My father has some thoughts of removing me to Oxford for my health', wrote William from Cambridge; but although he stayed for a time with another Dunelmian, Robert Eden, at Lincoln College, there is no evidence that he was ever a student there. He was subsequently entered at the Middle Temple in the chambers of Charles Sanderson and died suddenly in 1721.[1] Meanwhile the younger boy had been sent to a business house in Amsterdam, Jacob Lernwoods & Son, to learn business methods. While there he was commissioned by his brother to buy some standard editions of classical texts and 'some pieces of music to your mind'— Robert was a keen musician. The sudden death of the elder brother brought a change in the family plans: the younger son was promptly switched to law and for a time took over his brother's room at the Middle Temple.[2]

Throughout their school and college careers the father himself was a tireless and incomparable educator. He would not tolerate slovenliness in letter-writing or lack of method in keeping accounts. 'My Billy's letter of 13 Xber 1718 to

---

[1] He was formally entered in July 1717. *Middle Temple Admission Register* (ed. Sturgess), i. 280. There is some evidence that he wanted to become a clergyman and that his father had consented.

[2] He was admitted to the Inner Temple in November 1721. *Calendar of Inner Temple Records* (ed. Roberts), iv, 87. To transfer from one Inn to another was not uncommon at that time. Charles Sanderson was at the Inner Temple in 1717 and at the Middle Temple in 1726, though there is no record of his admission.

which I gave him a very sharp answer which I intended only for his advantadge and not to gratify any resentment of my own', runs a quaint endorsement on a letter from Cambridge. 'I cannot take this as any account', he wrote to the younger son, 'pray make it more regular by putting in a date.' He advised him to get into the habit of putting down every day's expense in one sum at night 'which is easily done by putting twenty shillings in your pocket at a time and at night reckon what remains'. There followed more advice about the necessity of hiding money from chambermaids and on having it secure about the person when he went abroad. Again, he had hoped to have a full account of Robert's impressions of Cambridge and when he received instead a lame one coupled with a dun, the boy heard about it. 'Nay, nay, Bobby it is your want of thought [not "the unsteadiness of your eyes", as he had alleged] that has occasioned so great a neglect. It is hard that I must find a memory for you all while I have the burden of providing for you laying heavy upon me.' But although Cotesworth was irritable and sharp-tempered he nursed no ill will: 'Answer that letter', he wrote two days later, 'and I will forgive all faults and you shall be my dear Bobby still.' More sharp reproof followed a little later.

I shall for the future leave it to your own discretion when and what you write to me for you have already had as much instruction and direction as I have time to give you. I know no more of what progress you make in the several sciences and amusements than if you had not cost me one penny. Whether you are fit to take from school or not, I know only by guess. I know your genius to learn any thing is very good, but of your application and proficiency I know nothing . . . wishes this last letter had been as handsomely and correctly writ as a former one, so it had saved me a groat besides the disturbance of seeing you so giddy as not to know what it is you are writing. I was in hopes that by your frequenting the Coffee House you would by this time have been able to have pickt me a piece of news now and then, as whether Alberoni and all the High Priest's schemes are broke and so a Spanish war prevented and our great trade into that part of the world saved or we must fight another 30 years for it.

Indeed, it would almost seem as if an element of steady insistence, short of nagging, is an essential ingredient in the educative process. 'Now is the precious time which, if lost, can never be regained, therefore, dear Bob, let me prevail on you to use the utmost endeavours to make the very best on't.' Or again, in the last year of his life, 'I am in a poor way and though easier, I am going. Be diligent in your reading, have a care of Physick, Remember your Brother, I am your affectionate father.' Colonel Liddell sent much the same sort of advice to his favourite nephew, Henry Ellison, who was also at the Middle Temple. 'Now that you are about to come into the world on your own bottom, I earnestly recommend it to you not only to persevere but to redouble your diligence in this last year. I need not tell you how great an advantage it will be to you both in reputation and in your calling to see a sober and diligent young man in an age when virtue and industry are hardly known.'

Above all, Cotesworth sought to impress upon his children the importance of sticking together as a family. 'Your kind affection and concern for each other will make me forget all my labours and give me the greatest pleasure I am capable of enjoying. Use diligence to furnish yourselves with knowledge; keep and hold fast your integrity and virtue and you may rest satisfied of my utmost endeavours to procure for you the rest of the means of happiness.' This may well serve as the epitaph on his lair-stone.

## CHAPTER IX

# Diversions

> People must have a great Itch for gaming or be much
> at a loss for something to kill time if so silly a game
> as Roly Poly can have its followers; it will be difficult
> for an Act of Parliament to prove effectual and be
> able to conquer such a monster which, hydra-like,
> will have new heads starting up as fast as the old ones
> are cut off.                             (*H. T. Carr*, 1741)[1]

ALREADY in Cotesworth's day the quality of life in polite
circles was surprisingly rich and varied. There was
much coming and going especially for young people—visits
and assemblies and later 'junkettings' and 'routs'. On such
occasions young ladies, previously coached by a dancing
master, danced in their stockinged feet and the stockings were
pure silk. The accounts with fashionable London dress-
makers and milliners for rich white Mantuas 'pink satin
lin'd', black velvet and 'corded Rosetta', and fans were
accepted by parents with quiet resignation.[2] 'You may perhaps wonder at so much finery', wrote Elizabeth Cotesworth
to her brother who was to place the order, 'but my Father
was so good as to talk of our visiting York Races this year.'
'The two young Ladys' Mantes etc are upon ye Green
because that Couler is now very much wore among the
Gentry', wrote one Bridget Seymour in the summer of 1711,
'the 30 yards of Rosetta was ye only good silk I could buy
at that price: it will wash and scour like any linnen.' The

---

[1] Ellison MSS.

[2] 'Tis said the women in the City are most extravagantly gay', wrote Sir William Chaytor
to his daughter in 1701, 'and old Mr Heather said they were rich in gold and silver brocades
with their petticoats laced to the knees and those that wears silk lace are all of a breadth to
the knee. The head [i.e. hat] moderate high and the rufles not so deep as formerly, the
firbilo as high as to be seen and not much puffing out.' 'Indian silks are all worn and perticularly
that they call chinses. Lady Sherrard in her French dress, her hair, like my peruge on her
forehead and her hair all in tufts round and abundance of small black ribbons and some colour'd
and her stomacker all ribbons. They think that fashion will not hold, its too hot for sumer.'
Chaytor MSS. Bowes MSS. 40747, §§ 103, 162.

quieter days at home were spent 'flowering' the broad cravats for their brothers or embroidering the 'stuff' furniture, and, for the more adept, making their own gowns and dresses.[1] In the better houses, maids were not finally engaged until they had produced samples of their needlework and many of the mistresses themselves plied the needle ceaselessly making shirts for the boys, knitting stockings or embroidering the table linen.[2] 'My wife finished the sowed work in the drawing-room', noted Sir Walter Calverley in 1716, 'it having been three years and a halfe in doing. The greatest part has been done with her own hands. It consists of ten panels.' Then it is clear from the book bills and private libraries that young people often read some of the most recent books and plays, especially if an elder brother was conveniently placed in town for getting them. Besides the *The Spectator* and the *Guardian* young Cotesworth's book bill for 1719–20 included *The Rehearsal, The Careless Husband, The Tender Husband, The Fair Penitent, Tamerlane* (all plays), a set of Wycherley, besides such things as Bossu's *Epick Poetry* (French edition), *Satcheverell's Tryal*, and the *Complete Country Dancing Master* in two parts—not to mention more serious works. When he was at Cambridge he sent his sister Clarendon's *History*, three enormous folio volumes, and three volumes of plays. In 1725 Miss Elizabeth asked Robert 'to send us Shakespeare's plays [there was a promise that they would be returned at the first opportunity] in the latest edition of Pope'. 'Pray get me Burnet's *History* which you subscribed for and send it by sea', Colonel Liddell instructed his nephew Ellison.[3] 'The want of newspapers shortens our sight that we cannot see neither what the ould pope nor the Great Turk are a doing', was Charles Cotesworth's quaint way of asking his famous brother to forward any newspapers to Egglesburn in Teesdale. Again, an entry in Ralph Ward's Journal for November 1755 runs 'Had the Votes from Mr.

---

[1] Miss Chaytor asked her father to 'send one of the gentilest patterns to flower my brother a long crevat at the ends'.    [2] The maids at Park House spun lint.
[3] Chaytor read Burnet's *History of the Reformation* in the Fleet. In 1732 Ellison subscribed to two volumes of Bourne's *History of Newcastle*.

Mathews ye first time from whom am to have ym every week so long as ye Parlmt sits.'

In polite society the cruder pastimes were dying out. 'If Harry will divert himself with cocks when he comes home', wrote Sir William Chaytor in 1700, 'tell him he may have the cock spur saw in my drawer and I would not abridge him of any things for a pleasant innocent diversion.' More than once during that first winter in the Fleet he expressed a hope that the weather would permit 'watching the cocks in the pit', and once he reported that Frampton had lost over £1,000 'of his cocks'. Sir Walter Calverley when he was a young man went frequently 'to the Cockings' and was usually successful at the 'mains'. That cock-fighting continued in certain sporting circles and among the lower orders is clear from Hogarth's print and Boswell's *London Journal* but one finds surprisingly little mention of it in the later correspondence and my impression is that, in genteeler circles, it was dying out in the second half of the century. Possibly Mr. Carr's profound social observation which appears at the head of this chapter is an indirect acknowledgement of the fact. 'The lads and lasses are playing at stoolball', wrote Chaytor from the Fleet, 'and George [his servant] has taught them to play at tuts.'

Children could always amuse themselves provided there were enough of them together and provided adults were content to be mainly spectators. In the autumn of 1741 the three Ellison children were left with their aunt and uncle Carr at Cocken while their parents were in London and at Bath.

Our Bett and your Harry agree well [reported Carr] but she is rather the stronger and would become the breeches. Last night they dressed up in one another's cloths. Mr. Mitford's wig under his cap made him appear like a French lady and Bett looked like a little impudent Irish soldier and danced with her namesake to your boy Ned's fiddle and so comically that my wife who has been confined to bed these six days by the Piles could not help laughing heartily at them.

The children mimick Mr. Liddell's hare hunting on the other side of the water [the river Wear] [he reported later] the young ones yelp it finely as hounds and as Bays in the *Rehearsal* makes a red Ribband tied round the arm signify fighting, so your daughter Betty and Bella by twisting a hazle switch about them signify riding and are turned into horsewomen.

In another letter he asked his brother-in-law to send 'copies of a good round hand—I believe some of the Stationers sell in print from copper-plate'. 'Bryons, the bookseller', he added 'sold a printed copybook called *The British Penman* (by Johnson) which is good, also Nicolas' *Young Penman* copybooks', but these were not meant purely for diversions.

Music was undoubtedly the principal diversion for adolescents—at least that is the conclusion to which the evidence points—it was certainly so with Miss Chaytor, the Cotesworths, and the Ellisons. 'If we can spare moneys', Lady Chaytor wrote, she proposed to let Ann have singing lessons from Mr. Nichole, an Italian master in London, adding somewhat unkindly, 'it will help to make up the want in her face'. In due course the master arrived. 'Mr. Nichole comes punctually and gives Nanny encouragement enuff, says he will make her sing as well as any and that she has a mellancholly voice fit to sing Te Dcums and Anthems.' Later, he proposed to bring 'a pair of harpsicalls for her to sing to as they would advantage her voice'. But alas! after her father was taken up she confessed that she never sang more.[1] The prisoner in the Fleet enjoyed singing for he wrote in 1701:

Went to St. Paul's where I heard the best anthems that ever I heard in my life; they begin to imetate the Italian.

And then, for Nanny's benefit,

Why should not we imetate the great Master of Music, Mr. Nichole, and lay down the instrument when the jarring house of the Law disturbs the harmony. A nice ear can find out the least false note and a well-composed will bring in the hand, the voice and the thought to

---

[1] At York, on his way to London, Chaytor 'diverted himself by hearing a young woman's voice, which though it be innocent, puts me below the gamutt'. For gamut, see *O.E.D.*

complete the tune and make an agreeable consort. Such a discord there is among the buffoon fiddlers of the law that one would think Bartholomew Fair is kept at Westminster Hall for there are all the vices acted upon the stage—drinking, whoreing, cheating and all mercenary trade are held there by charter.

Cotesworth somewhat grudgingly paid ten guineas for a new spinnet for his son William when he was at the Middle Temple though he thought it 'a female instrument' and nearly as much every year for Hannah to have lessons on it when she was in London. Robert, the younger brother, played the flute and was a member of a select musical club, started by fellow graduates and students at the Temple, which met at the Crown and Anchor, 'over against St. Clements'. 'I have sent Robbin Robson to you with his bagpipes', his sister wrote in 1725 'which I hope will convince Mr. Hassel it is very good musick'. This friend was Robert Hassell who was on intimate terms with the leading musical celebrities of the day and collected and published opera himself. He eventually married the sister of a member of the club, Miss Betty Ord of Newcastle.

April 27th, 1727.

Dear Bob,

I shall be glad to hear how you like your Flute. I thought it was a very good one and had some inclination to get me one of the same, but as I have two pretty good ones already I shall take time to consider of it unless you write me word that it proves extraordinary. Here is a Dantzicker come to town that is a prodigious player of the German Flute and generally reckoned the very first man in the World. I have not yet heard him but hope I shall to-morrow night at our Club. To-night is acted for the first time an Opera of Bononcini, called Aztyanax.[1] It has been twice put off on account of Cuzzoni who is very ill. Faustina too was lately ill and they took occasion to act Otho. Admetus has had a great Run much above its merits in my opinion. For it is not so good as Rodelinda and two or three more, but has been more followed and cryed up than any of them. It will be published this week. . . .

---

[1] Bononcini was a rival of Handel. Scholes, *Oxford Companion to Music*, s.n. *Admeto* had an unusual run of nineteen nights. Parry, *Studies of Great Composers*, 44–49.

May 10<sup>th</sup>.

. . . As for the Songs that you desire, I expect to have the Opera of Admetus[1] published in a few days; and I know there are several in it that will do very well. I have at length bought 5 or 6 of Handel's Operas and intend to put that among the rest, and as soon as I get it I will set to work to lay out some for you. Besides their being many of them very good, they will have the additional pleasure of being new to you.

I was last week at the first acting of a new Opera of Bononcini called Astyanax. There were some very good songs in Cuzzoni's part, but most miserably murdered; for my cousin Cuzzoni's voice was prodigiously out of order and Faustina's Partisans say very confidently that she will never recover it. Some say it is a great cold, others the Pox, and some that she is breeding. Whatever it be, the Connoisseurs are at their wit's ends about it. . . . Since my last I have heard Quants play on the German Flute.[2] It is impossible to tell you how I was pleased, but you may imagine that he outplays all other players of the German Flute as much as Robin the Piper outplays the meanest Piper in Northumberland.

Whenever Henry Ellison or any of his friends happened to be in town they invariably reported on the latest opera.

April 7, 1728.

I heartily condole with you upon the very low taste the People of Fashion have fallen into to desert the Opera and Old House where a man of sense might be so well entertained for the Beggar's Opera which all seem to agree to be hardly fit for the delight of children. But it seems to me to be still more odd that what everybody condemns, everybody should countenance. I hope by this time yourself and the Ladies are pritty well satisfied with all these things and begin to think again of Park House where I shall be extremely glad to see you all again.

I visit like death and the Doctor all sorts of places [wrote Dr. Cooper in February 1734]. I was most rapturously entertained at the Opera in the Hay market last Tuesday. Carestini who never appear'd before this winter is allowed by all the judges to exceed Senisino so much that no comparison can be made between them. I have

---

[1] Parry, *Studies of Great Composers*, 44–49.

[2] Johann Joachim Quantz (1697–1773) who taught the flute and composed for Frederick the Great. Scholes, *The Great Doctor Burney*, i. 204 n., 233–4.

not as yet heard Senisino and when I do, they are both so excellent in their way, that my opinion could go for very little, tho' I assure you Carestini warm'd me in such a manner as I had little imagination of.

I need not repeat to you [he wrote a fortnight later] that Operas, masquerades, plays and taverns make up so many points of the circle of which our joys in this great town are cheifly composed: the completion of which narrow circumference is probably ended in things not worth a beginning, as thinking is not the business of this place, I should be sorry to be out of the fashion.

I doubt we are in a bad way for this winter for Hendal [*sic*] is proud and saucy and without him nothing can be done for us that is good [wrote Sir Henry Liddell in November 1735]; they have a new performer from La Pieta at Venice who sings with good judgement and a very tolerable voice for a second.

[A month later he wrote wishing to] do justice to Verracini [in view of an earlier report that] his new opera will not do. The Opera pleases very well [he now wrote] Faranelli has not so good a part as might be wished, but Senesini shines greatly in it.

Nor was this enthusiasm for music a passing mood. When the *Beggar's Opera* was revived a quarter of a century later, Joshua Geekie reporting it to Ellison added, 'Miss Brent, a young scholar of Arne's, taking the part of Polly; she sings so very fine that I shall not understand a word of her songs'. It is scarcely surprising that the children of Henry Ellison and Hannah Cotesworth were musical—Hannah junior played the guitar and sang; in 1762 her banker-brother in town sent her Giardini's song 'which was inserted in the Opera of Love in a Village', together with other music.

This same northern circle appreciated the stage almost as much as the opera. Sir Henry Liddell and his friend young Cotesworth exchanged views on a critical appreciation of Young's new play in the summer of 1721,[1] and it is evident from Mr. Carr's letter about the juvenile theatricals at Cocken that he must have seen *The Rehearsal* himself.

We have no further expectation of new Theatrical Entertainments,

[1] Edward Young, *The Revenge.*

the year being so far advanced [he wrote in 1732]. There was a new piece called Baye's Opera, an attempt at something in the manner of *the Rehearsal*, but by all accounts a most wretched one. There was a talking eagle and a singing ass introduced into it but the poor fellow who had studied the asse's part was not permitted to appear after the first night. I don't doubt but you have heard what success Rich has met with by acting the dog. You'l be apt to think the Town's gone mad.

There is a new Tragedy now acting wrote by the author of Euridice[1] [he wrote in February 1739]; it was well supported by Lord Chesterfield, Mr. Pope, Mr. Littleton etc. at the first night and has some good scenes in it, but is not a very extraordinary play. 'Tis called Mustapha; the chief characters are an ambitious step-mother, a suspicious father and a faithful son who falls a sacrifice to the artful intrigues of the Empress and Grand Vizier in spight of the assistance of his half-brother who assists him to the utmost. Some particular passages which were thought to touch the present time were much applauded.[2]

Towards the end of her long life, a remarkable tribute was paid to Lady Ravensworth by the theatre-going public.

Lady R. had ventured to the Play [wrote Henry Ellison in 1781] attracted by the fame of the superior merit of Mrs. Siddons who, in her opinion, is intitled to all the praise and admiration she has received. From this testimony you will conceive an High idea of her merit. You can have no adequate notion of her powers till you see her. Mrs. Crespigny, I was told in London, went to the theatre rather prejudiced against her, criticized and found fault at the beginning, but soon began to doubt her own judgement and was actually in Hysterics before the conclusion of the play. In speaking of this subject, I must not omit the distinguished reception which Lady R. met with at the Playhouse, the Audience applauding her as she entered, a compliment I do not remember to have been paid to any individual, not in a public character.[3]

Perhaps we may here record a contemporary tribute paid by a northerner to that great northern artist, Hogarth. 'We never had a duller season', wrote Mrs. Liddell in 1736, 'ye Gunpowder Plot against Law and Equity has been ye only

[1] David Mallet.    [2] i.e. the feud between George II and Frederick, Prince of Wales.
[3] Ellison MSS.

subject of late and all allow the scene of confusion amongst the Gentlemen of the Gown was droll. I could like to see it represented by Hogart.'[1]

To turn now to more masculine pleasures. There was what Sir Gilbert Gerard called an "onest clubbe' in Durham city in the early years of the Restoration but what it did apart from 'bending the elbow' is not clear. 'My Saterday's wine reproved me eno' (without your wife)', wrote George Liddell, 'for I was not well till yesterday morning's coursing with canny Frank set me to rights.' The Carr and Ellison children must often have seen him. In 1743 Sir Henry Liddell wrote to Ellison that he had got him a young greyhound out of Norfolk 'that will be fit to enter this year and is a thorough well bred one'.

Liddell's uncle, Bright of Badsworth, near Pontefract, was a famous breeder of beagles, spaniels, and foxhounds. In this line of business he was an acknowledged master and his dogs were in great demand. He reserved for Ellison two young beagle bitches in 1730 'between 18 and 19 inches high . . . as good as can be' (in his view 21 inches was too big): 'It is not heels that makes a dog run hard but his nose and mettle.' At the same time he forwarded this advice,

> Put the puppies out to single Quarters and not in a town where they will come to nothing by being either stole, eaten up with mange, go mad, or other accidents attend them . . . and I will answer for it that they will find you more game and kill you more than all the beagles you have.

When the dogs were sent a month or so later the number had increased to four, each with its name and identification. 'Curious' he thought of for 'neice Kate because she is a good humour'd merry grig, a little boisterous in her caresses, not to be withstood by any person of less substance than herself'; 'Netty' for Miss Cotesworth and so on. All four he pronounced 'a good humour'd inoffensive tribe, but rather

[1] The reference is to Yorke's Mortmain Act. In December 1735 Robert Ellison remarked that his lodgings in Cannongate resembled the Harlot's Progress—'broken-back chairs and others wanting legs'. 'My tea equipage is extremely like hers—a broken tea-pot lid and a pewter gill pot for milk.'

too awful [i.e. easily cowed], therefore must not be roughly
dealt with, though they are as cunning as the devill'. He was
not certain 'if they are guilty of sheep—nobody could tell
that—at Quarters they are all staunch from sheep but when
two or three wild things come together nobody knows what
they may do'. He advised Ellison to keep only four pups out
of a litter. In the previous winter he had been commissioned
by Ellison or Colonel Liddell to recommend 'a groom that
could hunt a pack of beagles' and, accordingly, he recommended one Jack Smith as huntsman who understood 'the
due casting of a hare but I know not what language he has;
we are setting out to find a fox on the other side of the river'.
The Badsworth breed of beagles and foxhounds were supplied to the Earl of Carlisle and the Scottish Elphinstones.[1]
Indeed, it occurred to Colonel Liddell in 1730 that presents
of pedigree dogs would prove acceptable to his electoral
friends at Berwick—a novel and ingenious form of political
corruption. His brother Bright replied that had he known
this two months before he could have supplied them 'most
elegantly'; even so, he thought he might possibly spare a
couple or two. He needed not to have apologized for being
a poor letter-writer: where dogs were concerned he was a
master. Had he been at Park House in December 1747 a
dreadful calamity would probably have been avoided.[2] By
contrast, Ralph Ward of Gisborough condemned his neighbours, Jefferson and Saunderson, for 'the idle trade of keeping a pack of hounds and hunting'—an attitude that was
surely rare at the time.[3]

The interest in horses in the eighteenth century surpassed

[1] *H.M.C. Carlisle MSS.* 162, *supra.* In 1738 Sir Wm. Middleton of Belsay supplied
George Bowes with 19 'cupple' of hounds and 3 'tarriers'.
[2] The dog 'Tinker' was supposed to have gone mad. He attacked a servant who went to
fetch him from Mr. Ord's—'the skirts of his wide coat were torn all to pieces'. He quarrelled
with the turnspits 'so we have hung them', wrote the steward. And 'Robin told me he saw
Tinker catch hold of one of the cats on Sunday night so we have killed them all': only 'the
setting dog Midge, who had the mastery of Tinker' was unscathed. Nor was that all. Before
the offender was shot he hung on to the tail of the chestnut horse. 'We cannot perceive that
the horse is wound[ed]. Robin has swimmed him in Tyne till very weak and afterwards took
a great quantity of blood from him and ordered something [three powders and Dr. Mead's
drink] for him at Mr Kiplings.' [3] MSS. Journal, loc. cit.

all else, from the despised 'pad' that trotted 'hard', and those relay teams that drew the stage-coaches and covered such distances that, in Cotesworth's view, no single rider could equal without killing his horse, to the elegant pacers harnessed to a gentleman's private coach—the overall cost of which was fully comparable to a Rolls-Royce limousine[1]—and the racing thoroughbred. Already in Chaytor's day racehorses were bred and trained at Croft and Middleham in the North Riding before going to Newmarket—his 'gossip' was interested in the business.[2] Sooner or later everyone, even the ladies unless they were prepared to ride 'double' all their days, was interested. In his first term at Cambridge William Cotesworth wrote to his father:

I hope my writing that my mare was scarce able to carry me out of the dirt is not attributed to any fickleness in my temper for both you and Mr. Johnson told me last Xmas I was grown too big for her. If I was so then I am much certainly more so now having grown of late very prodigiously. I weighed about a month ago in my waistcoat nine stone. I did not sell her because I was offered money for her in summer when she's the best mare in England, nor would I have dared to sell her without asking your leave. I must endeavour to plunge through the Cambridge Roads (which are famous for being the worst in England) as well as I can with her, but my complaint was not without a good deal of reason. If I was to chuse an horse again I would buy as tall a one as I could conveniently meet with and one that trotted well, I being persuaded that a little pacing horse is a mere bauble

Later, when he was at the Middle Temple, his father gave strict orders that he must, on no account, attempt to ride down to Newcastle along with the stage-coach in which his brother and sister were travelling—that would be to kill his horse. Cotesworth strongly recommended that the party should hire a private coach as he himself had done in 1717[3]—

[1] Thomas Godsal of London supplied one to Ellison in 1762: the total cost including package and insurance was £136.

[2] 'My gossip that sees so many tricks at Newmarket may have reason to suspect every man', wrote Chaytor. He himself had a famous breed of horses. In travelling to London to join her husband, Lady Chaytor 'rode single to York, none being so kind as to afford me a double horse'.

[3] From a famous coachman Joshua Perry of York. In 1727 Robert Cotesworth commis-

one could be had for £15 or so to do a single journey between London and Newcastle, rather than risk not getting a seat in the stage-coach on any particular day. Places in the stage-coaches were bookable and chance travellers at termini and still more those who planned to join the coach at intervening places were often left behind. On the other hand, under-graduates or students at one of the Inns of Court who rode up to town on their own horses were faced with the dilemma of selling them at Smithfield where the chance was that they would lose heavily, or of renting a stable (at a price) and the animal eating its head off until the owner was ready to make the return journey.[1] But, like some pre-war tourists, some hit upon an obvious solution.

Besides, what opportunities offered to a smart young lady on horseback! 'I was riding out this morning and was so hot that I was obliged to pull of my Great Coat', wrote Miss Peggy Bowes from Bath in January 1733. 'Ye Prince came into the Field that I was in and sent one of his Gentlemen and desire that I would joine Compeney with him which I did. He ask me a great Many Questions and if I came here for my Health and how ye Waters agree with me; what was my name and if I had a Father alive. I told him I had the Misfortune to be born after his death: he said that was his case. He ask what Country I was one. I told him; he said yt he had hard yt there has fine Horses thare and yt he believes it since I rid so pritty one and ask if I had broake her myself or bort her. I told him my Brother gave me her. He said was I sister to Mr Bowes Member of Parliment. I told him I was. He said he had hard yt Gentleman kape runing Horses and that he sumetimes sold; and if he had any now he would be oblige[d] to him if he could recomend him to one: it is

sioned him to buy a nicely matched set of coach-horses. Perry replied that there were 'good fairs' at Bedford and Northampton in March; he would have to be there a few days before the fair 'or I may as well stay at home for the LONDON Jockeys is always a day before and I would have a start of them'.

[1] 'No sort of horse will sell here unless a fine hunter or a very large fine pad', wrote Chaytor from London, 'for men have such fancies for horses here.' 'If Harry brings a good one up to town he shall have the name of a jockey.'

for his own riding. If my Brother has not disposed of Gigg
he would be a very proper horse for him, for he does but ride
a low horse. He dont care but to buy of a Gentleman, afrad
ye horses should have ill tricks, still being but Week. I realy
think he dont sit above half a yard hight upon ye Horss.'
'He rides out every day and he told me yt he found great
benefit by it and the Waters. He seams to love to rid fast,
he is very affable and takes all ye pains that is posable to
oblige everyone and speaks English very much. He desire
yt if he spock any word rong yt he would take it as a favour
if I tould him it for he had a great desire to Larn ye English
toung.' The young lady's spelling was not all it should be
but she had made a hit.

Sir Henry Liddell, writing from Newmarket in 1729,
said that there was more company there than ever was
known, though he himself did not 'enter at all into horse
racing and as for the Hazard Table, Thank God, I dread
it'.[1] In 1736 Major Cuthbert Ellison wrote from Ireland
wanting 'the character of Lambton's Grey Mare which
has run by the name of Miss Doe and sometimes by that
of Shylooks. Last summer she won at Penrith by the
name of Smiling Betty and at Morpeth and Carlisle by the
name of Miss Doe'—an elusive lady. In particular he wanted
to know if she was sound, free from eye sores, 'what form she
is reckoned in and what character she bears amongst the
sportsmen', also the lowest price her owner would take. He
said he wanted the information for a friend. There were
great numbers of local race-meetings in the north at this
time—in 1721 the town of Newcastle gave a gold cup to be
run for on the Town Moor[2]—and there was a racecourse on
Gateshead Fell. By no means all the field were thorough-
breds. As a special favour Henry Ellison allowed Robin,
his groom, to ride one of the coach-horses at Chester races

---

[1] His friend Cotesworth wrote in 1720 'the horse races are over here. I know not what
other people thought, but I did not think there was much diversion.' George Saville thought
horse-racing 'actually a loosing trade . . . calculating *all the money* spent in training and you
will find it far exceeds all the money won in Plates'. Benham, *Records of the Lumleys*, 260.

[2] Brand, i. 434; ii. 513.

in 1731, though 'it is a thing I would not have him expect to practice'. It is arguable that the elusive anonymity of a mixed field added greatly to the sport, though it is doubtful if a coach-horse, however good, would stand much chance against one of Mr. Bowes's horses that had cost upwards of £150. The following letter from Colonel Liddell, dated 1725, points to the need for proper 'stewards'—a thoroughly eighteenth-century title—on such occasions.

We had great squabbling yesterday about the Gold Cup which was brought back undelivered. Sir William's [Middleton (?)] people claim it alleging that White was distanc'd tho' I dont hear any gentleman of that opinion, Alderman Fenwick and Cuddy Swinburne both eye-witnesses. It may occasion warm work and perhaps a lawsuit.

One northern worthy made a name for himself by his racing prowess:

No news from the Channel or Germany [wrote General Ellison in June 1759] but hear from Newmarket that our countryman, Shafto, has gained a complete victory, having rode 50 miles yesterday morning in less that one hour and fifty minutes. Tis imagined he has won from £8,000 to £10,000 by this Feat of activity. One may say he grows rich at a great pace.[1]

The *annus mirabilis* of the century of horseflesh! The hero was Jenison Shafto. In the following year, his kinsman Robert entered for the local stakes, the parliamentary election for the county of Durham, and notwithstanding some lather and drum-beating in episcopal and ducal circles, bore all before him.[2] In another historic year, thirty years later, young 'Cuddy' Ellison and his brother at a 'prep' school in High Wycombe, on hearing they had a twin brother and sister drank a glass of wine to celebrate the occasion and

---

[1] Ellison MSS. 'Early in the morning Jenison Shafto started against time to ride 50 miles in two hours, in the course of which he used ten horses and did it in two seconds under eleven minutes of the time prescribed by the articles to the astonishment of all present.' *Gentleman's Magazine*, xxix. 291. In a letter to her brother in May 1771 Mrs. Airey referred to 'the melancholy exit of poor J. Shafto; the cause is still only guessed at: people are apt to assign the change of fortune upon the Turf & elsewhere'.

[2] For the allusions see my article in *History*.

added 'I am sure if Cuddy and I had been at home we should have mounted Steady'.

Both Carr and Ellison were keen anglers; the latter, a quiet, contemplative man made annual expeditions to Wooler for his 'favourite diversion'. He got his tackle from London, though his lawyer friend, Geekie, who executed his commissions, confessed 'that he scarce knows a trout line from a jack line'. Carr was more knowledgeable. At Grindon he fished perch in the river and carp in a pond, with 'grass baited with a lob worm: carp not having been used to be taken by the angle they would even bite at a perch hook tied upon Gimp'. In the spring of 1733 he sent Ellison a box of tackle and a live-bait pan, and since the latter had confessed to being a stranger to 'tack fishing', forwarded some instructions.

The common way of laying live baits by lapping your line upon a forked stick I suppose you are acquainted with. The hooks upon which the greas is are true Kirby and most of them were made for the May fly and I got the shanks broke off; the rest I was forced to send are of another sort for Kirby is so idle and has so many people pursuing him for Hooks that it might very probably have been winter before I could have procured so many of him. Mr. Mompesson has been a month getting a dozen of him for the May fly. Your rod is finished all but varnishing but is too long to be sent by the carrier and therefore I shall get Mr. Goodchild to send it carefully down by sea.

Rods were evidently not yet made in sections. In the reference to Kirby we have a glimpse of another expert in his own line.[1]

I'm sorry you had so little diversion at Wooler [Carr wrote in 1737] after the trouble of so long a journey it is a greater disappointment which you should endeavour to remedy by learning to fish with flye and then on clear water and a bright day which won't do for worm, would answer the purpose very well. I am attempting it and when I come to settle at Cocken, hope to make myself a proficient that way for there is plenty of Dace to practice upon in the warm season of the year.

---

[1] 'Nobody sells Kirby hooks but he himself', wrote Geekie,

He hoped his friend would frequently share the diversions
of that place with him:

There is fine gudgeon fishing for the ladies. Jonathan took several
there last week with an angle as large as any I have seen in the Thames
and there are a great many of them that I design getting a punt made,
which is one of the flat bottom boats used by the Fishermen on the
Thames on purpose for that diversion.

It is surprising that there is no mention of salmon fishing in
the correspondence.

What needlework was to the womenfolk, gardening was
to the men. Both Carr and Ellison were keen gardeners, the
former was attracted by the more formal garden with an
artificial lake, and was fond of shrubs and evergreens, though
the hard winter of 1739–40 played havoc with them.[1] What
most impresses one about the annual seedsmen's bills at
Park House are the names and the great variety of flowers[2]
and vegetables grown, as 'Battersea' cabbage, 'Hackney',
'Cokermuth', and 'Early Dutch' turnips, 'Brown Dutch'
lettuce, 'Roam spinage'; also, the specialization in espalier
fruit-growing on paradise stock—'the true French sort, not
Dutch, which are not more than codlings'—'apricocks',[3]
peaches and nectarines, and the early use of glass.[4] When
Carr migrated to Mobberley Hall in Cheshire he was able
to compare the local varieties of apples and pears with those
he knew at Durham.

For my part, as the planting season is coming on I am thinking about
my gardening and recollect that you had a remarkable good apricot on
your south wall in the kitchen garden: if your gardener has budded
from that tree I should be glad of a couple for I find a greater variety
of fruit than I had supposed there was. I cannot pretend to judge of the
produce of my garden in so wet a summer and the peach trees are most
of them old. I have new planted one wall with peach trees and another
with Plums. Cherries ripen very well in the orchard upon standards

[1] Ellison confessed that he had 'no great veneration for greens'.
[2] e.g. bulbs from Holland, 'sweet-scented' peas, and carnations.
[3] Two young 'aprecoks' were planted at Croft.
[4] e.g.' Bell-glasses' and hot-bed frames. In 1730 the London seedsman, Henry Woodman,
told his client that 'he had built a greenhouse, a conveniency I very much wanted'.

and Buree and Cresanne pears I have too many of upon the walls, designing to supply the place of some of them with other sorts. The grapes this year will scarce be fit for tarts. Apples our soil is reckoned to be very good for and I found the Non-Pareils last year much better than any which were the produce of the gardens about Durham.

Two years later he wrote again,

Having had two years' experience of the goodness of a seedling pear of this county called the Aston from the town where the original tree grows, I am desirous of supplying my friends with it and shall send from Manchester on Thursday next by Fryer Todd, a parcel directed to Mr. Sill to be left at James Thompson's, containing 10 trees, two of which are for Mr. Airey and I thought if you had a mind to have 2 at Hebburn and 2 at Gateshead, there would be 2 left for you to send to Ravensworth and 2 for Mr. Robert Ellison. I think it so delicate a melting pear that if it equal'd the Beuree[1] in size it might very well rival it: however it has this advantage over it that it does not require the help of a wall to bring it to perfection tho' a wall will increase the bulk of it to be equal to that of the Cressane which it resembles so much that if they were mix'd together, it must be a pretty nice observer who could separate them. Off an espalier they will be less and off a standard tree still smaller, but better tasted off either than off a wall and indeed one may almost lay it down as a general rule that all fruits which will come to sufficient maturity without the assistance of a wall, will be better flavor'd than if they had had it. The fruit is now ripe and having them of my own both off a standard and off East and West walls, I can pretty well judge of them. In this county it is much the best off a standard.

These men knew what they were talking about.

Their keenness is illustrated in another letter of the same date from Dr. James Baker, Ellison's lifelong friend who was now living in London.

... have given a Paper to my Brother [the merchant] for lettuce and cucumber seed from Turkey, Melon from about Marseilles and for some Dutch Asparagus wch he will endeavour to procure for you. There is a new fashion'd Melon called (I think) Cantaloup.[2] When this

---

[1] S. Switzer supplied Ellison with a 'Burée de Roys' and nine other varieties of pears in 1734.

[2] Cf. Lord Chesterfield, *Letters* (ed. Bradshaw), ii. 901, 916, *passim*. Melons were grown at Park House in the seventeen-thirties.

summer at Sheen, at Bro: Andrews, I crossed the River at Thistle-worth just opposite to my Brother's (and very near to Sion House), with my nephew and another Gentleman, we went into the kitchen garden and I had some discourse with the Head Person. I saw his Hot Beds, and a very particular Melon, not much bigger than an Ostrich's egg, much ressembling the Colour of a Toad and with spots and streaks very like one. The Gardener, seeing we took Notice of it, carried us to a Tool-House, where some were cut that morning for the Family. One that was chopt by the wet bad season fell to our Lot. We wanted not Courage and Manhood to attack it, and were well rewarded for our Bravery. The Colour and Flavour were far beyond any I ever tasted and I fancy, notwithstanding the blemish, equal if not superior to any of the others, cut at the same time. Here my Presence of mind fail'd me or I would have begged a few seeds. Speaking of the sort to Mr. Burton of the City, he had heard of it and told me it might be got from Holland, and I have added it to the list I gave my Brother.

I have been at severall great Seed Shops, but did not ask if they had any Cantaloups, only in general inquired *what* sorts of Melon-seed they had, but alas Cantaloup was wanting in all. I hear there is a shop in Lombard-street w^ch being in the heart of the City and near the Change possibly I may meet with somewhat curious there. This new sort (some say) comes from one of the hottest parts of the East Indies.

'Colour and flavour far beyond any I ever tasted'! 'I can't forbear repeating my Thanks for your fine Present of Plants in the Autumn', wrote Bishop Butler to George Bowes in 1752, 'my Park [i.e. at Auckland] being a favourite article with me as, before I had one, my garden was.'

No eighteenth-century garden was complete without bees as honey was invaluable for winter coughs. 'I am sorry the bees do not cast', wrote Sir William Chaytor from the Fleet, 'I shall take care of the honey I have. I think it help to keep my spirits up sometime.' It was Nanny, his daughter, who handled the stocks. 'We have took five hives and not above three quarts of honey', she wrote at the end of the summer of 1707. It is clear that they relied on 'casts' (swarms) to keep up their stocks as the method of taking the honey then involved the destruction of the colony, a procedure which

Joseph Warder strongly disapproved a few years later.[1] A hive of bees was bought from a local carpenter for 15s. (more than the price of a fat sheep) for Park House soon after Cotesworth went to live there and every year Mrs. Ellison sent her sister presents of honey for the children. Half a century later the stocks at Gateshead Park had apparently died out and immediate steps were taken to get a hive from beyond Haltwhistle. William Tinlin, the sub-agent and tenant of Broomhouses, was commissioned to inquire for one; in mid-September he reported that he had bought 'an excellent good top swarm which I wish were safe at Gateshead. The man I bought it of[f] advises to let it stand eight or ten days after it is taken, he says the come [comb] will stifin and carry better and I think it looks in reason it may be so, therefore I await further instructions.' Another anonymous expert! The trepidation of an otherwise over-assertive Tinlin is palpable. There were numerous articles and contributions on bee keeping in the *Gentleman's Magazine*. The Yorkshireman, Henry Best, gave instructions on the taking of swarms and on winter feeding in his *Farming Notes*. Richard Bradley in his *Book on Gardening* (1727) noted that the Germans 'are so industrious as to move their colonies of bees from place to place, many miles distant on purpose to bring them to flowry places'. In 1775 Daniel Wildman, a Londoner, published his standard treatise on bees,[2] copies of which were to be found in most country houses. Before the end of the century Mrs. Shute Barrington, wife of the Bishop of Durham, hit upon the happy idea of giving each cottager in one village in the diocese a hive of bees. It was her contribution to the Society for Bettering the condition of the Labouring Poor and was probably the best effort in a surprisingly varied philanthropic activity.

[1] Bradley notes (p. 287) that a colony could fill 'a common boxhive' with honey in six weeks. The price of honey in 1741 was 10d. a lb. M‹cKillop, *The Background of Thomson's Seasons*, 44.

[2] *A Complete Guide for the Management of Bees*. Wildman, who lived at 326 Holborn, invented new types of flat-topped hive, made of mahogany or glass, in place of the old-fashioned straw skeps. In his new glass hives he was able to make important discoveries, e.g. he states that he had 'frequently observed copulation' to take place in the hive, though he remained convinced that the queen is 'not the breeder of the whole stock'.

Although the people who visited Bath and other fashionable watering-places spoke of the diversions at these places, originally visits were made strictly on doctor's orders. In 1690, for example, Sir John Sudbury was told that the choice before him was Tunbridge Wells or death, and although like the Assyrian Naaman, he protested and suggested the mightier waters of Epsom, the prophet was unmoved.[1] There were certain seasons of the year when the waters were most potent and although 'Spa' waters could be had in bottles that was not the same. Sir Henry Liddell visited Bath in the autumn of 1713 and readily owned the benefits he had received:

I have not bin so regular to the Bath as you imagin [he told Cotesworth] yet I believe the waters have not don me less service than if I had spent as many houres at ye Cross Bath pump, popett shoes [shows], Gaiming tables or in the Walks and Dancing roome as the nicest observers of all the Divertions of that place.

His 'brother' Stockdale died at Bath in 1730 and his own son, the colonel, in 1740. All the Ellisons appear to have been dyspeptic. The general, an expert on gout, visited Bath regularly for half a century;[2] his brother Henry was advised to go there by Dr. Lowther in 1741 who wrote,

As I find the waters had disagreed so much with you of Late, so that must be occasion'd by something besides the water since that agreed with you for some time and I wish that this may not be imputed to your want of Exercise. A confin'd air and a most Relaxt Season, that is great Rains and Foggy weather, as I find from others that you have had, for which reason in my last I desired that when you returned to Bath that you would take Country Lodgeings about two or three miles out of Town and so ride to the Pump in the morning and Drink the water Cool and return to the Country in the Evening. I could wish the Lodgeings might be situated upon a Hill to the South or West and

---

[1] Hunter MSS. xii, § 140.

[2] He told his brother 'if Lord Ravensworth's gout is only in his foot, I should not be sorry if he had a short fit, provided 'twas regular'. And again, some years later, 'The first visit is usually a short one. The swelling, inflammation and pain in your foot are symptoms of what is called the true or genuine gout. Favourable as they are and salutary as some think this sort of gout is, you will excuse my giving you Joy of the acquisition.' *Diary of Dudley Ryder* (ed. Matthews), 240–3, gives an account of the pump-rooms. Cf. Smollett, *Humphry Clinker*.

once a week I would take a Moderate Dose of Tincture of Rhubarb. I wonder you did not mention to me your Cold Bathing when you Drunk the waters, which I think I did not hear till within these two days; and this I fancy might be the occasion of their Disagreeing with you, as your weak habitt could not bear in the same twelve hours those suddain Contractions and Dilitations what with the Cold Water outwardly and the Rarefaction of the warm Inwardly.

'This town is astonishingly increased since I was last here', wrote General Ellison in 1773, 'the Circus and Crescent in the high part are really magnificent buildings, as the New Public Rooms likewise are, and extremely well contrived for their intended purposes. These Public Rooms were built by a Subscription at the expense of not less than £24,000. Great as the sum is, the Subscribers say they could not have laid out their money to greater advantage, but projectors are generally too sanguine.'

The rise of the northern watering-places, Scarborough, Bridlington, and, somewhat later, Harrogate and Moffat, deserves special mention. Visitors came to Croft and Butterby to drink the waters in Chaytor's day. 'There is no Company at these Wells but ourselves and two other water Drinkers', wrote Colonel Liddell from Harrogate in May 1733. 'Do you know that Padlocks are in Fashion here?', wrote Dr. Lowther from Scarborough two months later, 'which I think a very rong place for them as it may expose them to perpetual rust and besides the waters cost both partys so that there is no great Danger of Bold attacks.' Among the company there at that time were the Duke and Duchess of Rutland, Cibber, Sir G. Clifton, Sir Henry Slingsby, and Mr. Riselby 'with their families'. 'Here is in short a vastt Deall of Company here in so much as to make the place disagreable; our two pritty neighbours are here the Ramsden's, I think I never saw a more Regular place we have no Gallantry and I think less Drinking so that Bacchus and Venus meet with few Customers.' Five years later Mr. Carr of Cocken reported that his brother had gone there, 'There is a report that the tide affects the water very much so as to give it a brackish taste. . . . However whilst it has its Reputation to recover I find the neighbouring places are making a push. Bridlington has advertized a Spa water and I hear the Hartlepool people have got their genteel Alderman to subscribe for the building a Long Room there, but the town is so inconsiderable that it can scarce afford lodgings. The former, I believe, is a good town.' Dr. Baker, who was at Scarborough in the summer of 1745, reported that an innkeeper in the town, named Cass, keeps coaches 'with which he travells this whole Country over almost with Spaws as they are called'—clearly a forerunner of the sight-seeing tour. Baker reported also that the company was thinning 'eight Coaches went away this morning and some young Ladys, I hear, in a most dolorous plight. O dear Scarboro'!'

In 1742 Carr reported 'My brother is gone to Buckston Wells in Derbyshire to try those waters, but I fear his complaint is really the stone, the jumbling stony roads having increased his disorder. The place, he says, is a melancholly situation, the accommodations bad, and little company but invalids which makes me think his stay will be but short.'

Curiously enough, the reports of other northern visitors to Buxton were invariably unfavourable. The Miss Ellisons were there two years running, 1781–2, and on both occasions found the distinguished historian, Dr. Robertson of Edinburgh, with his wife and two daughters at the same lodging. 'Buxton has given me a thorough dislike of a public place in summer', wrote one of the Miss Ellisons, '. . . the most dismal of all Places.'

Yesterday brought us the acquisition of the Family of Dayrolles (the head made famous by being Lord Chesterfield's correspondent) . . . fear they will not stay long as they seem most heartily to despise the place and every thing it affords. Being their opposite neighbours at Table we cannot help hearing them utter the great dislike they express to every thing they meet with. One circumstance seems worthy of being conveyed even to the distance you are at which is that they are perpetually complaining of the stink here and are going to regale their noses at Harrogate. Among these dreary Hills you may believe I can only have Buxton ideas.

Evidently fashionable society could be just as outspoken on boarding-houses as modern holiday-makers are.

It will have been noted that the emphasis hitherto had been on drinking the waters. The cult of sea-bathing dates from about 1760, and with it came the rise of places like Tynemouth and Allonby—'the beach is as good as Wey-mouth', a later visitor reported. The Bates family regularly went to Tynemouth in August. 'They are building barracks in the Castle and quite spoiling your favourite spot', wrote Elizabeth Ellison in the summer of 1783. In 1766 General Ellison reported that the elderly Lady Ravensworth was sea-bathing. In 1781 his niece stayed with Lady Georgiana Smyth at Scarborough where the family had taken 'a whole house upon the cliff' for the season. She confessed that she had done more bathing than usual and had great benefit from it. She concluded wisely 'I find this place is exactly what people chuse to make it'.

I have consulted all the Doctors and Surgeons relating to ye illness in my face [wrote Bowes from London in 1718] and finding that none of y^m are able to cure me, I design, God willing, to set out for my own country in six or seven days, hoping that the air may have a better effect on me, wch if it doe not, I will immediately depart for Naples where I am sure that ye Heat of the climate will do me more good than all the Physick of LONDON.

Travel abroad was the latest diversion in which northerners began to indulge. In 1716 W. B. Bowes went to Switzerland, Rome, and Naples. Sir Henry Liddell visited Paris in 1729 and Rome a few years later.[1] Mr. and Mrs. Ellison went to

---

[1] Bowes MSS. 40747, § 171. Liddell's uncle, the colonel, wrote: 'he gives an Account of the Fireworks there which were very Magnificent. He sayes there were but 300 Ticketts and those given to the Princes of the Blood, Cheif Nobility and foreign Ministers. That only three were given to the English viz, to M^r Pointz, L^d John Russell and L^d Cardross. L^d Car-michael had not one which gave him great offence at M^r Pointz as he had as good pretensions as the other two. Sir Harry bid 5 Guineas but there was no purchasing. However, the very day a servant brought him one which he sold him for 12^s & was the only one sold. After the works were played off, they had a Dance by four of the best Dancers. Then a supper from 12

Spa in the Netherlands in 1742. An entry in Ralph Ward's *Journal* for July 1755 reads 'Mr. Hall returned from his travels in France and Italy where he had been near five years'. Henry Ellison, junior, went to France and intended to go to Italy in 1765 but was taken seriously ill in Paris, and his younger brother, Robert, poet and banker, lived in Switzerland for two years.

The 'Grand Tour' was already fashionable in Pope's day[1]—

> Led by my hand he saunter'd Europe round,
> And gather'd ev'ry vice on Christian ground,
> Saw ev'ry Court, heard ev'ry King declare
> His royal sense of Op'ra's or the Fair.

Richard Wharton of Durham did it in 1774 and John Christian of Unerigg, near Maryport, seven years later. In 1779 Richard Burdon of Castle Eden toured Sicily and returned via Munich where he saw the valuable collection of pictures.[2] John Christian went to Prague and Vienna two years later. The Salvins of Croxdale were in Paris during the Revolution and were reported to be 'violent democrats'.[3] H. G. Liddell visited Lapland in 1786 and brought back two Eskimo women.[4] This account will close with H. T. Carr's letters from Rome.[5]

Rome.<br>15th December 1739. (Old Style).

After passing through great variety of country, some as agreable, other parts as wild as can be imagined, we are at last got fix'd up in our Winter Quarters at Rome where there is a great deal more company

to 3. In another Apartment a Fine Concert. Then in the Grand Salle (built on purpose) a Ball which was begun by the Prince of Conti and ye Duchess of Luxemburg who danced two Minuetts. As soon as they had done a dispute arose who was next in Blood, during wch Sir Harry advanced to ye Circle and took out ye finest and most Beautifull Lady (the Dutchess of Pequigny) who, he says, by the sweetness of her looks, he knew could not deny him the Honour & with a bold Englishman's assurance danced the Third Minuett. I think the young Gentleman was very Gallant.' The French comments are not recorded.

[1] *Dunciad*, bk. iv. 310–14.    [2] Egerton MSS. 2002, § 28.
[3] Wharton MSS. (Durham University Library).
[4] He wrote to Lady Ravensworth that he was setting out for Sweden for a couple of months from 'a desire to see the Northern parts of Europe'. There is no suggestion of a wager. Cf. *D.N.B.*    [5] Ellison MSS.

than usual of our nation and more expected every day; and indeed for
people who have any taste for Antiquities, Statuary, Painting or Musick
here is sufficient entertainment for almost every hour. As to the appearance of the Town itself considering the very great number of palaces
that are in it, I beleive most people are disappointed, for setting aside
the Churches, Fountains, Pillars and Obelisks which are of themselves
a great ornament, the rest does not answer one's expectation, the lower
part of fine Palaces being frequently let off and divided into little
shops and Greatness and meanness are so jumbled together (as we often
see them in life in the same person) that the appearance they make
upon the whole is but very indifferent, and even where the Palaces are
not so disguised, the contiguous houses, being often ill built, there is not
any of them which strikes the eye at once like Grosvenor or St. James'
Square or several other squares and streets we have in London.

The inside of their Churches surpasses Imagination, every Age adding fresh ornament and no riches being spared to complet them.

As to the outside of St. Peter's, I think it does not equal St. Paul's
when you come near it, it rather resembles a Palace than a Church,
the Cupola being thrown so far back that the eye does not take it in,
but I am getting into too large a subject so shall drop it quite and return
to our affairs in North of England. . . .

. . . Sorry the harvest suffered by the heavy rains. Cold weather seems
to have been everywhere. From the beginning of October before we
left Lions and all the way upon the road 'til we came here, we had very
severe cold weather, now and then very hard frosts which pinched us
thoroughly for upon the road (except now and then at a large town)
we met with but very indifferent accommodations. Bad beds without
curtains, perhaps only a window shutter, to keep out the cold, thin
coverlets and no place to make a fire in, exposed us now and then a
good deal to the mercy of the season, but we both escaped colds all the
way. . . .

We have lately had some very fine weather here. On the 11th
December (Old Style) our shortest day, the sun shone here bright and
warm 'til 4 p.m. and 'tis now an exceeding fine day. . . .

Rome.
7th May 1740.
I have deferred answering yours sometime in hopes that a change of
scene here might afford something entertaining to give you an account
of, but the old Cardinals are still shut up in ye Conclave and, if any credit

is to be given to common report, as far from agreeing in the choice of a Pope as ever. 'Tis said they are now inquiring into ye management of Cardinal Corsini, the late Pope's nephew, and endeavouring to discover clearly the methods which have occasioned so great a scarcity of coin at this place, that the Bankers are forced to pay the greatest part of their Bills by Paper Notes of the value of so many crowns each and that 'tis with difficulty one gets silver for a Zequine, a piece of gold under the value of 10 shillings. A sede-vacante has usually been reckon'd the best worth a foreigner's seeing of any thing Italy can afford, but under that notion must certainly be included all the ceremonies attending the commencement of the new Popedom, for hitherto we have had nothing very extraordinary at least not enough to make amends for our being deprived of the Operas and Comedies and other diversions of the Carnival, as well as of the Musick and ceremonies of Holy Week which they said would have answered our expectation if there had been a Pope to have officiated, but now they were all suspended, except the baptising a Jew, washing the feet of pilgrims and some processions of penetents and lousy pilgrims. The most entertaining scene we had in Lent was owing to a little contrast. In the Piazza Navona, which I can compare to nothing so well in London as Covent Garden, being a fine square and a Market too, a Mountebank was holding forth to his Auditory in one place, a man with a monkey shewing tricks in another, in a third an old grey-headed conjuror sitting exhalted on a high stool telling of fortunes through a long tube alternately put to the ear and mouth of the cunning Doctor and inquisitive cully, each surrounded by their several admirers; when at the same time entring at another part, behold a Jesuit with a crucifix in his hand and a large cross carried before him. He mounts a few steps and harangues the crowd so successfully in his turn that the Mountebank, the Man with the Monkey, and the fortune teller are all struck dumb and deserted by their audience who flock to the Priest and at last attend him in solemn procession singing *Ora pro Nobis* to a Church at some distance, where entering, the Priest goes up to the Altar whilst they with the other part of the Congregation arrived there before, fall down upon their knees in the middle of the Church and have disciplines made of knotted cords put into their hands by persons appointed to distribute them: immediately after a solemn service is alternately sung by Priest and people in a melancholy tone, the door is shut and all candles put out, and the Jesuit then preached again: (the evening I attended there out of curiosity) his Discourse was upon the

Passion of our Saviour, at proper intervals they groan, they sigh, they howl, they thump their breasts with their hands and lash their backs some with these cord disciplines, others more devout with iron chains brought with them for that purpose! The Sermon and the Discipline ending, they sang again; candles were brought in and the door opened when being fully satisfied I withdrew home. I should have told you before that in one of their processions of Penitents there were some who disciplined themselves severely, beating their breasts and thighs with a wooden instrument stuck with iron teeth which enter'd the flesh and made them raw and bloody whilst a person, immediately following, from a sponge threw vinegar upon the wound.

The Season now coming on and having gone through our course of Antiquities and Palaces, in about ten days we propose going to Viterbo to drink the waters there which are to perform miracles: before that course is finished, I fear, the weather will be too hot for us to think of travelling homewards, though hitherto we have had no reason at all to complain of the warmth of the sun. We have undoubtedly avoided most severe weather by being out of England, but I really have met nothing yet in this climate to deserve much commendation. The weather is as uncertain as in England and the change affects one more, the air being more subtle and penetrating. Last week snow fell even upon the low Hills. Severe hail storm yesterday which will damage the vines. Indeed, the Italians say they never remember so bad a winter and spring as this. The elms are but just leaved now, but I observe the walnut tree and standard figs as well as the Oriental Plane which in England are late, have put out their young leaves too. . . .

We are now very thin at the English Coffee house, several being already gone from Rome and more going every week; three weeks will almost clear it. Sir Robert Walpole's youngest son is still here. We were much rejoiced with Admiral Vernon's success in the West Indies and hope in a little more time to hear a good account of the men of war which are at Cadiz.

# Epilogue

I HAVE tried in the foregoing pages to say something of a complex and changing society whose outlook was conditioned by coal. If little has been said on shipbuilding, iron-, rope-, and glassworks it is principally because the notable developments in these industries came later in the century, while the rapid growth of the chemical, engineering and allied trades belongs to the nineteenth century. Already, by 1750 the predominant industrial and social character of the north-east was set as in a mould. The mining industry, especially in the days of 'the pick-and-shovel' miner, tends to breed certain characteristics—qualities of skill, endurance, resource, and comradeship which may be obscured or begrimed by coarser traits. In the eighteenth century the pitman was often 'painted as black as his coals'. Moreover, the industry tends to produce social inequalities within itself because of the marked gradations in skill and earnings between the skilled hewer on piece-rates and the 'datale' hand, or between the engine-man and the lamp-cleaner. In the eighteenth century the miners constituted the *élite* of the working classes. Cobbett commented on the substantial comfort of the Durham colliers. It is no part of our present purpose to analyse the causes of the subsequent retrogression.

Of the quality of the civilization produced by the complex industrial changes of the century in the stately mansions of the gentry and the finely proportioned houses of the merchants on the Sandhill or up Westgate, I tried to say something in the opening chapters. Of that in the colliery villages another shall speak. Sir Charles Trevelyan writing to Gladstone in December 1885 in what proved to be his last letter to his old colleague, congratulated him on the results of the first general election under a democratic suffrage.[1]

[1] Add. MSS. 44334, § 241.

Wallington,
Cambo.
December 11. 1885.

The pure white record of Northumberland and Durham in the Times County Map of the Elections balancing Cornwall at the other end, impels me to a word of congratulation. These are suffrages worth having—I have long considered the Cornish the best specimen of the Celtic race, attributable in part perhaps to their early commercial intercourse with civilised foreigners and to the co-operative system on which they have always worked their mines. And, as for our Northumberland Hinds, I wish you could see them at the annual Garden Party we give to our Tenants and Workpeople and their Families. There is a remarkable blending of classes within this neighbourhood. The children of Farmers and Workmen are educated together. They freely intermarry and the Shepherds are small farmers already, with one or two cows and flock of hired sheep—and constantly rise to be independent tenant farmers on the usual footing. The application of Chamberlain's ['Unauthorised'] programme would be a decidedly retrograde process in these parts. These people are quiet and reserved in manner, but thoughtful and purposelike. The books in our village library are thumbed and soiled so as to be often illegible, but of late years, the newspapers have been their favourite reading, so that they were quite prepared for the exercise of the franchise and voted for the Liberal candidates in overwhelming majorities. Our mining population is of the same general character, but as the Pit villages are real urban communities and they work in large numbers together, they have more ready intelligence. Our new Mining M.P.[1] was taken fresh from the 'hewing', the most arduous work of all. He has a powerful physique and stentorian voice—and what is more to the purpose, a large fund of quiet good sense. I feel sure that he will improve into becoming at least Mr. Burt's equal.

True, rural Northumberland which Trevelyan knew, is not industrial Durham. In the former the great bulk of the population is still 'native', whereas the Durham coal-field attracted large numbers of displaced persons in the course of the nineteenth century and continues to export its best products. Trevelyan's tribute to their purposefulness and 'quiet good sense' may yet stand.

[1] Charles Fenwick. Thomas Burt was M.P. for Morpeth.

# William Cotesworth and the Fifteen

*Extracts from the correspondence of Henry Liddell to William Cotesworth*[1]

[Henry Liddell to Wm. Cotesworth at Gateshead]

22 September 1715.

. . . A particular friend of yours was spoke to by two great men to know if he could recommend any notable person in your Parts who could be trusted and on whose intelligence one might depend, said none was so capable as W.C. He desired when you had any that it might be directed to Mr. Edward Curtt at Baker's Coffee House in Exchange Alley or to our friend ye Corner of Bedford Row where you eat venison. He was the man that spoke to me and he would lay it before the Secretary. You need not putt any name and depend whatever is wrote will be kept secret. T. Forster and five other Members are ordered into Custody. Could you not dive into some of their Projects? Pray consider of this matter. Can you hand any intelligence from Scotland? 'Twould be an extraordinary service to yr King and Country. . . .

27 September.

. . . Young Crowley is taken up and offer'd £100,000 bail but would not be accepted. Harvey of Combe is in custody of a messenger. One fairro, a Jew, is taken for conveying letters under his liver [*sic*] to ye Pretender's friends who is still at Bar le Dus. [Dr.] Sleigh is just come from ye Coffee House . . . tells that ye scheme laid was that this Harvey was to have seized St. James, Wyndham Bristol, Packington was to have rais'd his men at Worcester and joined Kynaston in Shropshire. Your neighbour was to have secured ye Town [Newcastle] and Tinmouth Castle, some others were to have attempted ye Tower and Bank. The Plot was certainly as deep a one as ever was laid and was to be executed as yesterday. The Govt knows ye very bottom of ye whole; in a little time you will hear of abundance who have absconded from their

---

[1] N.B.—I found a typed copy of this correspondence at Hedgeley Hall, Powburn, Northumberland. I have not yet succeeded in tracing the original letters which once formed part of the Cotesworth collection; and I therefore cannot vouch for the accuracy of the transcripts.

usual place of abode. Some will have that Mr. Sh[ippe]n made ye first discovery, others that a young Roman Catholic gentleman, but all this is but guess'd work. . . . You have your Lord Lieutenant[1] ere this sure among you, your Northumberland Expedition will be hamer'd out. . . .

6 October.[2]

. . . Your letters are very kindly received and laid before ye Secretary by a certain great friend of ours from Herts. [Lord Chancellor Cowper] . . . Forasmuch as I can gather they depend more upon you than all ye Rest. . . .

. . . Has two Commissions from ye two Secretaries. 1st They desire you will inform them if Tom Fors[ter] be gon over to Lord M[a]r, also that there are some English Gentlemen gon lately Northwards on their way to that Lord as is supposed, iff possible to learn their names. 2nd They will have from you ye State of Northumberland with your opinion what force would be necessary to prevent any Disturbance in that or your Country, as also what would be requisite to secure ye Peace of your Corporation. 3rd You are further requested to send your thoughts freely and that what relates to Public Business might be in a paper by itself that it may be kept by them to refresh their memory.

10 October.

. . . It's said that ye County of Somerset tho' the highest in principle of any have begun to cry 'Peccavi'. . . .

The zeal of your Magistrates, if unfeigned, is beyond what could ever have bin expected. Your early dispatch was wonderfully well received and will be kept secret. I am surprised that your Ld. Lieut. did not send you down armes. Pray how stand your keelmen affected? A letter which says 'tis suspected a certain Bart[3] was amongst ym, but I can't imagine a man of his noble fortune would run a Risque more than probable of loosing all.

Mr. Fr[eke] says there has bin a desperate design at Bristol but prevented by ye help of the Militia and another in Devonshire but as ye Govt. are perfectly apprized 'tis odds will never come to Light.

---

[1] Lord Scarborough replaced Bishop Crewe.

[2] On 7 October Dr. John Bowes wrote from Durham, 'We are like to have great troubles in the north. Lord Wedrinton and Lord Derwent Water are up in Northumberland with their parties. I am in great pain and concern not only in general for England and the Church but for some effects of yours which pray advise me what to do with. I intimated some fears of what might happen from ye Rising in Scotland and therefore hope I shall receive some orders from you.' To Lady Bowes. Bowes MSS. 40747, § 127.

[3] ? Sir John Clavering of Axwell. Compare Brand's account of the loyalty of Newcastle in 1715, ii. 509–11.

A report from the Secretary's Office that the Duke of Argele writes more sanguinely than he ever did.

A Lady at Kensington[1] . . . is in contact with Mons^r Bernsdorf (who communicates direct) to His Majesty.

13 October.

. . . You will have 3 or 4 Regiments of Dragoons and a Battalion of Foot with all Expedition. I do assure you a good Kensington Lady has solicited for speedy succors and pressed harder than any whatever for ye Relief of her own Countrey. . . .

15 October.

While the Rebels lye undisturbed in ye Open Countrey it gives incouragement to People to join ym daily and is a President for other Countyes to rise in hopes of ye like business. You can't imagine how he [the Lord Chancellor] came in with that project of yours, said it was the best concerted of any he had heard off and would be of ye most effectual service to ye Govt. . . . My Lady . . . applyes to ye fountain head. Goe on and prosper.

18 October.

. . . I take your letters to Bedford Row where 'tis perused and ye most Remarkable pieces of it he sets down in a piece of Paper if too long for his Memory and away he goes to ye Proper Officer. . . . I can tell you that you will be ye Topp favourite of that family. I can't omit acquainting you that ye Lady told me that whatever Ld. Scarboro' should propose for your particular, that her Lord would second it and she would exert herself in your favour. . . . When this Hurlyburly was over, Govt. seemed resolved to make a large Reform in yr port [Newcastle] and elsewhere. . . . Had in mind Honest John of Cleadon. My Lady has taken minutes of the Troops you think necessary and you are to have two or more cruisers off your coast to Berwick as occasion may require. . . .

I look upon it [the Rising] as a stratagem, their March to Morpeth to try if you would be tempted to part with Hotham's Regiment in order to attack ym and then when the Town was clear off ym to shut ye Gates upon ym. . . .

You may rest satisfied that any sollicitation for a General Pardon will be in vain.

---

[1] ? Lady Yorke.

Tuesday. (? October).

... Lord Lumley expressed himself frankly upon ye Matter of ye North and told us that ye Saving of ye Town [Newcastle] was in greatest measure owing to the Collonel and yourself. Lord L[umley] threatens to make some of your Newcastle people smart. . . . He was inquisitive if any officers either Custom House or Excise were not zealous for ye Govt., that Mr. Walpole had desired to be acquainted with ym and he would take care to sett those matters Right.

20 October.

... They all agree with you that ye best Pollicy is not to press ye Oaths at this unsettl'd juncture.

... A Report that a few Highlanders are got over to North Berwick. ...

... Your Collector [? of Customs] is now a profess'd Whig. Oh, Will, ye Holy men have damnably poyson'd by much ye Greatest part of ye Nation. However, if we gett over this Decisive stroke (which I don't much doubt) ye Throne will be thoroughly establish'd.

The High Sheriff has written that Robert Lawson of Chirton refus'd to appear or in so much as send a horse to ye Dep[uty] Com-[missioner] upon his Summons. . . . Takes ye Lord Chancellor's opinion who is gone into Herts. [Later ordered to] send and seize his horses for H.M. service leaving him only what was not fit for use and after-[wards] he should be prosecuted for neglect. The non-attendance of many of ye half-pay officers is by no means warrantable and will not escape notice.

[Cotesworth was now instructed] to enclose letters to Charles Allanson in Bedford Row and ye business will be as well don that way as ye former, perhaps better.

27 October.

... Do you really think your keelmen right and tight and may be depended on occasion? . . .

1 November.[1]

Your Intelligence is so much in vogue that no sooner ye Post is come but I have great men's Vallets waiting for ye Produce of your

---

[1] On this same day Dr. John Bowes wrote to his kinswoman: 'We have good news from the North by express from Lord Scarboro'. The foot of the Rebels are deserting, and the Horse are closely pursued by General Carpenter who hopes to give good account of 'em. This news is authentic. Your sons are well at Newcastle where they are better than in any other place in the North as all friends says.' Bowes MSS. 40747, § 129. He had already dispatched £1,000 in bills to London and could now write 'Whatever becomes of us, you and your Money that I had in Custody, I hope is, in this time, in bills with you and will be duely paid.'

Packett. However I can assure you 'tis not to above 2 that I will trust them out of my hands and 'tis a high favor don to those I read ym to and those are very few in Number.

My father and I went to impart [your news] to ye D of Devon-[shire], thence to Mr. Walpole and took Ld. Somers in our return, but were disappointed at each. I do imagin they were all summon'd to Counsell, so we lost our labour. . . .

Ye cantoning ye Troops as proposed [by you] is looked upon as ye Produce off a sollid judgement. When things come to calm and these Burlys are over, you may assure yourself a lasting security may be reasonably expected.

5 November.

. . . I had feared the necessity of a winter campaign but yesterday's post has eas'd us of that since ye Rebels seem'd to steer another course than thro' your country. Report [today], if true [that], Genl. Carpenter has entirely routed ye foot: then I may venture to say the game is up. Two months more will clear the stage. You can't imagine what Industry was used to support ye faction which could be by no one way more effectually than by distressing ye Bank and sinking Credit. There had been a run since 24th July daily and especially ye last three weeks so that the Directors were oblig'd to call in 20% from those that subscribed to ye Circulation and a second call which puts a greater stop to Trade of all sorts.

8 November.

. . . They have ordered one of their Chief Inspectors from Whitby ride [William Selby] to visit strictly and have a watchful eye on ye behaviour of the Officers along ye coast: that he had directions to wait on you and receive your instructions.

. . . People who have not obeyed ye High Sheriff's summons and some opposed his authority [you are] to report to London. . . .

Sorry General Carpenter should have met with a foyle; had he pursued the same Rout ye Bogg trotters took, I am satisfied he could never have come up with them and must have alarmed [?] ye young Horse and ye men would have had much ado to have subsisted. They [the rebels] will lay wast wherever they come, but you may depend 'ere they be well in Lancashire you will find Genl. Wills ready to receive ym with 7 Regiments of Regular Troops and 'tis supposed Carpenter will not fail pursuing his march towards them as expeditiously as possible. . . . Hopes ye Transports are off ye Yorkshire coast.

10 November.

. . . What is ye Meaning of your Militia disbanding at this time of Day? Do you think yourselfs safer without such an arm'd force or that the danger is over? I think there is as much reason as ever to be on guard. . . . Is your [Ld.] Lieut in ye Misst, if so what occasion has been given for his Dissatisfaction? This method of proceeding shocks people. . . .

Queen Besse's Day [12 November].

. . . Can't omit taking notice that when I went to Ld. Townshend's levy [levée], he was mighty inquisitive if I knew one Alderman *Wise* in Newcastle and was very desirous of his character. I told his Lordship he meant Ald. White who was as vigorous and active for ye present Govt as any within those walls. Again he repeated Ald. Wise. I then replied there was one Andrew Wise an Irish Papist (formerly bookkeeper to Sir Wm. Creagh who was ye first Popish Mayor in that Corporation)[1] a man capable of insinuating himself with ye meaner sort.

. . . Yesterday two expresses from Preston . . . that the Rebels had surrendered at Discretion . . . computed at 4–5000 men, 1700 whereof were ye Highlanders and Northumbrians, ye rest what they had pick'd up in their Rout[e] and were joined by ye disaffected of Lancashire. 'Tis said there are several H[igh] C[hurch] Drs. among them who are order'd up immediately along with ye Chief of ye Rebels to Town. You see a joy thro'out ye City which can't be well paralleld and ye Court show no less satisfaction. This Noble Action has nipp'd ye designs of ye Enemys in ye Budd so that they can't expect a plentyfull crop.

. . . The Bart [Liddell's father] is looking for a chapter in Ezekiell.

[Nov. 12] Mr. Honeywood[2] who is zealous and hearty and prudent withall . . . has just come from ye Secretary's Office.

19 November.

. . . What you propose about ye Militia would be of singular use at this time. They could not fail of Picking up abundance of Strollers which tho' no corporal punishment were inflicted on ym, yet were they but mark'd so as to be known, a watchful eye might be sett on ym again[st] another time.

. . . Ye Justices have begun with their commissions by order of

---

[1] In 1687. Brand, ii. 498.
[2] Robert Honywood, M.P. for Essex. He married a daughter of Francis Bowes. Bowes MSS. 40748, § 16.

Council and had deliver'd in their rolls to ye Clerk of ye Peace where it has laid sometime. In Essex they began earlier so that 'tis hoped these presidents will spread all over ye Nation. . . .

24 November.

[On receiving news from Lancashire] . . . struck to see that no greater care is taken of ye Prisoners of note than to let them slip thro' their fingers . . . sees some of them come to town. . . .

[Concerning reinforcements for Newcastle]. I can tell you for your comfort you will see a parcell of clever Blades, middle stature, but well-set and excellently well armed. I doe answer that your young secretary will not be kept in ye house ye day they march into your Town.

There is a Flying report that ye Pretender landed in Scotland two days after ye battle.

Now 'tis hop'd this Hurricane is over and shortly we can expect a calm.

8 December.

The two great men told my Cosen that your letters were ye best Intelligence and clearly stated beyond what they had from any other hand [and hint at] a promise of Reward.

10 December.

. . . Yesterday came ye Prisoners from Preston. I saw your Bensham Landlord Clavering, look'd very pityfully; Hall of Otterburn ye same; Forster was muffl'd up in a blew coat. . . .

15 December.

. . . Pity your health would not permit you to take a Lancashire journey . . . both [your friends] extol your Industry, zeal and clever way of expression. My good friend 'twixt you and me I doubt there is not so good an Harmony between ye two Secretaries and our two friends first mentioned, (viz) ye Lady at Kensington. 'Tis only my surmise. These two are but young statesmen comparitively, but yet rely upon their own notions much. . . .

P.S. The Bishop of Lincoln is like to succeed ye Old Rock.[1]

The poor Dutch forces have undergone a fatiguing march. If your Corporation had any sort of zeal for ye Govt. they might shew it by expressing their charity to those poor souls. . . .

24 December.

. . . Lord W. Young is a very devout man so I would not give him

[1] Archbishop Tenison.

any disturbance at present touching what regards your Custom House
. . . will wait a more seasonable opportunity. . . .

4 January 1715/16.

. . . I was pump'd by several to know how fast Ld. Wm. [Poulett]
was ingag'd. My answer was Ye Gentleman was in Possession of too
plentiful a fortune, I thought, to ingage himself [i.e. to the Jacobites].

. . . Your proposed method of managing ye Forfeited Estates more
advantagiously to ye Crown.

. . . Good God what an age do we live in! I thought that when we
had what we waited for—a Whig Administration, yt then all injurys
cry'd out of before wou'd be redress'd. But it seems some others besides
Priests are just ye same. . . . I have discover'd so many tricks within
these two months that there is no trusting save three or four of our
friends. . . .

Could not you recommend proper surveyors out from Tees to
Berwick?

7 January.

. . . John Hunter of Northumberland, a prisoner at Wigan. I believe
that Hunter is ye same person that used to carry arms from Scotland
into our parts before ye Union. If it be ye same his father and he lived
at Shillow Hill, as I remember, or some such name. . . .

The Preston prisoners have been very uppish ever since their confinement on what account, I know not. They say Marr will be able to
release ym but those are distant views. Phil Hodgshon is ye most dejected,
he says plainly we shall be buoy'd up with hopes of a Pardon till we are
hang'd.[1]

9 January.

. . . Lechmere carried up a message to ye House of Lords that he
would undertake to impeach ye Earl of Derwentwater. Accordingly,
ye Commons did resolve to begin with ye two English and five Scottish
Lords taken at Preston.

P.S. This day ye Commons went upon prolonging ye Suspension
Act. No speech in opposition save from Mr. Shippen. . . .

The 7 Lords carried to ye Tower from ye H. of Lords today. In
their answers they confess'd the articles of Impeachment and threw
themselves on ye King's Clemency.

---

[1] He was attainted of high treason. The Commissioners of Forfeited Estates allowed the
claim of Matthew White for £467. 17s. 10d. in respect of a mortgage on Hodgshon's estate.
Add. MSS. 40843, § 31.

25 January.

Your Town was unworthy off so honest a man as Jurin as you very well remark. Posterity will have ocasion to curse those who have had any hand in making him uneasy in ye Post he was possess'd off.[1] But what can be expected from such a sett of governors and to be succeeded by such a Wretch who is not worthy off wiping his shoes is no less admirable. By this they seem resolv'd that the next generation shall continue in ye same Obscurity. Ignorance is ye Mother of Devotion. Oh, Blessed Mother Church! You have named that Person that poysons all and yet I wish he can be outed. . . .

As to ye blew coat Excise man I have bin speaking till I am weary. Lately I discours'd Roger Gale about him [who] says he Mr. C. should know that I am a stranger to that Town and a young Commissioner [of Excise]. However, if we would send him an Information he would out him in spight off Will. C. had not ye Gentleman this man represented to him as well among many others. But he [Gale] is a slippery spark.

As to ye Victualling and Clothing [contract] 'tis my admiration what interest those gentlemen have to obtain it, by what underhand means they work. As I take it those undertakers are generally comended to the Commissioners of the Treasury where I have not ye least interest, having bin soliciting an augmentation of sallery, as all in the office had save another and myself, but without success. . . .

Letter from Liverpool that young Pierson [a local Jacobite] has been wrought upon by a sister who is with him, to confess and has sworn to as well as sign'd ye Information, since that is, I believe, they will try ye ruse of sending a copy (lest it should miscarry) till after ye Tryalls. . . .

2 February.

. . . I should make a wretched Courtier, but, God be thank'd, my sole subsistence does not come from that Quarter. We have too many Saints among us, which whilst they continue to act as they doe, I should wish rather for a sinner, who acts according to his Profession, an open Game. . . .

Soon after ye guilty Lords [are tried] Lansdowne will be tried and after him cuming Mortimer. . . .

Hunter of Swallwell had his horse taken away by—Wilson, Lady Bowes' viewer and 3 or 4 others.

[1] Master of the Grammar School, Newcastle.

Ld. W. Y[oung?] just now tells me that your officer Sachevrell is turn'd out by their Board: they balloted for successor, it fell to Sir Thomas Frankland's lot. Ld. W. Y. told me if it had fallen to his lot he would have taken one of your recommends.

7 February.

. . . Your obliging their [Newcastle] great Bells to ring aloud till next morning would sufficiently proclaim our success thro'out that neighbourhood. . . .

If ye speak to ye Treasury, there ye have a saint who never fails of a friend ready to popp in, there again ye are frustrated. The only method that seems feasible is by applying to Mr. W[alpole] who has his heart and hands so full off Publick affairs that you may make 20 fruitless journeys without seeing his face: yet delays are dangerous. . . .

Some Lancashire prisoners nearly escap't from Newgate by fileing 4 iron barrs. . . .

9 February.

There is no getting speech of Walpole by such scrubbs as we. . . .

25 February.

Dont you frett yourself to pieces about ye Publick. What you hear from hence is generally false. The faction have a new Lye every day. There are secret Springs in all Govts which are not to be fathom'd.

# APPENDIX B

# 'Tenant Right' at Durham[1]

The Order set down by the Right Hon^ble the Lords of the Queen's M^atie's Privy Council and by the Lord President and others of Her M^atie's Council in the North Parts Between the Dean and Chapter of Durham and their Tenants, the seventeenth day of August in the XIX^th year of Queen Elizabeth.          (Allan MSS. vii. 231)

Where heretofore great contentions have arisen Between the Dean and Chapter of Duresme on the one part and sundry of their Tenants in the County Palatine of Durham claiming to hold their Farmholds by Tenant right on the other part as well before the right Hon^ble the Lords and others of the Queen's M^atie's Privy Council in the North Parts as also att the Comon Laws of this realm, for the ending of which troubles and for a quietness hereafter to be had and for the continuance and maintenance of the Service of the Inhabitants of that Country due to the Queen's M^atie, her heirs and successors. It is now ordered and decreed by the right Hon^ble privy Council as by certain Articles hereafter ensueth:

First, wherein their former suites and troubles the said Tenants claimed to hold their Farmholds by Tenant right and that the Dean and Chapter alleged them to be only their Tenants att will because some of them had taken no leases by a long time and yet it appeared by the Ancient Register and book of the Leases made by the Predecessors of the said Dean and Chapter shewed to that said President and Council in the North parts That the lands in contention belonging to that house had many times been letten for years by Lease and also by a tryall att the Common law by which it held same the said lands and Tenements should not be holden by tenant right.

Therefore it is ordered and decreed That all the same Tenants at Will claiming by Tenant right shall relinquish and give over for them, their heirs and assigns for ever all their titles, rights and claimes of Tenant right in the premises and every part thereof.

(2) And for so much as upon debating of the matter it appeared and could not be denied by the said Dean and Chapter but that the said

---

[1] See Chapters I and IV.

Tenants be bound by the custom of that Country and the Orders of the borders of England for anest Scotland to serve Her Ma^tie ... att every time when they be commanded in War and like manner upon the frontiers or else where in Scotland by the space of Fifteen days without wages which they shall not be able to do if they should be overcharged with great Fynes or raising of rents. Therefore, and for other Godly, charitable and Lawfull considerations it is further ordered and decreed That every of the said tenants shall from henceforth have and enjoy their several farmholds with Chappter terms according to the intent of these said Articles and draught of an indenture or Lease hereafter set down and expressed and accordingly shall take Leases of the said Dean and Chapter and shall pay their rents at the day and times accustomed and that every Tenant shall pay, do and make all rents, services, repiarations and customs as the tenants of every such tenement or farmhold hath heretofore done, paid or made for the said farmhold or of right ought to have done, paid or made.

(3) And it is further ordered that the eldest son of every tenant, if he sue for the same within one year next after the Death of his Father and for default of such son, the son and heir of the eldest son and for default of that son and heir of the eldest son, the brother of the eldest son if he be living or else his son and for default thereof the brother of the last tenant if he be then living or else his son suing for the same as before shall be admitted Tenant of the said tenement ... paying only that year's fyne at the most to the said Dean and Chapter and making yearly such rents and services, repairations and customs due for the said tenement. And this order is to be observed for ever. And if the Tenant fortune to have no son or son's son nor brother nor brother's son as is aforesaid, then it shall be in the Election of the said Dean and Chapter to choose their tenant and to let him the same for his life in form aforesaid. The true meaning of this Article is that if the son, brothers or other be within age at the time of the death of the Tenant, then if he by his Guardian, Tutor or friend make suit for the said Tenement he shall be thereunto admitted tenant.

(4) Notwithstanding the said former orders it is ordered that if any of the said Tenants be married and his wife living after his death that she shall have and enjoy the farmhold her husband died possessed of, during her widowhood without paying any fine, paying and doing the rents etc. If she [re]marry then her husband to pay two years' fyne and he and she to enjoy the said farm during the wife's life, she and also her husband yearly paying and doing the rents, repairations etc. And that

after her death the son of her former husband that was Tenant and in default of such son, such other persons as are before named according to the true meaning of the limitation before mentioned in the third Article shall be admitted tenant for his life if he sue for the same.

(5) And it is further ordered that no forfeiture of any of the said Tenants so to be letten for term of life as is abovesaid shall be taken but only for Treason, Rebellion, Wilfull Murder or Felony convicted, attainted or outlawed by the laws of this Realm. And the same to be forfeited to be taken in form abovesaid.

(6) And it is also ordered and declared that these articles abovesaid are ment and to be intended only for such tenants and tenements as be accounted tenants at will and tenements occupied or claimed to be holden or occupied by custom of Tenant Right and not to such Tenements as heretofore are or have been occupied and claimed by Lease for terms of years or for a term of life or lives within the space of thirty years past.

(7) And it is also agreed and ordered that all those part[icular] Articles and orders together with the Draught of the said indenture shall be entered and remain as of record in the Book of Orders of the Privy Council and decrees of the said Lord President and Council of the North Parts. And also in the Chancery Court of Duresme to the intent the same shall remain and be manifest to such of the tenants as shall have cause or need to sue for the same.

(8) And it is further ordered and agreed that for the more full ratifeing and confirming of these Articles and Orders to abide and continue for ever and that the said Dean and Chapter hath assented to the same. In testimony and approbation thereof the said Dean and Chapter shall unto this order, Articles and Draught set their commonseal.

Given at York this day and year above written. (1577).

\* \* \* \* \*

The Reports and Sayings of sundry aged persons touching the Customarie service of th'inhabitants of the Countie of Durisme and as they have seene it used in their tymes. 21 Martii 1581.

(Hunter MSS. 22, § 5)

First when there was any likeliehood of Invasion of this Realm by the Scotts and knowledge thereof given by the Lord Lieutenant, Lord Wardens or others having charge of the frontiers to the B[pp] of Durham, the Earle of Westmoreland, or in their absence to the Chancellor, Sheriffe and Justices of Peace, open proclamation was made that all able men meet for the warrs above sixteene and under three score yeares, both on horseback and on foote, should make theire repaire to Gateside beacon in their best and most defensible arraie for the warrs, with victualls for Ten daies, att a certain daie and houre appointed. Att which all men appearing there according to the proclamation (if occasion soe required that all must goe on) everie gentleman takeing to him his owne servants and teñants, joined themselves some to the Bishopp, some to the Earle of Westmoreland, if they were there; yf not, then to the Sheriffe or other of the worshipfullest of the Countrie that were there as they were affectioned and the common people and meane freeholders drewe themselves to such as they did hold thire lands upon, or were teñants to, as all that were the B$^{PP}$'s tenants to him or to his officers, the Erle of Westmoreland freeholders and tenants to him and his officers, the house of Durham tenants to the Stewards of their lands: th'inhabitants of Barnard Castle to the steward of that Lordship and the rest to the Sheriffe of the Shire; and after muster taken by the officers aforesaid all men went forward until by the officers of the borders they were placed as they were thought requisite; and soe they continued till the daies accustomed were expired, but if in the meane time they were coñmanded either to invade Scotland or to stay longer on the frontiers then ten daies to be accounted from their coñminge to Newcastle, they were imediately to enter into wages either soe soon as they passed the marches or that their 10 daies were ended. But if it seemed not convenient that all should goe and that the Lord Lieuteñnt or Warden called but for a number certaine, then that nomber was levied indifferentlie of everie mann's tenants and farmers according to the proportion of there Lands and they were chosen and appointed in this manner. The Queene's tenants by the Stewards of Barnard Castle Lordship or his deputie who had alsoe the leading of them. The B/$^{PP}$ of Durham tenants by such his officers or servants as it pleased him to appoint. And likewise the Erle of Westmoreland's tenants by such as pleased him to assigne: the House of Durham teñants by the Steward of their Lands: and the rest of the Countie by the Sheriffe and Commissioners or one of them. Theise men to goe forward as aforesaid, everie Companie under theire own Leader and if the Sheriff goe in person all under him as their generall and the chardges of this service certain to be borne indifferentlie by th'inhabitants of the Countrie. And for the better, speedie and most indifferent execucon of the premises, precepts were accustomd to be by the Commission$^{ers}$ for the musters directed to the officers or to the Stewarde of Barnard castle for the Queene's Majestie's teñants and freeholders within his office, to the Erle of Westmoreland's officers for his teñants as to the Constable of Rabie for that Lordship, the Constable of Branspeth for that Lordship, the Stewards of the Deane's lands for their teñants. And the chargs of the Leaders of theis men to be borne by their Lords if their ordinarie officers who they had for the same, went not themselves; that is to say, if the B/PP appointed any other of his gentlemen or servants then his Sheriffe he beareth their chargs; likewise the Erle of Westmoreland if either his Constable of Rabie or Brancepeth did not goe, as it often chanced they did not, being otherwise imploied: experience of the general going was after ye L^d Eure was killed[1] at which time it is said both the B/PP and the Erle of Westmoreland did goe in there owne persons, and the first time that anie can remember that the Countrie was inforced to staie on the borders more than ten daies was either att that time or nighe thereabouts and upon this ocãsion it is supposed the borders being unfurnished by reason of the overthrowe given by the Scotts wherein Sir Raph Ewre, L[ord] Warden, Sir Brian Stanton and others were slaine, a new supplie could not be gotten out of Yorkshire and other places before th'end of Ten daies. The B/PP and others earnestlie desired their contriemen to staie for fouer or five daies longer, which they did considering the necessitie of the time which was so thankefully taken that everie man at his departure had in reward V^s (shillings) which was supposed by many which were there at that tyme and are yett lyvinge to have bene the King's Majestie's benevolence. But since that time, fourteene daies have beene required, but not allreadie assented unto and being att some times commanded to stay longer they have had wag[e]s for so manie daies as they have served more than ten. And that this hath bene charged by some meanes not well knowen and when anie musters were to be taken, either generall or special, the officer of Barnard castle had a precept and mustered that Lordship within it selfe and made certificate to the general Commissioners of the execucon of this precept. In like manner did the Earle of Westmoreland either himselfe or by his Commandement, his officers within the Lordship of Rabie and Brancepeth and theire members and made like certificate to the general Commissioners of his or their proceedings. Item whensoever anie Souldiers were taken within this Countie either to invade Scotland, to lie in garrison in Barwicke or on the borders, theise souldiers ever had Coate monie, that is to say eche man 3^s/4^d for his Coate and Conducte.

---

[1] At Ancrum Moor in 1545. *Arch. Ael.* (1950), 66–68.

# A List of the Principal MSS. Material used in the Present Study

Allan MSS. (Durham Cathedral Library).

Baker–Baker MSS. (Department of Palaeography and Diplomatic, University of Durham).

Bishops' Registers (Bishops Chandler, Butler, Trevor, Egerton) Auckland Castle, County Durham.

Bowes MSS. (British Museum, Add. MSS. 40747–8).

Carlisle MSS. (Castle Howard, Yorkshire).

Chaytor MSS. (Witton Castle, County Durham).

Cookson MSS. (Department of Palaeography, University of Durham).

Cotesworth MSS. } (Public Library, Shipcote, Gateshead).
Ellison MSS.

Gateshead Parish Registers and Vestry Books (St. Mary's, Gateshead).

Gowland MSS. } (Durham Cathedral Library).
Hunter MSS.

Journal of Ralph Ward (The University Library, Durham).

Newcastle Papers (British Museum Add. MSS.: various).

Ravensworth MSS. (Trench Hall, Ravensworth Castle, County Durham).

Register of Leases. (Dean and Chapter Archives, Durham).

Ridley MSS. (Blagdon Hall, Northumberland).

# Index

PRINTED IN
GREAT BRITAIN
AT THE
UNIVERSITY PRESS
OXFORD
BY
CHARLES BATEY
PRINTER
TO THE
UNIVERSITY